# 冯汉骥全集 ⑦

## 人类学卷

冯汉骥 著　　张勋燎 白 彬 主编

巴蜀书社

# THE CHINESE KINSHIP SYSTEM[①]

## Foreword

### Abbreviations

e = ego                          h = husband, husband's

①　It is hard to express the extent of my indebtedness to Professors F. G. Speck, A. I. Hallowell and D. S. Davidson for their guidance, inspiration and interest in my work. My gratitude is especially due to Prof. A.I. Hallowell who has directed my work and examined the manuscript several times, making important corrections and improvements each time. His suggestions were so valuable that it was necessary for me to rewrite and rearrange the first part of the work entirely.

　　I am also most grateful to Prof. C. K. M. Kluckhohn and Dr. C. M. Arensberg for their careful reading of the manuscript and corrections. For criticism and assistance in the preparation of the manuscript, I am most indebted to my friend Mr. Paul K. Benedict, who has made corrections and improvements practically on every page. To Dr. Leslie Spier, editor of the *American Anthropologist*, I am indebted for permission to incorporate in the section on Teknonymy, material I have contributed to that Journal. I must also thank Prof. Serge Elisse'eff and Prof. J. R. Ware for sponsoring its publication in the *Harvard Journal of Asiatic Studies*. To the Trustees of the Harvard Yenching Institute, I wish to express my deep gratitude for the fellowship grant which made the completion of the work possible.

f = father, father's          w = wife, wife's

m = mother, mother's          o = older

s = son, son's                y = younger

d = daughter, daughter's      > older than

b = brother, brother's        < younger than

si = sister. sister's

*Example:* m f b s d > e signifies mother's father's brother's son's daughter older than ego.

## Definition of Terms

All terms are used in their customary meanings, as found in anthropological and sociological literature. A few terms are used here with a specialized connotation in connection with the Chinese social system. They are the following:

*Family:* used always in the sense or the "extended family" of the Gross- Familie, and equivalent to the Chinese term chia 家, or chia ting 家庭.

*Sib:* a group of people possessing a common sibname (patronym), descended from a common male ancestor, no matter how remote, and characterized by a feeling of relationship. Descent is strictly patrilineal, and the group is strictly exogamous. An organization for the common welfare of all its members, and ancestor worship, may or may not be present. It is equivalent to the Chinese term, *tsung tsu* 宗族.

*Sibname:* used in the sense of a patronym or surname which all members of a sib possess in common, and equivalent to the Chinese term *hsing* 姓.Descent of the sibname is strictly patrilincal.

*Sib relative*: relatives who belong to the same sib and possess the same sibname as ego. It is equivalent to the Chinese term *tsung ch'in* 宗亲，or *tsu jên* 族人 "clansmen."

*Non sib relative:* relative who belongs to a sib other than ego's and bears a sibname other than ego's. It is equivalent to the Chinese terms *wai ch'in* 外亲 and *nei ch'in* 内亲 combined; or the old legal term *ch'in shu* 亲属.*Wai Ch'in* refers to relatives through women of the sib married out, and the affinal relatives of father, father's father, and ascending. *Nei ch'in* refers to ego's own affinal relatives.

## Chronology

The following chronology is given for those who are not familiar with Chinese history since it is impossible to give the Western date in every instance. The tripartite division does not correspond to the traditional Chinese historical divisions but has been adopted here simply with reference to the evolution of the kinship system.

*Ancient Period:* first millennium B.C., which includes the following dynastic periods:

Chou dynasty, or the feudal period. ca, 1100-249 B.C.

Ch'in dynasty, 248-207 B.C.

Former Han dynasty, 206 B.C.-24 A.D.

*Transitional period:* first millennium A.D., which includes the following dynastic periods:

Later Han dynasty, 25-220 A.D.

Wei dynasty, 220-264 A.D.

Chin dynasty, 265-420 A.D.

Sung dynasty, 420-479 A.D.   Northern Wei dynasty, 399-534 A.D.

Ch'i dynasty, 470-502 A.D.   Northern Ch'i dynasty, 550-577 A.D.

Liang dynasty, 502-557 A.D.

Ch'ên dynasty, 557-589 A.D.

Sui dynasty, 58l-618 A.D.

T'ang dynasty, 618-907 A.D.

Wu tai, 907-960 A.D.

*Modern period:* second millennium A.D., which includes the following dynastic periods:

Sung dynasty, 960-1279 A.D. (This is the Sung dynasty to which the writer will always refer in the present treatise, not to the one mentioned above under 420-479 A.D.)

Yüan dynasty, 1280-1368 A.D.

Ming dynasty,　　1368-1644 A.D.

Ch'ing dynasty,　1644-1911 A.D.

〔 Other contemporary dynastic periods are omitted here since they are not referred to in this work. 〕

*Ancient system:* system of the ancient period, i.e., the system in the *Êrh Ya*, supplemented by the *I Li*, the Li Chi. and other contemporary sources.

*Modern system:* system of the modern period. i.e. the present Chinese system.

# Introduction

The interest of the Chinese themselves in problems of kinship was manifested quite early. This interest is primarily a practical one, for the whole Chinese social structure is built upon the basis of the "extended family" organization, which in turn is based upon the systematization of the mutual relationships among its members. If the whole social structure is to function harmoniously, the kinship system, which expresses and defines the rights and obligations of individuals to each other, must first be adjusted. This ideology is further fostered by the teachings of Confucianism, so that kinship becomes a subject of perennial interest.

The systematic recording of relationship terms goes back as far as the

*Êrh Ya,*[①]a work of the third or second century B.C. (according to the more conservative dating), in which the terms are carefully classified and arranged. Subsequent works of a similar nature all contain special chapters on kinship nomenclature, e.g., the *Shih Ming* 〔ca. 200 A.D.〕 and the *Kuang Y'a* 〔ca. 230 A.D.〕—to mention only two of the comparatively earlier ones. These works record later terms which are not present in the *Êrh Ya* and in a sense bring the *Êrh Ya* system up to the date of each compilation. This practice has continued down to the present day.[②]Even larger encyclopaedic works devote special sections to this subject, e.g., the *T'ai p'ing yü lan* (983 A.D.) has ten chapters,[③] and the *T'u shu chi ch'eng* 112 chapters,[④] on kinship nomenclature. Naturally, not all this material is relevant, and much of it belongs to belles lettres. In the ch'ing dynasty a series of special works on kinship terms appeared, the most important and extensive of which are the *Ch'êng wei lu* 称谓录 of LIANG Chang-chu 梁章钜 〔1775-1849〕, and the *ch'in shu chi* 亲属记 of CHÊNG Chen 郑珍〔1806〕. Both of

---

①    Tradition has it that the *Êrh Ya* was compiled by Chou Kung〔?-1105 B.C.〕and augmented by Confucius 〔551-479 B.C.〕, *Tzǔ* Hsia 子夏〔507-? B.C.〕, Shu-sun T'ung 叔孙通〔ca. 200 B.C.〕and others. It is not the work of one hand, nor of one period , but developed gradually during the first millennium B.C. Cf. B. KARLGREN, *BMFEA* 3(1931). 44-49. The section on Kinship Terms 释亲 probably dates from ca. 200B.C.Cf. 尔雅新研究 by NAITŌ Torajiro. in 先秦经籍考 2.163-184.

②    Most works of the 训诂 class have a section on kinship terms, e.g., the *P'ien ya*骈雅〔under 5.释名称〕, *Shih ya* 拾雅, etc., and even works on dialects like the *Hsu fang yen*续方言 of HANG Shih-chun 杭世骏〔1696-1773〕, and the *I yu* 异语 of CH'iEN Tien 钱坫〔1744-1806〕devote special sections to kinship term variants.Other dictionaries, starting from the *Shuo wên*. contain kinship terms too, but they are not systematically arranged.

③    太平御览, 511-521, 宗亲部.

④    图书集成, 明伦汇编：家范典, 1-112.

these works comprise collections of old terms, and are more or less in the *Êrh Ya* tradition. Of the two, the *ch'eng wei lu* is much wider in scope, but the arrangement of material is rather loose. The *ch'in shu chi* considers only the lineal relatives through father, and the ordering of data is more in keeping with the view of orthodox Confucianism. ①

By far the most important class of materials is formed by the ritual works, the *Li*. In these works kinship is not treated as a subject by itself but in connection with other subjects; an exception is the *ch'in shu chi*, a lost section of the *Li*, which dealt primarily with relationship terminology.② These ritual works are important sources for the functional study of the Chinese kinship system because they deal with kinship in action. Such are the *I Li* and the *Li Chi*, works of the second half of the first millenium B.C., that treat kinship in extenso, especially in connection with mourning rites, ancestor "worship," and other aspects of ritual. In all later works on ritualism—too numerous to mention here— kinship is the basic subject of discussion.

In addition, there are numerous miscellaneous works in which discussions on kinship terms occasionally occur. These are among the most

---

① Other important works are the *T'ung su pien* 通俗编〔ch. 4: 伦常，ch: 18. 称谓〕of CHAI Hao 翟灏，?-1788; the *Hêng yen lu* 恒言录〔ch,3: 亲属称谓类〕of CH'iEN Ta-hsin 钱大昕，1727-1804; the *Chêng su wên* 证俗文〔ch.4〕of Ho I-hsing 郝懿行 1757-1825; and the *Kuang shih ch'in* 广释亲 of CHANG shên-i 张慎仪. There are many other works of a less extensive nature but they rather duplicate each other.

② As quoted in *Pai hu t'ung* 8. 19b, the *Ch'in shu chi* 亲属记 is very similar in nature to the *Êrh Ya*.

important sources from the standpoint of the evolution of the Chinese kinship system, because generally it is here that one finds recorded the newly introduced terms (dialectical or unconventional) which, as a rule, are ignored by the ritual and other formal literature. Very often one finds in them enlightening discussions concerning the introduction and origin of new terminologies.

Thus, the interest in the study of kinship terminology is not new among Chinese scholars, and actually they sometimes made explanations which might rank with modern sociological interpretations , but the systematic socio-anthropological study began with Lewis H. Morgan.[1] Morgan's data were supplied by Robert Hart, an Englishman in the employ of the Chinese Maritime Customs. Despite the faulty nature of Hart's material, and notwithstanding Morgan's evolutionistic predilections, which invalidated most of his conclusions, the Morgan Hart work has remained the basis for most subsequent speculation. Since then has appeared a number of miscellaneous recordings, some in legal treatises or linguistic primers, others in lexicographic works, but, with one exception, none is worthy of serious consideration. This exception is the work of T. S. Chen and J. K. Shryock.[2] The Chen Shryock study is based chiefly on two modern dictionaries, the *Tz'ŭ yüan* and the *Chung hua ta tzŭ tien*. This material,

---

[1] *Systems of Consanguinity and Affinity of the Human Family,* 1870, Part Ⅲ , ch.Ⅳ. 413-437.

[2] "Chinese Relationship Terms," *American Anthropologist* 34 (1932) . 623-664.

although inadequate and unreliable, has been used to good advantage by the authors. George W. Bounakoff [1] seems to have made a stupendous attempt to synthesize all the material in European languages in the light of Morgan's hypothesis.

The limitations of all these European works are obvious. First, the terms relied upon have been collected by untrained persons from "uninformed" informants. Secondly, the writers have not made use of the vast amount of easily available Chinese documentary material—indeed, they seem unaware of the existence of such material. Consequently, most of these studies are marred by numerous inconsistencies and errors. The writers could seldom determine the exact nature of a term, because few ever sectioned out the multiple strata of terminology in the Chinese system. [2]

The present study is based chiefly upon the author's own collection of terms from the primary Chinese sources. All material consulted has been examined critically to insure correctness in terminology and interpretation.

---

[1] *Terms of Reationship in Chinese: An Ethnographical Linguistic Study* 〔N. J. Marr Institute of Language and Mentality, Academy of Sciences, USSR. 1936〕. I have not seen the original work (in Russian) but only the English "Analytical Summary." So far as I can make out, it is mainly based on secondary English sources with the exception of *Êrh Ya*, which is also available in English. Although he has used most of the European sources, he seems to have overlooked the tables of Gustave SCHLEGELn:*Nederlandch-Chinesech woordenboek met de transcriptic der Chi'ecsche karackters in het Ts'iang tsiu dialekt,* Leiden, 1886-90, vol. I, p. 1343, *Chineesche GesLachtboon.* The important issue, however, is his methodology which is based upon the Marxian conception of history and the Japhetic theory of language of H. I. Marr. Combining these with the evolutionary stages of L. H. Morgan, he arrives at the "collective beginnings" of Chinese society !

[2] Originally the present work included a section called "Critical Review of Early Studies." As it was not in a way constructive and occupied considerable space,it has been deleted.

The method of approach is primarily historical and linguistic①—partly because it is precisely these aspects which are the most engaging characteristics of the Chinese system and at the same time the least understood, partly because preliminary work of this sort is prerequisite to an understanding of the more implicit aspects of the system. The field of investigation is limited to the historical period, approximately the last twenty five centuries, within which the system has been fully documented. If kinship system changes occur at all, two thousand years should be long enough for their manifestation.②

## Principles of Terminological Composition

The principles governing the composition of terms are both linguistic and sociological. Linguistically, they are formed according to the syntactical principles of the Chinese language; sociologically, their connotations are determined by the relationships which they express and the circumstances

---

① By *linguistic*,I mean the usual and the formal approach to the study of kinship systems, i.e., by an examination of the kinship terms themselves, the structural whole they present, and the underlying principles involved.

② This paper is one of the studies made by the author under a fellowship grant by the Trustees of the Harvard- Yenching Institute, to whom he wishes to express his gratitude. The author is also deeply indebted to Professors A. I. Hallowell, F. G Speck, and D. S. Davidson for constant guidance, suggestions and improvements in this work; to Prof. C. K. M. Kluckhohn and Dr. C. M. Arensberg for their careful examination and corrections of the MS.; to MR.Paul K. Benedict, who has made improvements and corrections on almost every page. The author also wishes to thank Professors S. Elissee'ff and J. R. Ware for suggestions and assistance and especially for sponsoring publication in this Journal.

under which they are used. The multitude of Chinese relationship terms can be reduced to four fundamental classes, namely, *nuclear terms*, *basic modifiers*, *referential modifiers*, and *vocatives*. Nuclear terms express the nuclear group of relationships and, linguistically, are independent of modifiers. Each nuclear term possesses a primary meaning and one or more secondary meanings. The primary meaning is assumed when the term is used independently, and, when it is used in combination with other elements, the secondary meaning or meanings become paramount. Basic modifiers for the most part express collateral relationship and generation status and can not be used independently as kinship terms. The nuclear terms form the basis for kinship extensions and the basic modifiers locate the exact place of the relative in the total scheme. The combinations and recombinations of these two classes of elements constitute the modern standard system which is the norm of all other terminologies. The referential modifiers modify the standard system into proper forms for referential use in specific applications. Vocatives, aside from their primary usages, transform them into direct forms of address between relatives.

The following is an analysis of these four classes of elements and an exposition of the principles governing their composition and application. In the analysis of the nuclear terms the primary connotations (according to the modern standard system) are given first and then followed by the secondary meanings.

## Nuclear Terms

Tsu 祖: [2] father's father. Ancestor. Used in combination with other elements for all ascendants higher than the father's generation.

Sun 孙: [3] son's son. Descendant. Used in combination with other elements for all descendants lower than the son's generation.

Fu 父: [4] Father. Male of higher generation status. Male sex indicator for higher generations. Suffixed to terms of all male relatives of generations higher than ego.

*Tzŭ* 子: [5] Son. Male of lower generation status. Male sex indicator for lower generations. May be suffixed to terms of male relatives of generations lower than ego, but its use is optional.

Mu 母: [6] Mother. Female of higher generation status. Female sex indicator for higher generations. Suffixed to terms of all married female relatives of generations higher than ego.

Nü 女: [7] Daughter. Female of lower generation status. Female sex indicator for lower generations. Suffixed to terms of all female relatives of generations lower than ego.

Hsiung 兄: [8] Older brother. Male of the older brother's status. Indicator of seniority within the generation of ego. Used in combination with other elements for male relatives of the generation of, but older than ego.

Ti 弟: [9] Younger brother. Male of younger brother's status, Indicator of juniority for males within the generation of ego. Used in combination with other  elements for male relatives of the generation of, but younger than ego.

*Tzǔ* 姊: [10]  Older sister. Female of the older sister's status. Indicator of seniority for females within the same generation of ego. Used in combination with other elements for female relatives of the generation of, but older than ego.

Mei 妹: [11]  Younger sister. Female of the younger sister's status. Indicator of juniority for females within the same generation of ego.Used in combination with other elements for female relatives of the generation of, but younger than ego.

Po 伯: [12]  Father's older brother. Indicator of seniority. Applicable to terms from ego's generation and ascending, using the direct male lineal line as a standard of comparison.

Husband's older brother. Cannot be extended in this sense.

Shu 叔: [13]  Father's younger brother. Indicator of juniority.Applicable to terms  from ego's generation and ascending, using the direct lineal line as a standard of comparison.

Husband's younger brother. Cannot be extended in this last sense.

Chih 侄: [13a]  Brother's son. Indicator of descent from male collaterals. Used in  combination with other elements for descendants of male relatives of the generation of ego.

*Shêng* 甥: [14] Sister's son. Indicator of descent from female collaterals. Used in combination with other elements for descendants from female relatives of the generation of ego.

Ku 姑: [15] Father's sister. Indicator of relationship comparable with father's sister's. Indicator of descent from father's sister, or from female relatives comparable with father's sister's relationship.

Husband's sister. Cannot be extended in this last sense.

Chiu 舅: [16] Mother's brother. Indicator of relationship comparable with mother's brother's. Indicator of descent from mother's brother, or from male relatives comparable with mother's brother's relationship.

Wife's brother. Cannot be extended in this last sense.

I 姨: [17] Mother's sister. Indicator of relationship comparable with mother's sister's. Indicator of descent from mother's sister, or from female relatives comparable with mother's sister's relationshop. Wife's sister.[17] Indicator of relationship comparable with wife's sister's. Indicator of descent from wife's sister, or from female relatives comparable with wife's sister's relationship.

Yo 岳: [17a] Wife's parents. Indicator of relationship comparable with wife's parents, such as their cousins.

Hsü 婿: [18] Daughter's husband. Husband. Indicator of connection by marriage with ego's female relatives of the same generation of ego and descending.

Fu 夫: [19] Ego's husband. Husband. Indicator of connection by marriage with ego's female relatives of the same generation of ego.

Ch'i 妻: [20] Ego's wife. Wife.

Sao 嫂: [21] Older brother's wife. Female of older brother's wife's status. Indicator of connection by marriage with ego's male relatives of the generation of, but older than ego.

Fu 妇: [22] Son's Wife. Wife. Indicator of connection by marriage with ego's male relatives of the generation of, but younger than, ego and descending generations.

## Basic Modifiers

Kao 高:High; revered. Modifying indicator of the fourth ascending generation.

Tsêng 曾:Added; increased Modifying indicator for the third ascending and descending generations.

Hsüan 玄:Far; distant. Modifying indicator for the fourth descending generation.

T'ang 堂:Hall; the ancestral hall. Modifying indicator for the second collateral line from the second generation and descending. Ascending vertically, for father's father's brother's children and father's father's father's brother's children, that is, for paternal uncles and aunts once removed and paternal granduncles and aunts once removed. When extended to non sib relatives, it indicates, in a similar way, the third collateral line.

Ts'ung 从: To follow; through. It is used synonymously with *t'ang*. *t'ang* is a later term and its use is restricted. Wherever *T'ang* is used, *ts'ung* may be substituted, but not vice versa.

Tsai ts'ung 再从:To follow again, or to follow a second time. Modifying indicator for the third collateral line from ego's generation and descending. Ascendingly, for paternal uncles and aunts twice removed.

Tsu 族:Sib; tribe. Modifying indicator for relationships from the fourth collateral line and beyond.

Piao 表:Outside; external. Indicator of descent from father's sister, mother's brother and mother's sister. Similarly extended to all relatives descended from those whose terms include either *ku* (father's sister), *chiu*(mother's brother) or *i* (mother's sister) .

Nei 内:Inside; inner ;wife. Indicator of descent from wife's brother, or from relatives comparable with him, e.g., his male sib-cousins.

Wai外：Outside. Reciprocal modifier indicating mother's parents and daughter' s children.

The above generalizations are based on the connotations of the modern standard terminology. They are abstracted from the whole range of the nomenclature, with every term taken into consideration. Yet, because of the multitude of possible combinations for every Chinese character, exceptions are inevitable. These exceptions, few and relatively insignificant, will be evident when the  whole system is reviewed.

## Terminological Composition

In the building of terms, the terminology for the nuclear group of relations is taken as a structural basis, with the exception of parent child and husband wife terms, which are used as sex indicators.[1] All modifying elements indicating collateral relationship and descent are prefixed,[2] in succession, to the chosen basis, with the element expressing the nearest relationship nearest the basis and that expressing the farthest relationship furthermost, until the desired relationship is reached. All sex indicators are suffixed. If the generation category of the structural basis is not apparent, as in *chiu* and *i*, the sex indicators also function as generation indicators; here, too, they are always suffixed.

In choosing the structural basis for a term of a relationship, the factors to be considered are, first, generation and second, descent. Take, for example,

---

[1]　The sex indicators are fu 父，mu 母 tzǔ 子，nu 女，fu 夫，fu 妇,hsi 媳,hsü 婿. Failure to recognize this set of terms has resulted in much misunderslanding of the system. The first to disspell this misunderslanding was perhaps H. P. WLLKINSON,Chinese Family Nomenclature, *New China Rev.* (1921) 159-191. He writes: The initial error of the writers . . . was . . . in taking the sex indicators for male and female appended to varying 'descriptive' appellations of kindred as the name of a class,—that of ' sons' and ' daughters.' "A. L. KROEBER, quite independently, also discovered that" these last four terms (i.e. fu 父,mu 母，fu 夫，fu 妇)merely denote the sex of the person referred to, when they are added to other kinship terms... Process in the Chinese Kinship System, *American Anthropologist* 35(1933) 151-157.

[2]　The terms "prefixing" and "suffixing" are employed here in a loose sense, since there are no true "prefixes" and "suffixes" in Chinese (with the  exception, perhaps,of a few elements, notably the nominal suffixes). Here they merely indicate that a certain indivisible element (character) is placed before or after another indivisible element (character) in syntactic relationship.

the term for the father's father's sister's son's daughter's son. This is a complicated one, since the descent has shifted from female to male, and then back to female. Disregarding descent, let us first consider the generation. The individual concerned is of the son's generation. Instantly the basis is reduced to the alternatives *chih* or *wai shêng.* His immediate relationship with ego is through a female relative of ego's generation; therefore, the term *chih* is eliminated and only *wai shêng* remains. Furthermore, his relationship is a non- sib but consanguineal one, and descent is from father's father's sister, a relationship comparable with father's sister's; therefore, the qualifying elements *ku* and *piao* should be added. He belongs to the third collateral line of non sib relatives; therefore, the collateral modifier *t'ang* is applicable. Together, these elements form the term *tang ku piao wai shêng*—a term as exact as can be desired. To express a female relationship of the same kind, add *nü* to the above term, making it *t'ang ku piao wai shêng nü* 〔that is, f f si s d d〕. To express a female relationship by marriage, substitute *fu* for *nü;* for a male relationship by marriage, substitute *hsü.*

The elements which make up a compound term should always be interpreted in their extended, that is, their secondary, meanings, and should never be understood in their primary meanings. The amalgamation of all the extended meanings makes up the new connotation of the term so compounded. This phenomenon is a feature of Chinese syntax. Failure to understand this has been the source of much misinterpretation.

The following illustrations represent practically the whole range of the structural bases. They are chosen with a view to including the widest variety of combinations, in order to elucidate the nature of terminological formations. The scope, however, is naturally limited, and fuller information must be sought in the tables.

**Examples.** The *italics* represent the nuclear term used as a structural basis, and the *roman,* the added modifiers:

| | | | | | |
|---|---|---|---|---|---|
| tsu | | f f | ku piao po | fu | f f si s > f |
| po tsu | mu | f f o b w | shu | | f y b |
| T'ang shu tsu | fu | f f f b s < f f | t'ang shu | mu | w of f f b s < f |
| po | | f o b | tsai Ts'ung shu | fu | f f f b s s < f |
| t'ang po | fu | f f b s > f | ku | fsi | |
| t'ang ku | fu | f f b d h | t'ang *tzŭ* | fu | h of f b d > e |
| ku piao ku | mu | f f si d | t'ang i piao *tzŭ* | fu | h of m f b d d > e |
| chiu | | m b | mei | | y si |
| T'ang chiu | fu | m f b s | i mei | | w y si |
| t'ang piao chiu | fu | m f f si s s | t'ang i mei | fu | h of w f b d < w |
| i | | m si | i piao mei | fu | h of m si d < e |
| t'ang i | fu | m f b d h | t'ang i piao mei | | m f b d d < e |
| tsai Ts'ung i | mu | m f f b s d | chih | | b s |
| hsiung | | o b | tsu chih | nü | f f f b s s s d |
| ku piao hsiung | | f si s > e | tsai Ts'ung chih | hsü | f f b s s d h |
| t'ang ku piao hsiung | | f f si s s > e | wai shêng | | si s |
| sao | | o b w | T'ang wai shêng | nü | f b d d |
| chiu piao sao | | w of m b s s e | t'ang ku piao wai shêng | | f f si s d s |
| t'ang chiu piao sao | | w of m f b s s > e | sun | | s s |
| ti | | y b | chih sun | nü | b s d |
| t'ang ti | fu | w of f b s < e | T'ang chih sun | | f b s s s |
| tsai Ts'ung ti | | f f b s s < e | wai *shêng* sun | hsü | si s d h |
| *tzŭ* | | o si | | | |

In building terms for the third and fourth ascending and descending generations, the terms of the second ascending and descending generations are used as a basis, generation indicators are added to them. Modifiers of descent are usually added first, before the generation modifiers are prefixed. Examples:

| tsu | | f f | sun | | s s |
|---|---|---|---|---|---|
| tsêng tsu | mu | f f m | tsêng sun | nü | s s d |
| tse`ng po tsu | fu | f f f o b | tsêng chih sun | fu | b s s s w |
| kao tsu | fu | f f f f | hsüan sun | | s s s s |

The above represent the compositional principles of the standard system.[1] The standard terms are universal and form the patterns on which other terms are built or formed. They are for the most part used in formal— i.e., genealogical, legal and ceremonial literature. In ordinary applications, they must be properly qualified by modifiers according to the specific situations under which they are used.

## Referential Modifiers

The referential modifiers actually reflect the Chinese social code of etiquette, as well as the Chinese psychology concerning the proper attitudes to be assumed in social intercourse. It is a sign of politeness and refinement to pay due respect and compliments to others, and, appropriately but not exaggeratedly, to maintain for oneself a more or less humble position. This is precisely the attitude that conditions the application of kinship terms.

---

[1]   Some would call it "literary system," in the broad sense of the term.

The referential modifiers are also a manifestation of the consciousness of membership in the relational group. The complimentary and depreciatory modifiers cannot be applied indiscriminately; their application is prescribed by the identification with one relational group in contrast with another. Compliments may be applied more loosely, but depreciatives can be used only to those whom one strictly considers members of one's own relational group.

These two attitudes are fundamental in the application and understanding of the whole terminology.

The referential modifiers are governed by definite rules concerning their applications, and are always prefixed to the standard terms. With respect to their nature and usages, all of them can be broadly grouped under the following categories: 1. Complimentary, 2. Depreciatory, 3. Self reference, 4. Posthumous.

*Complimentary.* These elements are used in referring to the relatives of the person to whom one is speaking or writing. They consist of the following three elements: i. Ling 令: Illustrious, worthy, honorable. It may be prefixed to any standard term, except in instances where special stems are provided. ii. Tsun 尊: Honorable, venerable. Used synonymously with *ling*, but restricted in that it refers only to relatives of higher generation or status than that of the person to whom one is speaking. iii. Hsien 贤: Virtuous, worthy. Used alternatively with *ling*, but restricted in that it refers only to relatives of lower generation and status than that of the person to whom one is speaking. There are a few exceptions to this rule, e.g., *hsien shu*, "your virtuous paternal uncle."

Whenever one is in doubt as to whether *tsun* or *hsien* should be prefixed, he uses *ling. Ling, tsun* and *hsien* have the sense of "your" used in a polite way.

Complimentary modifiers should be prefixed when speaking to persons not related to oneself. They should not be used between sib relatives, except, when speaking to those of lower generations, in reference to their superiors. This latter practice is really teknonymy. The complimentary modifiers should be prefixed when reference is made to the relative of a non sib relative to whom one is speaking, if that individual is not a connecting relative. If he is a connecting relative and of higher generation than the speaker, the usual standard or vocative kinship term should be used. As a rule, one does not compliment those with whom one has close and direct relationships.

*Depreciatory.*① These modifiers are prefixed to the standard terms in referring to one's own relatives of the same sibname, when speaking or writing to others. "Depreciatory" is used here in the sense of "modest" or "of one's own." They consist of the following three elements: i. Chia 家:

---

① "Depreciatory" is used in contrast to "Complimentary." As the elements *chia* and *shê* show, "depreciatory" is used in the sense of "of my own family" or "of my own sib."

Family, dwelling, household. It is prefixed to the terms of all sib relatives of higher generation and status than ego. ii. Shê 舍: Cottage, shed, household. It is prefixed to the terms of sib relatives of the generation of, but of lower status than, ego (as younger brother); and principally in reference to sib relatives of the first descending generation, and sometimes all descending generations. It should never be used in reference to relatives in the direct lineal line, e.g., for one's own children. iii. Hsiao 小: Minor, junior, small, diminutive. Prefixed to the terms of sib relatives of lower generation than that of ego, principally in reference to one's own children, grandchildren, etc. With the exception of the lineal descendants, *shê* and *hsiao* can be used synonymously.

*Chia, shê* and *hsiao* have somewhat the sense of "my" used in a modest manner. It is important to note that depreciatory modifiers are not applicable to relatives of a different sibname.[1] They are not even applicable to one's father's married sisters or one's own married sisters because these women have adopted their husband's sibnames and are no longer considered as members of one's own family or sib, and therefore they are not to be "depreciated."[2]

---

[1] There is a general term that can be applied to any non sib relative, i.e., *pi ch'in* 敝亲 , "my poor〔or unworthy〕relative."

[2] *Yen shih chia hsün* 风操篇 ,2.5a 凡言姑,姊,妹,女子子,已嫁则以夫氏称之,在室则以次第称之.言礼成他族,不得云家也.

*Self reference.* [1] These modifiers are prefixed to the terms used by ego to refer to himself before another relative, either in speaking or in writing, e.g., a nephew refers to himself before an uncle, or vice versa. They consist of the following two elements: i. Yü 愚: Simple, rude, stupid. It can be prefixed to the terms when used by ego to refer to himself, principally as a relative of higher generation to one of lower generation. ii. Hsiao 小: Junior, minor. It can be prefixed to the terms when used by ego to refer to himself, principally where a relative of lower generation address one of higher generation.

Neither *yü* nor *hsiao* are applicable to oneself where addressing a relative of the direct lineal line, e.g., father and son, grandfather and grandson, etc., where special terms are provided for such purposes.

*Posthumous.* These modifiers are prefixed to—excepting a few special stems for this purpose—the standard terms when used in reference to one's own dead relatives, especially for parents, grandparents, father's brothers, etc. They consist of the following two elements: i. Wang 亡: "Deceased." Prefixed to terms of all relative when dead. ii. Hsien 先 "The late,""the former." Prefixed only to terms of relatives of higher generation or status than ego, when dead.

When referring to the dead relatives of others the complimentary

---

[1] "Self-reference" modifiers are in a certain respect indistinguishable from "deprecatory" except in context. It is especially true of the element *hsiao*. They are separated here for the purpose of exposition.

modifiers must again be prefix to these modifiers. This practice is not common; usually a circumlocutory expression is employed.

There are a number of special stems which are used with the referential modifiers. They will be pointed out in the tables in each connection. For the sake of clarity and brevity, all terms qualified by the referential modifiers, or formed with special words, will be called in later discussion either complimentary , depreciatory, self reference, or posthumous terminologies.

## Vocative Terms

Vocatives are used as forms of addressing relatives direct in person. In literary address, i.e., in writing, the standard terms must be used. Vocatives must not be used together with referential modifiers. The latter can only be prefixed to standard terms.

Vocatives are limited to relatives of higher generations than ego, and to those of the same generation as, but of higher age status than ego. Relatives of lower generations and age status can be addressed by name, or by using the standard terms as vocatives, if the occasion should arise. All vocatives are formed from three groups of terms: grandparent terms, parent terms, and older sibling terms.

*Grandparent terms*. The grandparent vocatives vary a great deal with local usage. As they have not been systematically recorded, it is rather difficult to determine the most prevalent ones.*Yeh yeh*, *wêng* or *wêng wêng*, *kung or kung kung,* for paternal grandfather, *P'o* or *P'o P'o, nai nai,* for paternal grandmother, may be considered the most common. No matter which terms are adopted in local usage, the adopted local terms are extended consistently throughout the whole system like these forms. In their extension, they are suffixed to the standard terminology by dropping the *tsu fu* and *tsu mu,* e.g., for *po tsu fu* (f f o b) the vocative is *po wêng,* or *po kung.*

*Parent terms.* Parent terms are less variable than grandparent terms. *Tieh, yeh,* and *pa pa* for father; *ma* and *niang* for mother. *Pa pa* is never, and *niang* is seldom, used in extensions.

Tieh 爹：Vocative for father. Used to form vocative terms for male relatives of the first ascending generation in place of *fu.*

Ma 妈: Vocative for mother. Used to form vocative terms for female relatives of thc first ascending generation in place of *mu.*[1]

The above rules will not apply in instances where special vocatives are provided. These terms may also be omitted in certain cases where they are unnecessary, just as *fu* and *mu* are sometimes omitted.

*Older sibling terms.* Ko, or ko ko 哥哥: Vocative for older brother. Used for conjugating vocative terms in place of *hsiung* for male relatives of the generation of , but older than ego.

*Chieh,* or *chieh chieh* 姐姐：Vocative for older sister. Used for

---

[1]　*Ma* and *mu,* in their extensions, indicate a married status, and cannot be applied to unmarried female relatives.

conjugating vocative terms in place of *tzǔ* for female relatives of the generation of, but older than ego.

It is the vocative nomenclature that varies dialectically. At present, this variability mostly involves the grandparent and parent terms, the older sibling terms showing very little variation. But no matter how variable the dialectical vocatives may be, the above conjugation rules can be applied simply by replacing the given forms with local terms.

The vocative terms are used more loosely, i.e., they are more "classificatory" than the standard terminology. When two relative speak face to face the exact relationship is always understood; it is only in referential usages that the more exact terms are needed. The prevalent use of sibnames,[1] personal names, titles, and numerical order of seniority and juniority[2] for particularizing each relative in vocative address also makes the accurate system rather too cumbersome.

---

[1] Sibnames are used only for particularizing non-sib relatives and women married into the sib.

[2] The ancient method of denoting seniority and juniority by *po* 伯, *chung* 仲, *shu* 叔, and *chi* 季 has long been obsolete. A purely numerical order is used today. If ego's father is one of six siblings, A,b, C, D, e, and F (capitals indicate males, small letters, females), the numerical order of *ta* 大, *êrh* 二, *san* 三, *ssū* 四, *wu* 五 and *liu* 六 will be applied to them, respectively. *Ta* is used in the sense of "eldest." *Jih chih lu*, 23. 38a: 今人兄弟行次,称一为大,不知始自何时.汉淮南厉王常谓上大兄,孝文帝行非第一也.If ego's father is D, then ego will call A *ta po*, b *êrh ku*. C *san po*. e *wu ku*, and F *liu shu*. If ego's father is A, then ego will call b *êrh ku*, C *san shu*, D *ssǔ shu*, e *wu ku*, and F *liu shu*. The terms *po* and *shu* change positions in accordance with the relative order of ego's father, but the numerical order remains constant.

There is another method of assigning the numerical order, viz., by separating the male and the female series. As in the above case, A, C, D, and F will be assigned *ta*, *êrh*, *san* and *ssǔ*, respectively, and b, e will be given *ta*. *êrh* respectively. The method used depends upon local custom and family whim.

## Supernumerany Terms

There are a few groups of terms which may be called "super numerary,"[1] viz., the sacrificial, epitaphic, literary and alternative names. These are referred to in the tables.

Sacrificial terms were used in ancient times for the direct lineal ancestors when offering sacrifices to them. There are only a few such terms, but they are now obsolete. Epitaphic terms are used on epitaphs and monuments. Strictly speaking, there are only two such terms, *k'ao* 考 for father and *pi* 妣 for mother. It is only the sons who erect epitaphs for their parents. Sacrificial and epitaphic terms are often confused with terms modified by "posthumous" modifiers. They are frequently used interchangeably, since they all refer to dead relatives, although in slightly different senses. Nevertheless, there are some very interesting changes which are of historical significance.

Literary terms are those used only in literary compositions, usually non-vocative and non-referential. Many of them are old obsolete terms but still retained in literary usage. Alternative terms are those that can be used synonymously with the prevalent forms. The adoption of the one or the other depends entirely upon local custom and individual proclivities.

---

[1]　"Supernumerary" is employed here in the sense used by E.W.GIFFORD in his discussion of California Kinship Terminologies, *UC-PAAE* 18, 1922-1926. It is not a happy term, and is adopted here only for want of a better one.

# Structural Principles and Terminological Categories

The architectonic structure of the Chinese system is based upon two principles: lineal and collateral differentiation, and generation stratification. The former is a vertical, and the latter a horizontal, segmentation. Through the interlocking of these two principles, every relative is rigidly fixed in the structure of the whole system.

## Lineal and Collateral Differentiation

The methods of differentiating collaterals differ in the ancient and the modern systems. In the ancient system, the *Êrh Ya* and *I Li*, each collateral line is differentiated by following the terminology of the kin nearest to the lineal line from whom this line originated; e.g., father's father's father's brother is called *tsu tsêng* wang fu, and his descendants down to ego's generations are differentiated by prefixing the term *tsu* to their respective terms; father's father's brother is called *Ts'ung tsu* wang fu, and all his descendants down to ego's generation are differentiated by prefixing the term *Ts'ung tsu*. This method is also applied to more remote collateral lines.[1]

In the *Êrh Ya* system there is no term for brother's sons and their

---

[1]　Cf. CHÊNG Chên: 补正尔雅释亲宗族,*Ch'ao ching ch'ao 'wên chi*,1.1a-4b.

descendants, nor is there any term for father's brother's son's sons and their descendants, nor for father's father's brother's son's son's sons and their descendants. It seems that the sons of brothers and sib brothers merge into one another, i.e. brother's sons are one's own sons. On the other hand, the *Êrh Ya* gives the term *ch'u* [1] for sister's son (man speaking), *li sun* [2] for sister's son's son (man speaking); *chih* [3] for brother's son (woman speaking), *kuei sun* [4] *for brother's son's son* (woman speaking). In the strict patrilineal sib organization of the Chou period, even one's own sons are differentiated from one another as regards the order of succession, hence it is difficult to see why there are no terms to differentiate one's own sons from brother's sons and sib brother's sons, while, on the contrary, terms are provided whereby the man may differentiate his sons from his sister's sons, and the woman may differentiate her sons from her brother's sons. [5]

The differentiating of collaterals in the modern system is far more complete and consistent, but is carried out on a different principle. The

---

[1]  *Êrh Ya:* 男子谓姊妹之子为出.

[2]  Ibid.: 谓出之子为离孙.

[3]  Ibid.: 女子谓昆弟之子为侄.

[4]  Ibid.: 谓侄之子为归孙、

[5]  It is very doubtful whether the *Êrh Ya* system is complete. It also has no terms for f si s s, m b s s. and m si s s. By inference, f si s s and m b s s can be called *ch'u,* since sister's husband, f si s, and m b s are called *shêng,* and sister's son is called *ch'u.* But the absence of terms for m si ss is rather disconcerting; these terms cannot all be merged into the terms for ego's own sons. or into any others. For some reason or other the compilers of the *Êrh Ya* seem not to have been interested in the terms for descendants or collaterals of the same generation. On the other hand, the *Êrh Ya* system, as it stands, seems to stress the terms on the matrilineal side of descending generations. Whether or not this is a survival of an earlier matrilineate is a matter of interpretation, since other evidence is inconclusive.

generation stratum of ego is used as a basis, and the collateral modifying terminology is extended vertically downward and upward. E.g., father's brother's sons are called *T'ang hsiung ti*, their sons and grandsons are called *T'ang chih* and *T'ang chih sun,* respectively. Upwards, *T'ang* is extended to father's father's brother's son, e.g., *t'ang po fu* and *T'ang shu fu*; and to father's father's father's brother's sons, e.g., *T'ang po tsu fu* and *T'ang shu tsu fu*. Other collateral lines, e.g., *tsai Ts'ung* and *tsu*, are similarly extended.

The development of the modern principle of differentiation began in the Han period. First came the differentiation of one's own sons from brother's sons by employing the terms *yu tzǔ* or *Ts'ung tzǔ*.[①] During the Chin period the term *chih* was permanently changed from a woman's term for brother's son to a man's term for brother's son. *T'ung t'ang*[②] was first used during the fifth and sixth centuries for denoting the second collateral line, and was later abbreviated to *T'ang*. *Tsai ts'ung* came into use a little later, and *tsu* is an old term used in a slightly delimited sense. With these important collateral modifying terminologies perfected, the whole process was completed about the end of the first millennium A.D.

---

① Cf. Table I, NO. 125.

② Cf. Table I, NO. 41.

DIAGRAM I

Ancient System of Collateral Differentiation

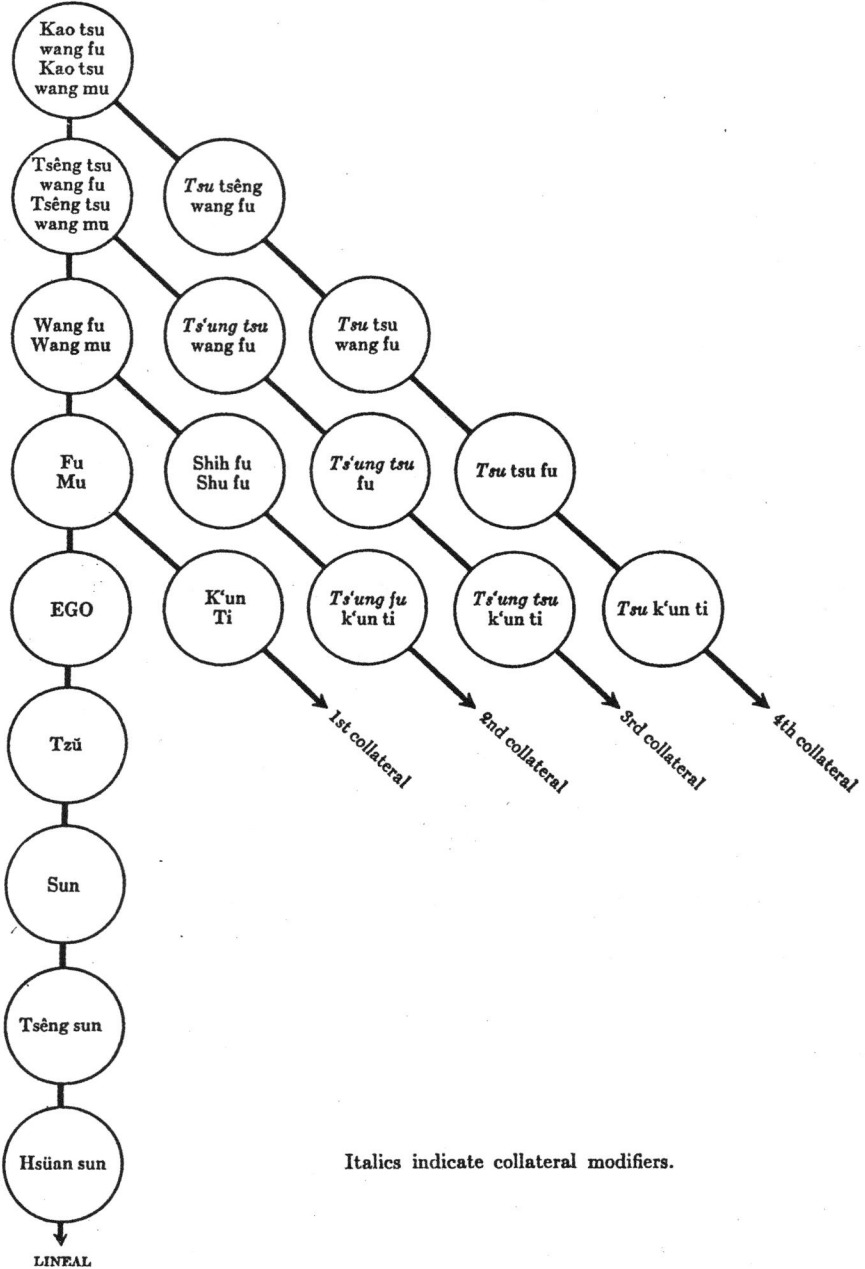

Kao tsu wang fu Kao tsu wang mu

Tsêng tsu wang fu Tsêng tsu wang mu

*Tsu* tsêng wang fu

Wang fu Wang mu

*Ts'ung tsu* wang fu

*Tsu* tsu wang fu

Fu Mu

Shih fu Shu fu

*Ts'ung tsu* fu

*Tsu* tsu fu

EGO

K'un Ti

*Ts'ung fu* k'un ti

*Ts'ung tsu* k'un ti

*Tsu* k'un ti

1st collateral

2nd collateral

3rd collateral

4th collateral

Tzŭ

Sun

Tsêng sun

Hsüan sun

Italics indicate collateral modifiers.

LINEAL

DIAGRAM II

## Modern System of Collateral Differentiation

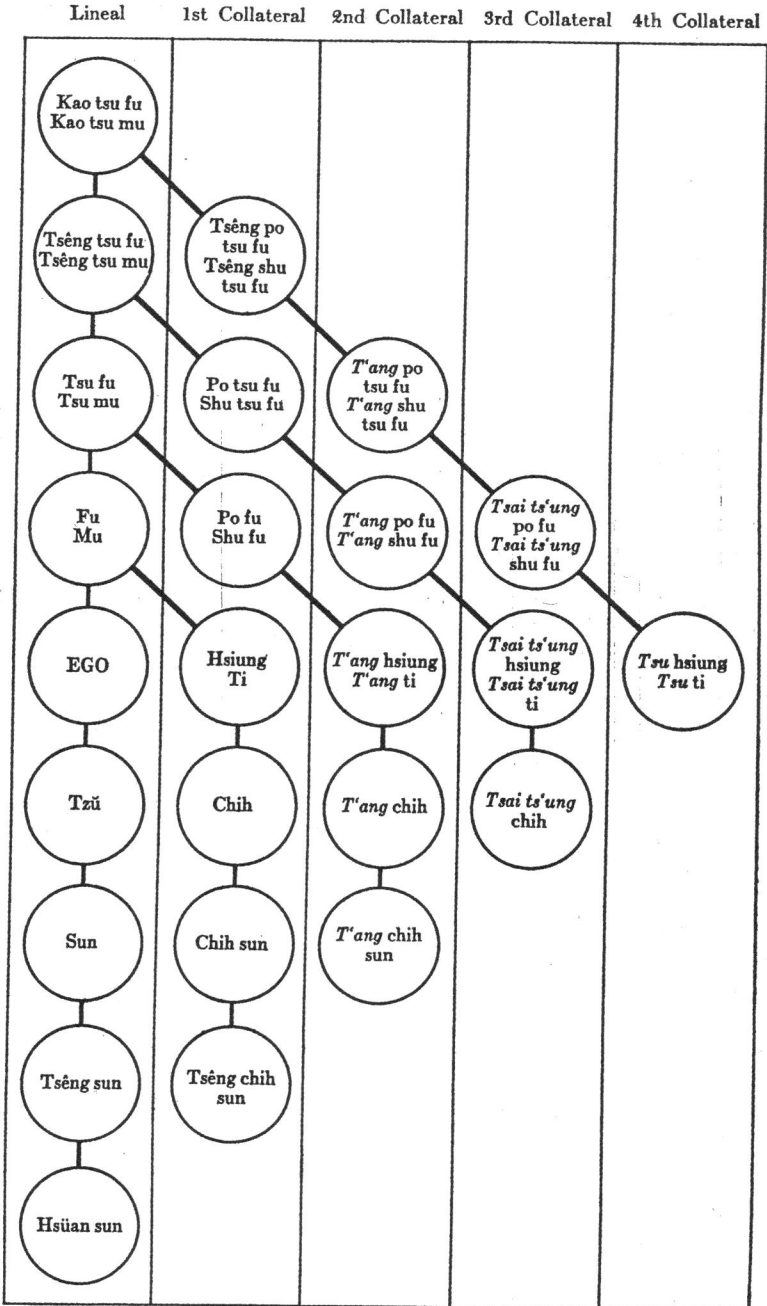

| Lineal | 1st Collateral | 2nd Collateral | 3rd Collateral | 4th Collateral |

Kao tsu fu
Kao tsu mu

Tsêng tsu fu
Tsêng tsu mu

Tsêng po tsu fu
Tsêng shu tsu fu

Tsu fu
Tsu mu

Po tsu fu
Shu tsu fu

T'ang po tsu fu
T'ang shu tsu fu

Fu
Mu

Po fu
Shu fu

T'ang po fu
T'ang shu fu

Tsai ts'ung po fu
Tsai ts'ung shu fu

EGO

Hsiung
Ti

T'ang hsiung
T'ang ti

Tsai ts'ung hsiung
Tsai ts'ung ti

Tsu hsiung
Tsu ti

Tzŭ

Chih

T'ang chih

Tsai ts'ung chih

Sun

Chih sun

T'ang chih sun

Tsêng sun

Tsêng chih sun

Hsüan sun

Italics indicate collateral modifiers.

## Generation Stratification

All relatives in the system are stratified in successive generation layers. This stratification performs the important function of fixing the exact location of relatives in the system, in conjunction with the principle of collateral differentiation.

In diagram III, the vertical columns represent collaterals and the horizontal columns represent generations. When one set of columns is superimpose upon the other, the two afford pigeonholes for every relative in the system. Each relative is then rigidly fixed, and not subject to fluctuations. The generation strata are maintained by the use of generation modifiers. The modifiers are, in most cases, adapted from the nuclear terms from the direct lineal line, since in counting generations the lineal relatives are always used as absolute standards of measure. This adaptation of nuclear kinship terms as generation indicators has been interpreted as partial merging of collaterals and lineals. Given our present knowledge of the system, this interpretation is not tenable.

Since generation is an important structural principle, it must not be disrupted, lest the structure break down. The most serious, if not the only, disruptive factor in this principle is intergeneration marriage. To counteract this influence, generation has become an important factor in the regulation of marital relations. A Chinese is not required to marry any of his or her relatives, but if such marriages do occur between relatives both parties must belong to the same generation stratum. In other words, a Chinese may marry any person outside of his or her own sib; if the parties are related, they must be of the same generation, irrespective of age.

This rule seems to have been less stringent in ancient times. During the Chou period a feudal lord could take his wife's paternal nieces as concubines, or even as wives after his wife's death. The Han emperor, Hui Ti(194-188 B.C.), married his older sister's daughter,[①] and the T'ang emperor, Chung tsung (705-710 A.D.), married his paternal grandaunt's daughter.[②] These instances are severely condemned as incestuous by later historians and moralists,[③] but they were not so condemned by contemporaries. On the other hand, these instances may have been anomalous; it may be only because the marriages involved emperors that they went unpunished and uncriticized. But, in either case, they do show the laxity of the generation rule during the earlier period.[④]

There can be no doubt that the generation rule was much stressed even

---

① *Han shu* 外戚列传，97A5a〔孝惠张皇后〕宣平侯敖尚帝姊鲁元公主，有女，惠帝即位，吕太后欲为重亲，以公主女配后为皇后......

② *T'ang shu*.76 19b: 中宗和思顺圣皇后赵......父环，尚高祖常乐公主，帝为英王，聘后为妃.

③　WANG Ming-shêng (1723-1797 A.D.) discussed these instances in his 十七史商榷（广雅书局本）86.2a:as the most flagrant violations of the "relationships of humanity," 人伦之极变.

④　The *T'ung tien* discussed two instances of difficulties in mourning obligations arising from inter generation marriages, 95. 12a: 族父是姨弟为服议；and the hypothetical case, 95. 5b-6b: 娶同堂姊之女为妻,姊亡服议 .It seems that inter generation marriage between distant relatives was tolerated during the first half of the first millennium A.D.

during the Chou period,[1] since the recorded marriages show that the inter generation type of marriage was the exception rather than the rule. [2] Its stiffening was gradual, and culminated about the middle of the first millennium A.D. The period of intensive development of the principle seems to have been about the third and fourth centuries A.D., because it is during this period that the generation indicators in personal names became popular. The T'ang Code (ca. 600 A.D.) contains clauses which definitely prohibit marriage between relatives of different generations. [3] All subsequent codes contain such interdictions, and cite cases. From the end of the first millennium A.D. to the present, not only have inter generation marriages been rigorously forbidden by law, but popular sentiment against them runs so high that even a teacher marrying his or her pupil, or a person marrying a friend's daughter or son, is condemned.

The underlying concept is the desire to keep constant the generation layers of relatives and to prevent their disruption. If the generation of one relative is disrupted by marriage, then all the positions of the relatives

---

[1] Both the *tsung fa* and the *sang fu* institutions, which were developed during this period, stress the separation of generations. *Sang fu* will be dealt with later. As to *tsung fa*, the subdivisions of *tsung* into minor *tsung* 小宗, for the most part, depends upon the counting of generations.

[2] The instances of primaty inter-generation marriages can be counted on the fingers. LIANG Yü-shêng〔*P'ieh chi*, 2.2a〕says: 楚成王取文芈二女,(左僖廿二),晋文公纳嬴氏(僖廿四),皆以甥为妻者,可谓无别矣.嗣后妻甥者,汉孝惠取张敖女,章帝取窦勋女,吴孙休取朱据女,俱楚录入员颛晋重作之俑也.

[3] *T'ang lü shu* I 户婚 14.2a: 若外姻有服属,而尊卑共为婚姻……以奸论 This is followed by expositions of this clause, and by another clause of the same nature but more specific. 尊卑 means "relatives belonging to different generations."

connected with him would also be disrupted, and the system would lose its accuracy of description and thus defeat its own purpose.

## Categories

Kroeber's essay on the *Classficatory Systems of Relationship*[1] does not invalidate the use of classificatory and descriptive designations in anthropological discussion; its contribution lies in the establishment of categories that are inherent in all systems. These categories constitute a convenient means for examining the working processes of any system. It is impossible to tabulate the whole Chinese system into one table, but we may take the nuclear terms and tabulate them in the light of the eight categories suggested by Kroeber. It must be understood that these nuclear terms are also used in secondary meanings, qualified by modifiers. In this tabulation only their primary meanings are considered.

Now let us consider the system as a whole, together with the nuclear terms under each category.

---

[1]　*Journal, Royal Anthropological Institute of Great Britain and Ireland 39*(1909).77-84.

## DIAGRAM III

| | Descended from females through males | | | | LINEAL | Descended from males through males | | | | |
|---|---|---|---|---|---|---|---|---|---|---|
| | 4th Collateral | 3rd Collateral | 2nd Collateral | 1st Collateral | | 1st Collateral | 2nd Collateral | 3rd Collateral | 4th Collateral | |
| | | | | | Kao tsu fu, Kao tsu mu, | | | | | IV |
| | | | | Tsêng tsu ku fu, Tsêng tsu ku mu, | Tsêng tsu fu, Tsêng tsu mu, | Tsêng po tsu fu, Tsêng shu tsu mu, | | | | III |
| | | Piao tsu fu, Piao tsu mu, | Ku tsü fu, Ku tsu mu, | Tsu fu, Tsu mu, | Po tsu fu, Po tsu mu, Shu tsu fu, Shu tsu mu, | T'ang po tsu fu, T'ang shu tsu fu, T'ang ku tsu mu, | | | | II |
| | T'ang piao po fu, T'ang piao shu fu, T'ang piao ku mu, | Piao po fu, Piao shu fu, Piao ku mu, | Ku fu, Ku mu, | Fu, Mu, | Po fu, Po mu, Shu fu, Shu mu, | T'ang po fu, T'ang shu fu, T'ang ku mu, | Tsai ts'ung po fu, Tsai ts'ung shu fu, Tsai ts'ung ku mu, | | | I |
| | Tsai ts'ung piao hsiung, ti, Tsai ts'ung piao tzü, mei, | T'ang piao hsiung, ti, T'ang piao tzü, mei, | Piao hsiung, Piao ti, Piao tzü, Piao mei, | Tzü, Tzü fu, Mei, Mei fu, | EGO | Hsiung, Sao, Ti, Ti fu, | T'ang hsiung, T'ang ti, T'ang mei, | Tsai ts'ung hsiung, ti, Tsai ts'ung tzü, mei, | Tsu hsiung, Tsu ti, Tsu tzü, Tsu mei, | I |
| | | T'ang piao chih, T'ang piao chih nü, | Piao chih, Piao chih nü | Wai shêng, Wai shêng nü, | Tzü Nü, | Chih, Chih nü, | T'ang chih, T'ang chih nü, | Tsai ts'ung chih, Tsai ts'ung chih nü, | | I |
| | | | Piao chih sun, | Wai shêng sun, | Sun, Sun nü | Chih sun, Chih sun nü, | T'ang chih sun, T'ang chih sun nü, | | | II |
| | | | | Wai shêng tsêng sun, | Tsêng sun, Tsêng sun nü, | Tsêng chih sun, Tsêng chih sun nü, | | | | III |
| | | | | | Hsüan sun, Hsüan sun nü, | | | | | IV |

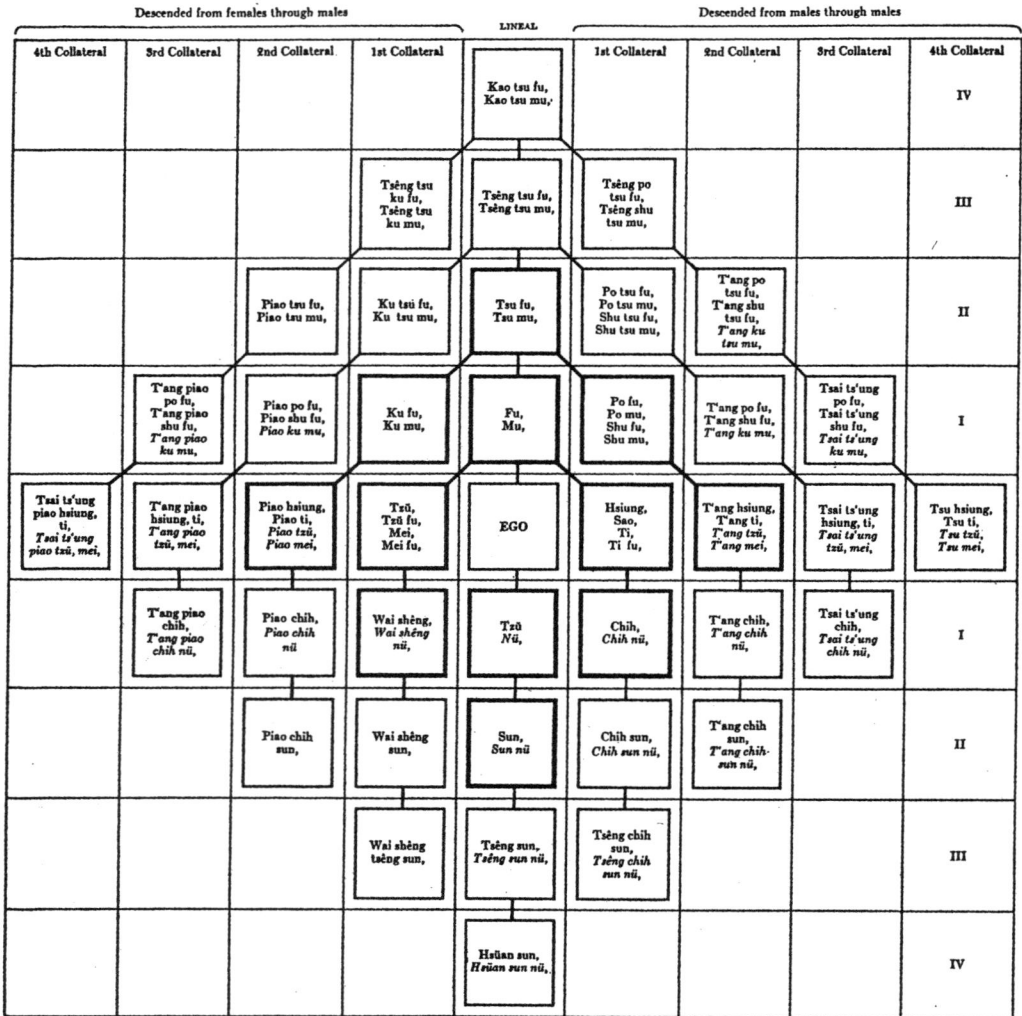

The heavy squares represent the nuclear group of relatives. Those in italics, indicate their descendants have not been carried over into the next generation, e. g., the children of *nü* are *wai sun* and *wai sun nü* but not given in the following square. The Roman numerals represent ascending and descending generations.

| Terms / Categories | 夫 fu | 嫂 sao | 妻 ch'i | 婦 fu | 婿 hsü | 岳 yo | 姨 i | 舅 chiu | 姑 ku | 甥 shêng | 姪 chih | 叔 shu | 伯 po | 妹 mei | 姊 tzŭ | 弟 ti | 兄 hsiung | 女 nü | 母 mu | 子 tzŭ | 父 fu | 孫 sun | 祖 tsu | Total | Percentage |
|---|---|---|---|---|---|---|---|---|---|---|---|---|---|---|---|---|---|---|---|---|---|---|---|---|---|
| Generation | * | * | * | * | * | * | | | | | | * | * | * | * | * | * | * | * | * | * | * | * | 18 | 78.27 |
| Blood or marriage | * | * | * | * | * | * | | | | | | * | * | * | * | * | * | * | * | * | * | * | * | 18 | 78.27 |
| Lineal or collateral | * | * | * | * | * | * | * | * | * | * | * | * | * | * | * | * | * | * | * | * | * | * | * | 23 | 100 |
| Sex of relative | * | * | * | * | * | * | * | * | * | * | * | * | * | * | * | * | * | * | * | * | * | * | * | 23 | 100 |
| Sex of connecting relative | * | * | * | * | * | * | * | * | * | * | * | * | * | | | | | | | | | | | 13 | 56.53 |
| Sex of speaker | | | | | | | | | | | | | | | | | | | | | | | | 0 | 0 |
| Age in generation | * | * | | | | | | | | | | * | * | * | * | * | * | | | | | | | 8 | 34.78 |
| Condition of connecting relative | | | | | | | | | | | | | | | | | | | | | | | | 0 | 0 |

NUCLEAR RELATIONSHIP TERMS CLASSIFIED ACCORDING TO KROEBER'S CATEGORIES

i. *The difference between persons of the same and of separate generations*. This category is rigorously observed in the whole system through the use of generation indicators. Generation is not only an important structural principle in the system but is also an important regulator of marriage and a determinator in the application of vocatives. But in the nuclear terminology it is represented by only 78.3 percent of the terms. In the terms po, shu, ku, chiu, i the generation category is overridden. This merging of generations is not inherent in the system, but has been produced through the disruptive force of teknonymy, which will be discussed later.

ii. *The difference between lined and collateral relationships*. This category is strictly fixed in the whole system. Collateral lines are differentiated by special modifiers. Practically all the basic modifiers exist solely for the function of developing this category. In the nuclear nomenclature it is represented by 100 percent of the terms.

iii. *The difference of age within one generation*. This category is only partially represented in the system. It is fully represented in ego's own generation, whether male or female. Among the ascending generations it is operative only among the male relatives, with the exception of the wives of male relatives. Among the descending generations it is not operative at all. In the nuclear terminology it is represented by only 34.8 percent.

W. H. R. Rivers attributed the differentiation of age within one generation to the practice of tribal initiation, i.e., older brothers will be initiated before younger brothers.[①] Whether or not this be correct, it is the only general explanation seriously advanced. In ancient China there are vestiges of initiation rites, especially as recorded in the *I Li*[②] and *Li Chi.*[③] Whether or not these ancient initiation rites have anything to do with the expression of this category is by no means certain. Chinese authors usually connect it with the sib organization, *tsung fa*, since in this organization the older brothers have absolute priority over the younger brothers in the transmission of office and property, and special privileges in the sacrificial rites to ancestors and in carrying on the line in general.[④]

iv. *The sex of the relative.* This category is consistently carried out in the whole system through the employment of sex indicators. In the nuclear terminology the representation is 100 percent.

v. *The sex of the speaker.* This category is entirely inoperative. The sex of the speaker is always understood but never expressed. But there are traces of this category in the ancient system. E.g., in the *Êrh Ya* and the *I Li,* the term *chih* is exclusively used as a woman's term for brother's children. A few other terms may have been used only as women's or men's terms, but here we are less certain.

---

① W.H.R.Rivers, *Social Organization,* ed.by W.J.Perry,1924,p.189.

② 士冠礼.

③ 冠义.

④ Ch'êng Yao-t'ien 程瑶田 (1725-1814):*Tsung fa hsiao chi* 宗法小记 1.la:宗之道，兄道也.大夫士之家，以兄统弟，而以弟事兄之道也.Ibid.1.1b:尊祖故敬宗，宗之者，兄之也.故曰:宗之道，兄道也.

vi. *The sex of the person through whom the relationship exists.* This category is fully expressed in the system through the use of special modifiers. E.g., *piao hsiung ti* may mean father's sister's sons, mother's brother's sons, or mother's sister's sons. But if we say *ku piao hsiung ti, chiu piao hsiung ti* and *i piao hsiunq ti*, the terms are exact, and refer to father's sister's sons, mother's brother's sons and mother's sister's sons, respectively. There are lapses in the vocative usages, since the exact status of the connecting relative is always understood and never expressed.

vii. *The distinction of blood relatives, from conecticn by marriage.* With the exception of the terms *chiu* and *i*, this category is consistently expressed. The merging of mother's brother (consanguineal) and wife's brother (affinal) into *chiu*, and of mother's sister (consanguineal) and wife's sister (affineal) into *i*, is due to the influence of teknonymy. In the vocative usages the terminology is looser, because of the mutual adoption of each other's terms by husband and wife.

viii. *The condition of life of the person through whom relationship exists.* This category is present, but usually is not consistently expressed. The most common distinction is between the dead and living relatives, by the application of special modifiers. There are a few distinct terms for this purpose for parents, grandparents, paternal uncles, etc. Other conditions of life of the relative are not expressed, or are indicated only by circumlocutory expressions.

Certain of these categories (ii, iv, vi and possibly vii) are essential to the maintenance of a strict unilateral—patrilineal in Chinese descent. It is also exactly these categories that find their fullest expression in the Chinese system. The great nicety in the distinction of dead and living ancestors (category viii) in the ancient terminology may have been due to ancestor worship, which is less prevalent now.

## Reciprocity

In kinship systems there is usually the factor of reciprocity to influence the expression of certain categories. Reciprocity is of three kinds: logical or conceptual reciprocity, verbal reciprocity, and self reciprocity, i. e., both conceptual and verbal.[1] It is not, on the whole, a feature of the modern Chinese system, since, to a certain extent, it is incompatible with the consistent expression of certain categories and exactitude in the discrimination of relatives.

In the ancient system there are traces of conceptual reciprocity. The *I Li*[2] *says*, "They call me *ku*, I call them *chih*." Inversely it is also true: "They call me *chih*, I call them *ku*." *Ku,* as used in the *rh Ya* and the *I Li*, means father's sister, and *chih* means brother's child (woman speaking) , both male and female. In other words, *ku* "indicates the sex of the relative but not of

---

① Cf. the definition of reciprocity suggested by A. L. *KROEBER, California Kinship systems,* UC: *PAAE* 12, 9. 340, note l; Zuni Kin and Clan, *Anthropolgical Papers,AMNH* 18 (1919). 78-81.

② 丧服 32. 1b: 传曰:侄者，何也? 谓吾姑者，吾谓之侄.

the speaker," whereas *chih* "does not recognize the sex of the relative indicated, but does imply the sex of the speaker."[1] Therefore, *ku* and *chih* each involve a category which the other does not express. *Ku* and *chih* in their ancient usages are true conceptual reciprocals.

The *Êrh Ya* also states, "They call me *chiu*, I call them *shêng*,"[2] *Chiu* is here used in the sense of mother's brother, and *shêng*, sister's child. But the reverse does not hold true. Actually this statement contradicts the other terms recorded in the *Êrh Ya* itself, since *shêng* was used in the sense of father's sister's son, mother's brother's son, sister's husband (man speaking), and wife's brother. The *Êrh Ya* also gives another term, *chu*, for the same relative, sister's child. It is very likely that the above statement is a later interpolation, since *chiu-shêng* was probably reciprocal from the Han to the T'ang periods.[3] The whole problem is complicated by the question of cross cousin marriage and teknonymy, which will be dealt with later. In short, *chiu-shêng* could not have been reciprocal in the ancient system, but *shêng* was itself partially reciprocal, i.e., in the male sex only.[4]

These are the only traces of reciprocity that can be detected in the ancient system. The tendency toward the consistent use of categories later

---

[1]  A. L. KROEBER, *Classificatory System of Relationship* 81.

[2]  This statement also occurs in the *I Li,* 丧服 33.9a: 传曰: 甥者, 何也? 谓吾舅者, 吾谓之甥.

[3]  During this period *chiu* was used for mother's brother alone, and *shêng* dropped all its other connotations and became simply a term for sister's child, e.g., *wai-shêng*.

[4]  That is, *shêng* is used reciprocally between mother's brother's son, father's sister's son, sister's husband (M.S.), wife's brother, and male ego. They call male ego *shêng,* and male ego also calls them *shêng*.

became so strong that even these few vestiges of ancient reciprocal terms have entirely disappeared from the modern system.

## Factors Affecting the System

In the course of development from the ancient to the modern system there has been a slow but persistent tendency toward systematization and more exactly descriptive efficacy in nomenclature. This tendency has to a large extent been conditioned by the sociological lines along which Chinese society is organized, and has to a lesser extent been intentionally fostered by ardent ritualists and framers of etiquette. On the other hand, there are also potent social forces which work against overrationalization and oftentimes throw certain parts of the system out of gear by undermining certain categories. The systematizing forces are the sib organization and the mourning system. These two factors have supplemented one another in moulding the kinship system to their own pattern. The disrupting forces are the Chinese marriage customs and, most potent of all, teknonymy. The ritualists served as a stabilizing agency in vigilantly conserving the nomenclature[①] with a view to the exactitude of mourning specifications and

---

① For example, *chu* and *ku* as terms for the husband's parents have been obsolete since the turn of the first millenium A.D., but they are still used in this sense in ritual works. *Chiu* was extended to include wife's brother ca. 900 A.D., but one never finds *chiu* used in this sense in formal literature.

the needs for maintaining sib solidarity. But generally they were powerless against the popular tendencies in kinship usages, and very often were forced to accept the already established terms and attempt to harmonize and incorporate them into the whole system.[1] Thus, in the Chinese system there is a seeming embodiment of a well considered plan while, at the same time, there are many incongruities. No matter how much we may discredit "mock kinship algebra," to borrow a phrase from Malinowski,[2] it is pertinent to inquire into the conflicting forces which have moulded, and are today shaping, the Chinese system.

## The Sib:Descent and Exogamy

Kinship ties necessarily begin within the family as a procreational unit. These primary ties, as we may call them, [3] are biologically the same in all societies,[4] though, functionally, they may differ from culture to culture.[5] But kinship ties do not rest within the reproductive family. They are extended to a much wider circle of individuals who are actually or

---

[1]  E.g., *i* was extended to include mother's sister ca. 500 B.C. During the next seven or eight centuries, the new and old terms were used interchangeably. About 400 A.D. *i* was standardized as term for both mother's sister and wife's sister.

[2]  Kinship, *Man* 30 (1930). 17. 19-29.

[3]  B. MALINOWSKI would call this "the initial situation of kinship": preface to Raymond FIRTH's *We, The Tikopia*〔1936〕x.

[4]  I.e., the divisions into father, mother, son, daughter, brother and sister, members of the strictly procreational family, exist in all kinship systems.

[5]  E.g., the relationship of "father" to the rest of the procreational group in a patrilineal society may be radically different from that in a matrilineal society.

reputedly related to those of the procreational family. In this process of extension certain groups of related individuals are emphasized and certain others minimized, although their degree of relationship may be exactly the same. The basis of this variability in the grouping of kin is the subject of much, perhaps unduly much, anthropological discussion. And naturally so, for it is precisely this variability in kinship patterning that differs so widely among different peoples—particular systems grouping relatives in quite different ways. The character of the kin groups emphasized likewise reflects the wider ranges of the social structure of which the kinship system is part.

In the Chinese kinship system, relatives in the male line receive emphasis; the formalized basis of which is the exogamous patrilineal sib.

Sib organization is called *tsung fa* in Chinese, literally, the "law of kindred." The *tsung fa* was bound up with the feudal system,[1] which was swept away in the course of the third century B.C. The sib organization, however, has survived to the present day, although in a much attenuated and modified form. The postfeudal development of the sib reached its climax in the third to the eighth centuries A.D., when it is usually termed *Shih tsu* or *tsung tsu*. The causes of this excessive development were many, but primarily it represents a reactionary growth following the abolition of the feudal system. The larger and more prominent sibs took the place of the

---

[1] For the sib organization of the feudal period, cf. WAN Kuang-T'ai 万光泰, *Tsung fa piao* 宗法表; WAN Ssǔ-ta 万斯大, *Tsung fa lun* 宗法论; and Ch'êng Yao-T'ien 程瑶田, *Tsung fa hsiao chi* 宗法小记. For a more modern study, cf. Sun Yao 孙曜, Ch'un Ch'iu shih tai chih shih tsu 春秋时代之世族〔1931〕.

feudal nobility, both in monopolizing governmental offices and in maintaining social prestige.[1] Their influence began to decline during the T'ang period. This was, on the one hand, due to the suppressive measures of the T'ang rulers and, on the other hand, to the social upheavals precipitated by the decline of the T'ang dynasty.[2] At the present time sib organization, for most people, is less vital than formerly, but its traditions and influences still permeate the whole of Chinese social life.

*Tsung fa* itself has been well studied, and we need here consider only those two of its characteristics which have direct influence upon the alignment of relatives, viz., patrilineal descent and exogamy. With the *tsung*, the sib, each line of descent is strictly patrilineal, not only in the transmission of the sibname but also in the transmission of office, property, etc. It is also primogenitary: the eldest brother has priority over the younger brothers.[3] The *tsung* is absolutely exogamous. Marriage within it is impossible, even after a "hundred generations." It is also strictly patrilocal.[4] Evidence is far from conclusive as to whether or not Chinese society passed through a prior

---

[1] Cf. *Kai yü Ts'ung k'ao,* 六朝重世族,17 1b-9a.

[2] Cf. *T'ung Chih* 通志：氏族略序,25.1.

[3] In the transmission of hereditary titles, the primogenitary principle holds but the property is divided equally among the brothers, although the eldest brother usually receives an extra share. It is only in the ceremonies in the ancestral halls that the primogenitary line has absolute priority over all collateral lines.

[4] When, for want of male issue, a son-in-law is adopted as son, he adopts the wife's sibname and lives with her parents. He is in every way treated as a son. The children or the third generation revert to his original sibname 三代回宗, but usually one male child is allowed to carry on the wife's line.

matrilineal phase.① Exogamy, however, was predominately a Chou institution,② and its development was rather late. Ancient authorities attest that during the Hsia and Shang 〔ca. 1700-1100 B.C.〕 periods members of the same sib could marry after the lapse of five generations.③ The institution of strict sib exogamy was traditionally attributed to Chou Kung 〔ca.1100 B.C.〕, who instituted it for the maintenance of sib solidarity. Nevertheless, there is abundant evidence to show that even during the Chou period this interdiction was neither universal nor strictly enforced.④ It was only after the overthrow of the feudal system and the transformation of the sib organization that absolute sib exogamy gradually prevailed. From the middle of the first millennium A.D. to the present this rule has been vigorously enforced by law.⑤

The moulding effect of the exogamous patrilineal sib is seen in the dichotomy of relatives in the system. Relatives are divided, along sib lines, into sib relatives 〔tsung Ch'in〕 and *non-sib relatives* 〔wai Ch'in or nei

---

① The existence of an early matrilineal state constitutes the underlying hypotbasis of many recent works on ancient Chinese socicty, e.g., M. GRANET'S *La civilisation chinoiae*. Paris, 1929. and Kuo Mo-jo's 中国古代社会研究，1931, The evidence they have marshalled is suggestive rather than conclusive.

② *Li chi* 大传,34.7b: 系之以姓而弗别，缀之以食而弗殊，虽百世而昏姻不通者，周道然也.*T'ung Tien*, 96.2a,cites,晋范汪祭典：且同姓百代不婚,周道也.

③ *T'ai p'ing yü lan* 太平御览〔1808〕鲍氏 ed., 540.7b-8a. citcs 礼外传. The five generations include the generation or ego. Even then, it is still very doubtful whether the Hsia and yin peoples had any exogamy at all.

④ CHAO I says〔*Kai yu Ts'ung k'ao,* 31. 2b-3a〕, 同姓为婚，莫如春秋时最多 and cites many cases to support his thesis. He concludes, 此皆春秋时乱俗也,汉以后此事渐少.

⑤ E.g., in *T'ang lü,shu* i 14. 1a:诸同姓为婚者，各徒二年，缌麻以上以奸论. Cf. Pierre HOANG, *Le mariage chinois au point de vue Lêgal.*〔1898〕43-53.

Ch'in〕. All sib relatives belong to the same sib of ego and possess the same sibname. Paternal relatives descended from females through males or females are non sib relatives. Maternal and affinal relatives all belong to the non sib group.

To maintain this distinction between the sib and non-sib groups, the terminology must be bifurcated in such a way that the paternal relatives descended from males through males are differentiated from those descended from females through males. This is carried out by differentiating the father's brother's sons 〔T'ang hsiung ti〕 and their descendants from father's sister's sons〔piao hsiung ti〕 and their descendants; brother's sons 〔chih〕 from sister's sons〔wai shêng〕; son's sons〔sun〕from daughter's sons〔wai sun〕; and so on, ascendingly, descendingly, and collaterally This bifurcation is necessary, since father's sister, sister, daughter, or any female sib relative who through sib exogamy has married into other sibs, and their descendants, belong, on account of patrilineal descent, to different sibs from ego.

Nevertheless, the emphasis upon the sib relatives is not so manifest in the whole kinship system as it might be. A partial explanation lies in the minute differentiation in the terminology, which to a certain extent has obscured this grouping. If we look at the application of the depreciatory modifiers, however, this emphasis at once becomes apparent. Only sib relatives are to be depreciated, inasmuch as they are regarded as members of one's own group. Non-sib relatives are not to be depreciated, since they are felt to be outside of one's own group.

Conceptually, sib relatives are considered nearer than non-sib relatives, even though their degree of remoteness from ego may be exactly the same. This is best expressed in the mourning obligations. The mourning period for paternal grandparents is one year, but for maternal grandparents only five months; for paternal uncle one year, and for maternal uncle five months; for father's brother's son nine months, and for mother's brother's son only three months. More instructive is the difference in mourning periods for a female sib relative before and after her marriage. The mourning period for father's unmarried sister, ego's unmarried sister, unmarried daughter, and brother's unmarried daughter, is one year; after their marriage, the mourning period is decreased to nine months, i. e., it is lessened by one degree. Therefore, we see that as long as these females remain unmarried they belong to ego's sib, but after marriage they belong to their husband's sibs. This transference through marriage has lessened their bond with the sib and, consequently, with ego. ①

The nomenclature of the non sib relatives is perhaps more expressive of this dual division of relatives. The differentiation between paternal grandparents ﹝tsu﹞ and maternal grandparents ﹝wai tsu﹞, paternal

---

① The mourning obligations of an unmarried female to her paternal relatives are just the same as those of her brother. After marriage, all these obligations are lessened by one degree, and, reciprocally, obligations of these relatives to her are also lessened by one degree.

uncle 〔*po* and *shu*〕 and maternal uncle 〔*chiu*〕, paternal aunt 〔*ku*〕 and maternal aunt 〔*i*〕, is, of course, a regular feature of a system based upon exogamous social grouping. But the interesting phenomenon is the merging of the father's sister's, mother's sister's, and mother's brother's descendants in the single term, *piao*.[1] *Piao*, as a term in itself, means "outside" or "external." The descendants of father's sister, and of mother's sister and brother, although consanguineal relatives of distinct affiliation, are all non-sib relatives, and hence their merging in the term *piao* is understandable.

The introduction and development of *piao* is also of historical interest. In the ancient system of the *Êrh Ya* and the *I Li*, father's sister's sons and mother's brother's sons were merged in the term *shêng,* through cross -cousin marriage. [2]mother's sister's children, being parallel cousins, stood alone as *ts'ung mu hsiung ti* 〔for males〕 and *Ts'ung mu tzŭ mei* 〔for females〕. During the first two centuries A.D., with cross-cousin marriage already long in abeyance, father's sister's sons were designated as *wai* 〔outside〕, e.g., *wai hsiung ti,*[3] and mother's brother's sons as *nei* 〔inside〕, e.g., *nei hsiung ti.*[4] At about the same time[5]*chung* and *piao*

---

[1] The *ku piao, chiu piao* and *i piao* are the three first-degree *piao* relationships of the Chinese system.

[2] See discussion under CROSS COUSIN MARRIAGE,below,pp.1167-1170.

[3] *I Li* 丧服, 33.9b: 姑之子. 郑注：外兄弟也.

[4] Ibid., 33.10b: 舅之子. 郑注：内兄弟也.

[5] *Hou-Han shu* 郑太传, 100.2-3a:……公业惧，乃诡词更对曰：……又明公将帅，皆中表腹心.

were used as equivalents of *nei* and *wai*, since *chung* means "middle," "inside," and *piao* means "outside," "external."

During the last few centuries of the first millennium B.C. and the first few centuries A.D., mother's sister's sons were usually designated by the newly extended term *i*, e.g., *i hsiung ti*, although *ts'ung mu hsiung ti* was still permissible.

From the fourth to the seventh centuries A.D. constant confusion was produced through the use of the terms *nei* or *wai* for mother's sister's children, and, consequently, a confusion of relatives involving father's sister's, mother's brother's and mother's sister's descendants.[①] The reason for this may lie in the fact that these relatives, although of clear affiliation, all belong to the non-sib group and are distinct from the exogamous partilineal sib group. During the T'ang period, the *chung* was dropped and *piao* alone was applied to all these relatives.[②] Thus *piao* became a general indicator for non-sib consanguineal relations descended from relatives of higher generations than ego.

---

① E.g.,*T'ung Tien,* 95.9a-12b: 为内外妹为兄弟妻服议：(The instance involved is neither mother's brother's daughter,nor father's sister's daughter,who ought to be *nei* or *wai*, respectively, but mother's sister's daughter) 晋徐众论云：徐恩龙娶姨妹为妇，妇亡，而诸弟以姨妹为嫂，嫂叔无服，不复为姨妹行丧. The 海录碎事 (cited by *Ch'êng wei lu,*3.20a) states: 唐人两姨之子，相谓为外兄弟. And 山堂肆考，角集，47b:两姨之子为外兄弟，姑舅之子为内兄弟，一说，姑子称舅子为内兄弟. The use of *nei* and *wai* is so confusing that even these encyclopaedists do not know which usage is correct.

② During the sixth century the subject of *piao* relationships became so popular that even genealogies were compiled for them, e.g. *Wei shu* 高谅传，57.5a:谅造亲表谱录四十许卷，自五世以下，内外曲尽，览者服其博记.

This conceptual as well as nomenclative dichotomy of relatives is a definitive expression of the exogamous patrilineal sib principle. At the same time, this principle has been modified by another factor-mourning rituals -resulting in the elaborate differentiation of collateral lines in the sib group, rather undermining its original function. But an understanding of this principle is most essential for a grasp of the system as a whole, since it is not only a potent moulding force but is as well a controlling factor in many important kinship usages, i.e., the depreciatory and complimentary terminologies.

## Mourning Grades

The Chinese mourning system is based upon the sib organization for its discrimination against non sib relatives, and on degree of relationships for the assignment of mourning grades. Mourning for sib relatives vanishes at the fourth degree 〔fourth collateral〕 and at the fourth generation, both ascending and descending from ego.[①] There is, consequently, in the kinship system a sharp differentiation of the first four collateral lines, and an indefinite grouping of all further collaterals in the *tsu* relationship.

Mourning, *sang fu* in Chinese, is a colossal subject in itself; here we can only touch upon those fundamental aspects that are prerequisite to an elucidation of its influence upon the kinship system. *Chan ts'ui* (three

---

① *Li Chi* 大传，34.7b: 四世而缌，服之穷也.

years), *tzŭ ts'ui* (one year), *ta kung* (nine months), *hsiao kung* (five months), and *ssŭ ma* (three months) are commonly known as the *wu fu*, "five grades of mourning." Actually, the number is greater than five. The specifications of these grades have fluctuated much from period to period; certain grades have been dropped or added in conformity with the excentricities of particular periods. Although the specifications may thus have changed, the fundamental principles which underlie these specifications have remained constant.

All the paraphernalia expressed by the above terms[1] are mere accessories, the fundamental units of mourning being the "mourning periods." The basic unit is the *year*. All other degrees are either *chia lung* 〔increased mourning〕, or *chiang shai* 〔decreased mourning〕, relative to the basic unit. These principles are best expounded in the *San nien wên* of the *Li Chi*, [2] which says:"Why is it that the mourning period for the *nearest kin* is one year? Because the interaction of heaven and earth has run its round; and the four seasons have gone through their changes. All things between heaven and earth begin their processes anew. The rules of mourning are intended to resemble them." "Why should there be three years mourning 〔for parents〕? The reason is to make it more impressive, *chia lung,* by

---

[1] 　The terms *chan ts'ui. tzŭ Ts'ui, ta kung,hsiao kung,* and *ssŭ ma* specify the kind of apparel to be worn at the mourning for a particular relative.

[2] 　三年问, 58. 3a-4b. For translations in European languages,cf.J. LEGGE, *Li Ki* Sacred Books of the East 28.393-4; and S. COUVREUR, *Li Ki*〔1913〕, 580-586.

doubling the period, so that it embraces two round years." ①"Then why have the mourning of nine months? The reason is to prevent excessive grief." Therefore three years 〔actually twenty-five months counted as three years〕 is the highest expression, *lung*, of mourning. Three months and five months ② are the lowest, *shai*. One year and nine months are the norms. Heaven above gives an example; earth below, a law; and man between, a pattern. The harmony and unity that should characterize men living in their kinships are hereby completely shown."

Mourning starts from the nearest kin with the basic unit of *ch'i*, one year. The nearest kin have three. According to the *Sang fu chüan*,③"the relation between father and son is one; between husband and wife is another; and between brothers is a third." With the three nearest kin, with the basic unit of *Ch'i*, and with the principles of *chia lung* and *chiang shai*, the whole system is correlated with the kinship system as in Diagram IV (see p. 201).

The process is as follows: The mourning period for father is *Ch'i*, one year; for grandfather, *ta kung*, nine months ;for great grandfather, *hsiao kung*, five months; and for great great grandfather, *ssŭ*, three months. This is called *shang shai*, "ascending decrease." The mourning period for son is

---

① Twenty-five months are counted as three years, hence the "three years"mourning is only two years and one month.

② "Five months" are counted as two seasons, which should be six months. The substitution of five for six reflects an ancient Chinese aversion for even numbers. Thus, the basic periods are: three months (one season), five months (two seasons), nine months (three seasons), and one year (four seasons).

③ *I Li* 30. 8b-9a.

*Ch'i*, one year; for grandson, *ta kung*, nine months; for great grandson, *hsiao kung*, five months; and for great great grandson, *ssǔ* three months. This is called *hsia shai*, "descending decrease." The mourning period for brother is *Ch'i*, one year; for father's brother's son, *ta kung*, nine months; for father's father's brother's son's son, *hsiao kung*, five months; and for father's father's father's brother's son's son's son, *ssǔ*, three months. This is called *P'ang shai*, "horizontal decrease."

The *chan ts'ui*, three years, mourning for father is *chia lung*, increased mourning; basically it is only one year. The one year, *Ch'i*, mourning for father's father and father's brothers, is likewise *chia lung*, since basically it is the *ta kung* grade, nine months.

All non-sib relatives, whether consanguineal or affinal, are given the last grade of mourning, *ssǔ ma*, three months, no matter how closely related they may be.[1] They are subject also to the principle of *chia lung*; e.g., in the ancient mourning specifications, the mourning grade for mother's sister is *hsiao kung*, five months, but for the mother's brother it is only *ssǔ ma*, three months;[2] the former is *chia lung*, and the latter is not. Basically they are all *ssǔ ma*.[3]

Mourning grades of a simpler kind must have existed long before the

---

[1]　*I Li* 丧服, 33.2a: 外亲之服皆缌也 .Cf. *Jih chih lu* 5.35-7.

[2]　In modern mourning specifications motber's brother is increased to five months,*hsiao kung*.

[3]　For the actual specifications one must consult the ritual works of each period. The above are merely general statements of principle.

Chou period, but their elaboration began only when they fell into the hands of the Confucianists.[1] Using the family and sib as the bases for their ideological structure, these literati elaborated the mourning system with a view to the maintenance of sib solidarity. In the course of this elaboration of the mourning system they also standardized its basis, the kinship system, for a carefully graded system of mourning rites requires a highly differential kinship nomenclature, lest an awkward incommen surability ensue. This is especially apparent in the comparison of the *Êrh Ya* and the *I Li* systems. The *Êrh Ya* system, when compared with the system recorded together with the mourning rites 〔 *Sang fu chuan* 〕 in the *I Li*, is inconsistent and less differential in many respects. Certain classical scholars naively tried to amend the *Êrh Ya* with the *I Li* system, since they considered the *Êrh Ya* system below the standard of Confucian ideals of kinship[2] They failed to see that the *Êrh Ya* represents an early state of the system, and the *I Li* a later but rationalized system worked over to conform with the mourning system.

There is no doubt that the *Êrh Ya* system was already to some extent rationalized through Confucian influences, but it is much less so than that in the *I Li*. With the Confucian ideals firmly implanted in the Chinese social

---

[1] Certain scholars believe that the three-year mourning for father was a Shang custom, and that the Ju 儒, who practiced it during the Chou period and later evolved into Confucianists, were descended from the Shang dynasty people. Cf. Hu Shih: 说儒, 胡适论学近著, 第一集, 19-23,90-94. For an opposite view cf. FÊNG Yu -Ian. *The Origin of Ju and Mo*, CHHP 10.279-310.

[2] Cf. 补正尔雅释亲宗族, by 郑珍, *Ch'ao ch'ing ch'ao* 〔*wen chi*〕. 1a-4b.

structure from the second century B.C. on, the mourning rites were increasingly elaborated and popularized,[1] and concomitantly the kinship system, until both reached their apogée during the T'ang period.

The elaborate mourning rites are a distinctive feature of Chinese ceremonial and social life. Under their influence the Chinese kinship system, through the increasing emphasis laid upon collateral differentiation and generation stratification, was transformed from a classificatory system based upon an exogamous sib organization into one of the descriptive type.[2]

---

[1]　Cf. 三年丧服的逐渐的推行, by Hu Shih, op. cit., 95 102.

[2]　Kingsley DAVIS and W. Lloyd WARNER have made some very pertinent remarks concerning the use of "classificatory" and "descriptive" in connection with kinship analysis (Structural Analysis of Kinship, *American Anthropologist,* 39: 2〔1937〕, 291-315). They have also formulated a new set of categories for the structural analysis of kinship, with which, I think, few students will agree. The present writer disagrees with them in many points on their interpretation of the Chinese system. Since, however, this MS is going to press as their article appears, it is not possible to elaborate this remark.

## DIAGRAM IV [1]

| IV | Kao tsu | 4 | | | | | |

Mourning Grades:
1 = ch'i, one year
2 = Ta kung, nine months
3 = Hsiao kung, six months
4 = Ssŭ ma, three months

I, II, III, IV indicate generations removed from ego

Ascending decrease →

| IV | Kao tsu | 4 |
| III | Tsêng tsu | 3 | Tsêng po tsu Tsêng shu tsu | 4 |
| II | Tsu | 2 | Po tsu Shu tsu | 3 | T'ang po tsu T'ang shu tsu | 4 |
| I | Fu | 1 | Po Shu | 2 | T'ang po T'ang shu | 3 | Tsai ts'ung po Tsai ts'ung shu | 4 |
| | EGO | | Hsiung Ti | 1 | T'ang hsiung T'ang ti | 2 | Tsai ts'ung hsiung Tsai ts'ung ti | 3 | Tsu hsiung Tsu ti | 4 | Horizontal decrease → |
| I | Tzŭ | 1 | Chih | 2 | T'ang chih | 3 | Tsai ts'ung chih | 4 |
| II | Sun | 2 | Chih sun | 3 | T'ang chih sun | 4 |
| III | Tsêng sun | 3 | Tsêng chih sun | 4 |
| IV | Hsüan sun | 4 |

Descending decrease →

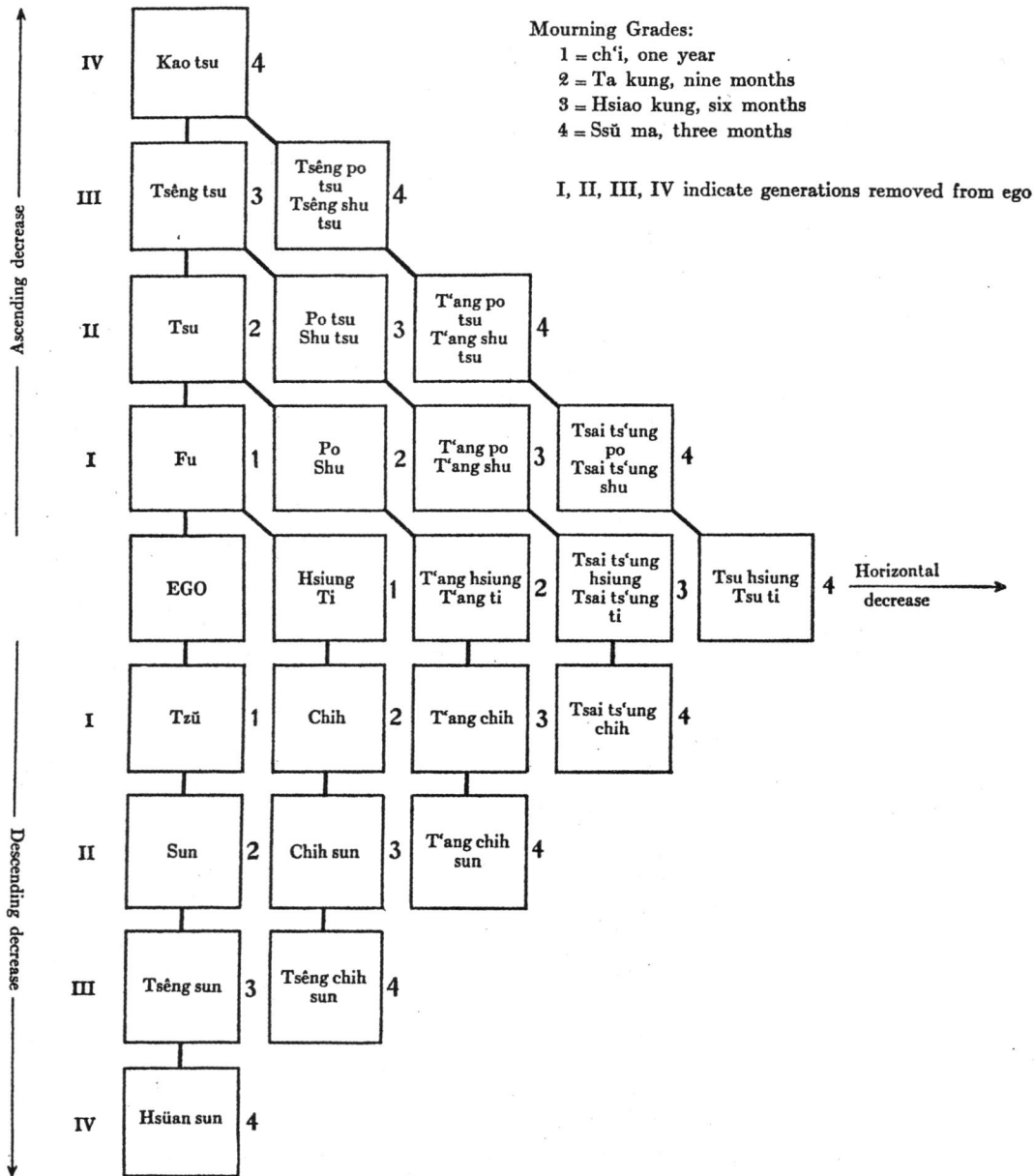

[1] Since the author is merely outlining the basic mourning system, only the male relatives are given. A complete specification would require eight to twelve diagrams.

## Cross–cousin Marriages

Cross-cousin marriage is permitted, but not encouraged, in modern China. Generally, it is discountenanced not on the ground that the blood relationship is too close but on the ground that older relatives might be estranged as a result of difficulties which might arise between the young married couple, or vice versa. On the other hand, however, it is desirable, because it increases the number of relationships and knits the bond more closely.[1] Theoretically and ritually, it has been disapproved since the beginning of the first century A.D.[2] Legal prohibition, however, came rather late, the first definite clause being found in the Ming Code.[3] Since the enforcement of this law proved rather difficult, in the Ch'ing Code this interdiction was invalidated by another clause, immediately following it, which allowed such marriages.[4] It must be noted that in modern

[1]　As the popular saying goes, 亲上加亲.

[2]　*Pai hu t'ung,* 10. 16a:外属小功以上，亦不得娶也,.是春秋传曰，讥娶母党也.袁准,of the Chin dynasty, says,〔*T'ung Tien,* 60. 16b 17a,内表不可为婚议〕曰：今之人内外相婚,礼欤？曰：中外之亲，近于同姓，同姓且犹不可，而况中外之亲乎！古人以为无疑，故不制也.今以古之不言，因谓之可婚.此不知礼者也.These statements probably read too much into the old ritual works.

[3]　*Ming lü chi chieh,* 6. 17a: 若娶己之姑舅两姨姊妹者，杖八十，并离异. The clause in the T'ang Code〔*T'ang lü shu* 1.14. 2b〕，其父母之姑舅两姨姊妹……并不得为婚……is sometimes expanded to include prohibition against cross cousin marriage. Cf. *Jung chai sui pi (hsü pi),* 8.12. The clause seems to indicate only parents' cross cousins，not one's own cross cousins; if so, the interdiction is against inter generation marriage rather than cross cousin marriage. But the *T'ung tien* (95. 11a) seems to show that during the T'ang period marriage with cross cousins and mother's sister's daughter was actually prohibited.

[4]　G. JAMIESON, Translations from the *General Code of laws of the Chinese Empire,* Chapter 18: "A man cannot marry the children or his aunt on the father's side, or of his uncle or aunt on the mother's side, because though of the same generation they are within the fifth degree of mourning." But a little later in the *Li,* it reads:"…… In the interest of the people it is permitted to marry with the children of a paternal aunt or of a maternal uncle or aunt." *China Review* 10 (1881-82) , 83. Cf. also Sir G. T. STAUNTON, *Ta Tsing Leu Lee* (1810), 115.

China the kinship system is not the primary regulator of marriage; the important factor is sib exogamy supplemented by the generation principle. Thus, not only marriage with cross-cousin, but also with parallel cousin by mother's sister is allowed.[1] No statistical data for cross cousin marriage are available at present, but my general impression is that the percentage is very small. In any event, cross-cousin marriage is in no way reflected in the modern kinship system.[2]

The ancient system as recorded in the *Êrh Ya* and the *I Li* reflects a preferential type of cross cousin-marriage in certain kinship equations.[3]The

---

[1] The practice of marriage with the mother's sister's daughter began at least as early as the third and fourth centuries A.D.E.g., *T'ung Tien* 95. 9a cites the discussion of 徐众 of the Chin dynasty concerning the mourning obligations of dual relationship for mother's sister's danghter who married one's own older brother. A great many useless discussions have been lavished on this subject.

[2] T. S. CHEN and J. K. SHRYOCK in their "Chinese Relationship Terms", *American Anthropologist* 34: 4, 623-669, interpretable in terms of cross-cousin marriage the fact that the father's sister's children and the mother's brotber's children are designated by the same terms (see Chen Shryock Table I. terms 85-92, and Tabe IV, terms 17-24, and note 33). But I do not see where the marriage element enters. The terms merely indicate cross-cousinship and nothing more. In order for these terms to be interpretable in terms of cross-cousin marriage, either the mother's brother or father's sister's husband must be addressed by the same term as that used for wife's father, or sister's husband or wife's brother addressed in cross-cousin terminology in fact, any usage that will bring in the marriage element. Unfortunately, no terminology of this sort exists in the modern system. Hence, the authors' interpretations involving cross-cousin marriage in notes 33, 34,39, 42, 61, 64, 65 and 67, are untenable. Furthermore, these interpretations are based on incomplete and faulty data. E.g., the important modifier piao is omitted from the terms of mother's sister's children, thus making mother's sister's daughters merge with wife's sisters. Mother's sister's children are *piao,* just as mother's brother's children and father's sister's children are *piao.* Not only cross-cousins are designated by *piao,* but also parallel cousins through mother's sister. This consideration completely invalidates the cross-cousin interpretation. Actually, since, as the authors have ably shown, the abandonment of the cross-cousin marriage custom was responsible for the development of the modem system, how can the modern system still be interpreted as indicative of that usage?

[3] The first to interpret the *Êrh Ya* system in terms of cross cousin marriage was M. GRANET, *La civilization chinoise.* 187. The thesis was further developed by sheu and Shryock, op. cit. 629-630.

terms concerned are the following: ①Chiu 舅: a. mother's brother, b. husband's father,② c. wife's father,as *wai chiu*.③ Ku 姑: a. father's sister, b.husband's mother, c.wife's mother, as *wai ku*. Shêng 甥: a. father's sister's sons, b.mother's brother's sons, c. wife's brother,④d. sister's husband (man speaking) .⑤These terms indubitably manifest cross cousin marriage of the bilateral type, couple with sister exchange, The latter practice is shown especially in the term *shêng*, which means wife's brother and sister's husband.

Indirect evidence can be obtained from the arrangement of the *Êrh Ya*. Here the terms on kinship are arranged into four groups: i. Tsung tsu 宗族, Relatives through father. ii. Mu tang 母党, Relatives through mother. iii.

---

① In the following notes some of the old Chinese interpretations of the extensions of these terms are given. They are not necessarily correct, but they do serve to show the traditional Chinese conceptions.

② The old interpretation of the extension of *chiu* and *ku* to include husband's father and mother is as follows: The one who is as venerable as father, but who is not the father, is mother's brother, *chiu*. The one to whom one is as attached as much as to mother, but who is not the mother, is father's sister, *ku*. Husband's parents are of similar relationship, hence we call them *chiu* and *ku*. Cf. *Pai hu T'ung,* 8. 20b: 称夫之父母谓姑舅何? 尊如父而非父者，舅也.亲如母而非母者，姑也.故称夫之父母为舅姑也.

③ Wife's parents are called *wai chiu* (outside *chiu*) and *wai ku* (outside *ku*), that is to say, the wife is an outsider who comes to one's own family and makes it her own family too. She calls the husband's parents *chiu* and *ku*. The husband, in reciprocating, calls her parents *wai chiu* and *wai ku,* as a sign of equality for both parties. *Shih Ming:* 妻之父曰外舅，母曰外姑，言妻从外来，谓至己家为归,故反此义以称之，夫妇匹敌之义也.

④ Wife's brothers are called *wai shêng* (outside *shêng*) because their sister marries ego and becomes ego's wife, hence her male siblings are the *shêng* of an outside sib. *Shih Ming:* 妻之昆弟曰外甥，其姊妹女也，来归己内为妻，故共男为外姓之甥.甥者，生也.他姓子本生于外，不得如其女来在己内也.

⑤ Kuo P'o's commentary on the term *shêng*, in the *Êrh Ya*, says that these four individuals are of equal status, hence they reciprocally call one another *shêng*.四人体体，故更相为甥. This conception of 敌体, equal status, between the relationships of *shêng*, has been the basis of most later interpretations; e.g., 姑之子为甥,舅之子为甥，妻之昆弟为甥，姊妹之夫为甥解，by 俞樾，诂经精舍自课文，春在堂全书本.

Ch'i tang 妻党, Relatives through wife. iv. Hun yin 婚姻, Relatives through husband. It is interesting to note that father's sister's sons, mother's brother's sons, sister's husband (M.S.), and sister's sons are all listed under Group iii, *ch'i tang*. The grouping of these relatives of quite distinct affiliations under *Relatives through wife* clearly demonstrates that the *Êrh Ya* system is built upon the practice of cross cousin marriage.

## Sororate

The sororate was operative during the feudal period, at least among the feudal lords.[1] The *Êrh Ya* gives the term for sister's husband 〔woman speaking〕 as *ssŭ*, literally "private." This is sometimes interpreted as evidence of the sororate, since a woman considers her sister's husband her "private."[2] The validity of this reasoning is rather dubious, without other terminological corroboration. *Ts'ung mu*, the term in the *Êrh Ya* and the *I Li* for mother's sister, has also been interpreted as a reflection of this usage.

---

[1]  Cf. M. GRANET, *La polygynie sororale et le sororat dans la Chine féodale,* 1920. The author overworks his material to arrive at forced conclusions, but most of the relevant data are collected in this little work. The thesis is also incorporated in his later work, *La civilization chinoise,* in which he has utilized the antiquated anthropological theory that the sororate and levirate represent survivals of an early fraternal group marriage.

[2]  Cf. CHEN and SHRYOCK, op. cit., 628. The *Shih Ming* interprets *ssŭ* in quite a different way. Female ego's sister's husband is called *ssŭ*, private, because this man has *private* relations with female ego's sister: 姊妹互相谓夫曰私，言其夫兄弟之中，此人与己姊妹有恩私也 .On the basis of this old interpretation, the *ssŭ* does not concern female ego at all, and so is scarcely evidence for the sororate.

*Ts'ung mu* literally means "following mother."[①] But the term is best interpreted as a counterpart of *ts'ung fu*, a term for father's brother; hence *ts'ung* indicates the collateral line rather than potential motherhood.

Throughout the historical period, including modern China, the sororate has been practiced, but, since the possibilities are reduced by infant betrothal, its occurrence has been sporadic only. The single reflection in the modern system comes in the term *i*, which means mother's sister, father's concubine, wife's sister, and concubine. This identification seems irrefutable, yet another explanation is possible. A man calls his friends *hsiung*, older brother, and *ti*, younger brother, as a sign of courtesy and intimacy. A woman also calls her female friends *tzŭ*, older sister, and *mei*, younger sister, for the same reason. It is perfectly natural for the wife to call and consider her husband's concubines *mei*, and actually she does. The term *i* may thus be extended without recourse to the actual sororate at all. Similarly, *i* is usually used by children for the father's concubines, [②] and by servants for the master's concubines, in both instances as a complimentary term.

---

① LIU Hsi (ca. 200 A.D.), in his *Shih Ming*, interprets *tsung mu* in the following manner: mother's sisters come to marry the father as *ti* 娣, hence they are of the status of *tsung mu*. Even if they do not marry the father, the term is still applied to them. This, I believe, is the earliest known sociological interpretation of kinship terminology. Whether or not it is correct is quite another matter.

② The *T'ung su p'ien* [ 18. 17a-17b ] states that the father's concubines are called *i*, because of the old *yin* marriage custom. *I* was originally a term for several sisters who married the same husband. In later times, the *yin* custom was discontinued but concubines are actually equivalent to the *yin*. Therefore, although father's concubines are not mother's sisters, *i* can still be applied to them. This sociological interpretation is rather erroneous. The *yin* marriage custom had nothing to do with the term *i*, and the *yin*'s were never called *i*, but always *chih* 侄 and *ti* 娣.

Where the sororate is practiced extensively, it may be accompanied by marriage with the wife's brother's daughter, because if the wife has no marriageable sister her brother's daughter is a good substitute. There are indications of such a practice in feudal China among the nobility.

When a feudal lord married, his bride was accompanied by eight bridesmaids called *yin*, who were his future concubines.[1] The *yin* were recruited in the following manner. The bride and the eight *yin* were divided into three groups, with three women in each group. The first group consisted of the bride, one of her younger sisters or younger half-sisters, *ti*,[2] and one of her older brother's daughters, *chih*. These three women constituted the principal group. Two other feudal states of the same sibname as the bride each supplied a principal *yin*, a *ti*, and a *chih*.[3] Thus there were three groups and nine women in all. The contribution to the *yin* by other states had to be entirely voluntary, and could not be solicited,[4] for it was not proper to ask

---

[1]    *Kung-yang chuan* 庄公十九年，8.1b 2a: 媵者何？诸侯娶一国，二国往媵之，以侄娣从. 侄者何？兄之子也，娣者何？弟也.

[2]    Whether *ti* 娣 meant the bride's actual younger sisters, or her younger half sisters, i.e. her father's *yin*'s daughters, is a matter of speculation. Probably *ti* meant only her younger half-sisters, since there is abundant evidence to show that the daughters of the principal wife, *fu jên*, were always married out as *fu jên*, and *yin*'s daughters always married out as *yin*. In this way the noble-born and low-born were always kept constant 贵贱有常. This interpretation tallies with the uses of *i* and *ti* in the *Êrh Ya*. Cf. 毛际盛: *Shuo wên chieh tzǔ shu i* 说文解字述谊 (聚学轩丛书本), 2.44a.

[3]    *Tso Chuan* 成公十八年，26.23a: 卫人来媵共姬，礼也. 凡诸侯嫁女，同姓媵之，异姓则否. This may have been the general rule, but there were exceptions.

[4]    *Kung-yang chuan* 庄公十九年，8.2a: 何休注：言往媵之者，礼. 君不求媵，二国自往媵夫人，所以一夫人之尊.

children of others to become the dishonorable *yin*.①

This elaborate system for the selection of the *yin* served to insure a large number of descendants for succession in the feudal lord's office.②A niece, rather than a second younger sister was included in the *yin* in order to create a difference in the blood, so that if the two sisters failed to bear issue, a niece of different blood might bear a son. Similarly, the two other groups of *yin* were selected from two different states, in order that their blood would be still more dissimilar and the chances of having an heir would thus be tripled.③ Sib relatives were selected for the *yin* with a view to preventing jealousy and intrigue within the harem.④

The *yin* custom was not strictly what is usually termed "secondary marriages." All the women were married at once, though if a *yin* were too young she could "wait her years in her parental state" until grown up, and was then sent to the bridegroom;⑤ but this was rather unusual. In theory, a feudal lord married only once in his life;⑥ if the principal wife, *fu jên*, died a yin might act for the *fu jên* in her ceremonal and social capacities but

① *Pai hu t'ung*,10.12a:所以不聘妾者何？人有子孙，欲尊之，义不可求人为贱也……妾虽贤不得为嫡.

② Ibid, 10,11a:天子诸侯一娶九女者何？重国广继嗣也.Ibid., 13b,大夫成功受封，得备八妾者，重国广嗣也.

③ *Pai hu t'ung*,10.11b:不娶两娣何？博异气也.娶三国女何？广异类也.恐一国血脉相似，以无子也.

④ Ibid., 备侄娣从者，为其必不相嫉妒也.一人有子，三人共之，若己生之也. *Kung-yung chuan*, 庄公十九年, 8.2a:何休注：必以侄娣从之者，欲使一人有子，二人喜也.所以防嫉妒，令继重嗣也.因以备尊尊亲亲也.

⑤ *Kung-yang chuan* 隐公七年, 3.8a:叔姬归于纪.注：叔姬者，伯姬之媵也.至是乃归者，待年父母之国也.

⑥ Ibid., 庄公十九年, 8.2a:诸侯一聘九女，诸侯不再娶.

could not assume the title of *fu jên*.[1] Actually, the *yin* had very little legal status, and were only "legalized mistresses" of the feudal lord.

The ministers, *Ch'ing ta fu*, of the feudal lords could have one wife and two concubines, but could not take the wife's sisters or nieces as *yin*.[2] There are discrepancies in the interpretation of this rule in the classical works, and in a few instances the ministers followed the feudal lords' example and took the wife's younger sister and niece as concubines.[3] The scholar class, *shih*, i.e., the lower ruling class, were allowed one wife and one concubine.[4] Opinions differ as to whether or not this one concubine could be the wife's younger sister or niece. According to Ku Yen wu (1613 1682), a scholar could not take his wife's younger sister or niece as concubine.[5] All commoners were allowed only one woman, at least in theory.[6]

To judge from the evidence, the *yin* custom may have been only a kind of "legalized incest," whereby the emperor and feudal lords might assure themselves of an heir. Some of the lower nobility, however, might have

---

[1]  *Tso Chuan* 隐公元年，2.2b 3a:孟子卒，继室以声子.杜注：诸侯始娶，则同姓之国以侄娣媵，元妃死则次妃摄治内事，犹不得称夫人，谓之继室.This rule was not absolute, cf. *Pai hu t'ung*,10–19。

[2]  *Pai hu t'ung*, 10.17b:卿大夫一妻二妾何？尊贤重继嗣也.不备侄娣何？北面之臣贱，势不足尽人骨肉之亲也.

[3]  E.g., *Tso Chuan*, 35.18a:初臧宣叔娶于铸，生贾及为而死，继室以其侄.

[4]  *Pai hu t'ung*, 10.18a:士一妻一妾何？下卿大夫礼也.丧服小记曰：士妾有子，则为之缌.

[5]  *Jih chih lu*, 5.34b:贵臣贵妾条.

[6]  This is what was called 匹夫匹妇.In fact, under the feudal system,the title to all land was held by the feudal lord, and the common people worked under a "serf" system；no one could afford two women unless he belonged to the ruling class.

followed suit later. It is not difficult to see why such a highly arbitrary custom could not have become very prevalent even among the nobility; not only was the supply of women limited, but the practice actually ran counter to the generation principle ideology of this period. For example, a feudal lord was not allowed to marry the noble women of his own estate, because, theoretically, everyone within his feudal state was his subject, and if the lord were married to any woman in his own state her parents would automatically be a generation higher than he and thus could no longer be his subjects. To avoid this contradiction, a feudal lord was required to marry outside his own state.[①] *yin* marriage was swept away with the feudal system during the third century B.C. Since the beginning of the Western Han period〔B.C. 206-A.D. 8〕, the practice has never again been recorded, either among the royalty or the nobility.[②]

When we turn to the ancient kinship system, we find there a peculiarity which seems to reflect the practice of marriage with the wife's brother's daughter. In the *Êrh Ya* sister's sons are called *chu* (M.S.). In a later passage, the same relative is called *shêng*. It has been remarked above, in connection with cross cousin marriage, that in the *Êrh Ya*, *shêng* is principally used for father's sister's sons, mother's brother's sons, wife's brothers, and sister's

---

[①]　*Pai hu t'ung*, 10.15a: 诸侯所以不得自娶国中何? 诸侯不得专封, 义不臣其父母.春秋传曰: 宋三世无大夫, 恶其内娶也.

[②]　Some students have even suspected that the yin marriage custom was a mere invention of the Han scholars.

husband (M.S.). This use of *shêng* to mean sister's sons does not comply very well with the generation principle stressed in the *Êrh Ya*.[1]

There is also a peculiar usage of *shêng* in the works of Mencius 〔B.C. 373-289〕. Mencius used *shêng* to mean daughter's husband.[2] It seems that the overriding of the generation principle in the use of *shêng*, was a phenomenon that appeared rather late in the feudal period. *shêng* was applied, during the feudal period, to 1. father's sister's sons; 2. mother's brother's sons; 3. wife's brothers; 4. sister's husband (M.S.); 5. sister's son (M.S.); 6. daughter's husband.

The first four connotations can be interpreted in terms of cross cousin marriage of the bilateral type, together with sister exchange. The last two meanings seem to demand a cross cousin marriage of the above type, together with a marriage with the wife's brother's daughter. In a case of this sort, both sister's husband and sister's son can marry ego's daughter, and ego's daughter's husband will be identified with both sister's husband and sister's son. However, in view of the fact that marriage with the wife's brother's daughter was only a "legalized incest" among the nobility and never a prevalent practice, teknonymy is a more plausible, and a simpler, explanation. Both sister's son and daughter's husband will be *shêng* to ego's own son, if cross cousin-marriage is assumed; ego simply adopts the son's

---

①     The only other term is the *Êrh Ya* which overrides generations, is *shu* 叔 ,for father's younger brother and husband's younger brother.

②     *Mêng tzǔ*, 10A. 10b:舜尚见帝，帝馆甥于贰室……

term in addressing them.

On the whole, the influence of the sororate, both on the ancient and modern kinship systems, has been rather negligible. Insofar as the evidence goes, the sororate, both in ancient and modern China, is only a permissive type of marriage, that is to say, ego's marriage with one woman does not affect the status of marriage of her sisters, nor does it affect ego's own marriage status.

## Levirate[1]

The junior levirate certainly exists in a few parts of modern China, at least among the poorer classes,[2] but, even in the few places where it is practiced, it is not considered respectable. A man adopts this only as a last resort in getting a wife. If necessary, he can sell his brother's widow and use the "bride-price" to marry another woman. Legally, marriage with the older

---

[1]　Sir James Frazer has insisted upon the intimate co-existence of the sororate and the levirate (*Totemism and Exogamy*, 1910, 4. 139-150). R. H. LOWIE also says: "The connection would undoubtedly appear to be even closer were not much of our information on marriage rules of primitive tribes of rather haphazard  character. That is, it may safely be assumed that in not a few' instances it is sheer negligence or defective observation that has made writers report one of the two customs without the other." (*Primitive Society*, 1920, p. 36.) lf this correlation is valid, we should find the levirate in China as a correlative institution.

[2]　Cf. *China Review*, 10〔1881-2〕, 71, The levirate in China. Also. HUANG Hua-chieh 黄华节, Shu chieh sao 叔接嫂, *Eastern Miscellany*, 31: 7〔1934〕, 妇20-21. P. G. Von Möllendorff once remarked, "I have not heen able to find the slightest trace of it (levirate), and it can never be of the same importance with the Chinese as with other people (e.g. to keep the family property), as posthumous adoption, the Chinese substitute for it" fully meets the object. *The Family Law of the Chinese*〔1896〕, 17.

brother's or younger brother's widow is stringently prohibited; ① the punishment is strangulation for both parties. G. Jamieson has doubted its existence in China at all under such heavy penalties. ②

Whether or not the junior levirate existed in ancient China is quite problematical. Granet cites two cases from the *Tso Chuan*, but these can hardly be interpreted as evidence for the levirate.③ Chên and Shryock say that "the relationship terms indicates only the junior levirate, in which an older brother marries his deceased younger brother's wife. A wife calls her

---

① This law was first explicitly stated in the *Ming lü chi chieh* 6.20, promulgated during the period Hung-wu. 1368-1398 A.D. (latest revision, 1610 A.D.). In all earlier codes the levirate was prohibited under a more general clause, e.g., in the *T'ang lü shu i*, l4, 3a: 诸尝为祖免亲之妻而嫁娶者，各杖一百．缌麻及舅甥妻，徒一年．小功以上以奸论．妾各减二等，并离之．Under this clause, the levirate is out of the question.

On the other hand, the explicit clause in the Ming Code against the levirate may be a reaction to its introduction into China through the Mongols of the yuan dynasty. Cf. 李鲁人：元代蒙古收继婚俗传入内地之影响．大公报，史地周刊，No.8,April 10,1936,(Sheet 11),p.3.

② *China Review* 10.83 says: "In view of the severe penalty for it, it is scarcely possible that the levirate can be practiced in any part of China."

③ *La civilisation chinoise*, 424-425. The two cases cited are: Pi Wu Ts'un〔LEGGE, *Chinese Classics*, V: ii, 773〕; *Tzǔ Yüan and Hsi Kuei*〔Ibid, V: i, 115〕. In the first case, Pi Wu Ts'un, who was going to war and intended to marry a woman of better status, refused his father's proposal on the pretext that his father would be able to marry his younger brother to the woman in question. The woman proposed by his father not only cannot he regarded as his wife, but not even as his fiancée. In the second case, Tzǔ Yüan already had the full authority of the state of ch'u, and did not need to marry his older brother's widow in order to acquire his brother's authority, as Granet's theory demands. On the other hand, Hsi Kuei was a noted beauty and Tzǔ Yüan's attempted Seduction was motivated by lust. Unfortunately for Granet's thesis, Tzǔ Yüan did not succeed in seducing her, and was soon killed.

According to the ancient mourning specifications, sister-in-law and brother-in-law are not subject to mourning obligations, hence Granet considers his hypothesis confirmed inasmuch as relatives without mourning obligations may marry. But mere mourning obligations do not prevent marriage, e. g., cross-cousins have mourning obligations to each other but, according to Granet's theory, they are prescribed to marry!

What we need are actual instances of the levirate-not this ambiguous and anomalous kind of material which may he interpreted to support any kind of hypothesis. Granet is laboring to use the sororate and levirate as proof of an earlier fraternal groupmarriage which is in itself a hopeless hypothesis.

husband and her husband's older brother (possible husbands) by the same term, *po*, but uses a different term for his younger brother." [1] The authors are somewhat confused in this. Where only the older brother can marry the younger brother's widow, the practice is termed the "senior" levirate, not the "junior" levirate. The "senior" levirate alone is not found in Asia. Either both forms of the levirate are practiced by the same people, or the junior levirate alone is practiced, as in India, southeastern Asia, and northeastern Asia. There is also an anachronism in the connotations of *po* cited by the authors. In a few places in the "Book of Odes," *po* is interpreted as meaning husband, [2] but this usage is not found in literature after 500 B.C. On the other hand, the use of *po* to mean husband's older brother did not begin until the tenth century A.D. [3] Thus, *po* meaning husband and *po* meaning husband's older brother not only are not contemporaneous, but are separated by a hiatus of fifteen centuries! Historically minded though the Chinese may be, I do not see how one can interpret this terminology in terms of the levirate.

　　Chattopadhyay has interpreted the differentiation of older and younger

---

[1]　　CHEN and SHRYOCK, op. cit. 628-629.

[2]　*Shih Ching,* 3C. 7a-8b: 伯兮朅兮，邦之桀兮；伯也执殳，为王前驱.自伯之东，首如飞蓬，岂无膏沐，谁适为容……The *po* used here is sometimes interpreted as meaning husband, but it is uncertain whether *po* is a relationship term for husband, or a reference to the official title the husband holds, or simply a word meaning "the brave and handsome one." To judge from the context, the last is the preferable interpretation.

[3]　　T'ao Yo 陶岳, *Wu tai shih pu* 五代史补(豫章丛书本), 5.8a:〔李〕涛为人不拘礼法，与弟瀚虽甚雍睦，然聚话之际，不典之言，往往间作.瀚娶礼部尚书窦宁固之女，年甲稍高，成婚之名，窦氏出参涛，辄望尘下拜.瀚惊曰：大哥风狂耶? 新妇参阿伯，岂有答礼仪? 涛应曰：我不风，只将是亲家母.

brothers in India in terms of the junior levirate. [1]Such an interpretation is extremely weak, unless supported by other terminological corroboration. If the junior levirate explains the differentiation of older and younger brothers, it certainly does not explain the differentiation of older and younger sisters, which is also characteristic of most Indian systems. Whether or not the *tsung fa* adequately explains the expression of the category of age in generation in the Chinese system, as advocated by the old Chinese authors, we do not know; certainly this expression cannot be explained by the junior levirate, which is of so sporadic occurrence in China.

## Teknonymy

We have already discussed several types of marriages that are relevant to the determination of minor kinship peculiarities. With the exception of cross cousin marriage, the influence of the others, both on the ancient and modern systems, has been rather negligible. These problems will be further discussed here in connection with teknonymy and other peculiarities in the system, in order to ascertain the actual determining factor or factors.

As has already been shown, generation is an important structural principle in the Chinese system. It also regulates marriage among relatives, and plays an important role in the functioning of Chinese social and

---

[1] Chattopadhyay, Levirate and Kinship in India. *Man*,22 (1922), 25. W. Lloyd WARNER, Kinship Morphology of Forty-one North Australian Tribes, *American Anthropologist* 35. 66 makes a similar interpretation.

ceremonial life as a whole, since the dealings between relatives are in many respects based upon generation differences, so also in the assignment of mourning grades, etc. Since  generation is such an important factor in the system, we should  expect it to be consistently expressed in terminology. Yet there are  some notable exceptions. mother's brother and wife's brother are  designated by the same term, *chiu*; mother's sister and wife's  sister by the same term, *i*; father's older brother and husband's  older brother by the same term, *po*; father's younger brother and  husband's younger brother by the same term, *shu*; father's sister  and husband's sister by the same term, *ku*; etc. These peculiarities are  of significance, because originally the generations of these  relatives were clearly differentiated by distinct terms, and only in  the course of time were they gradually merged into each other.

First, let us take the connotations of the term *chiu*, and the  terms for the wife's brother, during the various periods, and  arrange them in a single table, as follows:

| Period | Connotations of *chiu* | Terms for wife's brother |
|---|---|---|
| I  1st Millennium B.C. | mother's brother<br>husband's father<br>wife's father | *shêng* |
| II  1st Millennium A.D. | mother's brother | *fu hsiung  ti* |
| III  2nd Millennium A.D. | mother's brother<br>wife's brother | *chiu* |

The various connotations of the term *chiu* in Period I are perfectly intelligible from the point of view of cross cousin marriage, as discussed above. In such a marriage, the mother's brother and husband's father is the same person, so also the mother's brother and wife's father. In Period II the cross cousin marriage was dropped, and consequently the meaning of *chiu* became confined to mother's brother.

The terms for the wife's brother are different for each of the three periods. In Period I wife's brother was called *shêng*甥. *Shêng* also meant, in this period, father's sister's son, mother's brother's son and sister's husband (man speaking) .[1] This is also explicable in terms of cross cousin marriage of the bilateral type, coupled with sister exchange. In Period II, because of the disappearance of this type of marriage, *shêng* was no longer applicable to any of these relatives and new terms were introduced to take its places. *Fu hsiung ti* is the term used for wife's brother.[2]

In Period Ⅲ the term *chiu* (mother's brother) was extended to include wife's brother. The first use of *chiu* in this new meaning is to be found in the *Hsin T'ang Shu*. In the biography of Chu Yen-shou, we read: "Yang Hsing -mi's wife is the older sister of Chu Yen-shou……Hsing-mi 〔luring Chu

---

[1] Cf. *Êrh Ya*.

[2] The term is purely descriptive. *Fu* 妇 means wife, *hsiung ti* means brother (older and younger). *Pei Ch'i Shu* 崔昂传, 30.9b-10a:崔昂直臣，魏收才士，妇兄妹夫，俱省罪过。*Ibid*,郑元礼传,29.6b:但知妹夫，疏于妇弟.*Ch'i hsiung ti* 妻兄弟 and *nei hsiuny ti* 内兄弟 were also permissible at this time. Cf. Table Ⅲ.〔From this point the editors have been forced to substitute the symbol for some frequently recurring characters. In this instance the missing characters are No. 11 on p. 155.〕

Yen-shou into a trap〕says, 'I have lost my eyesight and my sons are too young. Having *chiu* 〔meaning Chu Yen-shou〕take my place, I shall have no worry.' ' "[1] This is certainly a curious extension of the use of *chiu*, for, through all the previous vicissitudes of the term, the generation element had always been preserved. This overriding of the generation principle certainly warrants an explanation.

A strictly sociological interpretation would point to a marriage with the wife's brother's daughter. In Period I *chiu* also meant father in law; since, in this interpretation, the wife's brother is a potential father in law, the extension of the term *chiu* to include him would be perfectly logical. However, there are several difficulties in such an interpretation. In the first place, historical evidence does not seem to support this hypothesis. wife's brother's daughter marriage in connection with the yin custom was never a preferred form, nor, as stated above, was it common even among the feudal nobility. Moreover, it disappeared together with the feudal system during the third century B.C., and has never been practiced since. Secondly, *chiu* had ceased to mean wife's father at least a thousand years before it was extended to mean wife's brother. These two temporal considerations, involving a hiatus of more than a millennium, are irreconcilable with such an interpretation. Thirdly, such a marriage contradicts the generation

---

① *Hsin T'ang shu* 朱延寿传，189.10a：田頵之附全忠，延寿阴约曰：公有所为，我愿执鞭．頵喜．二人谋绝行密.行密忧甚，绐病目，行触柱，僵.妻，延寿姊也，掖之.行密泣曰：吾丧明，诸子幼，得舅代，我无忧矣.〔The missing character is No. 16 on p. 156.〕

principle; wife's brother's daughter is one generation lower than ego; and thus, in the Chinese system, is within the incest group. Legally, inter generation marriage between all relatives became definitely prohibited at least half a millennium before *chiu* was extended to mean wife's brother.[1] In the face of these objections, the above interpretation is untenable.

It is significant that Chinese scholars had been employing teknonymy to explain this terminological anomaly long before the introduction of the term into anthropological discussion by E. B. Tylor.[2] Ch'ien Ta hsin〔1727-1804〕, one of the most penetrating classical scholars of his time, attributed this extension of the meaning of *chiu* to the gradual, imperceptible effect of the practice of teknonymy.[3] wife's brothers are *chiu* to one's own children. The father, adopting the language of his children, also calls his wife's brothers *chiu*. This process can clearly be seen in the above mentioned instance of Chu Yen-shou. Yang Hsingmi called Chu Yen-shou *chiu*, at the same time mentioning his own sons. One can infer that, after long teknonymous usage, the term *chiu* established itself and finally displaced the older term.

Whether or not this hypothesis can be sustained depends upon the

---

[1]  The T'ang Code, compiled and promulgated during the period A.D. 627-683,stringently prohibits inter -generation marriage: *T'ang lü shu i* 13.2.

[2]  On a Method of Investigating the Development of Institutions , *Journal, Anthropological Institute*, 18 (1889), 245-69.

[3]  *Hêng yen lu*, 3.13b: 予按……后世妻之兄弟独得舅名，盖从其子女之称，遂相沿不觉耳.

additional evidence we can adduce for its support, or, in other words, upon whether or not it can explain all the peculiarities of the same nature in the system. Let us now turn to the examination of those terms by which the wife addresses her husband's brothers: *po* for the husband's older brother, and *shu* for the husband's younger brother. But *po* was originally a term for father's older brother, and *shu* for father's younger brother. This overriding of generations is quite aberrant, from any point of view. Insofar as I am aware, there is no social or marital usage in China, nor is there any comparable usage that ethnographic data suggest, which could give rise to such a terminology.

From the historical point of view, the terms for these relatives were different at different periods. In the *Êrh Ya* the father's older brother is called *shih fu*. From the second century B.C. down to the present *po fu* has been the standard term, but from the fourth century A.D. on, *po* alone also has been in use.[1]

In the *Êrh Ya* husband's older brother is called *hsiung kung*.[2] During the succeeding centuries *hsiung chang* was commonly employed.[3] Ca. the tenth century A.D. *po* was extended to include husband's older brother.[4]

---

[1]　*Li Chi* 曾子曰，18.10a:已祭而见伯父叔父.*Yen shih chia hsün* 风操篇 2.6b:古人皆呼伯父叔父，而今世多单呼伯叔.Cf. *Hêng yen lu*, 3.6-7.

[2]　夫之兄为兄公.

[3]　*Shih Ming*. 夫之兄……俗间曰兄章.Cf.Table IV,term 5.

[4]　See p. 1179, note [3].

In the *Êrh Ya* the father's younger brother is called *shu fu*. This term has continued in use without any radical change down to the present; as in the case of *po*, above, from the fourth century A.D. on *shu* alone has also been in use. *Shu* is also used in the *Êrh Ya* for husband's younger brother. This usage is rather unusual, inasmuch as it overrides generations and thus contradicts its own statement of principle, that "husband's siblings are affinal siblings."[①]

As has been stated above, no possible explanation for this blending of generations can be found in marriage forms; the only possible alternative is teknonymy. Husband's brother's are *po* and *shu* to female ego's own children. The mother, adopting the terminology of her children, also calls them *po* and *shu*. This case tremendously strengthens our hypothesis, since no other known social factor or form of marital relationship can adequately explain these usages.

A similar situation exists in the terminology for father's sister and husband's sister, both called *ku*, and mother's sister and wife's sister, called *i*.

As has already been pointed out, *ku* is used in the *Êrh Ya* for father's sister, husband's mother, and wife's mother 〔e.g., *wai ku*〕, as a result of cross-cousin marriage. When cross-cousin marriage declined, *ku* was usually employed for father's sister alone. In the *Êrh Ya*, husband's older

---

① *Êrh Ya*: 妇之党为婚兄弟，婿之党为姻兄弟.〔The missing character is No. 18 on p. 156.〕

sister is called *nü kung*, and younger sister *nü mei*.[1] Somewhat later *shu mei* was used for the husband's younger sister. [2] In the fourth century A.D. the term *ku* began to be extended to include husband's sisters.[3] The factors behind this extension cannot be exactly ascertained, although the marriage rules and social customs of the period concerned are fairly well known. The extension could not have been due to marriage with the wife's brother's daughter, in which case the husband's sister would be elevated to the position of the husband's father's sister; the above-cited objections to a similar interpretation of *chiu* also apply here. Furthermore, other features do not follow either terminologically [4] or conceptually.[5] Teknonymy remains the best explanation since husband's sisters are *ku* to female ego's own children.

Originally *i* was used, as in the *Êrh Ya*, for wife's sisters. In the *Êrh*

---

[1]　夫之姊为女公，夫之女弟为女妹.〔No.11 on p.155.〕

[2]　*Hou Han Shu* 曹世叔妻《班昭》传，114,8b:妇人之得意于夫主，由舅姑之爱己也；舅姑之爱己，由叔妹之誉己也.〔First and second are no. 16 on p.156; last ,No.11 on p.155.〕

[3]　The earliest occurrence of the term *hsiao ku* for husband's sister is in the famous poem 古诗为焦仲卿妻作(*Yü T'ai hsin yung chi*,1.17b):却与小姑别，泪落连珠子.新妇初来时，小姑始扶床，今日被驱遣，小姑如我长.The literature on the dating of this poem has already become enormous. Hu Shih tends to date it earlier than most others, about the middle of the third century A.D., cf.现代评论，6:149.9-14:孔雀东南飞的年代.Others tend to date it much later, about the fourth and fifth centuries A.D.

[4]　E.g., among the Miwok, where marriage with the wife's brother's daughter is reflected in twelve terms〔E. W. GIFFORD, *Miwok Moieties*, University of California Publications in American Archaeology and Ethnology, 1916, p. 186〕, but these are all lacking in the Chinese system.

[5]　Among the Omaha, marriage with the wife's brother's daughter is reflected in the conceptual identification of the father's sister, the female ego, and the brother's daughter〔A. LESSER, Kinship Origins in the Light of Some Distributions, *American Anthropologist* 31 (1929), 711-712〕, but it is not indicated in the terminology. In the Chinese system the generations of father's sister, husband's father's sister, and the husband's sister are clearly distinguished conceptually, although the terminology fails to differentiate them.

*Ya* mother's sisters are called *Ts'ung mu*. The earliest use of *i* to mean mother's sister is found in the *Tso Chuan*. In the twenty-third year 〔B.C. 550〕 of Duke Hsiang, a passage reads, "*I*'s daughter of Mu Chiang."[①] By checking the relatives connected with Mu Chiang, one finds that the term, *i*, here does not mean wife's sister 〔or married sister, woman speaking〕 as it should, but mother's sister. As a matter of fact, the passage should read, "*Ts'ung mu*'s daughter of Mu Chiang," not, "*i*'s daughter."

Theoretically, the sororate, together with a marriage with the father's widows, would adequately explain the usage. In this combined type of marriage, the father marries mother's sisters and ego marries wife's sisters. Ego again marries father's widows after his decease. Then mother's sisters become equated with wife's sisters. This explanation seems fantastic but has some support, since a man's secondary wives (concubines) may also be called *i*, i.e., mother's sisters, wife's sisters, and secondary wives are all grouped in one class. It is well known that the sororate was practiced among the feudal nobility, but, as regards the inheritance of father's widows, there is no authenticated evidence.[②] Indeed, such a marriage would have been

---

① *Tso chuan* 襄公二十三年, 35.18a.

② M. Granet cites the case of Duke Hsüan 〔718-700 B.C. 〕of Wei who married his father's concubine I Chiang (*La civilisation chinoise*, p. 401). Apparently, Granet is not aware of the fact that Ku Tung-kao 顾栋高 〔1679-1757〕has convincingly shown that I Chiang had not previously been Duke Hsüan's father's concubine (*Ch'un Ch'iu ta shih piao* 春秋大事表, 清经解 ed, 50. 3a-4b: 卫夷姜晋齐姜辨).Even if it be admitted that this is an authentic instance of step-mother and step-son marriage, nothing is proved thereby, since the instance is quite anomalous. Not only are such anomalies recorded in quite a few instances from the Ch'un Ch'iu period, but also examples of incest, involving actual blood relationship, like grandmother and grandson,brother and

abhorrent to the ancient Chinese. We learn that the old writers detested the Hsiung-nu, pastoral nomads of the northern steppes, who married their fathers' widows, and never failed to mention this as an excuse for derision.①

K'ung Ying-ta 〔A.D. 574-648〕 explained the extension of *i* to include mother's sister (Ts'ung mu) as due to the psychological similarity between these relatives.② Mother's sister's are *i* to one's father, just as wife's sisters are *i* to oneself. The son, imitating the language of his father, also applies *i* to his father's *i*. In short, this case seems to demand a psychological explanation, together with reverse teknonymy.

The connotations of *shên* are likewise of significance. Father's younger brother's wife and husband's younger brother's wife are both called *shên* in the vocative. In the *Êrh Ya* father's younger brother's wife is called *shu mu*, which is the standard term today. *Shên* first came into use during the Sung period; it is usually regarded as a contracted pronunciation of *shih mu*.③ Its extension to include husband's younger brother's wife was effected about

---

sister, cf. 王士廉：左淫类记.But Granet has omitted these. Indeed,such anomalies are always cropping up in Chinese history, even in quite recent times,e.g., the T'ang Emperor Kao-tsung〔650-684〕married his father's concubine Wu Chao 武 曌 later known as the notorious Empress Wu of the T'ang dynasty, and the Emperor Hsüan-tsung〔712-756〕married his son's concubine Yang Yü-huan, well known to Europeans as the foremost beauty of China. One wonders how Granet would interpret these instances.

① *Shih Chi* 匈奴列传, 110.2a: 父死妻其后母,兄弟死皆取其妻妻之. The Hsiung-Nu customs of marrying father's widows other than one's own mother and the levirate were so well known to the ancient Chinese that they frequently mentioned them as a sign of the moral inferiority of the Hsiung-nu.

② *Tso Chuan* 襄公二十三年, 35.18a.

③ *Ming tao tsa chih,* 13b :王圣美尝言，经传无婶字......考其说,婶字乃世母二字合呼也. *Shih mu,* pronounced as one word ,because *shim*, or *shên*.

the same period.[1] No possible marital relationships could give rise to such an equation of relatives, nor could any other sociological factor. Teknonymy offers the simplest solution. Husband's younger brother's wife is the *shên* of female ego's children.

The origin of the terms *kung*, for husband's father, and *P'o*, for husband's mother, has never been investigated. The old term for husband's father is *chiu*, and for husband's mother, *ku*, both of which reflect cross-cousin marriage. During the first millennium A.D. a large number of terms were introduced for the designation of these two relatives, since *chiu* and *ku* were no longer applicable after the discontinuance of that particular type of marriage, but *kung* and *p'o* finally gained prevalence.[2]

On the other hand, *kung* and *P'o* are prevalent grandparent terms.[3] Why the wife should apply grandparent terms to the husband's parents is rather perplexing. This terminology is most susceptible to marital irregularities, but we cannot see what marital form, no matter how startling, could be involved here. But if we assume teknonymy, the situation immediately explains itself.

The foregoing cases comprise the most significant terminological

---

[1]  *Tzŭ wei tsa chi* 紫薇杂记, of Lü Tzu-Ch'ien 吕祖谦, 1137-1181 A.D.〔*Shuo fu* 说郛, 19〕2a: 吕氏旧俗，母母受娣房婢拜，以受其主母拜也. 娣见母母房婢妮，即答拜，是亦毋尊尊之义也……母母于娣处自称名，或去名不称新妇，娣于母处则称之. *Mu mu* is used in the sense of husband's older brother's wife, and *shên* in the sense of husband's younger brother's wife.

[2]  See Table IV, terms 1 and 2.

[3]  See Table I, terms 13 and 14.

anomalies, and constitute about all the instances in the Chinese system, both ancient and modern, where the generation principle is openly violated. In every case we have tried to explain these exceptions by facts and hypotheses which have proved illuminating in the discussion of analogous phenomena elsewhere. But we have found none of them applicable to the Chinese situation; rather, we have found teknonymy the only satisfactory explanation.

There can be no doubt that teknonymy is the determining factor in all these cases, but one may ask whether teknonymy is universal in China and of sufficient antiquity to have been involved in producing such effects in kinship terminology. The universality of this practice in China is unquestionable; the frequency of its use, however, might have varied in time and place. At times the practice was so accentuated that the ordinary forms of address became hardly intelligible.[1] In many regions, e.g., Wusih, Kiangsu, the bride ordinarily addresses her husband's relatives as if she were one generation lower. The teknonymy practiced is usually of the type that omits the child's name, just as in English a man may call his wife simply "mother." This type is especially efficacious in producing the irregularities just discussed.

As regards the antiquity of teknonymy, we must depend upon historical

---

[1]　E.g., the extreme instance of the practice of teknonymy in South China, as recorded in the *Ch'ing hsiang tsa chi* 青箱杂记, by Wu ch'u-hou 吴处厚 ca .1080 A.D.〔涵芬楼 ed.〕3.2b-3a,of the Sung period ,which reads：岭南风俗相呼不以行第，唯以各人所生男女小名呼其父母.元丰中〔1078-1085〕,余任大理丞，断宾州〔modern 宾阳县 in Kwangsi〕奏案，有民韦超，男名首，即呼韦超作父首.韦邀男名满，即呼韦邀作父满.韦全【男】女名插娘，即呼韦全为父插.韦庶女名睡娘，即呼庶作父睡，妻作姊睡.

evidence. The earliest instance that can be interpreted as teknonymy is recorded in Kung-yang's commentary on the *Spring and Autumn Annals* 〔Ch'un Ch'iu〕. In the sixth year of Duke Ai 〔B.C. 489〕 is recorded an instance concerning Ch'ên Ch'i. He, in referring to his wife, says, "The mother of Ch'ang ...'"[①] Ch'ang is known to have been Ch'ên Ch'i's son. The teknonymous usage here is indubitably clear. This instance, in the fifth century B.C., is more than a millennium earlier than most of the cases we have discussed above, except those involving *i* and *shêng*, which are about contemporaneous. On the other hand, if we make allowance for the conservative spirit of the classical writers in recording colloquial language, it is reasonable to infer that teknonymy is much older than this documentary evidence would indicate.

The influence of teknonymy on kinship terminology is quite apparent. Gifford, in discussing similar usages in the English and Californian kinship terminologies, has cogently remarked: "There must be, in other kinship systems, many analogous cases 〔cases analogous to the English teknonymy of calling husband "daddy" and wife "mother"〕, some of them crystallized into invariable custom like the Luiseňo case, cases which require no startling form  of marriage for their explanation, but which could be readily understood as our own, if we were but familiar with the family of the group

---

① *Kung-yang chuan* 哀公六年，27.12a：诸大夫皆在朝，陈乞曰：常之母，有鱼菽之祭，愿诸大夫之化我也.

in question." ①

In the very limited literature on teknonymy, various theories have been put forth to account for its origin, but no serious attempt has been made to use it in explanation of other social phenomena. Teknonymy as a usage is based on kinship and kinship nomenclature—a circumlocutory way of expressing embarrassing relationships. Through long and intensive use, why should it not have produced certain peculiarities in kinship terminologies, as other social usages are reputed to have done? The Chinese cases are especially illuminating. It would require a series of marital or other special practices to explain the peculiarities of *chiu, po, shu, ku, i, shên, kung, p'o* and *shêng*, whereas they can uniformly be explained by the single principle of teknonymy.

## Historical Review of Terms

The Chinese method of counting relationships starts with the three

---

① *Californian Kinship Terminoloyies 265.* In the Chinese instances the situation is so apparent that even so amateur an observer as Hart has been led to remark: "The nomenclature employed in the designation of two brothers-in-law and two sisters-in-law, i.e., by a wife toward the brothers and sisters of her husband, and by a husband toward the brothers and sisters of his wife, seems to have its origin in the names applied to such people by the children (their class children, or nephews and nieces) born of the marriage. Thus an individual's wife's brother is the *kew* 〔 = *chiu* 〕 of that individual's children, and that individual in speaking of him as his brother-in-law, employs the same word, *kew*, to designate him as such, so with the other." 〔 Morgan, *Systems...*, p. 413. 〕 Morgan, however, engrossed in his evolutionary "stage building," entirely overlooked this pertinent remark.

nearest kin, i.e., parent-child, husband-wife, and brother-sister, and extends out in all directions. Whenever one comes to the question of Chinese kinship extensions, one always stumbles upon the problem of *chiu tsu* 九族,"nine grades of kindred." This is a much discussed but vague term, which first occurs in the *Book of History*.[1] Its interpretation comprises two major theories, representing two different schools of classical commentators. The Modern Script School interprets the *chiu tsu* as follows: The four groups of relatives of the father; plus the three groups of relatives of the mother; plus the two groups of relatives of the wife.

The four groups of relatives of the father are: 1. With ego in the center, counting four generations above, four generations below, and the four collateral lines each counting four generations from the lineal line from males through males. 2. Father's sisters, when married, and their descendants. 3. Ego's sisters, when married, and their descendants. 4. Ego's daughters, when married, and their descendants.

The three groups of relatives of the mother are: 5. Mother's father and mother.6. Mother's brothers. 7. Mother's sisters.

The two groups of relatives of the wife are: 8. Wife's father. 9. Wife's mother.

---

[1] *Shu Ching* 尧典, 2.7b: 以亲九族.Whether this is the earliest use of the term or not is very questionable, since the antiquity and authenticity of the 尧 典 is much questioned. However this is the focal point of later controversies. 顾颉刚 has a very penetrating discussion of the *Problem of Chiu tsu* 九族问题, in 清华周刊 37: 9-10, 105-111.

This interpretation is not followed by the Ancient Script School of classical commentators, who believe the *chiu tsu* includes only the sib relatives but not the non-sib relatives. Therefore, according to their interpretation, the *chiu tsu* takes into account only the first of the above nine groups of relatives. That is, the *chiu tsu* means simply nine "generations," viz., the four ascending and the four descending generations, with *ego* in the middle. Naturally because of the collective responsibility of the individual's social actions, many students tend to narrow down the interpretation in order to lessen the social and legal complications. The *chiu tsu* problem, however, is purely an academic and historical matter.

In the present work the classification of the *Êrh Ya* is generally followed. The actual extent of the terminology listed, however, is entirely dictated by the needs of modern research and by the material available, although all those relatives within the Chinese mourning grades are included. The sib relatives are emphasized, but such emphasis is unavoidable in a system based strictly upon a patrilineal social grouping, where many of the terms for non-sib relatives are merely extended combinations from those for sib relatives.

The relatives are divided into two main groups and subdivided into four tables. The two main divisions are Consanguineal Relatives and Affinal Relatives. Under Consanguineal, there is a subdivision into Relatives through Father and Relatives through Mother; and under Affinal, into Relatives through Wife and Relatives through Husband. Under each group are also listed persons connected through marriage, that is the "in-law's"; this is a conventional practice.

In the tables the modern standard terminology is given first under each entry; these terms represent the system as it now stands. The slight variant combinations in some of the compounded terms have been carefully collated against one another from contemporary sources. In collating, two criteria were adopted: the statistical and inferential; i.e., if two or more forms are equally common, that form inferentially most in keeping with the working principles of the system is given as the standard form, and the others are given as alternatives. These variations are rather insignificant, and, in view of the number of people using the system and the geographical extent of the system, quite inevitable.

Under each standard term are given the historical terms in their chronological order. Their exact nature, whether alternative, literary, or dialectical[1] is indicated, together with their modern status.[2] Following them come the referential and vocative terminologies. If no terms are given, it is understood that they can be formed from previously stated formulae. No stereotyped order is followed, but generally the treatment varies according to the nature of the material and in keeping with special circumstances.

Citations illustrating the use of terms are given in the notes. It is

---

[1] Dialectical differences in Chinese kinship terminology have been somewhat exaggerated. Many of them are mere local variations in pronunciation which do not affect the morphology of the system.

[2] I.e., the exact connotation and nature of the term in modern usage, if it is still used.

possible only to give citations for the earliest occurrence of a new term, or for an old term used in a new meaning. In some cases, the most typical instances are cited. These citations are of importance, since only through them can the exact nature and chronology of a term be determined.

In the tables I have attempted to record as fully as possible the whole range of terms. [1] Thus, under the father's father no less than twenty terms are given, under various usages and periods, and in some instances the number is still greater. Of course, not all terms can be so treated, especially terms for distant relatives, which are compounded from the basic terminologies, but the slight variations in any possible combinations are given. A full recording of the whole nomenclature and the determination of the exact nature of each term are indispensable conditions for the proper understanding and interpretation of the system, since most of the early misunderstandings are the result of partial and mixed renderings of the system comprising forms from different strata of the terminology.

## Consanguineal Relatives

*Relatives through Father Table* **I**

### I. **Generation of the father's father's father's father**

---

[1] Terms that are idiosyncracies and have no general currency are excluded. E.g., the Emperor Hsüan of the Northern Chou dynasty did not like others to use the term *kao*, so he changed the term *kao tsu* to *chang tsu*, and *tsêng tsu* to *tz' ŭ chang tsu:Pei shih* 周宣帝纪, 10.32a: 又不喜听人有高者，大者,……改……九族称高祖者为长祖，曾祖为次长祖 .Terms of such nature will not be considered.

### 1. Kao tsu fu 高祖父 f f f f

In the Classics *kao tsu* was sometimes used to mean any ancestor ascending from grand-father.[1] In the 17th year of Duke Chao 〔525 B.C.〕 in the *Tso Chuan*, the first ancestor was called *kao tsu*.[2] In another place the ninth ancestor was referred to as *kao tsu*.[3] King K'ang 〔1078-1053 B.C.〕 called King Wên and King Wu *kao tsu*, but actually they were his great -grand-and grandfathers.[4] Apparently, during the Chou period, if the actual father's father's father's father is meant, *wang fu* must be added, like the *kao tsu wang fu* used in the *Êrh Ya*. The term *kao tsu* does not occur in the mourning relations of the *I Li*[5] and it is surmised that any lineal relative ascending from *tsêng tsu* may be called *tsêng tsu*.[6]

During the T'ang period *kao mên*[7] was used, but infrequently;it was

---

①   *Jih chih lu*, 24.1a: 汉儒以曾祖之父为高祖，考之于传，高祖者，远祖之名尔.

②   *Tso chuan* 昭公十七年，48. 5a: 郯子曰……我高祖少皞挚之立也……

③   Ibid.,昭公十五年，47.11b:王曰……且昔而高祖孙伯黶司晋之典籍，以为大政，故曰籍氏.The term 高祖 is meant for the ninth ancestor of 籍谈 It is also used in the same way in the *Shu Ching*, e.g., 盘庚 9. 17a: 肆上帝将复我高祖之德. The term *kao tsu* refers to Ch'êng T'ang (1765-1760 B.C.?).

④   *Shu Ching*,康王之诰，19.3a：无坏我高祖寡命.

⑤   In the 丧服传 of the *I Li*, since there are no mourning specification for f f f f, the term for him does not occur. In the ritual works, the first use of *kao tsu* for f f f f is the 丧服小记 of the *Li Chi*, 32.7b:有五世而迁之宗，其继高祖者也.

⑥   *Mêng Ch'i pi t'an*,3.3a:丧服但有曾祖曾孙，而无高祖玄孙.曾、重也. 自祖而上，皆曾祖也；自孙而下，皆曾孙也；虽百世可也. Very probably the use of *kao tsu* for f f f f, and *tsêng tsu* for f f f is due to the development of the sib organization of the Chou period but originally both of them meant simply "distant ancestors." Cf. 丁山：宗法原考，*CYYY*, 4:4 (1934), 399-415, in which he considers that during the Shang and early Chou periods, exact relationships are only counted to two generations both above and below.

⑦   *Chin shih ts'ui pien* 段行琛碑，101.11b:……高门平原忠武王孝先，*Ch'êng wei lu*, 1.4a, 按高门，高祖也.

most likely a posthumous term. The posthumous and temple term used in the *Li Chi* is *hsien kao*.[①] The term is no longer used in this sense. Since the Yüan dynasty (1280-1367) *hsien kao* had been used as an epitaphic term for father.

2. Kao tsu mu 高祖母 f f f m

Kao tsu wang mu 高祖王母 is the term used in the *Êrh Ya*.

3. Kao tsu ku mu 高祖姑母 f f f f si

Kao tsu wang ku 高祖王姑 in the *Êrh Ya*.

4. Kao tsu ku fu 高祖姑父 f f f f si h

No term is given in the *Êrh Ya*. In tracing relationship through women of the father's sib married out, the terms for these women are usually employed; the terms for their husbands, only infrequently.

5. Tsêng tsu fu 曾祖父 f f f

Ⅱ. **Generation of the father's father's father**

As a form *tsêng tsu* may be used alone. *Tsêng tsu wang fu* is the term

---

① *Li Chi* 祭法，46.8a-9：显考庙.疏：曰显考庙者，高祖也.Ibid. 檀弓，9.12a-13:殷主缀重焉.郑注：缀，犹联也.殷人作主而联其重，县诸庙也；去显考乃埋之.孔疏：显考，谓高祖也.

used in the *Êrh Ya. Tsêng ta fu,* [①] *ta wang fu* [②] and *wang ta fu* [③] have been common alternative terms since the sixth century A.D. *Tsêng mên* [④] was commonly used during the T'ang period. All these terms may be used posthumously. The ancient posthumous term is *huang kao,* [⑤] as used in the *Li Chi. Huang kao* was later used as a posthumous term for father, but has been prohibited since the Yüan dynasty, since *huang* implies "imperial."

The vocative is rather variable. *T'ai wêng* [⑥] and *tsêng wêng* [⑦] were common from the fourth to the ninth century A.D. *Wêng* means "venerable old man." *T'ai kung* and *t'ai yeh yeh* [⑧] are common modern vocatives.

---

① *Shih chi* 夏本纪, 2.1b:禹之父鲧,鲧之父帝颛顼, 颛顼之父曰昌意……禹之曾大父昌意及父鲧, 皆不得在帝位.*Ch'ang li chi* 崔评事墓铭, 24.1b:曾大父知道……〔Here and in two following notes supply No.4,on p.154.〕

② *Chü chiang wên chi* 裴光庭碑, 19.3b:大王父定……

③ *Chin shih yao li* 书祖父例, 7b:庚承宣为田布碑, 称曾祖为王大父.

④ *Hsin t'ang shu* 孝友程袁师传, 195.6b:……改葬曾门以来, 阅十二年乃毕. *Chin shih Ts'ui pien* 比丘尼惠源志铭, 82.13a-19b:曾门梁孝明皇帝…… Chien Ta-hsin〔*Chien yen T'ang chin shih wên po wei*, 6.13〕says :称曾祖为曾门, 未详其义.From what can be deduced from the evidence , *mên* 门 was a very common posthumous term in referring to lineal relatives from the second ascending generation and upward during the fourth to the eighth centuries A.D . Father's father was called 大 门 中, father's father's father's father was called 高门, so father's father's father was called 曾门.Its origin may be similar to the term 从兄弟门中 as explained by Yen Chih-t'ui.See p.1219,note ④.

⑤ *Li chi* 祭法, 46.8a 9:曰皇考庙.孔疏曰皇考庙者, 曾祖也.

⑥ *Nan Shih* 齐废帝郁林皇纪, 5.1a:太翁.

⑦ 曾翁: Since *wêng* was commonly used as vocative for grandfather, *tsêng wêng* and *T'ai wêng* were used for great grandfather. *Wêng* may also be used for any venerable old man.

⑧ 太公 and 太爷爷: *T'ai* means "great." *Kung* and *yeh yeh* are vocatives for grandfather; *t'ai kung* and *t'ai yeh yeh*, for great grandfather.

6. Tsêng tsu mu 曾祖母 f f m

In the *Êrh Ya*, *tsêng tsu wang mu*. The most common modern vocative is *t'ai p'o*, or *t'ai p'o p'o*.[①]

7. Tsêng po tsu fu 曾伯祖父 f f f o b

*Tsu tsêng wang fu* is used in the *Êrh Ya*, and *tsu tsêng tsu fu* in the *I Li*.[②] Both these terms also apply to father's father's father's younger brothers.

8. Tsêng po tsu mu 曾伯祖母 f f f o b w

In the *Êrh Ya*, *tsu tsêng wang mu*, and correspondingly *tsu tsêng tsu mu* in the *I Li*. Both these terms also apply to father's father's father's younger brother's wife.

9. Tsêng shu tsu fu 曾叔祖父 f f f y b

The vocatives of 7 and 9 are similar to 5, but differentiated by prefixing their numerical order or titles.

10. Tsêng shu tsu mu 曾叔祖母 f f f y b w

The vocatives of 8 and 10 are similar to 6, but differentiated by prefixing their sibnames or their husband's numerical order.

---

① 太婆 or 太婆婆: *p'o* or *p'o p'o* are vocatives for grandmother; *t'ai p'o*, for great grandmother. K'ung p'ing chung 孔平仲, ca. 1080 A.D., 朝散集,豫章丛书 ed.,2.19a:代小子广孙寄翁翁：太婆八十五，寝膳近何似?
② 　*I Li* 丧服, 33.6a:族曾祖父母.郑注：族曾祖父母者，曾祖昆弟之亲也.

11. Tsêng tsu ku mu 曾祖姑母 f f f si

*Tsêng tsu wang ku* is the term used in the *Êrh Ya*. Modern vocative, *ku t'ai p'o*.

12. Tsêng tsu ku fu 曾祖姑父 f f f si h

Modern vocative, *ku t'ai kung* 姑太公 or *ku t'ai yeh* 姑太爷.

### Ⅲ. Generation of the father's father

13. Tsu fu 祖父 f f

*Tsu* may be used alone to mean father's father, but it may mean any ancestor.[①] In the *Êrh Ya*, *tsu* was used synonymously with *wang fu*,[②] but *wang fu* is now more often used in the posthumous sense. Since the Han period *ta fu*[③] has been frequently used. Other early alternative terms, like *tsu chün*,[④] *tsu wang fu*[⑤] and *tsu wêng*,[⑥] are commonly met in literature. Another common early term is *kung*,[⑦] which in many localities is still used as a vocative.[⑧] Since *kung* is a common complimentary term for any older

---

①　*Jih chih lu*, 24.1a: 自父而上，皆曰祖. 书微子之命曰，乃祖成汤是也.

②　*Êrh Ya*: 祖，王父也.

③　*Shih Chi* 留侯世家，55.1a: 留侯张良者，其先韩人也. 大父开地……Ibid. 郑当时传，120.6b: 然其知交皆其大父行.

④　*K'ung ts'ung tzŭ* 居卫篇，2.45b: 子思既免，曰……祖君屈于陈蔡作春秋.

⑤　*Chin shih Ts'ui pien* 王文干墓志，113.62a: 奉天定难南朝元从功臣讳英进，公之祖王父也.

⑥　乐清县白鹤寺钟款识有祖翁祖婆之称. Cf. *Ch'êng wei lu*, 1.7a.

⑦　*Lü shih ch'un ch'iu*, 10.10a: 孔子之弟子从远方来者，孔子荷杖而问之曰：子之公不有恙乎?

⑧　Cf. *Ch'êng wei Lu*, 1.8a.

man, its connotation as a relationship term is indefinite. It is used to mean father, husband's father, etc. *T'ai kung*[1] is used in the *Hou Han Shu* to mean father's father, but is now used as a vocative for father's father's father.

The most common modern vocatives are *yeh yeh* 爷爷, *kung kung* 公公, *a wêng* 阿翁, *wêng wêng* 翁翁.[2] Their usage depends upon local custom.

The depreciatory term is *chia tsu* or, uncommonly, *chia kung*. The prefixing of *chia* to *tsu* to refer to one's own father's father dates from the Han period. It is sometimes condemned as incorrect and vulgar,[3] but is nevertheless in universal usage today.

The complimentary term is *tsun tsu fu*.[4] *Ta mên chung*[5] was used as a complimentary term during the fifth or sixth century A.D. It was most probably a posthumous term, and is not used today.

The ancient posthumous terms were *wang kao*[6] and *huang tsu kao*.[7] The former was probably more often used in connection with ancestral temples, and the latter, with sacrifices. This minute distinction might be due to the important role of ancestral worship and sacrifices in the sib organization

---

① 　*Hou Han Shu* 李固传, 93.14b:姊文姬【固女】……见二兄归……曰：李氏灭矣！自太公以来，积德累仁，何以遇此？ During the Han period, *kung* was sometimes used for father; *t'ai kung*, for father's father.

② 　*Shih shuo hsin yü*, 3B. 10a.

③ 　Cf. *Yen shih chia hsün* 风操篇, 2. 4b-5b.

④ 　Ibid., 2.5a-b:凡与人言，称彼祖父母、世父母、父母及长姑，皆加尊字. 自叔以下，则加贤字，尊卑之差也.〔Supply No. 4,p.154〕

⑤ 　Ibid., 2.6a:大门中.

⑥ 　*Li Chi* 祭法, 46.8a-9b:曰王考庙.孔疏:曰王考庙者，祖庙也.

⑦ 　Ibid. 曲礼, 3.22a：祭王父曰皇祖考，王母曰皇祖妣.

during the feudal period. During the fifth century A.D. *hsien wang chang jên* [1] was commonly used. None of these terms is used today. The modern posthumous terms are *hsien tsu* 先祖 or *wang tsu* 亡祖.

### 14. Tsu mu 祖母 f m

The term in the *Êrh Ya* is *wang mu* 王母, which corresponds to *wang fu*. Later terms, like *ta mu* [2] and *tsu p'o*,[3] more or less correspond to the terms for father's father. The depreciatory term is *chia tsu mu*, and the complimentary term, *tsun tsu mu*. The ancient posthumous term is *huang tsu pi*,[4] and the modern term, *hsien tsu mu*. *T'ai P'o* was once used as a vocative for father's mother but it is now used for father's father's mother. The most common modern vocatives are *p'o p'o* 婆婆 [5] and *nai nai* 奶奶.[6]

### 15. Po tsu fu 伯祖父 f f o b

Both the *Êrh Ya* and *I Li* give the term *ts'ung tsu tsu fu.*[7] It applies to both older and younger brothers of father's father.

---

① *Yen shih chia hsün* 书证篇, 6.15b: 今世俗呼其祖考为先亡丈人，又疑丈当作大.

② *Hsin shu* 俗激篇, 3.1b: 今其甚者，到大父矣，贼大母矣. *Han shu* 文三王传, 47.5b: 共王母曰李太后，李太后清平王之大祖也.颜师古注：大母，祖母也.

③ 祖婆：see p.1202 ,note ⑥.

④ *Li Chi* 曲礼, 3.22a: 王母曰皇祖妣.

⑤ K'ung p'ing chung 朝散集, op .cit., 代小子广森寄翁翁, 2.19a: 婆婆到辇下，翁翁在省里.

⑥ *Ch'in shu chi* 1 .6b: 嬭，按今读奴蟹切，曰嬭嬭.或以呼母，或以呼父母，或似呼伯叔母.嬭,is also written 奶. It originally meant mother and was read *ni* ,as in the *Kuang yün*, 嬭，楚人呼母.

⑦ *I Li* 丧服, 33.la: 从父父父父母.

*Po wêng* ① is a modern vocative. The vocatives of 13 may also be applied here by prefixing the numerical order or title.


### 16. Po tsu mu 伯祖母 f f o b w

*Ts'ung tsu tsu mu* is the term both in the *Êrh Ya* and the *I Li*.② Since the *Êrh Ya* also gives the term *ts'ung tsu wang mu* 从祖王母, in can be inferred that during the Chou period father's father's brothers may also have been called *ts'ung tsu wang fu*. During the Han period it was abbreviated to *ts'ung tsu mu*.③*po p'o* ④is a more modern term, and may be used vocatively.


### 17. Shu tsu fu 叔祖父 f f y b

Compare 15. In the *Kuo Yü* the term *ts'ung tsu shu mu*⑤ is used for father's father's younger brother's wife. It can be inferred that in ancient times *Ts'ung tsu sbu fu* may also have been used for father's father's younger brother, and *ts'ung tsu shih fu* for father's father's older brother, but this inference is by no means certain. Since the T'ang period *shu wêng*⑥ has been a common alternative term, and may be used in the vocative. The

---

① 伯翁，cf.，龚大雅，义井题记 in *Pa Ch'iung shih chin pu chêng*,117.12a-14b.

② Cf .p.1204, note ⑦.

③ *Li Chi* 檀弓，9.25b:敬姜曰：妇人不饰.郑注：敬姜者，康子从父父.

④ 伯婆.

⑤ *Kuo yü* 鲁语，5.12a:公父文伯之母，季康子之从父叔母也.〔First missing character is No.4,p.154.〕

⑥ *Ch'ang-li chi*, 23.,13a: 祭李氏二十九娘子文. Han Yü refers to himself as 十八叔翁 and to his wife as 十八叔婆. Ibid. 23. 12b: 祭滂文,where he refers to himself as 十八翁 and to his wife as 十八婆. They were offering sacrifice to his brother's grandchildren.

vocatives of 13 may also be applied here, according to local usage, by prefixing the numerical order.

18. Shu tsu mu 叔祖母 f f y b w

Compare 16 and 17. In the Han dynasties *chi tsu mu*[1] seems to have been used. According to another interpretation, *chi tsu mu* means father's father's brother's secondary wives,[2] but there is no means of checking this. Since the T'ang period *shu p'o* seems to have been a common vocative. *P'o p'o* may be used in the vocative for 16 and 18 by prefixing the numerical order of their husbands, or their own sibnames. [3]

19. Ku tsu mu 姑祖母 f f si

*Wang ku* 王姑 is the term given in the *Êrh Ya*.

20. Ku tsu fu 姑祖父 f f si h

21. Chiu tsu fu 舅祖父 f m b

---

① *Chin shih Ts'ui pien* 18. 1b: 收养季父母.

② Ch'ien Ta-hsin says〔*Ch'ien yen T'ang chin shih wên po wei*, 1. 26b〕that 其称季父母,犹言庶父母也.〔Supply *tsu*, ancestor.〕

③ *Yen shih chia hsün* 风操篇, 2.7b: 父母之世叔母，皆当加其姓以别之.

*Chiu tsu*① may be used alone. The inverted form *tsu chiu*② was used quite early; and *ta chiu* ③ was used during the Later Han period.

22. Chiu tsu mu 　○○母 f m b w

23. I tsu mu 姨祖母 f m si

24. I tsu fu ○○父 f m si h

The vocatives for the above can be constructed from the vocatives for grandparents, whatever forms are used, by prefixing *ku*, *chiu* and *i*.

25. T'ang po tsu fu 堂伯祖父 s of 7 or 9＞f f

26. T'ang po tsu mu ○○○母 w of 25

27. T'ang shu tsu fu 堂叔祖父 s of 7 or 9＞f f

28. T'ang shu tsu mu ○○○母 w of 27

───────────────

① 　*Lêng lu tsa shih* 冷庐杂识, by Lu I-t'ien 陆以湉， ca .1850 A.D. 笔记小说大观 ed. 2.25b: 今之称谓……称父之父为父父 .〔Supply *fu……chiu……chiu tsu.*〕

② 　*Chin shu* 应詹传, 70. 1b: 镇南大将军刘弘，詹之父父也.

③ 　*Hou Han Shu* 张禹传, 74.2a: 父父况, 族姊为皇祖考夫人……况……见光武, 光武大喜曰：今乃得我大父乎!〔Supply *tsu-fu.*〕

No term is given for 25 and 27 in the *Êrh Ya*, but *tsu tsu wang mu* 族祖王母 is used for 26 and 28. It is inferred that *tsu tsu wang fu* may have been used for 25 and 27. In the *I Li*, *tsu tsu fu* is used for 25 and 27, and *tsu tsu mu* for 26 and 28,[①] whereas in the *Êrh Ya* these terms are used for the son and the son's wife of either 25 or 27. The *I Li* is simply using an abbreviated form.

Vocatives of 15-18 may be applied here, respectively.

29. T'ang ku tsu mu 堂姑祖母 d of 7 or 29

In the *Êrh Ya*, *tsu tsu ku*. This term is rather inconsistent with the whole *Êrh Ya* system, since logically it should be *tsu tsu wang ku*. Perhaps the *Êrh Ya* was already beginning to use abbreviated forms.

30. T'ang ku tsu fu 堂姑祖父 h of z

Vocatives can be built up by prefixing grandparent vocatives with *ku*, and can further be differentiated by prefixing the numerical order of 29, or the sibname of 30.

31.Piao tsu fu 表祖父 f f f si s

32. Piao tsu mu ○○母 w of 31

The above two terms can be further differentiated by prefixing *ku, chiu*

---

① *I Li*, 33. 6a.

and *i*, e.g., *ku piao tsu fu* for f f f si s, *chiu piao tsu fu* for f f m b s, *i piao tsu fu* for f f m si s. Ordinarily, *piao tsu fu* is applied to them all. Usually these relationships are not continued socially after the death of the f f f si and f f m, unless it be that either of the parties strongly wishes to maintain them. Terms for their descendants will not be given in this table. If the relationships are maintained, terms could easily be constructed, e.g., the sons of 31 will be called *t'ang piao po fu* and *t'ang piao shu fu*, etc.

### IV. Generation of the father

33. Fu 父 father

*Fu* is primarily a standard literary term throughout, and is seldom used alone as a vocative. *Wêng*[1] was an old vocative. *A kung*[2] and *tsun*[3] were prevalent from the third to the sixth centuries A.D. About the fifth century A.D. members of some of the royal families called father *hsiung hsiung*,[4] a term for older brother. During the T'ang dynasty the royal family called

---

[1] *Shih chi* 项羽本纪，7.26a: 汉王曰……吾翁即若翁.

[2] *Nan Shih* 颜延之传，34.4b:……又非君家阿公.According to 王念孙〔*Kuang ya shu chêng*〕公 and 翁 are very similar in sound and may be dialectical renderings of a same term.

[3] *Sung shu* 谢灵运传，67.30a: 阿连才悟如此，而尊作常儿遇之.*Shih shuo hsin yü* 品藻篇，2B.30a: 刘尹至王长史许清言，时苟子年十三，倚床边听.既去，问父曰，刘尹语何如尊？ Ibid.9b: 谢太傅未冠，始出西诣王长史清言，良久，去后苟子问曰：向客何如尊？〔Supply *fu.*〕

[4] *Pei Ch'i shu* 南阳王绰传，12.6b: 兄兄.

father *ko*,[1] nowadays a universal vocative for older brother. Before this, *ko* had never been used in either of these senses.[2] It might be that *ko* was an old dialectical term for father, and that during this period it became confused with *hsiung*, thereupon losing its original meaning of father and acquiring the connotation of "older brother," but the matter is most perplexing.

*Yeh* 耶 is a vocative used from the sixth century A.D. on;[3] it is also written 爷.[4] *Tieh* 爹,[5] which may be a later variant pronunciation of *t'o* 爹,[6] a dialectical form of western Hupeh of about the same period, is now a common vocative. *Pa pa* is almost as commonly used as *tieh*; it first occurred in the *Kuang Ya*, which reads, "*pa......is father*."[7] The *Cheng tzǔ T'ung* considers *pa* a term of the southern aborigines,[8] and states that the

---

[1] *Chiu T'ang shu* 王琚传, 106.16b: 元宗泣曰：四哥仁孝. The *ko* is meant for the Emperor 睿宗. Ibid. 棣王琰传, 107.5a: 惟三哥辩其罪. The 三哥 is here used by 琰 in referring to his father, Emperor Hsüan-tsung. *Ko* was also used by the royal family of the T'ang dynasty to refer to oneself before the son. *Chêng wei lu*, 1.15a: states: 淳化阁帖有唐太宗与高宗书哥哥敕. 父对子自称哥哥. 盖唐代家法如是. 〔Supply *fu*.〕

[2] 哥 is defined in the *Shuo wên* as "to sing" or "a song".

[3] *Yen shih chia hsün* 文章篇, 4.10b.

[4] *Nan shih* 侯景传, 80.22b: 王伟劝立七庙......并请七世讳......景曰：前世吾不复忆，惟阿爷名标. The original form is 耶, and 爷 is a later form with classifier No. 88 added. For discussion cf. *Kai yü ts'ung k'ao*, 37.15; *Hêng yen lu, 3.2; and Ch'êng wei lu*, 1.15-16.

[5] *Ch'ang-li chi* 祭女挐女文, 23.14a: 阿爹阿八，使汝妳......祭于第四小娘子之灵. Cf. *Shu P'o*, 1.2b-3a, 呼父为爹.

[6] *Kuang ya*: 爹......父也, pronounced t'o. *Nan shih* 始兴忠武王憺传, 52.15b: 诏征以本号还朝，人歌之曰：始兴王，人之爹【徒我反】赴人急，如水火，何时复来哺乳我.荆土方言谓父为爹，故云. For discussion cf. *Kai yü Ts'ung k'ao*, 37.15.

[7] 爸......父也.

[8] *Chêng tzǔ T'ung*: 爸。The Miao and Yao tribes of southwest China still call father *pa*, or its slight variants. Cf. *Miao fang pei lan* 苗防备览 by Yen Ju-i 严如熤〔1843 绍义堂 ed.〕8. 6a, 9.2b, and 9.10a; *Ling piao chi man* 岭表纪蛮 by Liu Hsi-fan 刘锡藩〔1932, Shanghai, Commercial Press〕137.

aborigines call their elders *pa pa* 八八, or *pa pa* 巴巴, and that the Chinese lexicographers added the classifier 父 to form 爸. On the other hand, *pa* is also considered a later variant pronunciation of *fu* 父.[1]

The dialectical difference, insofar as the evidence goes, seems to indicate that *tieh* is predominantly a northern usage,[2] and *pa*, a southern;[3] but this explanation is by no means certain.

The *Kuang Yün* states that the people of Wu call father *chê*,[4] but according to the *T'ung Ya* father was called *lao hsiang* in Wu.[5] None of these terms seem to be in use today. The inhabitants of Fuchow call father *lang pa* 郎罢;[6] this usage dates from the T'ang period. Before that, *lang* alone also had the meaning of father;[7] hence *lang pa* may be combination variant of *lang* and *pa*. In modern usage in that place, however, *lang pa* is always used in the referential and never in the vocative.

*Fu Ch'in* 父亲[8] may be used as a literary vocative by the son in

---

[1]　Chêng Chên (*Ch'in shu chi*, 1.1b) says that 古读巴如逋，即父之重唇音，遂作巴加父. 今俗呼父或为巴巴，或为耙耙，或为八八，并此字.

[2]　*Kuang yün*: 爹，北人呼父.

[3]　*Chi Yün*: 爸，(部可切，又必驾切) 吴人呼父. The *Ch'êng wei lu*, 1.27a:also states that 吴俗称父为阿伯. *Po* 伯 may be a different rendering of *pa* 爸.

[4]　箸(正奢切)，吴人呼父. The modern pronunciation is the same of *yeh* 爷.

[5]　*T'ung Ya* 称谓，19.4b.

[6]　*Hua yang chi*,1.13a:囝，哀闽也. 自注.囝，音蹇，闽俗呼子为囝，呼父为郎罢. 郎罢别囝，吾悔汝生……

[7]　*Shu I*, 1.9b:古人谓父为阿郎. *Pei shih* 汲固传，85.4a:【李】宪即为固长育，至十余岁.恒呼固夫妇为郎婆.According to 朱父〔cited by *Ch'êng wei lu*, 1.26a〕盖北朝称父父郎也.

[8]　*Ch'in* 亲 means "relative", "parent".

addressing his father, as in a letter. In this connection, *ta jên* 大人① and *Ch'i hsia* 膝下②must be appended, making the term *fu ch'in ta jên Ch'i hsia*, a stereotyped form of literary address. In addressing letters, *Ch'i hsia* is used for either parent, whereas *ta jên* may be appended to any term for relatives of higher generations. *ch'i hsia* is primarily a literary parent term; its literal meaning is "like a child at your knees."

The father, in referring to himself before his children, may use *nai kung* 乃公， ③ *nai wêng* 乃翁④ and the more colloquial and modern terms *a tieh, a pa,* or *lao tzǔ* 老子. In certain localities *lao tzǔ* may also be used for father in general.⑤

The depreciatory term is *chia fu*, or *chia yen*.⑥ *Yen* literally means "the stern and respected one." *Chia chün*⑦ is also fairly common .*Chia kung*⑧ is a rather uncommon old term.

---

① 大人 literally means"big man" that is "senior" .It is frequently used  alone as a vocative , e.g., *Shih Chi* 越世家，41.11b; Ibid., 高祖本纪 8.32a.

② *Hsiao Ching* 圣治章，5.4b：故亲生之膝下以养父母……注：膝下，谓孩幼之时也.

③ *Han Shu* 陈万年传，66.17a：万年尝病，命咸教戒于床下 . 语至夜半，咸睡，头触屏风.万年大怒，欲杖之，曰：乃公教汝，汝反睡不听吾言，何也?

④ 乃翁 is somewhat equivalent to 乃公.*Nai* 乃 is used in the  sense of "your".

⑤ *Chêng tzǔ* t'ung: *s.v.fu*, father.

⑥ *I Ching*, 4.16a: 家人有严君焉，父父之谓也. *Hsiao Ching* 圣治章，5.1a:孝莫大于严父.

⑦ *Shih shuo hsin yü*, 1A.3a: 家君.Here the term *chia chün* is used both as a complimentary and depreciatory term. 〔From this point in Dr. Fêng's article the editors have been forced to revert to their usual practice of providing only indispensable citations from the Chinese. 〕

⑧ *Chin shu* 43.6b.*Chia kung* is no longer used in this sense;it is now used for mother's father.

The complimentary term is *tsun ta jen* 尊大人. *Tsun chün*,[1] *tsun kung*,[2] *tsun hou*,[3] *fêng wêng*, *fêng chün*,[4] in modern times are literary rather than vocative.

*K'ao* 考 is a posthumous term. In ancient literature it was also used for the living father, being synonymous with *fu*.[5]  At present, however, it is primarily an epitaphic term. At different periods *k'ao* was used with various modifiers to express special circumstances. In the *Chü Li* of the *Li Chi*, *huang k'ao*[6] is used as a posthumous term for father, but in the *Chi Fa* of the same work it is used as a temple term for father's father's father.[7] *Wang k'ao* is a temple term in the *Li Chi* for father's father in connection with sacrifices,[8] but during the T'ang period it was occasionally used as a posthumous term for father.[9]  *Huang k'ao* and *wang k'ao* have been prohibited for common use since the Yüan dynasty, being reserved only for

---

[1]  *Shih shuo hsin yü*, 2A. la; *Chin shu*, 75.5a. Sometimes *chün chia tsun* is used, e.g., *Shih Shuo hsin yü*, 2B. 34a.

[2]  *Chin Shu*, 82. 1b; Ibid., 92.23b.

[3]  *Shih shuo hsin yü*, 1A. 28b: 尊侯.

[4]  封翁 and 封君 were used originally for those who received titles through sons who had risen to high official positions. Later they became common complimentary terms.

[5]  According to the *Shuo Wên*, *k'ao* means "old." Thus it could be applied to any old man.  Its application to mean father is a later development and its use as a posthumous term is a still later specialization. Cf. *Ch'in shu chi* 1.5.

[6]  *Li Chi*, 5.22a.

[7]  Ibid. 46.8b 9a: 皇考.

[8]  Ibid . 46.8 9: 王考.

[9]  *Ch'ang-li chi*  24.10a.

the imperial family.① Thereafter the term *hsien k'ao* came into use as a universal epitaphic form.② But this term sharply contradicts the old usage, since in the *Li Chi*, *hsien k'ao* is used as a temple term for father's father's father's father.③

*Fu chün* 府君 is another popular epitaphic term. Originally, i.e., in the Han dynasty, only those who had been governors (*t'ai shou* 太守) could be called *fu chün* by their sons, but since the T'ang period the term has been used indiscriminately.④ The ordinary posthumous terms are *hsien fu* 先父, *wang fu* 亡父, *hsien ta fu* 先大夫, *hsien chün* 先君, *hsien tzǔ* 先子, *hsien chün tzǔ* 先君子,⑤ *hsien kung* 先公,⑥ etc. The complimentary posthumous terms are *tsun hsien chün* 尊先君 and *tsun fu* 尊府.⑦

The ancient temple term for father is *ni* 祢.⑧

---

① This prohibition is best illustrated in the *Yüan tien chang* 元典章, *1908* edition, 31. 16a-b.

② The term *hsien k'ao* 显考 was used for father much earlier than the Yüan period,e.g., *Shu Ching* (K'ang kao), 14.3a. It continued to be used down to the fourth and fifth centuries A.D. for parents both living and dead. *Hsien* means "great,""illustrious,"etc. Down to the Sung period, *hsien* is predominantly used in the posthumous sense. Cf. also the *Chin Shih Li*, 5. 55b.

③ 郑珍〔*Ch'in shu chi*, 2. 3a〕rather bemoans such contradiction.

④ Cf. *Hêng yen lu*, 3.3b-5b; Ch'êng wei lu, 1. 21a-b.

⑤ *Hsien chün* and *hsien tzǔ* originally were terms used during the feudal period by the nobility in referring to their deceased fathers. They became common terms at about the end of the period.

⑥ *Hou Han Shu* 93. 15a.

⑦ *Ch'ang li-chi* 21.6b.

⑧ *Tso Chuan* 32. 4b. *Ni* means "near","closer",i.e., the father is nearer than the father's father, etc. It is the same as 昵. Cf. also *Shu Ching* 10. 11a.

### 34. Mu 母 mother

*Mu*, like *fu*, is primarily a standard term and is seldom used in the vocative. Other ancient alternative terms are *yü* [1] and *wên*, [2] but these terms can be applied to any old woman. During the T'ang period, *niang tzǔ* [3] was used for mother but at the same time it was also used for any young woman. This usage seemed to be northern. *Niang tzǔ* is used in modern terminology sometimes as a husband's term for wife, sometimes for any young woman.

The most peculiar variant of the term for mother is *tzǔ tzǔ* 姊姊 which was used by the royalty of the Northern Ch'i dynasty; [4] *tzǔ* being a term for older sister. According to the *Shuo Wên*, the people of Shu call mother *chieh* and the people of Huai nan call mother *Shê*. [5] The older form of *chieh* 姐, according to the *Yü P'ien*, is written 她. In the 说山训 of the *Huai nan tzǔ*, *shê* is used for mother and Kao Yu comments that it is a Chiang Huai practice. [6] The *Shuo Wên* also states that *shih* 媞 was used for mother in Chiang Huai. Kuo P'o (267-324 A.D.) said that the people of Chiang Tung [7] called mother *shih* 姼, also pronounced *chih*, or *ch'ih*. *Shê, shih, chih* and

---

① 妪，*Shuo wên; Hsin Shu* 3.1b.

② 媪，*Shuo wên; Kuang ya; Han fei tzǔ* 10b. Also read *ao*.

③ 娘子，*Shu I*, 1.9b-10a; for its uses during the various periods, cf. *Kai yü ts'ung kao*, 38.1a–3a.

④ *Pei Ch'i shu* 9.4a.

⑤ Hsü Shên seems to consider 社 a variant of 姐.

⑥ *Huai nan tzǔ* 16. 12a-b. Chiang Huai is the area between the Yangtze and Huai Rivers.

⑦ Chiang Tung is a vague geographical term, approximately the lower Yangtze delta.

*Ch'ih* all seem to have been derived from the same root and probably represent variants of *chieh*.[1] Apparently, from the third century B.C. to the fourth century A.D., *chieh*, with its variant forms, was a very prevalent vocative for mother throughout the Yangtze valley. Even down to the thirteenth century A.D. mother was sometimes called *chieh chieh*.[2] On the other hand, from Han to T'ang times *chia chia* was frequently used for mother and might be another variant transcription of *chieh chieh*.[3]

Perhaps due to the close similarity of these two sounds—*tzŭ* and *chieh*—and to the vagaries of transcription, for a time *tzŭ* was used for *chieh*. *Tzŭ*, being the older and more literary term, triumphed over *chieh*, and the latter lost its original meaning and acquired the meaning of older sister, like *tzŭ*. This seems the only reasonable explanation, and, if true, means that we have here an exact parallel with *hsiung* and *ko*, as discussed above. Apparently, no marital relations are involved.

The universal modern vocative is *ma* 妈 or *ma ma*.[4] *Niang* 娘,[5] or *niang niang*, are also very commonly used in many localities. The *Kuang*

---

[1]  According to Chêng Chên (*Ch'in shu chi*, 1.6b) the ancient pronunciation of *chieh* 姐 and *shê* 社 was about the same and both were in the rhymes 鱼，虞，模 which are very close.  Hence he considers *shê* to be a dialectical variant of *chieh*.

[2]  *Ssŭ Ch'ao wên chien lu* 四朝闻见录，己集，by YEH Shao-wêng 叶绍翁，ca, 1220 A.D.〔知斋不足丛书 edition〕16a.

[3]  *Pei Ch'i shu* 12. 8b: 家家.

[4]  But cf .*Hsi shang fu t'an* 席上腐谈，by Yü Yen 俞琰〔宝颜堂秘笈 edition〕1.2a.

[5]  As explained before, *niang* can be used in various designations sometimes overriding generations.  Used as a vocative for mother, it was first noticed during the fourth and fifth centuries A.D.  *Nan Shih* 44. 5a-b; *Pei Shih* 64.13b-14a.

*Yün* says that the people of ch'u called mother *ni*.[1] The *Chi Yün* states that the people of Ch'i called mother *mi*,[2] and the people of Wu called mother *mi*.[3] *Ni* and *mi* may be early dialectical variants of *ma*. The Miao, Yao and Tung tribes of Southwest China still call mother *mi* or *ma*.[4] Whether the aboriginal terms influenced the Chinese, or vice versa, or whether they both have been derived from a common earlier form, we at present have no way to determine. Certainly *ma* is only a slightly differing version of *mu*.[5]

*Mu ch'in* 母亲 is sometimes used as a vocative, but more commonly in addressing one's mother in a letter; in the latter case, *ta jên* and *ch'i hsia* must be suffixed.

The depreciatory term is *chia mu*,[6] or *chia tz'ŭ*.[7] *Tz'ŭ* literally means "the affectionate one." *Tsun lao* [8]was used around the fifth century A.D., and *chia fu jên* was allowable during the Later Han times.[9]

*Ling mu* 令母,[10] *ling tz'ŭ* 令慈, *ling t'ang* 令堂, and *tsun t'ang* 尊

---

[1] 妳（嬭）: cf. *Ch'in shu chi*, 1.6. ch'u 楚 is the ancient term for the middle Yangtze valley and at present approximately the modern Hupeh and Hunan provinces.

[2] 娒. Cf. also the *Yü p'ien*. Ch'i is the old name for the modern province of Shantung.

[3] 媄. Wu is the ancient name for roughly the southern part of Kiangsu province.

[4] *Miao fang pei lan, op. cit.*, 8.6a, and 9.10a. *Ling piao chi man*, op. cit., 137.

[5] *Ch'in shu chi*, 1.7a.

[6] *Yen shih chia hsün*, 2.4b-5a. It seems that the prefixing of *chia* (house) to the terms of lineal ascendants to form depreciatory terms was not prevalent during Yen's time.

[7] This is the opposite of the term *chia yen*, "the stern one," for father. The mother is supposed to be affectionate and the father, stern.

[8] *Sung Shu* 91.15a: 尊老.

[9] *Hou Han Shu* 78.9a: 家夫人.

[10] *Ts'ai chung lang chi* 6.7b.

堂，① are the most common complimentary terms. *Tsun shang* ② and *tsun fu jên*③ were used from the fifth to the eighth centuries A.D. At present *tsun fu jên* is used as a complimentary term for another's wife. *T'ai fu jên*④ may be used for anther's mother when the father is dead. *An jên* 安人 and *kung jên* 恭人, originally terms for a titled woman, may be used loosely, if incorrectly, as complimentary terms.

The posthumous term is *pi*,⑤ as defined by the *Shuo Wên*. Yet this view is sometimes disputed, since in classical literature the term was often used indiscriminately for both living and dead mother. The modern usage follows the interpretation of the *Li Chi*, that *mu* is used when the mother is living, and *pi* when she is dead.⑥ *Huang pi*⑦ was an old sacrificial term but has been forbidden since the Yüan period. *Hsien pi*⑧ is exclusively an epitaphic term.

### 35. Po fu伯父 f o b

---

①    *Lu shih-lung wên chi* 10. 10a. *T'ang* 堂 is derived from *Pei T'ang* 北堂, a non-vocative, non-referential literary term for mother. Cf. *T'ung su pien*, 18.5a-5b.

②    *Sung shu* 91.15a: 尊上.

③    *Ch'ang-li chi* 29. 3b: 尊夫人.

④    This was originally used for a titled woman, e.g., *Han Shu* 4.12a-b: 太夫人.

⑤    妣. The *Êrh Ya* uses *mu* and *pi* synonymously.

⑥    *Li Chi* 5. 22b.

⑦    Ibid. 5.22a.

⑧    *Wang shih chung chi* 38a: 显父 This is, perhaps, the first use of *hsien pi*, but it is used for the living mother. Now *hsien pi* is used exclusively as a corresponding term to *hsien k'ao*.

The old term in the *Êrh Ya* and *I Li* is *shih fu*.[①]  In the *Li Chi*, *po fu*[②] is sometimes used in place of *shih fu*. *Po* itself means oldest, e.g., an oldest brother may be called *po hsiung*, and an oldest sister, *po tzǔ*. Since the Wei and Chin periods, *po* alone has been used as a vocative for father's older brother.[③] From the Sung period down to modern times, *po po* has been the most prevalent vocative. The posthumous term is *wang po* 亡伯. *Ts'ung hsiung ti mên chung*[④] is an old term used *circa* the fifth century A.D. but seldom heard today.

### 36. Po mu 伯母 f o b w

*Shih mu* is the old term used in the *Êrh Ya*, *I Li* [⑤] and *Li Chi*.[⑥]  *Po mu* is also used in the *Li Chi*.[⑦]

### 37. *shu fu* 叔父 f y b

---

① 　*I Li* 30.8b. *Shih* means "generation." That is, the father's older brother is the one in the father's "generation" to succeed to the grandfather.

② 　*Li Chi* 18.10a: 伯.

③ 　See p. 1185, note ①.

④ 　*Yen shih chia hsün* 2. 6a: 从兄弟门中. It literally means "within the gate of father's brother's sons", a circumlocution for expressing a mournful situation.

⑤ 　*I Li* 30.9b 10a.

⑥ 　*Li Chi* 18.15a.

⑦ 　Ibid., 43.2b.

*Circa* the latter half of the first millennium B.C., *chu fu*, [1] *ts'ung fu*, [2] and *yu fu* [3] were used for father's brothers, both older and younger. They are still used today as alternative terms but are primarily literary forms. *Ts'ung fu*, a contraction of *ts'ung tsu fu*, was also used for father's father's brother's sons.

*Shu fu* also was used in another sense in early times. The father's first younger brother was called *chung fu*, the second younger brother, *shu fu*, and the youngest, *chi fu*.[4] This usage was never common. *Chi fu* was also used for father's younger brothers in general, not necessarily his youngest brother.[5] *Ts'ung wêng* is a relatively late and uncommon term.[6]

Since the third century A.D. *shu*, *a shu*, or *shu shu* have been used as common vocatives.

Among the royal families of the Northern Ch'i and T'ang dynasties, father's brothers were called *a hsiung*; this may be a family peculiarity.

The depreciatory term is *chia shu fu*, or simply *chia shu*. Yen's *Family Instructions* states that it is incorrect to use *chia po* for father's older brother,

---

[1]    *Shih Ching* 9C. 2a: 诸父 . *Chu fu* is a very vague term, literally "the fathers."

[2]    *I Li* 31.17a: 从父昆弟 . Since father's brother's sons can be called *ts'ung fu k'un ti*, father's brothers can be called *Ts'ung fu*. Pei shih 22.8.

[3]    *Li Chi* 8.4b-5a: 犹父 . Since brother's sons can be called *yu tzŭ*, it is inferred that father's brother can be called *yu fu*, "like father."

[4]    *Shih Ming*: 季父 .

[5]    *Shih chi* 7.1b; *Ch'ang-li Chi* 23.9b; Han Yü refers to himself as *chi fu*.

[6]    *T'ang chih yen*, 3.1a: 从翁 .

since he is an elder of father and one dare not use *chia*.① This is somewhat over rationalistic; *chia po* is the most common form today. The complimentary term for another's father's younger brother is *hsien shu*, or *ling shu*.

The posthumous term is *wang shu*. *Ts'ung hsiung ti mên chung* is an old term both for father's older and younger brothers.

### 38. Shu mu 叔母 f y b w

This is also the term used in the *Êrh Ya*. *Chi mu* ② was used during the Han period, but rarely. The vocative *shên* ③ dates from the Sung dynasty. This term is not found in the classical literature, and is thought to be a contraction of *shih mu*. In modern times *shên shên*, *shên mu*, or *shên niang* have been commonly used as vocatives. Another common usage is by prefixing her sibname, or the numerical order of her husband, to *ma*. This also applies to 36.

### 39. Ku mu 姑母 f si

"Father's sisters are ku," defines the *Êrh Ya*. *Ku* is also used in the *I Li*.④

---

①   *Yen shih chia hsün* 2.5a.

②   *Hou Han Shu* 118.20a.

③   *Ming tao tsa chih*, 13b: 婶.

④   *I Li* 31.16b 17a. LIANG Ch'ang-chü (*Chêng wei lu*, 8.13a-14b) considers *ku tzǔ mei* a term for father's sister. As far as its use in the *I Li* is concerned, it should be interpreted as *ku* (father's sister), and *tzǔ* and *mei* (ego's own sisters). The other instances which Liang cites in support of the use of *ku tzǔ* for father's older sister, and *ku mei* for father's younger sister, are very questionable.

The vocative for father's unmarried sister is *ku*, or *ku ku* prefixed by her name or numerical order. When she is married, *ku ma* is the most prevalent form.

*Chia ku mu* is sometimes used as a depreciatory term. Yen's *Family Instructions* considered this usage incorrect, for when a woman was married out she was no longer a member of the family, so that *chia* could not be applied.[1]

## 40. Ku fu 姑父 f si h

*Ku hsü*[2] and *ku fu*[3] are used as alternative terms, mostly from the third to the sixth centuries A.D.

## 41. T'ang po fu 堂伯父 f f b s f

*Êrh Ya* gives the term *ts'ung tsu fu* for father's father's brother's sons, both older and younger than father. By inference from other usages, *ts'ung tsu shih fu* may be used for the former. Since the Han period, *ts'ung po*, or *ts'ung po fu* have been used.[4] During the fifth and sixth centuries A.D. the term *t'ung t'ang* was introduced, since agnate relatives of the same paternal grandfather offer sacrifices in the same ancestral hall. *T'ung t'ang* literally

---

[1] *Yen shih chia hsün* 2.5a.

[2] *Pei Ch'i Shu* 18.3b: 婿.

[3] *San Kuo Chih* 13.3a; *Nan Shih* 57.14a.

[4] *Chin Shu* 80. 1a.

means "the same hall." During the T'ang period the *t'ung* was dropped and only *t'ang* was used.[1]Later the term was extended to other collateral lines.

### 42. T'ang po mu 堂伯母 w of 41

As can be inferred from *ts'ung tsu fu* and *ts'ung tsu shih fu*, the older term would be *ts'ung tsu mu* or *ts'ung tsu shih mu*. Since the Han period *ts'ung po mu* or simply *ts'ung mu* have been used.

### 43. T'ang shu fu 堂叔父 f f b s < f

Compare 41. *Ts'ung tsu shu fu* may, by inference, be the older term. Since the Han period *ts'ung shu* or *ts'ung shu fu* [2] have been used as alternative terms.

In the vocatives of 41 and 43 the modifier *t'ang* is usually dropped, i.e., the vocatives of 35 and 37 may be applied here, respectively, modified by their names or numerical order.

### 44. T'ang shu mu 堂叔母 w of 43

*Ts'ung tsu shu mu* may be the older form. The later abbreviated form *ts'ung shu mu* may be used alternatively with *t'ang shu mu*. *T'ang shên* is a vocative extension of *shên*.

---

[1]　Ch'iEN Ta-hsin〔*Hêng yen lu*, 3.9a-b.〕

[2]　*Sung Shu* 52.5a.

45. T'ang ku mu 堂姑母 f f b d

The term in the *rh Ya* is *ts'ung tsu ku*, later abbreviated to *ts'ung ku*.[1] *Ts'ung* and *t'ang* are synonymous. The vocative for father's sister may be used here, modified by her name or numerical order.

46. T'ang ku fu 堂姑父 f f b d h

The vocative for father's sister's husband may be used here, modified by his sibname.

47. Tsai ts'ung po fu 再从伯父 s of 25 or 27 > f

*Tsu fu* is the term used in the *Êrh Ya* and *I Li*.[2] *Tsu po fu* may be used for this relation, but it can be applied to any male sib relative of the father's generation older than father, from the fourth collateral line onward so it is a rather loose term.

48. Tsai ts'ung po mu 再从伯母 w of 47

49. Tsai ts'ung shu fu 再从叔父 s of 25 or 27 < f

*Tsu fu* is used in the *Êrh Ya*, *Tsu shu*[3] and *tsung shu*[4] are later

---

① *Chin Shu* 51.2b.

② *I Li* 33.6a: 族.

③ *Chin Shu* 83.1a.

④ *Yin hua lu*, 2.2a: 宗叔.

alternatives, but used rather loosely. In the vocatives of 47 and 49, *tsai ts'ung* is usually dropped, leaving only *po* and *shu* modified by their names or numerical order.

50. Tsai ts'ung shu mu 再从叔母 w of 49

The vocatives of 36 and 38 may be applied to 48 and 50, respectively, modified by their sibnames or their husbands' numerical order, or by both.

51.Tsai ts'ung ku mu 再从姑母 d of 25 or 27

In the *Êrh Ya*, *tsu tsu ku* 族祖姑. In modern times, *tsu ku* 族姑 has been used alternatively, but in a rather loose fashion.

52. Tsai ts'ung ku fu 再从姑父 h of 51

53. Ku piao po fu 姑表伯父 f f si s > f

*Chung wai chang jên* [1] was used during the fifth and sixth centuries A.D. During the Sung dynasty *piao chang jên* [2] and *wai po fu* [3] were frequently used. Before the T'ang period, *chang jên* was used as a polite term for any old man; but since then it has been used as a synonym for *yo fu*, wife's father.

---

① 中外丈人, cf. *Yen shih chia hsün 2.8b*. Chung-wai is synonymous with *chung-piao*.

② *T'ai p'ing kuang chi* 太平广记〔1934, Peiping, 文友堂 ed.〕148. 4a.

③ Cf. 东观余论附录〔学津讨原 ed.〕5a.

54. Ku piao po mu 姑表伯母 w of 53

*Chang mu* [1] was used during the fifth and sixth centuries A.D., but is now used exclusively for wife's mother.

55. Ku piao shu fu 姑表叔父 f f si s<f

56. Ku piao shu mu ○○叔母 w of 55

57. Ku piao ku mu ○○姑母 f f si d

58. Ku piao ku fu ○○姑父 f f si d h

59. Chiu piao po fu 舅表伯父 f m b s<f

60. Chiu piao po mu ○○伯母 w of 59

61. Chiu piao shu fu 舅表叔父 f m b s<f

62. Chiu piao shu mu ○○叔母 w of 61

---

[1]   *Yen Shih Chia hsün* 2.8b. The use of *wang* 王 *mu* and *hsieh* 谢 *mu* is no longer intelligible. Perhaps their use is based on the most well-known sibnames of the time, Wang and Hsieh.

63. Chiu piao ku mu ○○姑母 f m b d

64. Chiu piao ku fu ○○姑父 h of 63

65. I piao po fu 姨表伯父 f m si s > f

66. I piao po mu ○○伯母 w of 65

67. I piao shu fu ○○叔父 f m si s < f

68. I piao shu mu ○○叔母 h of 67

69. I piao ku mu ○○姑母 f m si d

70. I piao ku fu ○○姑父 w of 69

The terms listed under 53 are applicable to 55, 58, 59, 61, 64, 65, 67 and 70 respectively, during the period mentioned above. In ordinary modern usage the modifiers *ku, chiu* and *i* are usually omitted, so that terminologically these relatives are not distinguished from one another. Conceptually, the exact relationship is always assumed.

## V. Generation of the speaker

71. Pên shên 本身 ego，a male.

A female would use the same terms, except for those provided in Table IV and certain terms in Table III.

72. Ch'i 妻 wife

*Ch'i tzŭ*[1] 妻子 is commonly used, but it may also mean "wife and children." In certain cases *fu* [2] is used synonymously with *Ch'i*, but it may be used to mean "woman" in general. In kinship usage *fu* is principally used for the wives of those who are of lower generations and age status.

*Fei*[3] is a very old term and so also is *nei chu,* [4] but the latter is rather uncommon. *Nei shê* [5] and *ju jên* [6] were commonly employed during the first half of the first millennium A.D. *Shih,*[7]*chia,*[8]and *shih chia* [9] are also very old terms, but are still commonly employed as literary forms

*Chieh fa*[10] and *chung k'uei*[11] are primarily literary terms. *Chieh fa* is

---

[1]    *Jih Chih lu*, 24. 5a.

[2]    *I Ching*. l. 33a: 妇.

[3]    妃*Êrh Ya*; *Shuo Wên*; *Shih Ming. Tso chuan* 5.19a; *Chan kuo ts'ê* 3.83a. *Fei*, as used before the Han period, is a term for "wife" in general. It is only during the Han period and since that *fei* is reserved for the wives of nobility and the Emperor's secondary wives. Cf. *ch'in shu chi*, 2.5b-6b.

[4]    *Tso Chuan* 42. 9b: 内主. *Nei chu* literally means "inside lord."

[5]    陈琳：饮马长城窟行〔*Yü T'ai hsin yung chi*,1.13a〕:内舍.

[6]    *Chiang wên-T'ung chih*1.1b: 孺人. *Ju jên* was originally a term for titled women during the feudal period, e.g., *Li Chi* 5.11b. It became a common term for wife during the third and fourth centuries A.D. Since then, it has reverted to its old connotation.

[7]    *I Li* 6.8b: 室 .*Li Chi* 28.20b.

[8]    *Shih Ching* 7B.5b: 乐子之无家 .*Tso chuan* 14. 10b.

[9]    *Shih Ching* 4A. 6b: 室家.

[10]   *Wên Hsüan*, 29. 14b:结发.

[11]   *I Ching* 4.17a: 中馈 .*Chung k'uei* literally means "the family larder"and is used metaphorically.

applied only to the first marriage principal wife; *chung k'uei* is also used as a literary complimentary term.

The wife, when speaking to the husband, calls herself *Ch'ieh* 妾, "your concubine"; or, *chi chou Ch'ieh*.① These abject terms are seldom, if ever, used except in literature. During the feudal period, a noble woman could on formal occasions, call herself *pei tzǔ*,②or *hsiao tung*,③ according to rank. These terms are now entirely obsolete. *Chün fu* ④ is a common form, but mostly used in poetry.

The husband calls the wife *hsien Ch'i*,⑤ or *niang tzǔ*,⑥and, more anciently, *hsi chün*.⑦These highly complimentary terms are rarely used in daily life, and are rather mere literary forms. *Ch'ing* is a reciprocal term, i.e., used alike both by husband and wife, and is now a predominately literary form of address. Husband and wife may call each other by name, or they may use no term at all and just refer to each other as "you," "he," and "she." After issue, teknonymy is the most common practice.

The depreciatory term is *nei*.⑧ *Nei tzǔ* 内子, *nei jên* 内人 and *pi nei* 敝

---

① 　*Shih Chi* 8.4a: 箕帚妾 ; i.e., a female with broom and dust basket ready to serve.

② 　*Tso Chuan* 15.2a: 婢子 .

③ 　*Lun Yü, 16.10a:* 小童 ; *Li Chi* 5.12a.

④ 　*Shih Ching* 13B. 6a: 君妇 .

⑤ 　贤妻 literally "virtuous wife".

⑥ 　*Pei Ch'i Shu* 39.5a: 娘子 .

⑦ 　 *Han shu* 65.5a: 细君 .

⑧ 　It is also a general term used for wife and concubine together, e.g., *Tso Chuan* 14.18b. Cf. *Hêng yen lu* , 3.9b- 10a and *Ch'êng wei lu*, 5.12b-13b.

内 are its derivatives. *Cho ching* [1] and *shih jên* [2] are more literary. The above terms are used mostly in refined society. *Chia li* [3] and *hsiang li* [4] are vulgar terms. *Hun chia,* [5] *hun shê,* [6] *lao P'o,* [7] and *chia chu P'o* [8] are vulgar and dialectical forms used mostly in the referential, and are not necessarily depreciatory.

The complimentary term is *fu jên* 夫人，originally a term for the wife of a man of rank. More intimately, *sao fu jên* 嫂夫人 may be used. *T'ai T'ai* is more colloquial. [9] *Ling shih* [10] and *ling Ch'i* [11] are literary in nature. In ancient times *nei tzǔ* [12] was used as a complimentary term, but is now exclusively used as a depreciatory term. *k'ang li* [13] is a literary form used

---

[1]  拙荆 is derived from the 荆钗布裙 of Mêng Kuang 孟光，wife of Liang Hung 梁鸿 of the Later Han dynasty. The variants are *shan ching* 山荆，*ching fu* 荆妇 and *ching jên* 荆人.

[2]  *Shih Ching* 2C. 6a: 室人.

[3]  "In the home." Cf. YAO k'uan 姚宽 ?-1161 A.D., 西溪丛话，学津讨原 ed., 2. 19b.

[4]  乡里，"in the country." *Nan Shih* 64. 16a: 谓妻杨，呼为乡里，曰：我不忍令乡里落他处，今当先杀乡里.

[5]  *Nan T'ang chin shih* 南唐近事 of Chêng Wên-pao 郑文宝，953-1013 A.D.〔宝颜堂秘笈 ed.〕3a-4b: 浑家;also *Liang Ch'i i kao* 梁溪遗稿，诗钞 of Yu Mou 尤袤 1127-1194 A.D.,〔锡山尤氏丛刊 ed.〕淮民谣，11b.

[6]  浑舍 is a variant of hun-chia.

[7]  老婆 "old woman."Cf. *Ch'êng wei lu*, 5.10a. This is the most common modern term.

[8]  *Hêng yen lu*, 3. 13b-14a: 家主婆.

[9]  Ho Liang-chün 何良俊，*Ssǔ yu chai Ts'ung shuo* 四友斋丛说〔纪录汇编 ed.〕6.52b-53a: 太太. Cf.also *T'ung su pien*, 18.8a. During the Ming period, *t'ai t'ai* was a term for the wives of officials of the 中丞 rank and higher.

[10]  令室.

[11]  *Shih Ching* 20B, 8b: 令妻.

[12]  *Yen tzǔ Ch'un Ch'iu*, 6.9a:内子. *Nei tzǔ* was used during the feudal period as a term for the wife of ministers of the feudal lords, e.g., *Li Chi* 44.16a. and *Shih ming*. Hence it is sometimes used as a complimentary term.

[13]  *Tso Chuan* 27. 2b: 伉俪.

to refer to another's wife, and, more commonly, to refer to both husband and wife as *hsien kang li*.

*Pin* ① and *ling jên* ② are posthumous terms for wife. *Tê pei* ③ is a posthumous complimentary term. It is also used as a literary form for the wife in the case of an aged couple.

### 73. Hsiung 兄 o b

The *Êrh Ya* used *hsiung* to explain *k'un*.④ The two terms apparently were synonymous in ancient times. Kuo P'o's (276 324 A.D.) commentary on the *Êrh Ya* states that the people of Chiang Tung called older brother k'un. The *Shuo Wên* does not give the character 晜, but gives the character NFEBE 㾪, and states that the Chou people used this term for older brother. NFEBE is probably its original form and 晜 and NFEBF , its variants. 昆 is a later borrowed form.⑤　In the *Shih Ching*, only the *Wang Fêng* (4A.9a) uses the term *k'un*, all others using *hsiung*. This fact is regarded as evidence that *k'un* is a Chou term.

In the *I Li* all male paternal cousins of the same sibname of ego and

---

①　*Li Chi* 5.22b: 嫔 .

②　*Chu tzǔ nien P'u* 朱子年谱 by Wang Mu-hung 王懋竑 1668 1764 A.D.〔粤雅堂丛书本〕2A.13a: 令人 .

③　 *Ch'êng wei lu*, 5.14a: 德配 .

④　*Êrh Ya*: 晜 .

⑤　 The *Shuo wên* lists the character 昆 but not with the meaning "older brother." 　The *Yü p'ien* gives 㾪 and states that it is the same as 昆 . Huang k'an 皇侃〔488-545 A.D.〕says, that *k'un* 昆 means "bright", "brilliant." Out of reverence the older brother is called *k'un* (论语义疏，6.2b-3a 古经解汇函 edition). This is rather a rationalization.

within the *Ta Kung* degree of mourning are given as *k'un ti*, and all male paternal cousins of the same sibname but beyond the *Ta Kung* degree of mourning, and all male cousins of different sibnames from ego are given as *hsiung ti*,[1] This illustrates the intentional differentiation and standardization of the degrees of relationship adopted by the ritual books in employing terms in other than their original connotation. *k'un* is entirely obsolete at present.[2]

The vocative is *ko* [3] 哥 or *ko ko* a euphonic duplication. *Ko*, as given in the *Shuo wên*, does not mean older brother at all; it means "to sing," or "a song." *Ko* was first used from the sixth to the eighth centuries A.D., to mean father and then in the ninth and tenth centuries A.D. it became a vocative for older brother.[4]

According to the *Fang Yên*, the people of Chin and Yang called older brother *po* or *p'o*,[5] The *Shih Ming* says that the people of Ch'ing and Hsü used the term *huang* 荒 .Until the fourteenth to the seventeenth centuries A.D. the peoples of the lower Yangtze delta still called older brother 况 *huang*.[6] 况 and 荒 are pronounced about the same. The ancient pronunciation

---

[1]  *Ch'êng wei lu*, 4.2b.

[2]  For a most complete and classical study of the difference between these characters,cf. 昆弟兄弟释异 by Tsang Yung 臧庸, 1767—1811, 拜经堂文集〔1930〕,1.

[3]  *Kuang yün*.

[4]  *Kai yü Ts'ung k'ao*, 37.25b.

[5]  *Fang Yen*, 10. 4a: 膀 Its pronunciation is very uncertain.

[6]  *Yen pei tsa chih* 研北杂志,by Lu Yu 陆友, ca. 1330 A.D.〔得月簃 edition〕49a.

of *hsiung* 兄 may have been *huang* 况, as the two characters are often used interchangeably.① The *Pai hu T'ung* uses 况 to explain 兄.

### 74. Sao 嫂 o b w

The *Êrh Ya* reads, "Woman calls older brother's wife *sao*," but it does not give the man's term. Whether or not *sao* was exclusively a woman's term we have no means of knowing. The *Shuo Wên* defines *sao* as "older brother's wife" but does not specify man or woman; it was most probably a term for both man and woman.②

### 75. Ti 弟 y b

The younger brother, when speaking to the older brother or sister, calls himself *pi ti*,③ or *hsiao ti*.④ The older brother or sister calls the younger brother *hsien ti*.,⑤ These were old usages; at present simply *ti* is used,

*Chia ti*⑥ was used as a depreciative from the third to the eighth centuries A.D. It is now incorrect to use this term. The present term is *shê ti*, and the complimentary term, *ling ti* or *hsien ti*.

---

① 　*Shih Ching*, 3A. 7a; Ibid, 18B. 1a: *Han shu*. 76. 6a. with YEN Shih-Ku's note.

② 　For example, *Chan kuo ts'ê* 3.6a.

③ 　*San kuo chih* 29. 26a (commentary): 鄙弟.

④ 　木兰诗: 小弟.

⑤ 　*Shih Chi* 86. 9a: 贤弟.

⑥ 　*Ts'ao tzǔ* Ch'ien chi 释思赋序, 1.5b; *T'ang shu* 162. 22b.

## 76. Ti fu 弟妇 y b w

*Ti hsi* 弟媳 is an alternative term. *Fu* and *hsi* are synonymous in relationship terminology. The older brother usually avoids the younger brother's wife, and vice versa. Conversation can be only formal, and a proper distance must be maintained.

## 77. Tzŭ 姊 o si

*Tzŭ* is now used chiefly in standard and literary contexts. It may be doubled as *tzŭ tzŭ*. The universal vocative is *chieh* or *chieh chieh*. Compare 34 for changes of *chieh*. *Chieh* may also be used for any young woman, e.g., *hsiao chieh*, which is equivalent to "Miss."

*Hsü* [1] was an ancient term for older sister, used in the state of ch'u ; *shao* [2] was used in Ch'i. *Mêng* [3] was an old term for father's concubine's daughter older than father's principal wife's daughter. Later, in certain regions, it was used to mean older sister in general.[4] *Nü hsiung* [5] may be used as a literary alternative for *tzŭ*.

## 78. Tzŭ fu 姊夫 o si h

---

① *Li Sao*〔*Wên Hsüan*, 32.9b〕媭 ; also *Shuo Wên*.

② *Kuang yün*: 媻

③ *Tso chuan* 2.2a: 孟 .

④ *Fang yen,* 12.1a.

⑤ *Shuo wên*: 女兄 .

The term in the *Êrh Ya* is *shêng*—a reflection of cross cousin-marriage. *Tzǔ chang* and *tzǔ hsü*① are modern alternatives. *Chieh fu* is more colloquial. Teknonymy is the most common practice as regards the vocative. If there is no child, brother terms are usually used.

The *Êrh Ya* says that sisters call each other's husband *ssǔ*,②"private"; this is considered evidence of the sororate. It has long been obsolete. In modern times, brother and sister use the same term.

## 79. Mei 妹 y si

*Ti*③ is said to be a woman's term for younger sister but this is by no means certain. During the feudal period *ti* had a special connotation in connection with the yin marriage. *Nü ti* ④ is a literary alternative term for *mei*. The *Shuo Wên* states that the people of ch'u called younger sister *wei*,⑤ which may be a variant of *mei*.

The depreciatory term *chia tzǔ* is used for older sister, and *shê mei* for younger sister. This use of these terms is continued even after the sisters are married, although theoretically this should not be done.

---

① 　*Hou Han Shu* 49. 12b: 婿；*Chin Shu* 39. 8a-b.〔No. 18 on p. 157.〕

② 　私. *Shih Ching* 3B.9a. The *Shih ming* gives the traditional, but rationalistic,explanation.

③ 　*Shih Ming*: 娣. This interpretation is followed by Chêng Chên in his *Ch'ao ching ch'ao wên chi*, 1.17b-18a. This view is hardly justifiable, however, on the basis of the *Êrh Ya's* use of *mei* and *ti*. The former is used both by man and woman; the latter, in reference to the yin costom of the feudal period, refers to younger sisters who have married the same man. Thus *ti* can also be applied to husband's younger brother's wife, as in the *Êrh Ya*.

④ 　*Shuo wên*: 女弟.

⑤ 　婿. Cf. also *Kung-yang chuan* 4. 7b.

80. Mei fu 妹夫 y si h

In the *Êrh Ya* the term is *shêng*—a reflection of cross cousin marriage. The *Êrh Ya* also says that sisters call one another's husbands *ssŭ* —a supposed reflection of the sororate. *Mei chang* and *mei hsü* are modern alternatives. For other usages, compare 78.

81. T'ang hsiung 堂兄 f b s > e

*Ts'ung fu k'un ti* is the term in the *Êrh Ya* and *I Li* [1] for the first male paternal cousins. Later it was abbreviated to *Ts'ung hsiung* [2] for the father's brother's sons older than speaker, and *ts'ung ti* [3] for those younger than the speaker. *Kung k'un ti* was used in the *Shih Chi*. [4] During the fifth and sixth centuries A.D. *T'ung T'ang* was substituted for *Ts'ung*, e.g., *T'ung T'ang hsiung* and *T'ung T'ang ti*. During the latter part of the T'ang dynasty the *T'ung* was dropped, only *T'ang hsiung* and *T'ang ti* being used. *T'ang and Ts'ung* can still be used alternatively.

82. T'ang sao 堂嫂 w of 81

83. T'ang ti 堂弟 f b s < e

---

①   *I Li* 31. 17a.

②   *Liang Shu* 31.1a.

③   *San kuo chih* 8.1a.

④   Shih Chi 49.6a:公.

84. T'ang ti fu 堂弟妇 w of 83

85. T'ang tzǔ 堂姊 f b d＞e

The older term is *Ts'ung fu tzǔ mei* for father's brother's daughters, both older and younger than speaker. The development is exactly parallel with that of 81, *T'ang hsiung*.

86. T'ang tzǔ fu ○○夫 h of 85

87. T'ang mei 堂妹 f b d＜e

88. T'ang mei fu ○○夫 h of 87

89. Tsai Ts'ung hsiung 再从兄 f f b s s＞e

The older term is *Ts'ung tsu k'un ti*, as used in the *Êrh Ya* and the *I Li*.[①] *Tsai Ts'ung* was substituted later. *Tsai* means "once again" or "a second time." *Ts'ung* is synonymous with the later term *T'ang*, which indicates the second collateral line. Hence *tsai Ts'ung* indicated the third collateral line.

90. Tsai Ts'ung sao 再从嫂 w of 89

---

① *I Li* 33. 1b: 祖.

91. Tsai Ts'ung ti 再从弟 f f b s s<e

92. Tsai Ts'ung ti fu 再从弟妇 w of 91

93. Tsai Ts'ung tzŭ 再从姊 f f b s d>e

94. Tsai Ts'ung tzŭ fu 再从姊夫 h of 93

95. Tsai Ts'ung mei 再从妹 f f b s d<e

96. Tsai Ts'ung mei fu 再从妹夫 h of 95

97. Tsu hsiung 族兄 f f f b s s s>e

The alternative and more exact term is *san Ts'ung hsiung* 三从兄. *San* means "third," and *Ts'ung* signifies second collateral. Hence *san Ts'ung* means the fourth collateral line, since *Ts'ung* begins the count from the second collateral line. This principle can be extended and the terms formed, e.g., *ssŭ Ts'ung*, *wu Ts'ung*, *liu Ts'ung*, indicating the fifth, sixth, seventh collateral lines, respectively. *Tsu* 族 is a vague term applied to all sib relatives from the fourth collateral line and beyond, without further discrimination.

*Tsung hsiung* ① is a modern alternative. *Tsung* 宗 is in a certain sense synonymous with *tsu* 族. *Ts'ung tsêng tsu k'un ti*② was used during the Han period; it is a rather clumsy device involving the enumeration of ancestors.

*Ch'in T'ung hsing*③ is the term given in the *Êrh Ya* for male paternal cousins of the same sibname, of the fifth collateral line. It is obsolete now; generally *tsu hsiung ti* is used, or, more exactly, *ssǔ Ts'ung hsiung ti.*

98. Tsu sao 族嫂 w of 97

99. Tsu ti 族弟 f f f b s s s＜e

100. Tsu ti fu 族弟妇 w of 99

101. Tsu tzǔ 族姊 f f f b s s d＞e

102. Tsu tzǔ fu 族姊夫 h of 101

103. Tsu mei 族妹 f f f b s s d＜e

---

① 宗兄 is just as indefinite as *tsu hsiung*, and can be applied to any older sibbrother from the fourth collateral line and beyond. But *tsung hsiung* was used during the feudal period by younger brothers to refer to the primogenitary eldest brother. *Li Chi* 19. 10b-11a.

② *Hsin Shu* 8.6a-b.

③ 亲同姓.

104. Tsu mei fu 族妹夫 h of 103

The vocatives for brothers and sisters, brothers'wives and sisters' husbands can be correspondingly applied to 8l-104, individualized by their names, numerical order, or sibnames. Depreciatory and complimentary forms can be formed in the regular way.

105. Ku piao hsiung 姑表兄 f si s > e

The old term in the *Êrh Ya* is *shêng*—a reflection of crosscousin marriage. During the Han period *wai hsiung ti*[1] and *Ts'ung nei hsiung ti*[2] were used for both the older and the younger. The term *piao* also dates from this period. *Shêng, wai hsiung ti* and *Ts'ung nei hsiung ti* are all obsolete now.

In the vocative *ku* is always dropped, leaving only *piao hsiung* or *piao ko*. *Piao hsiung* is more literary and formal, *piao ko* is strictly vocative. In certain localities *lao piao* 老表 is used.

106. Ku piao sao 姑表嫂 w of 105

Vocative *piao sao*.

107. Ku piao ti 姑表弟 f si s < e

108. Ku piao ti fu ○ ○ 弟妇 w of 107

---

[1]   *I Li* 33. 9b.

[2]   *Wên Hsüan*, 25.1a.

109. Ku piao tzǔ○○姊 f si d＞e

Vocative *piao chieh*.

110. Ku piao tzǔ fu○○姊夫 h of 109

111. Ku piao mei○○妹 f si d＜e

112. Ku piao mei fu○○妹夫 h of 111

113. T'ang ku piao hsiung 堂姑表兄 f f si s s＞e

114. T'ang ku piao sao○○表嫂 w of 113

115. T'ang ku piao ti○○表弟 f fsi s s＜e

116.T'ang ku piao ti fu○○○弟妇 w of 115

117. T'ang ku piao tzǔ○○○姊 f f si s d＞e

118. T'ang ku piao tzǔ fu○○○姊夫 h of 117

119. T'ang ku piao mei○○○妹 f f si s d＜e

120. T'ang ku piao mei fu○○○妹夫 h of 119

Terms 113-120 may also be applied to the children of father's father's brother's daughter. This is by inference only; no documentary usage has been noted.

## VI. Generation of the son

### 121. Tzǔ 子 son

*Tzǔ*, in ancient times, was used to mean child, either male or female. Thus it was often compounded with other elements to signify son, e.g., *chang fu tzǔ*.[1]*Êrh* [2] is synonymous with *tzǔ*; it is now used mostly as a diminutive, with no sex connotation, so that it has to be combined with other elements to express son, as in the modern term *êrh tzǔ*.[3] *Hsi* [4] is an old term for son, but also has the indefinite meaning of child; consequently, the forms *hsi nan* [5] for son and *hsi nü* for daughters are used. *Ssǔ* 嗣 [6] means "descendant," and is also used for son. During the feudal period *ssǔ tzǔ* [7] referred to the eldest succeeding son, but in modern terminology is

---

[1] *Shih Chi* 67. 19a-b: 夫子丈; literally, "male child".

[2] *Kuang ya*: 儿.

[3] *Shih Chi* 52. 2a.

[4] 息 means "to reproduce," or "to bear." Hence it is used both for male and female children. See p.1242, note [5], and p.1245, note [1].

[5] *Ts'ao tzǔ-chien chi* 8. 1.

[6] *Shu Ching* 4.7a.

[7] *Li Chi* 4.5a.

used for the adopted son. *Hsing*,① in ancient times, may be used for son but it may mean any descendant, being synonymous with *shêng*, ②"to bear." *Nu*③ is another old term.

*Ku* and *ni*④ were uncommon old, perhaps local, terms for son. *Tsai* 崽 ⑤ and *tsai* 囝 ⑥ are modern dialectical forms, apparently derivatives from *tzǔ*. 囝 may also be pronounced *chien*.⑦

*Tzǔ* can be combined with various modifiers to express the more exact and complicated relationships of sonship resulting from ancestor worship, inheritance, concubinage, divorce and remarriage, adoption, etc.

The son, in speaking to the father, calls himself *nan* 男, "a male issue." *Êrh tzǔ* 儿子 is more vocative, and *nan* is principally a literary form of address. During the mourning period the son refers to himself as *ku tzǔ*,⑧ *ai*

---

① *Shih Ching* 1C. 7a: 姓; and *Tso Chuan* 42. 32a.

② Since the ancient pronunciation of *hsing* is about the same as 生, they are used interchangeably. *Shih Ching* 20D. 7b.

③ *Shih Ching* 9B. 10b: 帑.

④ *Kuang Ya*: 瞉, 婗. Cf. 王念孙, 广雅疏证, 6B.4.

⑤ *Fang Yen,* 10. 1b.

⑥ *Chêng tzǔ t`ung, s. v.*

⑦ Chêng Chên (Ch'in shu chi, 2. 12b) says that the *Chi Yün* gives the pronunciation 九件切. This is incorrect and probably a confusion with 弄. But *chien* may be a T'ang pronunciation, e.g., in *Hua yang chi*, 1.13a. However, at present the character is pronounced differently in different localities. In Fukien, it is pronounced "chan", in Chekiang and Kiangsu. "lan", and in Kiangsi, Kwangtung, Hupeh and Hunan,' tsai'.

⑧ 孤, "orphaned son", used when mourning for the father when the mother is living.

*tzǔ,*[1] *ku ai tzǔ,*[2] *pu hsiao nan,*[3] or *chi jên.*[4]

The father calls the son *êrh tzǔ* both in the vocative and in writing. In speaking, usually only the name is used. In writing, the relationship term is used together with the name, as "*êrh tzǔ* so and so." This rule applies to relatives of all descending generations.

The complimentary term is *ling lang.*[5] Other combinations are *lang chün,*[6] or *hsien lang*[7]. *Hsien tzǔ,*[8] *ling tzǔ,*[9] and *ling ssǔ*[10] are alternative terms, somewhat more literary. *Kung tzǔ*[11] was originally a term for the sons of the feudal nobility and later for the sons of men of high official positions. But now it has become a general complimentary term almost as prevalent as *ling lang.* Another very common, rather vulgar, term is *shao yêh* 少爷, which also originally referred to the son of a man of rank or of an official, e.g., as used by the servants in referring to the master's son.

The depreciatory term is *hsiao tzǔ*, or *hsiao êrh.* More vulgarly *hsiao*

---

[1] 哀, "grieving son," used when mourning for the mother when the father is chung piao.

[2] This is used in mourning for either parent when both of them are dead. The differentiation began during the T'ang dynasty. Cf. *Kai yü Ts'ung kao*, 37. 8a-9b.

[3] 不孝男 "unfilial son."

[4] *Shih Ching* 7B. 3b: 棘人.

[5] 郎 is originally a title of office. During the Han period, high officials could appoint their sons *lang.* Thus *lang* became a complimentary term. *Cf. Ch'êng wei lu*, 6.3a.

[6] *Yü t'ai hsin yung chi*, 1.18b.

[7] 古文苑, *Ssǔ pu Ts'ung kan* ed., 10. 17a.

[8] *Wei Wu-ti chih* 43a-b.

[9] *Nan Shih* 59. 6a.

[10] *Mo Chi*, 2.12b.

[11] *Shih Shing* 1C. 6b; Ibid. 13A. 5a.

*Ch'üan* 小犬, "a little dog." *Chien hsi*① and *jo hsi*② are obsolete literary terms.

### 122. Tzŭ fu 子妇 s w

*Hsi fu* 媳妇 is a more colloquial term. *Hsi* 媳 was originally written 息，which means "son" or "child." During the Sung period the female classifier was added, forming 媳 .③Thus it became a distinct term for daughter in law. *Hsi fu* may be used for the wives of all the relatives of descending generations.

Son's wife is usually addressed with this name by her parents-in-law. The father-in-law sees her only on formal occasions, and usually maintains a proper distance. When the daughter-in-law gets older and has children, the parents-in-law may even use the grandchildren's term in referring to her—extreme extension of teknonymy.

### 123. Nü 女 daughter

*Nü tzŭ tzŭ*④ and *fu jên tzŭ* ⑤ are used in the *Li Chi* and *I Li* for daughter, in distinction to *chang fu tzŭ* for male child. *Ying* ⑥is said to have been an

---

① *Shih Chi* 43.32b: 贱息 .

② *Nan Shih* 46.10a: 弱息 .

③ Cf. *Ch'êng wei lu*, 8.17b-18a.

④ *I Li* 31.16b-17a. *Li Chi* 2.13b.

⑤ *I Li* 32.4a.

⑥ *Yü p'ien*: 婴 . It is usually a term for infant.

ancient term for daughter, but this is by no means certain.

*Nü êrh* is more colloquial. It is used both by parents and daughter, and is a general term as well. When the daughter writes to her parents only *nü* is used in referring to herself.

The complimentary terms are *ling yüan*,[1] *ling ai*,[2] *nü kung tzŭ* 女公子 and, more colloquially, *Ch'ien chin* [3] and *hsiao chieh*.[4] *Yü nü*[5] was used during the feudal period, but is no longer used in this sense. *Hsiao niang tzŭ* was commonly used during the T'ang and Sung periods.[6]

The depreciatory terms are *hsiao nü*, more vulgarly, *hsiao ya t'ou* 小丫头, "little handmaid." *Hsi nü*[7] is an old obsolete term, which could be used as a literary form. *Chia tzŭ* [8] was admissible during the Han period, but was never used in this sense in later times and nowadays is used as a depreciatory term for older sister.

### 124. Nü hsü 女婿 d h

---

[1]  令媛, *yüan* is a term for a beautiful girl and *ling yüan* is probably derived from *Shih Ching*, 3A. 5a.

[2]  令爱, your beloved one.

[3]  千金, "a thousand tales of gold," that is precious. *Yin p'ao sui pi* 音匏随笔, by TSAO Mou-chien 曹楙坚〔乙亥丛编 edition.〕8a.

[4]  小姐, was used during the Sung period as a term for young maid servants, or prostitutes. Cf. *Kai yü Ts'ung k'ao*, 38.12. At present it is used as a complimentary term for the daughter of another and for any young woman.

[5]  *Li Chi*, 49.3a: 玉女.

[6]  Cf. *Kai yü Ts'ung k'ao*, 38.1a.

[7]  *Shih Chi*, 8.4a: 息女.

[8]  *Yen shih chia hsün, 2.5a:* 家父.〔No. 10, p. 155.〕

Mencius uses the term *shêng*. The *Êrh Ya* uses the term *hsü*, which may also mean "husband" in general.[1]*Hsü* is combined with a variety of qualifiers to signify daughter's husband, e.g., *tzǔ hsü*,[2] *lang hsü*, and *hsü shêng*.[3]Other alternative terms are *nü fu*[4] and *pan tzǔ*.[5] *Chiao K'o*,[6]*tung ch'uang*,[7]*t'an ch'uang* ,[8] *k'uai hsü, chia hsü*,[9]and *mi Ch'in*[10] are mostly literary forms, used more or less in a complimentary way.

*Ch'ing* [11] was originally a dialectical form (Shantung) for daughter's husband, and later was commonly used as a literary term. The forms *tsu pien* 卒便 and *p'ing shih* 平使 are erroneous derivatives of *ch'ing*.[12] *Ch'ing* is also used to mean "husband" in general. *Ch'ing* and *hsü* were originally complimentary terms for a man of ability.

The complimentary terms are *ling hsü* and *ling T'a n. Ling T'an* is derived from *T'an ch'uang*, and is rather uncommon.

Depreciatory term, *hsiao hsü*.

---

1. Originally, it was a complimentary term for an able scholar.
2. *Shih Chi* 89.10a.
3. 婿 (*Ch'êng wei lu*, 8. 21b). [No. 14, p. 156. ]
4. *Chin Shu* 34. 8a.
5. 半子, half son. *Liu pin-K'o wên chi*, 外集，祭虢州杨庶子文，10.7.
6. 娇客，literally，"delicate" or "graceful guest." It is non-vocative and non-referential.
7. 东床，"the one who occupies the bed in the eastern chamber," is based on the anecdote of 王羲之，东床坦腹，*Chin Shu* 80. 1b. Cf. *Shih ch'ang T'an*, 1.3b.
8. 坦床.
9. 快婿 and 佳婿 mean practically the same thing. *Pei Shih* 34. 16b-17a.
10. *Chiu T'ang Shu* 159. 7a:密亲.
11. *Fang Yen* 3. 1a: 倩.
12. *Fang Yen, loc. cit.*, commentary. Kuang Ya, loc. cit.

125. Chih 侄 b s

The *Êrh Ya* gives no term for brother's son, man speaking. It is conjectured that brother's sons (man speaking) could be called sons, *tzŭ*. The *Li Chi* uses the term *yu tzŭ*, "like son," [1] but whether or not it is an established term is quite uncertain. During the Han dynasty the term *ts'ung tzŭ* [2] was commonly employed, but more commonly the purely descriptive forms *hsiung tzŭ* and *ti tzŭ* were used. There is evidence that brother's sons were simply called *tzŭ*.[3]

*Chih*, as used in the *Êrh Ya*, was a woman's term for brother's son. It is similarly used in the *I Li* (32.1b). The use of *chih* as a man's term for brother's son dates from the Chin period (265-420). This usage originated in north China and then became general.[4] The woman's term for brother's son was then prefixed with *nei*, thus forming nei chih, in contra-distinction to *chih*.

*Chih nan* is mostly a self reference term. *Yüan*[5] is a complimentary term, not commonly used. The common complimentary term is *ling chih*.

---

[1]  *Li Chi* 8. 4a.

[2]  *Shih shuo hsin yü*,1A,21b(commentary): 从子.

[3]  *Han shu* 71.4a-b; *Hou Han Shu* 90B. 18b: Tsai Yung refers to his father's younger brother and himself as *fu tzŭ*. It also must be understood that whenever one is referring to well known relationships, or in the vocative, the more inclusive terms *fu tzŭ* are usually used, otherwise the more exact terms.

[4]  *Yeh shih chia hsün* 2. 7a.

[5]  阮 as a complimentary term was based on the uncle-nephew relationship of 阮籍 and 阮咸. Cf. *Shih shuo hsin yü*, 3A. 38a.

### 126. Chih fu 侄妇 b s w

*Chih hsi fu* is more colloquial. As remarked above, *hsi fu* applies to the wives of all relatives of descending generations.

### 127. Chih nü 侄女 b d

*Chih* as used in the *Êrh Ya* and *I Li* is devoid of sex connotation, a feature characteristic of one of a pair of reciprocal terms. *Ku* and *chih* are conceptual reciprocals. When *chih* was transformed into a man's term. it ceased to be reciprocal and the sex indicator was suffixed, e.g., chih nü for brother's daughter.The inverted form *nü chih* may also be used. *Yu nü* and *Ts'ung nü* are the terms corresponding to *yu tzǔ* and *Ts'ung tzǔ*. *Hsiung nü* and *ti nü* are descriptive terms corresponding to *hsiung tzǔ* and *ti tzǔ*.

### 128. Chih hsü 侄婿 b d h

*I hsing*[①] is an unconmmon ancient term, rarely understood today. *Hsiung hsü*, "older brother's *hsü*," and *ti hsü*, "younger brother's *hsü*," are descriptive alternatives. *Chih nü hsü* is more colloquial.

### 129. Wai shêng 外甥 si s

The *Êrh Ya* gives the term *ch'u* and, in a later passage, *shêng*. *ch'u* is probably an older term than *shêng*, since *shêng*, but not *ch'u* , is used in the

---

① 　*Ta tai li chi*, 6. 7a: 异姓.

*I Li.*[1] *Wai shêng* came into use during the Chin dynasty; it is also written 外生.[2] *Chai hsiang* [3] is a term used, probably rarely, *circa* the first half of the first millennium A.D.

130. Wai shêng fu 外甥妇 si s w

131. Wai shêng nü 外甥女 si d

132. Wai shêng hsü ○○婿 si d h

133. T'ang chih 堂侄 f b s s

134. T'ang chih fu ○○妇 f b s s w

135. T'ang chih nü ○○女 f b s d

136. T'ang chih hsü ○○婿 f b s d h

---

① *I Li* 33. 9a.

② *Shih shuo hsin yü*, 3A. 3a (commentary).

③ 宅相，"house site," is of interesting origin. *Chin shu* 41.1a: Wei Shu was an orphan reared in his maternal grandmother's home, the Ning family. When the Ning's built a house, a geomancer prophecied that this house site, *Chai hsiang*, would have a daughter's son who would be great. Wei Shu's maternal grandmother considered this prophecy had been fulfilled, when Wei Shu, although young, was brilliant and precocious. Wei Shu then said, "I will fulfill the prophecy of this good house site, chai hsiang." *Pei Ch'i Shu* 29. 2b; *Shih ch'ang T'an*, 1. 3a.

137. T'ang wai shêng 堂外甥 f b d s

138. T'ang wai shêng fu ○○甥妇 f b d s w

139. T'ang wai shêng nü ○○甥女 f b d d

140. T'ang wai shêng hsü ○○甥婿 f b d d h

141. Ku piao chih 姑表侄 f si s s

142. Ku piao chih fu ○○○妇 w of 141

143. Ku piao chih nü ○○○女 f si s d

144. Ku piao chih hsü ○○○婿 h of 143

145. Ku piao wai shêng ○○外甥 f si d s

146. Ku piao wai shêng fu ○○外甥妇 w of 145

147. Ku piao wai shêng nü ○○○○ 女 f si d d

148. Ku piao wai shêng hsü ○○○○婿  h of 147

149. Tsai Ts'ung chih 再从侄 s of 89 or 91

150. Tsai Ts'ung chih fu ○○侄妇  w of 149

151. Tsai Ts'ung chih nü ○○○女 d of 89 or 91

152. Tsai Ts'ung chih hsü ○○○婿 h of 151

153. Tsu chih 族侄 s of 97 or 99

154. Tsu chih fu ○○妇  w of 153

155. Tsu chih nü ○○女 d of 97 or 99

156. Tsu chih hsü ○○婿 h of 155

## Ⅶ. Generation of the son's son

157.Sun 孙 s s

*Tzŭ hsing*[1] is an old obsolete term. During the Chin period *wan shêng*

---

[1]    *Shih Ching* 1C.7a; *I Li* 44.2b; *Shih Chi* 49. 2a.

晚生，"late born," was used for son, likewise, *hsiao wan shêng*, "little late born," for son's son.[①] *Wên sun* is a literary form derived from the Book of History;[②] it originally referred to King Wên's son's son. *Sun êrh* and *sun tzŭ* are more colloquial, *êrh* and *tzŭ* being diminutives.

*Chia sun* [③] was used as a depreciatory term during the Han period, but has never been used since and is now considered incorrect. The correct depreciatory term is *hsiao sun*.

*Sun* may be combined with various modifiers to express the exact relationships, e.g., *chang sun* for the oldest son's son, *shih sun* or *Ch'êng chung sun*[④] for the eldest son's eldest son, who must carry the three years mourning obligations in his father's place in the event that the father has died before the grandfather.

158. Sun fu孙妇 s s w

159. Sun nü 孙女 s d

*Sun*, as in the *I Li*, may be used to mean grandchild or any descendant from the second descending generation and down. In modern usage *sun nü* is employed in contra distinction to *sun*. The inverted form, *nü sun*, is also

---

① *Chin shu* 69. 7b; *p'ieh chi*, 4.2a.

② *Shu Ching* 17. 35a: 文孙.

③ *Yen shih chia hsün* 2.5a.

④ *I Li* 30. 12a:其适孙承重者.

permissible.

160. Sun hsü 孙婿 s d h

161. Wai sun 外孙 d s

162. Wai sun fu ○○妇 d s w

163. Wai sun nü ○○女 d d

164. Wai sun hsü ○○婿 d d h

165. Chih sun 侄孙 b s s

*Ts'ung sun* is a term found in the *Kuo Yü*.[1] *Yu sun* [2] was occasionally used during the T'ang period, and earlier, but is seldom used today, except as a literary form.

166. Chih sun fu ○○妇 b s s w

167. Chih sun nü ○○女 b s d

---

[1] *Kuo yü* 3. 7a.

[2] *Yüan shih Chang-Ch'ing chi* 54.4b.

168. Chih sun hsü ○○婿 b s d h

169. Wai chih sun 外侄孙 b d s

170. Wai chih sun fu ○○○妇 b d s w

171. Wai chih sun nü ○○○女 b d d

172. Wai chih sun hsü ○○○婿 b d d h

In local variations, *chih wai sun* 侄外孙 and *T'ang wai sun* 堂外孙 may be used for 169-172.

173. Wai shêng sun 外甥孙 si s s

The term in the *Êrh Ya* is *li sun* 离孙, literally "departing grandson." Whether or not there is any significance in this term one cannot say. Other ancient alternative terms are *Ts'ung sun shêng*[1] and *mi sun*.[2]

174. Wai shêng sun fu 外甥孙妇 si s s w

175. Wai shêng sun nü ○○孙女 si s d

---

[1]　*Tso Chuan* 60.20b.
[2]　Ibid 60. 17b: 弥.

176. Wai shêng sun hsü ○○孙婿 si s d h

177. T'ang chih sun 堂侄孙 f b s s

178. T'ang chih sun fu ○○○妇 w of 177

179. T'ang chih sun nü ○○○女 f b s s d

180. T'ang chih sun hsü ○○○婿 h of 179

181. Ku piao chih sun 姑表侄孙 f si s s s

182. Ku piao chih sun fu ○○○○妇 w of 181

183. Ku piao chih sun nü ○○○女 f si s s d

184. Ku piao chih sun hsü ○○○○婿 h of 183

185. Tsai Ts'ung chih sun 再从侄孙 s of 149

186. Tsai Ts'ung chih sun fu ○○○○妇 w of 185

187. Tsai Ts'ung chih sun nü ○○○○女 d of 149

188. Tsai Ts'ung chih sun hsü ○○○○婿 h of 187

189. Tsu sun 族孙 s of 153

190. Tsu sun fu ○○妇 w of 189

191. Tsu sun nü ○○女 d of 153

192. Tsu sun hsü ○○婿 h of 191

*Tsu chih sun* 族侄孙 may be used in substitution for *tsu sun* in terms 189-192, but the *chih* is not necessary.

## Ⅷ. Generation of the son's son's son

193. Tsêng sun 曾孙 s s s

According to old usages all descendants from the son's son's son and descending can be called *tsêng sun*, or *hsi sun*.[①] During the Han period *êrh sun* was probally used synonymously with *tsêng sun*.[②]

---

① 　*Chiu T'ang shu* 160. 19b.

② 　*Han Shu* 2.2b. The interpretations of the term *êrh sun* 耳孙 are quite divergent. Perhaps the interpretation of 李裴 is the more prevalent usage in the Han period but it by no means precludes its use in the other connotations. Cf. *Hsüeh Lin* 3. 10-11.

*Ch'ung sun* 重孙 is the modern colloquial term.

194. Tsêng sun fu 曾孙妇 s s s w

195. Tsêng sun nü 曾孙女 s s d

196. Tsêng sun hsü ○○婿 s s d h

197. Wai sun tsêng sun 外孙曾孙 d s s, or s d s

198. Wai sun tsêng sun nü ○○○○女 d s d, or s d d

199.Tsêng chih sun 曾侄孙 b s s s

200. Tsêng chih sun nü ○○○女 b s s d

201. Wai shêng tsêng sun 外甥曾孙 si s s s

202. Wai shêng tsêng sun nü ○○○○ 女 si s s d

## IX.Generation of the son's son's son's son

203. Hsüan sun 玄孙①s s s s

204. Hsüan sun fu ○○妇 s s s s w

205. Hsüan sun nü ○○女 s s s d

206. Hsüan sun hsü ○○ 婿 s s s d h

The following terms are found in the *Êrh Ya*; although of no practical use, they are given here because of their theoretical interest:

207. Lai sun 来孙 s s s s s

208. K'un sun 昆 ○ s s s s s s

209. Jêng sun 仍○ s s s s s s s

210. Yün sun 云○ s s s s s s s s

*Relalives through Mother Table* Ⅱ

Ⅰ. **Generation of the mother's father's father**

1. Wai tsêng tsu fu 外曾祖父 m f f

---

① 　*Jih Chih lu*, 5. 32b.

In the *Êrh Ya* the term is *wai tsêng wang fu* ○○ 王父.

2. Wai tsêng tsu mu ○○祖母 m f m

*Wai tsêng wang mu* ○○王母, as used in the *Êrh Ya*. Vocatives of the above two terms vary locally; they are largely based on the vocatives of 3 and 4, with generation modifiers.

**Ⅱ. Generation of the mother's father**

3. Wai tsu fu 外祖父 m f

*Wai tsu* may be used alone. The term in the *Êrh Ya* is *wai wang fu* 外王父. *Wai ta fu*[1] and *wai wêng*[2] are modern alternatives. The modern vocatives *chia kung*,[3] also pronounced *ka kung*, and *wai kung* were used as early as the fifth century A.D.

4. Wai tsu mu 外祖母 m m

*Wai wang mu* is used in the *Êrh Ya*. *Wai P'o*[4] is the most common modern vocative; likewise common is *chia P'o*, also pronounced *ka P'o*. *Chia mu*[5] was used during the fifth and sixth centuries A.D. Since *chia* at

---

[1] *Chang Yu-shih wên chi* 张右史文集, collected works of CHANG Lei 张耒(1052-1112 A.D.), *Ssŭ pu Ts'ung k'an* edition, 17.9b.

[2] *Yüan shih chang-Ch'ing chi* 9.5b.

[3] *Yen shih chia hsün* 2.8a.

[4] *Jung chai sui pi*, ssŭ pi 2.11a.

[5] *Yen shih chia hsün* 2.8a

that time meant "mother," *chia mu* meant mother's mother. *Chia mu* is now used as a depreciatory term for mother. *Liao liao*[①] is a dialectical form used in certain parts of North China.

5. Wai po tsu fu 外伯祖父 m f o b

6. Wai po tsu mu ○○○母 m f o b w

7. Wai shu tsu fu 外叔祖父 m f y b

8. Wai shu tsu mu ○○○母 m f y b w

*Ku wai tsu mu* may be used for the mother's father's sister, *chiu wai tsu fu* for the mother's mother's brother, and *i wai tsu mu* for the mother's mother's sister. These relationships are not maintained socially, but the terms show how they can be handled. Practically, there are many ways of solving this terminological problem, e.g., if the necessity for addressing these relatives should arise, one may adopt the terms of the mother's brother's son, who is the nearest relative of the same generation of ego on the mother's side.

---

① *K'ang-hsi tzǔ tien* 嫽. *Liao* is also read *lao*, and is synonymous with *ao*. YEN Chih T'ui〔*Yen shih chia hsün* 2.7b〕says that during his time the uncultured people called mother's parents by the same term as father's parents when the latter were all dead.

### Ⅲ. Generation of the mother

9. Chiu fu 舅父 m b

Or simply *chiu*, as used in the *Êrh Ya*. Since in modern usage, *chiu* also means wife's brother, the generation and sex indicator *fu* is necessary. *Po chiu* 伯舅 may be used for the mother's older brother, and *shu chiu* 叔舅 for the younger brother. These terms are now mainly literary. The mother's brothers and their family may be vaguely referred to as *wai shih* or *wai chia*.[1]

Vocatives are *chiu chiu, a chiu*, or *chiu tieh*. *Chia chiu* [2] was used as a depreciatory term during the fourth and fifth centuries A.D., but is not used today and is considered incorrect. *Ling chiu* and *tsun chiu* are complimentary terms.

10. Chiu mu 舅母 m b w

*Chin* [3] is an old vocative used during the Sung period, and is now rather uncommon. The modern vocative is *chiu ma*.

11. I mu 姨母 m si

In the *Êrh Ya* and the *I Li* the term is *Ts'ung mu*.[4] *I* originally meant "wife's sister." The first use of *i* for mother's sister is found in the *Tso Chuan*,

---

[1]  Literally "outer family." *Chin Shu* 41.1a

[2]  *Shih shuo hsin yü*, 3B. 32a.

[3]  *Shu I*, 1.9b: 妗 . *Ming t'ao tsa chih*, 13b.

[4]  *I Li* 33. 2a.

the 23rd year (B.C. 550) of Duke Hsiang.[1] This extension is attributed to the psychological similarity of these two relatives and to reverse teknonymy. Since the Han period *i* has entirely displaced the older verm *ts'ung mu*. *I* is also used for concubines a usage attributed to the sororate. The inverted form *mu i* may also be used.

Vocatives are *a i* or *i ma*.

12. I fu 姨父 m si h

*I fu,*[2] *i chang jên,*[3] or *i Chang*, were used during the first millennium A.D., but are uncommon today.

13. t'ang chiu fu 堂舅父 m f b s

*Ts'ung chiu* is used in the *Êrh Ya* and can still be used today, but more as a literary form.

14. T'ang chiu mu 堂舅母 w of 13

15. T'ang i mu 堂姨母 m f b d

---

[1]　*Tso Chuan* 35, 18a.

[2]　*Yen shih chia hsün* 3. 23a.

[3]　*Pei Shih* 47.7b-8a. *I chang jên* is now used to mean wife's mother's sister's husband.

16. T'ang i fu 堂姨父 h of 15

### Ⅳ. Generation of the speaker

17. Chiu piao hsiung 舅表兄 m b s＞e

*Shêng* is the term in the *Êrh Ya* a reflection of cross-cousin marriage. *Nei hsiung*[1] was a substitute used during the Han period; later it became confused with *wai hsiung,*[2] a term for father's sister's son. Today these terms are not used with the same meanings. *Nei hsiung* is now used for the wife's older brother, and *wai hsiung* for half brothers, by the same mother, older than ego. *Chiu tzǔ* [3] and *chiu ti* [4] are purely descriptive terms which were used *circa* 500 A.D.; at present they both mean "wife's brothers."

*Piao* was first introduced during the latter part of the Han period, after cross-cousin marriage had long ceased to be preferential. *Piao*, or *chung piao*,[5] was first used for mother's brother's and father's sister's children, and later was extended to include mother's sister's children.

In the vocative *chiu* is always dropped, leaving simply *piao hsiung* or *piao ko*, and, in certain localities, *lao piao*.

---

[1]　*I Li* 33.10a.

[2]　*Sung Shu* 93.4b-5a.

[3]　*Chin Shu* 34. 8b.

[4]　*Ch'ang-li Chi* 32.7b.

[5]　*San kuo chih* 11.20. *Chung piao* is equivalent to *nei wai*.

18. Chiu piao sao 舅表嫂 w of 17

19. Chiu piao ti ○○弟 m b s<e

20. Chiu piao ti fu ○○弟妇 w of 19

21. Chiu piao tzǔ ○○姊 m b d>e

22. Chiu piao tzǔ fu ○○姊夫 h of 21

23. Chiu piao mei ○○妹 m b d<e

24. Chiu piao mei fu ○○妹夫 h of 23

25. I piao hsiung 姨表兄 m si s>e

*Ts'ung mu k'un ti* is used in the *Êrh Ya* and *I Li* (33. 9a). *I hsiung ti* was used during the last few centuries of the first millennium B.C. and approximately the first half of the first millennium A.D.[1] It can still today be used as an alternative term.[2] *Wai hsiung ti* was sometimes used during

---

[1]　See discussion, pp. 192 193. *Nan shih* 57. 17a.

[2]　Cf. LIANG Chang-chü, *Ch'êng wei lu*, 3.20b. WANG Shih han 汪师韩, 1707-? A.D, considers *i hsiung ti* a northern peculiarity: *t'an shu lu* 谈书录,〔昭代丛书 ed.〕45a.

the T'ang period,[1] having resulted from a confusion with the term for mother's brother's sons and father's sister's sons, which finally led to the extension of the term *piao* and the partial merging of the three relationships.

26. I piao sao 姨表嫂 w of 25

27. I piao ti ○○弟 m si s＜e

28. I piao ti fu ○○弟妇 w of 27

29. I piao tzǔ ○○姊 m si d＞e

30. I piao tzǔ fu ○○姊夫 h of 29

31. I piao mei ○○妹 m si d＜e

32. I piao mei fu ○○妹夫 h of 31

33. T'ang chiu piao hsiung 堂舅表兄 m f b s s＞e

34. T'ang chiu piao sao ○○○嫂 w of 33

---

[1]　海录碎事 (cited by *Ch'êng wei lu*, 3. 20a).

35. T'ang chiu piao ti ○○○ 弟 m f b s s<e

36. T'ang chiu piao ti fu ○○○弟妇 w of 35

37. T'ang chiu piao tzǔ 堂舅表姊 m f b s d>e

38. T'ang chiu piao tzǔ fu ○○○○夫 h of 37

39. T'ang chiu piao mei 堂舅表妹 m f b s d<e

40. T'ang chiu piao mei fu ○○○○夫 h of 39

Terms 33-40 may also be applied to the children of father's mother's brother's sons, i.e., the children of 59-62 in table I, hence these terms are not given there. This extension is inferred only from popular usage, there being insufficient documentary evidence for collation. At any rate, when one considers non sib relatives on the third collateral line in as far as the third generation descending, the terminology becomes vague, and, indeed, an accurate system is not necessary here, since in almost all cases these relationships are not maintained socially.

41. T'ang i piao hsiung 堂姨表兄 m f b d s>e

42. T'ang i piao sao ○○表嫂 w of 41

43. T'ang i piao ti ○○表弟 m f b d s<e

44. T'ang i piao ti fu ○○表弟妇 w of 43

45. T'ang i piao tzǔ 堂姨表姊 m f b d d>e

46. T'ang i piao tzǔ fu ○○表姊夫 h of 45

47. T'ang i piao mei ○○表妹 m f b d d<e

48. T'ang i piao mei fu ○○表妹夫 h of 47

## V. Generation of the son

49. Chiu piao chih 舅表侄 m b s s

50. Chiu piao chih fu ○○○妇 m b s s w

51. Chiu piao chih nü ○○○女 m b s d

52. Chiu piao chih hsü ○○○○婿 m b s d h

53. Chiu piao wai shêng 舅表外甥 m b d s

54. Chiu piao wai shêng fu ○○○○妇 m b d s w

55. Chiu piao wai shêng nü ○○○○女 m b d d

56. Chiu piao wai shêng hsü ○○○○婿 m b d d h

57. I piao chih 姨表侄 m si s s

58. I piao chih fu ○○○妇 m si s s w

59. I piao chih nü ○○○女 m si s d

60. I piao chih hsü ○○○婿 m si s d h

61. I piao wai shêng ○○外甥 m si d s

62. I piao wai shêng fu ○○○○妇 m si d s w

63. I piao wai shêng nü 舅表外甥女 m si d d

64. I piao wai shêng hsü ○○○○婿 m si d d h

65. T'ang chiu piao chih 堂舅表侄 s of 33 or 35

66. T'ang chiu piao chih fu ○○○○妇 w of 65

67. T'ang chiu piao chih nü ○○○○女 d of 33 or 35

68. T'ang chiu piao chih hsü ○○○○婿 h of 67

69. T'ang i piao chih 堂姨表侄 s of 41 or 43

70. T'ang i piao chih fu ○○○○妇 w of 69

71. T'ang i piao chih nü ○○○○女 d of 41 or 43

72. T'ang i piao chih hsü ○○○○婿 h of 71

## Ⅵ. Generation of the son's son

73. Chiu piao chih sun 舅表侄孙 m b s s s

74. Chiu piao chih sun fu ○○○○妇 m b s s s w

75. Chiu piao chih sun nü ○○○○女 m b s s d

76. Chiu piao chih sun hsü ○○○○婿 m b s s d h

77. I piao chih sun 姨表侄孙 m si s s s

78. I piao chih sun fu ○○○○妇 m si s s s w

79. I piao chih sun nü ○○○○女 m si s s d

80. I piao chih sun hsü ○○○○婿 m si s s d h

Since most of these terms are extensions from table I, their historical development, vocative and complimentary usages can be inferred from there.

## Affinal Relatives

*Relatives through Wife-Table* Ⅲ

Ⅰ. **Generation of the wife's father**

1. Yo fu 岳父 w f

The term in the *Êrh Ya* is *wai chiu*, and in the *Li Chi* (52.27b), *chiu* is used alone for this relationship. As *chiu* also meant mother's brother during this period, the terminology reflects *cross cousin marriage*. During the Later Han period *fu kung*[1] and *fu wêng*[2] were prevailingly used, as purely descriptive terms. Whether or not *chang jên* 丈人 was used for wife's father during the Han period is by no means clear;[3] it became the prevailing term during the T'ang dynasty.[4] *Yo fu* and *chang jên* are the universal modern terms, and the use of the one or the other depends upon local custom. *Yo fu* is more formal and literary, *chang jên* is more colloquial. Sometimes the combined and abbreviated form *yo chang* is used. Another very common but non vocative and non referential term is *T'ai shan*, name of the eastern sacred mountain of the old Chinese Empire. There are many interpretations of the origin of the terms *yo fu, chang jên* and *T'ai shan*, of interest to those who are concerned with the origin of individual terms.

One interpretation of the origin of the term *yo* is that found in the *Chiao ssŭ chih* of the *Han Shu* (25A. 13a), viz., large mountains are called *yo shan*, and small mountains, *yo hsü*. Since mountains can be called both *yo* and *hsü*, and since *hsü* also means daughter's husband, the meaning of *yo*

---

[1] *Hou Han Shu* 71.11a.

[2] *San Kuo Chih* 1.22b-23a.

[3] *Han Shu* 94A. 25b-26a. In the *Nêng kai chia man lu*, 2.28, this erroneously considered to be the origin of *chang jên* for wife's father. The term *chang jên* used here merely means any older man; cf. Yen Shih Ku's commentary on this passage.

[4] *Chiu T'ang Shu*. 147.1b.

was transferred and *yo* became a term for wife's father.[1] Another interpretation goes thus: Yo Kuang of the Chin dynasty was the father of the wife of Wei Chieh; since these two men were the best known personages of their time, and since their relationship as father-in-law and son in law was much admired by the people, it is possible that *yo chang* 岳丈 is a corruption of *Yo chang* 乐丈.[2]

The story of the origin of the term *T'ai shan* is as follows: In the year 725 A.D. the Emperor Hsüan tsung offered sacrifices to T'ai Shan, "Mount T'ai." According to precedence, all those officials who participated in it, with the exception of the San Kung 三公, were promoted one rank. Chang Yüeh, the premier, was the marshal of ceremonies. This son-in-law, Chêng I, was promoted from the ninth rank to the fifth rank and was accorded the privilege of wearing purple robes. In the banquet of celebration the Emperor was surprised by his quick advancement. The professional court jester, Huang Fa-cho, remarked: "This is the influence of T'ai Shan!" This is popularly considered the explanation of the origin of the term.[3] But *T'ai shan* must already have had the meaning of father-in-law, since this joke is a pun, *T'ai shan* being interpreted both as wife's father and as Mount T'ai; i.e., Chêng I's unprecedented promotion was due to his participation in the

---

[1]　*Jih sun chai pi chi* 日损斋笔记 by 黄溍〔1277-1357 A.D.〕〔墨海金壶 edition〕10b.

[2]　*Chin Shu* 36. 13b; *Kai yü Ts'ung k'ao* 37. 20a.

[3]　Cf. *Shih ch'ang T'an* 1.2b.

sacrifices to T'ai Shan, or, in a satirical sense, to the influence of his father in law, Chang Yüeh.

Still another version of the origin of the terms *T'ai Shan* and *yo* relates that Mount T'ai, also called Eastern Yo, has a peak named Chang Jên. Since *chang jên* means wife's father, and Chang Jên is one of the peaks of T'ai Shan, *T'ai shan* has become a term for wife's father—a kind of punning and semantic transference. Furthermore, T'ai Shan is also called Yo, whence the term *yo* is derived.[1]

These are interesting speculations, any one of which is just as reasonable as any other. One point seems to be certain, viz., that no sociological factors or marital implications are involved. First, from the linguistic point of view, both *yo* and *T'ai shan* have never been used in any sense other than "venerable high mountain" and "Mount T'ai ." Second, as relationship terms, both of them are late introductions, not earlier than the T'ang period. If there were any sociological implications, they should be easily detectable.

The application of *chang jên* to wife's father, as remarked above, first became prevalent during the T'ang period. Before and during the Han periods it could be applied to any old man to whom one might wish to pay respect. From the fourth to the sixth centuries A.D. *chang jên* was used for mother's brother, mother's sister's husband and father's sister's husband,

---

[1]  *Kai yü Ts'ung k'ao* 37. 20a.

e.g., *chung wai chang jên*. Hence, its use for wife's father may be an alternative extension from the term *chiu*, which was used during this period for mother's brother and sometimes for wife's father. If this idea is correct, the use of *chang jên* may be an indirect survival from cross-cousin marriage.

*Wai fu*,[①] *ping sou*,[②] and *ping wêng*,[③] were alternative terms used during the Sung period. *Fu t'o* [④] is an old dialectal term used in southwest China during the Han period.

*Chia yo* is used as a depreciatory term, but theoretically it may be incorrect.

## 2. Yo mu 岳母 w m

*Wai ku* or *ku* alone are used in the *Êrh Ya* and *Li Chi* a reflection of cross cousin marriage. *Chang mu* and *T'ai shui* [⑤] are terms corresponding to *chang jên* and *T'ai shan*. Before the T'ang period, *chang mu* could be applied to father's and mother's married sisters, mother's brother's wife,

---

① Cf. *Ch'ien chü lu* 潜居录〔*Shuo Fu* 说郛, 32〕1b.

② *Tung P'o Ch'üan chi* 东坡全集, *Ssǔ pu pei yao* ed., 13. 7:冰叟.

③ *Yu huan chi wên* 游宦纪闻, by CHANG Shih-nan 张世南 (ca. 1200 A.D.)，知不足斋丛书本　6.2b.On *ping sou* and *ping wêng* see p. 1273, note ②.

④ *Fang Yen*, 6.7a:⊙女多.

⑤ 合璧事类 (cited by the *Ch'êng wei lu*, 7. 13a): 泰水. The term *T'ai shui* is really interesting. The opposite of *shan*, mountain, is *shui*, water. Water is here used in the sense of "rivers" or "lakes." Since wife's father is called *T'ai shan*. so *T'ai shui* is used for wife's mother. The *Ho pi shih lei* being a cyclopaedia compiled during the Sung period, the term must have been quite common during that time. At present it is not a very good term and employed mostly on non-vocative and non-referential occasions.

or the wife of any person whom one addressed as *chang jên*. *Mu t'o* [1] was a dialectal form corresponding to *fu t'o*.

*Yo fu* and *yo mu* may be used vocatively, but generally the husband adopts the wife's terms, addressing her parents with parent terms. Post issue, teknonymy is the most common practice.

In referring to wife's father's parents, circumlocution by enumeration of relations is common. In certain localities *lao chang jên* and *lao chang mu* are used in the referential. Inferentially and logically, *yo tsu fu* and *yo tsu mu* would be correct, but they are not used. In the vocative, one usually adopts the wife's terms.

3. Po yo fu 伯岳父 w f o b

4. Po yo mu 伯岳母 w f o b w

5. Shu yo fu 叔岳父 w f y b

6. Shu yo mu 叔岳母 w f y b w

Alternatively and more commonly, *po chang jên* is used for 3, *po chang mu* for 4, *shu chang jên* for 5, and *shu chang mu* for 6. *Lieh yo* [2] is

---

① Cf. *Fang yen* 6. 7a.

② *Ho pi shih lei* (cited by *Ch'êng wei Lu* 7. 13a), 列岳.

an uncommon complimentary term for 3 and 5.

wife's father's sister and her husband are called *ku chang mu* and *ku chang jên*, wife's mother's sister and her husband are called *i chang mu* and *i chang jên*, and wife's mother's brother and his wife, *chiu chang jên* and *chiu chang mu*, respectively.

## Ⅱ. Generation of the wife

7. Chiu hsiung 舅兄 w o b

*Shêng*, which is used in the *Êrh Ya*, reflects cross cousin marriage. The *Êrh Ya* also gives the term *hun hsiung ti*, "brothers by marriage" a purely descriptive term. The *Li Chi* [1] gives the term *ssǔ Ch'in hsiung ti*, also more or less descriptive, since *ssǔ Ch'in* literally means "private relations." *Fu hsiung ti*[2] and *nei hsiung ti*[3] were in use from the Chin to the T'ang dynasties, and can still be used as alternative terms. *Fu* and *nei* both mean "wife." *Chiu* was first applied during the tenth century A.D., through teknonymy.[4]

8. Chiu sao 舅嫂 w o b w

---

[1]　*Li Chi* 27. 11b.

[2]　See p.1182, note [2].

[3]　*Liang Shu* 12. 4a; *Chin shih Ts'ui pien* 101.26a. The use of *nei hsiung ti* for wife's brothers was confused with that for mother's brother's sons. It may be due to the influence of earlier cross cousin marriage terminology from which the new nomenclature still could not extricate itself.

[4]　See discussion pp. 216-220.

*Ch'i sao*[1] may be used, but is a purely descriptive term.

9. Chiu ti 舅弟 w y b

10. Chiu ti fu 舅弟妇 w y b w

11. I *tzǔ* 姨姊 w o si

12. I *tzǔ* fu 姨姊夫 w o si h

The term in the *Êrh Ya* for wife's sisters' husbands is *ya*[2] or *yin ya* as used in the *Shih Ching.*[3] *Yu hsü*[4] was used during the Han period and T'ung mên a little later.[5]*Liao hsü* originated as a local term in eastern China. *Lien mei* and *lien chin*[6] were first used during the Sung period. *Lien chin* is the most commonly used term at present; it probably originated as a local form in North China. *I fu*[7], as a term, is as old as any of those above, but more descriptive. These terms are used reciprocally, i.e., ego refers to his wife's sisters' husbands by any of these terms, according to local usage, and they

---

[1]  *Nan shih* 45. 13b.

[2]  亚 .

[3]  *Shih Ching* 12A. 3b: 姻亚 .

[4]  *Han Shu* 64A. 10b: 友婿 .

[5]  *Êrh Ya*: 同门，僚婿 .

[6]  *Luan chên tzǔ lu*, 懒真子录, by MA Yung-Ch'ing 马永卿, ca. 1110 A.D. 〔1920, Commercial Press ed.〕 2.5b: 连袂，连襟 .

[7]  *Ho pi shih lei*〔cited by *Ch'êng wei Lu* 7. 17a-b〕.

refer to him by precisely the same term. These terms are only used in the referential. Vocatively, brother terms are usually adopted, or teknonymy is practiced.

13. I mei 姨妹 w y si

*Ch'i mei*[1] and *nei mei* [2] are alternative and principally descriptive terms. *I*, as used in the *Êrh Ya*, is interpreted as meaning the wife's sisters who have married different men, and most probably it was originally a man's term.[3] *Ti* 娣 is used to mean sisters who have married the same man in connection with the yin marriage custom, and is more likely to be a woman's term.[4] *Hsiao i* is a modern colloquial expression.

14. I mei fu 姨妹夫 w y si h

15. T'ang chiu hsiung 堂舅兄 s of 3 or 5 >w

16. T'ang chiu sao ○○嫂 w of 15

---

[1]　*San kuo chih* 22. 1b.

[2]　Ibid. 9. 6a.

[3]　*Shih Ching* 3B. 9a; *Tso Chuan* 8.24a.

[4]　*Shih Ching* 18D. 5a. Cf. the *Shih ming*. It seems the term *ti* cannot be separated from the yin marriage custom. Accordingly, when the yin marriage ceased to be practiced, *ti* also ceased to function.

17. T'ang chiu ti ○○弟 s of 3 or 5 <w

18. T'ang chiu ti fu ○○弟妇 w of 17

19. T'ang i tzǔ 堂姨姊 d of 3 or 5 >w

20. T'ang i tzǔ fu ○○姊夫 h of 19

21. T'ang i mei ○○妹 d of 3 or 5 <w

22. T'ang i mei fu ○○妹夫 h of 21

wife's father's sister's children, wife's mother's sister's and brother's children are called *nei piao hsiung ti* for males, and *nei piao tzǔ mei* for females. It could be further differentiated by adding *ku, i* and *chiu*, e.g., *nei ku piao hsiung* for wife's father's sister's son older than wife.

### Ⅲ. Generation of the son

23. Nei chih 内侄 w b s

*Chih* was originally a woman's term for brother's child, being reciprocal with *ku*. Since the Chin period it has been used more as a man's term for brother's son, hence *nei* is prefixed, in contradistinction with *chih* alone. See Table I, 125. In contemporary usage, female ego would use *chih* for brother's son before marriage,  but after marriage she would use *chih* for husband's brother's son and *nei chih* for her own brother's son.

24. Nei chih fu  ○○妇 w b s w

25. Nei chih nü ○○女 w b d

26. Nei chih hsü ○○婿 w b d h

27. I wai shêng 姨外甥 w si s

*Ch'i shêng* [1] was used *circa* sixth century A.D. It is more or less descriptive, i.e., wife's *shêng*.

28. I wai shêng fu ○○甥妇 w si s w

29. I wai shêng nü ○○甥女 w si d

30. I wai shêng hsü ○○甥婿 w si d h

In certain local usages *i chih* may be substituted for *i wai shêng* in terms 27-30. Although illogical, it is permitted locally,

---

① *Liang Shu* 28. 2a.

## Ⅳ. Generation of the son's son

31. Nei chih sun 内侄孙 w b s s

The *Êrh Ya* uses the term *kuei sun,* which literally means "returning grandson." *Kuei sun* was probably a woman's term, since the *Êrh Ya* says that chih's sons are called *kuei sun,* and *chih* is primarily a woman's term in the *Êrh Ya.*

32. Ne chih sun fu ○○○妇 w b s s w

33. Nei chih sun nü ○○○女 w b s d

34. Nei chih sun hsü ○○○婿 w b s d h

35. I wai shêng sun: w si s s [1]

36. I wai shêng sun fu: w si s s w

37. I wai shêng sun nü: w si s d

38. I wai shêng sun hsü: w si s d h

---

[1] For characters. see Nos. 24–30 above.

In some local usages *i chih sun* may be substituted for *i wai shêng sun*. Terms 23 to 38 are used by husband and female ego alike.

## Affinal Relatives

*Relatives through Husband-Table* Ⅳ

I. **Generation of the husband's father**

1. Kung 公 h f

In the *Êrh Ya* the general term is *chiu*; when he is living, *chün chiu*[1] is used—a reflection of cross-cousin marriage. In modern ritual works, the compilers still use *chiu* for husband's father and refuse to employ the modern term *kung*. If they are afraid lest the term be misunderstood, they employ the descriptive nomenclature, e.g., *fu* of *fu* 夫之父 "father of husband" or *mu* of *fu* 夫之母 "mother of husband."

*Chang*[2] and *chung*[3] were used during and somewhat before the Han period. *Kuan*[4] was a local term in the lower Yangtze valley *circa* the end of the T'ang dynasty. All these terms seem to have been more or less local, and their degree of prevalence is uncertain. The modern term *kung* dates from about the fourth and fifth centuries A.D.;[5] it is also used in the doubled form *kung kung*.

---

[1]　*Êrh Ya*: 君舅 .

[2]　*Shih Ming*: 章 .

[3]　*Lü Shih Ch'un Ch'iu* 14.17a: 妐 .

[4]　*Nan T'ang Shu*〔by MA Ling〕25.2a: 官 .

[5]　Yü T'ai hsin yung chi 1. 16a 21a.

*Hsien chiu,*[①] *huang chiu,*[②] and *hsien tzǔ*[③] are old posthumous terms no longer used today.

2. P'o 婆 h m

*Ku*, and *chün ku* only when she is living, are the terms used in the *Êrh Ya* a reflection of cross cousin marriage. *Wei*[④] was used during the Han Period, and *wei ku*[⑤] is equivalent to *chün ku* of the *Êrh Ya. Chia*, or *a chia,*[⑥] are terms used *circa* the fourth and fifth centuries A.D. and surviving quite late as dialectal forms. *Mu*[⑦] was also used *circa* 500 A.D. *P'o* in ancient usage may mean any old woman; its use for husband's mother dates from the T'ang period. The use of *kung* and *P'o* for husband's parents might also be due to teknonymy, since from quite early times *kung* and *P'o* have commonly been used as grandparents' terms.

*Huang ku* and *hsien ku* are ancient posthumous terms.

## Ⅱ. Generation of the husband

3. Pên shên 本身 ego, a female

---

①   *Êrh Ya* : 君舅.

②   *I Li* 6. 1a-2b.

③   *Kuo Yü* 5. 9b: 先子.

④   *Shuo wên*: 威.

⑤   Wang Nien Sun〔*Kuang ya su chêng* 6B. 5〕: 威姑.

⑥   *Pei Ch'i Shu* 30.4b. *Nan shih* 33. 9a. The *chia* may be a different rendering of *ku*, as they may be pronounced about the same. Cf. *Yen shih chia hsün* 1. 14a.

⑦   姥 read 木五切 mu.

Ego, a female, might, in speaking to the husband's relatives, refer to herself as *hsin fu*, during the fourth and fifth centuries A.D.[1] This custom seems to have been in vogue as late as the twelfth century A.D.[2] At present, the proper relationship term should be used.

### 4. Fu 夫 husband

*Chang fu* 丈夫 and *fu hsü* are alternative terms. *Hsü* may be used alone for husband. *Lao kung*[3] and *nan jên*[4] are colloquial rather vulgar, terms.

Whether or not *shih*,[5] *po*,[6] *tzŭ*,[7] *chün tzŭ*,[8] *fu tzŭ*,[9] and *chia*[10] are actually ancient relationship terms for husband cannot be determined. They might be merely general complimentary terms for man used in the sense of "husband," or simply circumlocutory expressions. *T'ien*,[11] *so T'ien*,[12] and *kao chên*[13] are primarily literary forms; *kao chên* is used almost exclusively

---

[1]　*Shih shuo hsin yü* 2B. 40b 41a: 王平子年十四五，见王夷甫妇郭氏贪，欲令婢路上儋粪，平子谏之，并言不可.郭大怒，谓平子曰：昔夫人临终，以小郎嘱新妇，不以新妇嘱小郎. *Hsin fu* literally means "the bride."

[2]　*Shu I* 1. 12a.

[3]　This is used chiefly in southeast China, as in Kiangsu, Kwangtung, etc. It literally means "the old male."

[4]　A very common term used in the sense of "husband"; literally, "male."

[5]　*Shih ching* 3C. 3a: 士.

[6]　伯; see p.1179, note [2].

[7]　*Shih ching* 4C. 2b: 子.

[8]　Ibid. 7A. 5a.

[9]　*Mêng Tzŭ* 6A. 4a; *Hou Han Shu* 113. 9.

[10]　*Kuo Yü* 6. 8b; *Mêng Tzŭ* 6A. 6a.

[11]　*I Li* 30. 15b. *T'ien* (heaven) is used in the sense of the "positive" or "male" principle.

[12]　所天 is based on the above, employed only in literary usages, i.e., non-vocative and non-referential.

[13]　古绝句四首〔*Yü T'ai hsin yung chi* 10. 6a〕: 藁砧.

in poetry.

The wife calls the husband *liang*,[①] *liang jên*,[②] *lang*,[③] and ch'ing .[④] *Ch'in* is a common reciprocal term. All these words are old forms, now chiefly retained in literary usage and seldom, if ever, used in the vocative. The wife may call the husband by his personal name, or just "you,"[⑤] and most prevalently she employs teknonymy.

The depreciatory terms are *wai tzŭ*,[⑥] and *cho fu* 拙夫 or *yü fu* 愚夫. These terms are employed only in refined society. Ordinarily, the wife refers to her husband as *t'a* 他, meaning "he" or "him," or by teknonymous and circumlocutory expressions.

*Huang p'i*[⑦] is an ancient and now obsolete posthumous term.


## 5. Po 伯 h o b

*Hsiung kung* is used in the *Êrh Ya*. *Kung* 公 is often written 仫 or 妽, and is sometimes pronounced *chung*.[⑧] *Hsiung chang* [⑨] was commonly

---

① *I Li* 5. 8a.

② *Shih ching* 6C. 8a; *Mêng Tzŭ* 8B. 11b-12a.

③ *Chin shu* 96. 9b.

④ *Shih shuo hsin yü* 3B. 48b-49a: 卿.

⑤ *Yen shih chia hsün* 1.13b: 倡和之礼，或尔汝之.

⑥ Wife calls husband *wai* and husband calls wife *nei*; this practice dates from the middle of the first millennium A.D. Cf. *Hêng Yen Lu* 3.11a.

⑦ *Li Chi* 5.22a: 皇辟.

⑧ *Êrh Ya* commentary.

⑨ *Shih Ming*: 兄章.

used during the Han period. *Chang* is written 偉 or 嫜.

*Po* means principally father's older brother. Its extension to husband's older brother first occurred at about the end of the T'ang period.[1] This change can be explained on the basis of teknonymy. *Po po* is more colloquial.

## 6. Mu mu 母母 h o b w

*Ssŭ fu* is the ancient term used in the *Êrh Ya*,[2] and is scarcely known today. *Mu mu* first came into use during the Sung period.[3] It is sometimes written 姆姆; the pronunciation differs slightly in different localities.

## 7. Shu 叔 h y b

*Hsiao shu*,[4] *shu lang*,[5] and *hsiao lang*[6] are alternative terms that date from the fourth and fifth centuries A.D. *Hsiao shu* is more colloquial, *shu lang* and *hsiao lang* are more literary. *Shu* is used in the *Êrh Ya*.

In the lower strata of present-day society, the younger brother-in-law can usually "play jokes" with the older sister-in-law. This circumstance is primarily based on the popular assumption that the younger brother-in-law is always a minor and that the older sister-in-law assumes a kind of maternal

---

[1]　See p. 1179, note [3].

[2]　姒妇.

[3]　See p.1190, note [1].

[4]　*Shih Chi* 69.15b-16a.

[5]　*Wên Hsüan* 40. 6b.

[6]　*Chin Shu* 96. 9b.

attitude.

### 8. Shên shên 婶婶 h y b w

*Ti fu* is an ancient term.[1] *Ssŭ* and *ti* are also used in the *Êrh Ya* to mean sisters who married the same man; the younger calls the older *ssŭ*, and the older calls the younger *ti*.[2] This usage is probably connected with the yin marriage. When used for husband's brother's wives, the *fu* should be appended as it is in the *Êrh Ya* and *I Li* (33. 2a-b).

*Shên shên* was first used during the Sung period.[3] *Shên* was originally a term for father's younger brother's wife, and its extension to husband's younger brother's wife is certainly teknonymous.

Female ego and husband's brothers' wives may refer to each other as *ti ssŭ*, as recorded in the *Êrh Ya*, and as *hsien hou* [4] and *chou li*,[5] as used during the Han period. *Ti ssŭ* and *hsien hou* are now obsolete. *Chu li* is the prevailing term at present; it is reciprocal and used only in the referential.

### 9. Ku 姑 h si

*Ta ku* 大姑 may be used for the older sister, and *hsiao ku* 小姑 for the

---

[1]  Cf. *Êrh Ya*.

[2]  姒，娣.

[3]  Seep. 1189, notes [3], and seep 1190, note [1].

[4]  *Han Shu* 25A. 18b: 先后.

[5]  *Fang Yen* 12. 1a: 筑娌. *Chu* is a synonym of 妯.

younger sister, of the husband. On the other hand, *ta ku* need not necessarily indicate that the sister is actually older than the husband, since the female siblings may be counted in a separate numerical series. Hence *ta* and *hsiao* may only indicate the seniority and juniority among the husband's female siblings. In fact, *ta ku* and *hsiao ku* may be both younger than the husband. These terms are mainly used for the husband's unmarried sisters, but they may continue to be used after their marriage, though rarely.

In the *Êrh Ya*, husband's older sister is called *nü kung* 女公，and the younger, *nü mei* 女妹. *Shu mei* was used during the Han period.[1] *Hsiao ku* was first applied ca. the fifth century A.D. Since *ku* originally meant father's sister, its extension is attributable to teknonymy.

10. Ku fu 姑夫 h si h

*Ku fu* also means father's sister's husband, and its application to husband's sister's husband is undoubtedly teknonymous.

## Conclusions

Having discussed the system in its morphological and historical aspects, I shall here venture upon a few concluding remarks. It may safely

---

[1]　Cf. *Hou Han Shu* 114.8.

be asserted that during the last two thousand years the system has undergone a series of changes both in its structural principles and terminological categories, yet has retained many features of the old system. The latter stability seems to be related to the continuity of Chinese civilization as a whole. As regards the changes, there is, generally speaking, a broad historical correlation with the changes in the development of Chinese society. One notes that practically all the kinship changes occurred during the last two centuries of the first millennium B.C. and the whole of the first millennium A.D. During this period the system was in a state of flux. Many old terms were dropped, changed, or delimited in connotation. New terms were introduced, as if by way of experiment; some were incorporated into the system, others fell into oblivion. Almost all the new terms used in the modern system originated at this time. The whole system was finally stabilized during the T'ang period, after a thousand years of constant transformation and confusion.

This millennium likewise was a period of civil and social strife, the aftermath of the dissolution of the old feudal system. To be sure, the entire social structure was not suddenly transformed; many of the old social institutions lingered on, though in slightly modified forms.[1] Nevertheless, the evolution of the new social order was begun. It was a slow and gigantic

---

[1]　There are students who would even consider present China a fundamentally feudal society. This is somewhat an exaggeration and depends on one's definition of "feudalism."

process, accompanied by periods of alternating political and social tranquillity and chaos, of reactionary and progressive thought. This was an age of widening contacts with outside influences, especially from the third to the sixth centuries A.D., the "Dark Ages" of Chinese history, when nearly all the territory north of the Yangtze was overrun by less civilized peoples from the northern steppes; the resultant large waves of Chinese migration southward resulted in the efflorescence of the *shih tsu* 世族 organization and its excrescent manifestation in the *mên fa* 门阀 [1] system of official recruitment. The entire process is too complex a subject to be dealt with here, but it shows a general chronological correlation with the development of the kinship system. When the kinship system crystalized toward the end of the first millennium A.D., Chinese society still continued to evolve. The kinship system, being a more conservative institution and in some ways a stabilizing mechanism for other social institutions, has remained essentially the same as it was during the T'ang period.

The individual parts of the system have exhibited varying amounts and rates of change, i.e., the changes have been differential. The nomenclature for sib relatives has experienced relatively little alteration, although there have been refinements in the degrees of differentiation and, for some terms, changed connotations. This may be due to the fact that, although the old sib

---

[1]　*Mên fa*, as a system of official recruitment, is based on sib connections. Cf. 杨筠如：九品中正与六朝门阀〔1931〕.

system, *tsung fa*, has been transformed into the modern sib organization, *shih tsu*, the sib principle has remained the basis of kinship evolution. The increased descriptive efficacy represents merely refinements of superficial features of the system, correlated with the elaboration of the mourning ritualism.

Most remarkable changes have occurred in the terminology for non-sib relatives, especially in the nomenclature for affinal relatives, which Aginsky calls "basic terminology."[1] A glance at Tables III and IV will show how radical and complete the changes are. It is a generally accepted fact among social anthropologists that the affinal terminology is extremely sensitive to variations in marital relationships. But have the Chinese marriage regulations radically changed during this period? This question finds a simple answer in history. The most important factor in the regulation of marriage in China, from the first millennium B.C. down to the present, has been sib exogamy supplemented by the generation principle. It has been pointed out above that as time went on a gradual stiffening of this rule took place, but there was little actual change. In general, the effect of marriage regulations upon the kinship system has been so small that we are justified in ignoring it. We can also, in the manner employed before, dispose of the sororate and the levirate as moulding influences on the system.

---

[1] B. W. Aginsky. Kinship systems and the forms of marriage, Memoirs, American Anthropological Association, 45 (1935), 14.

Cross-cousin marriage, however, presents a very different problem, for it is upon this that the affinal terminology of the old system was undoubtedly based. If we assume that the decline in the frequency of this form of marriage resulted in the breakdown of the old affinal nomenclature, we must still explain the origin of the new terminology. These new terms are, in my opinion, not the products of new forms of marriage, but are the result of the operation of teknonymy. Marital relationships as a whole have had little influence upon the modern system. The reason for this may lie in the fact that the Chinese marriage regulations are purely restrictive, not prescriptive, i.e., aside from certain restrictions connected with sib-exogamy and generation, there is complete freedom of choice.

The morphological configuration of the Chinese system has puzzled many a student. Morgan, in generalizing on the system, vacillated between his Malayan and Turanian, saying that "it falls below the highest type of the Turanian form, and affiliates wherever it diverges with the Malayan."[1] Lowie, apparently using the same material, considered the Chinese system either a "generation" or a "bifurcate merging" system[2]—which is equivalent to saying that it is either Malayan or Turanian. T. S. Chen and J. K. Shryock, using Lowie's system of classification, call the Chinese system "bifurcate collateral." [3] Kroeber is of the same opinion, but says, "the Chinese system

---

①    Morgan, *System...* op.cit., p.413.

②    R. H. Lowie, Relationship Terms, *Encyclopa edia Britannica*.

③    Op.cit., p.627.

appears to consist of a 'classificatory', that is non-descriptive, base, which has been made over by additions into a 'descriptive' system similar in its working to the English one, in fact is more precisely and successfully descriptive than this."[①] Compare this with Morgan's remark that the Chinese system "has accomplished the difficult task of maintaining a principle of classification which confronts the natural distinctions in the relationships of consanguinity, and, at the same time, of separating those relationships from each other in a precise and definite manner."[②]

Actually, the Chinese system is not one that lends itself to any simple characterization in terms such as "classificatory" or "descriptive." It must first be understood in the light of its own morphological principles and historical development. In Morgan's definition of the terms, the Chinese system is both classificatory and descriptive. This is not an "inconsistency" from the point of view of Morgan's system, but a characteristic of a system moulded by diverse factors of a counteracting nature. It is the elucidation of these underlying factors that is of scientific import rather than any particular characterization. This problem has been approached through a detailed analysis of the changes which the Chinese system has undergone during the documentary period of its history. Insofar as the data have permitted, correlative sociological facts have been evaluated with reference to these

---

① Process in the Chinese Kinship, op. cit., p.151.

② Morgan, Systems... p.413.

changes and the nature of possible dynamic factors indicated.

## Chinese Works Frequently Cited

The following list has been prepared for the sole purpose of avoiding the constant repetition of bibliographical information in the text. The works are arranged alphabetically according to the romanized brief title as used in the text and notes. Since full bibliographical information is usually given in the notes for Chinese works cited only once or twice and for European works referred to, they are not given here.

Chan kuo ts'ê 战国策校注: commentaries by Pao Piao 鲍彪, *circa* 1150 A.D. and Wu Shih-tao 吴师道, 1283-1344 A.D.; Ssŭ pu Ts'ung k'an 四部丛刊.

Ch'ang li chi 昌黎先生集: Collected works of Han Yü 韩愈, 768-824 A.D.; Ssŭ pu pei yao 四部备要.

ch'ao ching ch'ao wên chi 巢经巢文集：Collected works of Chêng Chên 郑珍, 1806-1864 A.D.;清代学术丛书 edition.

Ch'êng wei lu 称谓录: by Liang Chang-chü 梁章钜，1775-1849 A.D.; 1875 edition.

Chêng tzŭ t'ung 正字通: compiled *circa* 1670 A.D. by Liao Wên ying 廖文英; 1670 edition.

Chi yün 集韵: compiled by Ting Tu 丁度, 990-1053 A.D., and others; *Ssǔ pu pei yao* edition.

Chiang Wên tʻung chi 江文通集: Collected works of Chiang Yen 江淹，444-505 A.D.; *Ssǔ pu Tsʻung kʻan* edition.

Chʻien yen tʻang chin shih wên pa wei 潜研堂金石文跋尾：by Chʻien Ta hsin 钱大昕, 1727-1804 A.D.; 1884 潜研堂全书 edition.

Chin shi li 金石例: by Pʻan Ang-hsiao 潘昂霄, *circa* 1300 A.D.; 徐氏随庵丛书 edition.

Chin shih Tsʻui pien 金石萃编: compiled by Wang Chʻang 王昶，1727-1806 A.D.; 经训堂 edition.

Chin shih yao li 金石要例: by Huang Tsung-hsi 黄宗羲, 1609-1695 A.D.;借月山房汇钞 edition.

Chin shu 晋书: by Fang Chiao 房乔, *circa* 630 A.D.,and others; 1894, 同文书局 edition.

Chʻin shu chi 亲属记：by Chêng Chên 郑珍, 1806-1864 A.D.; 广雅丛书 edition.

Chiu Tʻang shu 旧唐书: by Liu Hsü 刘昫, 887-946 A.D., and others; 1894. 同文书局 edition.

Chʻü-chiang wên chi 曲江文集: Collected works Of Chang Chiu-ling 张九龄, 673-740 A.D.; *Ssǔ pu Tsʻung kʻan* edition.

*Êrh ya* 尔雅义疏: Commentary by Ho I-hsing 郝懿行, 1757-1825 A.D.; *Ssǔ pu pei yao* edition. Since the section referred to is the short *Shih*

*Ch'in* 释亲, Relationship Terms, no page reference is given in the notes.

Fang yen 方言: by Yang Hsiung 扬雄, 53 B.C.-18 A.D. commentary by Kuo P'o 郭璞, 276-324 A.D.; *Ssŭ pu Ts'ung k'an* edition.

Han fei tzǔ 韩非子: by Han Fei 韩非, ?-324 B.C.; *Ssŭ pu pei yao* edition.

Han shu 汉书: by Pan Ku 班固, 32-92 A.D.; 1894, 同文书局 edition.

Hêng yen lu 恒言录: by Ch'ien Ta-hsin 钱大昕, 1727-1804 A.D.; 1884, 潜研堂全书 edition.

Hou Han shu 后汉书: by Fan Yeh 范晔, ?-445 A.D.; 1894, 同文书局 edition.

Hsiao ching 孝经注疏: 115, 阮刻十三经注疏 edition.

Hsin shu 新书: by Chia I 贾谊, *circa* second century B.C.; *Ssŭ pu pei yao* edition.

Hsin T'ang shu 新唐书: by Ou-yang Hsiu 欧阳修, 1007-1072 A.D., and Sung Ch'i 宋祁, 998-1061 A.D.; 1894, 同文书局 edition.

Hsüeh lin 学林: by Wang Kuan-kuo 王观国, *cirea* 1140 A.D.; 武英殿聚珍版 edition.

Hua yang chi 华阳集: by Ku k'uang 顾况, *circa* 8th and 9th centuries A.D.; 1855 双峰堂 edition.

Huai nan tzǔ 淮南子: attributed to Liu An 刘安, ?-122 B.C.; 1876 浙江书局 edition.

I ching 周易注疏: 1815 阮刻十三经注疏 edition.

I Li 仪礼注疏: 1815 阮刻十三经注疏 edition.

Jih chih lu 日知录集释: by Ku Yen wu 顾炎武, 1612-1681 A.D., commentary by Huang Ju-Ch'êng 黄汝成; 1872 湖北崇文书局 edition.

Jung chai sui pi 容斋随笔：by Huny Mai 洪迈, 1123-1202 A.D.; *Ssǔ pu Ts'ung k'an* 续编 edition.

Kai yü Ts'ung k'ao 陔余丛考: by Chao I 赵翼, 1727-1814 A.D.; 1790, 寿考堂瓯北全书 edition.

Kuang shih Ch'in 广释亲: by Chang Shên i 张慎仪, based on 钱塘梁氏残稿.梦园丛书 edition.

Kuang ya 广雅疏证: by Chang I 张揖, *circa* 230 A.D. ,commentary by Wang Nien-sun 王念孙, 1744-1832 A.D.; 1879, 淮南书局 edition. Since the section referred to is the *Shih Ch'in* 释亲, Relationship Terms, 6. 1-6, no page reference is given in the notes.

Kuang yün 广韵: revised by Ch'ên P'êng-nien 陈彭年, 961-1017 A.D., and others; *Ssǔ pu Ts'ung k'an* edition.

Kung-yang chuan 公羊注疏: 1815,阮刻十三经注疏 edition.

K'ung Ts'ung tzǔ 孔丛子: attributed to K'ung Fu 孔鲋, *circa* 200 B.C.; *Ssǔ pu Ts'ung k'an* edition.

Kuo yü 国语: commentary by Wei Chao 韦昭, 204-273 A.D.; *Ssǔ pu Ts'ung k'an* edition.

Li chi 礼记注疏: 1815 阮刻十三经注疏 edition.

Liang shu 梁书: by Yao Ssǔ-lien 姚思廉, ?-637 A.D.; 1894, 同文书

局 edition.

Liu Pin-K'o wên chi 刘宾客文集: Collected works of Liu Yü-hsi 刘禹锡, 772-842 A.D.; *Ssŭ pu pei yao* edition.

Lu Shih-lung wên chi 陆士龙文集: Collected works of Lu Yün 陆云, 262-305 A.D.; *Ssŭ pu Ts'ung k'an* edition.

Lun yü 论语注疏: 1815,阮刻十三经注疏 edition.

Lü shih Ch'un Ch'iu 吕氏春秋: attributed to Lü Pu wei 吕不韦， ?-235 B.C.; *Ssŭ pu pei yao* edition.

Mêng Ch'i pi t'an 梦溪笔谈: by Shên Kua 沈括, 1030-1094 A.D.; 津逮秘书 edition.

Mêng tzŭ 孟子注疏: 1815 阮刻十三经注疏 edition.

Ming lü chi chieh fu li 明律集解附例: compilation of 1585 A.D.,万历十三年;1908, 修定法律馆 edition.

Ming tao tsa chih 明道杂志: by Chang Lei 张耒, 1052-1112 A.D.; 顾氏文房小说 edition.

Mo chi 默记： by Wang Chih 王铚, *circa* 1120 A.D.; 1918 涵芬楼 edition.

Nan shih 南史: by Li Yen-shou 李延寿, *circa* seventh century A.D.; 1894 同文书局 edition.

Nan T'ang shu 南唐书: by Ma Ling 马令 *circa* 1100 A.D.; *Ssŭ pu Ts'ung k'an* 续编 edition.

Nêng kai chai man lu 能改斋漫录：by Wu Tsêng 吴曾, *circa* 1150

A.D.; 武英殿聚珍版 edition.

Pa Ch'iung shih chin shih pu chêng 八琼室金石补正: compiled by Lu Tsêng-hsiang陆增祥, *circa* 1850 A.D.; 吴兴刘氏希古楼 edition.

Pai ching T'ang wên chi 拜经堂文集: by Tsang Yung 臧庸, 1767-1811 A.D.;1920 上元宗氏石印 edition.

Pai hu T'ung 白虎通疏证: attributed to Pan Ku 班固, 32 92 A.D. ,and others; commentary by Ch'ên Li 陈立, 1809-1869 A.D.; 1875 淮南书局 edition.

Pei Ch'i shu 北齐书: by Li Pai-yao 李百药, 565-648 A.D.; 1894 同文书局 edition.

Pei mêng so yen 北梦琐言: by Sun Kuang-hsien 孙光宪, ?-968 A.D.; 雅雨堂丛书 edition.

Pei shih 北史: by Li Yen-shou 李延寿, *circa* 7th century A.D.; 1894 同文书局 edition.

P'ieh chi 瞥记: by Liang Yü shêng 梁玉绳, *circa* 1780 A.D.;清白士集edition.

San kuo chih 三国志: by Ch'ên Shou 陈寿, 233-297 A.D.; 1894 同文书局 edition.

Shih Ch'ang t'an 释常谈: anonymous; *circa* 1100 A.D.; 百川学海 edition.

Shih chi 史记: by Ssŭ-ma Ch'ien 司马迁, ?145-74? B.C.; 1894 同文书局 edition.

Shih ching 毛诗注疏: *Ssŭ pu pei yao* edition.

Shih ming 释名疏证: by Liu Hsi 刘熙, *circa* 200 A.D. ,commentary by Pi Yüan 毕沅, 1730-1797 A.D.; 广雅丛书 edition. The part referred to is the Section Ⅱ: *Shih Ch'in Shu* 释亲属, Relationship Terms. No page reference is given in the notes.

Shih shuo hsin yü 世说新语: by Liu I-Ch'ing 刘义庆, 403-444 A.D., commentary by Liu Hsiao-piao 刘孝标, *circa* 530 A.D.; *Ssŭ pu Ts'ung k'an* edition.

Shu ching 尚书注疏：1815,阮刻十三经注疏 edition.

Shu i 书仪：by Ssŭ-ma Kuang 司马光, 1019-1086 A.D.; 学津讨原 edition.

Shu P'o 鼠璞: by Tai Shih 戴埴, *circa* 1220 A.D.; 学津讨原 edition.

Shuo wên 说文解字: by Hsü Shên 许慎, *circa* 200 A.D., commentary by Hsü Hsüan 徐铉, 916 991 A.D.; *Ssŭ pu Ts'ung k'an* edition.

Sung shu 宋书: by Shên Yo 沈约, 441-513 A.D.; 1894 同文书局 edition.

Ta Tai li chi 大戴礼记: by Tai Tê 戴德, *circa* 100 B.C.; *Ssŭ pu Ts'ung k'an* edition.

T'ang chih yen 唐摭言: by Wang Ting-pao 王定保, 870-954(?) A.D.; 雨雅堂丛书edition.

T'ang lü su i 故唐律疏议: codified by Ch'ang-sun Wu-chi 长孙无忌, ?-659 A.D. and others. *Ssŭ pu Ts'ung k'an* 三编 edition.

ts'ai Chung-lang chi 蔡中郎集: Collected works of ts'ai Yung 蔡邕, 133-192 A.D.; *Ssǔ pu Ts'ung k'an* edition.

Tṣ'ao Tzǔ-chien chi 曹子建集: Collected works of Ts'ao Chih 曹植, 192-232 A.D.; *Ssǔ pu Ts'ung k'an* edition.

Tso chuan 左传注疏: 1815,阮刻十三经注疏 edition.

Tsung fa hsiao chi 宗法小记: by Ch'êng Yao-T'ien 程瑶田, 1725 1814 A.D.; 清经解 edition.

T'ung su p'ien 通俗篇: by Chai Hao 翟灏, ?-1788 A.D.; 无不宜斋 edition.

T'ung tien 通典: compiled by Tu Yu 杜佑, 735-812 A.D.; 1896, 浙江书局 edition.

T'ung ya 通雅: by Fang I-chih 方以智, *circa* 1650 A.D.; 立教馆 edition.

Wang Shih chung chi 王侍中集: Collected works of Wang Ts'an 王粲, 177-217 A.D.; 汉魏六朝百三名家集 edition.

Wei Wu-ti chi 魏武帝集: Collected works of Ts'ao Ts'ao 曹操，155-220 A.D.; 汉魏六朝百三名家集 edition.

Wên hsüan 六臣注文选：compiled by Hsiao T'ung 萧统, 501-531 A.D., commentary by Li Shan 李善, ?-688 A.D. and others. *Ssǔ pu Ts'ung k'an* edition.

Yen shih chia hsün 颜氏家训: by Yen Chih-T'ui 颜之推, 531-591 A.D.; *Ssǔ pu pei yao* edition.

Yen  tzǔ Ch'un Ch'iu 晏子春秋： attributed to Yen Ying 晏婴, ?-493 B.C.; *Ssǔ pu pei yao* edition.

Yin  hua lu 因话录: by Chao Lin 赵璘, *circa* 840 A.D.; 稗海 edition.

Yü  p'ien 玉篇: compiled in 543 A.D. by Ku Yeh-wang 顾野王 augmented in 760 A.D. by Sun Ch'iang 孙强, revised in 1008 A.D. by Ch'ên P'êng-nien 陈彭年, and others; *Ssǔ pu  Ts'ung  k'an* edition.

Yü  T'ai hsin yung chi 玉台新咏集: compiled by Hsü Ling 徐陵，507-583 A.D.; *Ssǔ pu Ts'ung k'an* edition.

Yüan  shih chang Ch'ing chi 元氏长庆集: Collected works of Yüan Chên 元稹, 779-831 A.D.; *Ssǔ pu Ts'ung k'an* edition.

〔原载 *Harvard Journal of Asiatic Studies*, Vol.2, No.2(1937), pp.141−275〕

# THE HISTORICAL ORIGINS OF
# THE LOLO

The Lolo[1] are an important non-Chinese people of Southwest China. They have been known under various names in the region where they are now found for nearly 2000 years. Their present number is unknown, although some have estimated it at about 3000000[2]. The Lolo of Ssŭch'uan have been estimated

---

[1]  罗罗。

[2]  This figure was set by Terrien DE LACOUPERIE, in " The Language of China before Chinese," *Trans. Philological Soc.*, 1885-56, p. 479. It was quoted by Frederick Stan, in " Lolo Objects in the Public Museum, Milwaukee," *Bull*, 1911, Vol.I, Pt.2, pp. 209-20. E. PITARD, in *Les races et l'histoire*, 1924, p. 495, quoted from Stan.YOUNG Ching-chi, in " A Brief Account of the Lolo," *Ling-nan Jour.*, Vol. I, pp.134-52, quoted from Pittard. This figure is too high, and although it occurs in a recent article, is nothing but a guess by Lacouperie. The editor of *Science*, in Vol. 18, 1934, p. 1672, estimated the number of Lolo in Ssŭch'uan at above 1000000, and this figure is supposed to be based on W. R. MORSE," The Nosu Tribes of Western Szechwan,"*Chin. Med. Jour.*, March, 1933. These figures are not based on counting, and are exaggerated. An investigation by the 中国西部科学院，特刊, No. 1, in 1935, states that the Black Lolo of Ssŭch'uan do not number more than 20000, and the White Lolo, not more than 80000. These figures are more reliable because they are based on an actual count of Lolo family groups in the 凉山 area.

to number 1000000, and occupy a territory of more than 11000 square miles. These estimates of population are much too high, and the total number of Lolo is about 1000000.

The Lolo are scattered over the mountainous country of Yunnan and the southwestern part of Ssǔch'uan. On the west, they extend almost to the valley of the Mekong. On the east, they have occupied in historic times the western districts of Kueichou. On the south, small scattered groups are found on the northern border of French Tonking.

In a northeastern thrust along the Ta-liang, or Great Cold, mountains which follow the northeastern course of the Yang-tzǔ River, they reach as far north as Chia-ting and Ya-chou, south of the Ta-tu River. This narrow strip is about 150 miles long, and somewhat less than 100 miles wide. The country is rugged, and is known as the home of the independent Lolo. On the west are the Tibetan, Sifan and Moso tribes. The Sifan are on the north, and a few scattered Shan and Miao tribes are on the southeast.

The region occupied by the Lolo is a southeastern extension of the Tibetan Plateau. It is crossed by the upper reaches of the Yang-tzǔ River and its tributaries. The rivers have many rapids, and are not navigable for any distance. The climate is temperate, but the winters are rigorous.

The geographic position of the Lolo makes them important not only for themselves, but as holding a key to the movements of peoples in Southeast Asia.

Although they possess a script,[1] they have not, so far as is now known, any historical literature. At present, the only sources for their past are meagre and sometimes inaccurate references in Chinese works.

The name Lolo first appears in the Yüan period; that is, it has been used for about 800 years. It was soon identified with Lulu, the name of a tribe of the Eastern Ts'uan barbarians of the fifth to the ninth centuries A.D.[2] It is not possible to check this identification, but the Mongols established a district called Lolo-ssŭ hsüan-wei[3] in the northern part of the Chien-ch'ang Valley.

At present, the names used by the Lolo for themselves vary considerably from tribe to tribe. The initial consonant is rarely *l*, there is a wide range of vowel fluctuation, and the second syllable is usually *so* or *su*. Sometimes the second syllable is omitted.[4] Foreign investigators have varied considerably in

---

[1]  The Lolo script is pictographic and modeled somewhat after the Chinese. Chinese sources say that it was invented by a Lolo named A-bi about A.D. 550. The Lolo have three legends concerning its invention. A-bi called it *wei-shu*(standard script); the Chinese called it *Ts'uan-wên*(script of the Ts'uan). It is used chiefly for religious documents, and can be read only by the *pi-mo* (shamans). Even these read only the script of their own tribe, as has been shown by V. K. TING, in 漫游散记, *Independent Review*, 1933, No. 85, p. 13, and No. 42, pp. 19-20, and by D'OLLONE, In *Forbidden China*, pp. 106-107. There is already a large literature on the Lolo script. The most recent and extensive work is by V. K. Ting, 爨文丛刊, 1936; see also YOUNG Ching-chi, *L'écriture et les manuscrits Lolos*, 1935.

[2]  炎徼纪闻4: 17a罗罗本卢鹿而讹. See also Pelliot,"Deux itineraires de Chine en Inde," *BEFEO* 4 (1904). 187.

[3]  罗罗斯宣慰司 cf. 新元史248: 8b.

[4]  Some of the variations are Mo-su, Mou-su, Ngo-su, Ne-su, Nei-su, No-su, No, Na, and Lei-su. In Ssüch'uan, they are called Man-tzü, or more courteously, Man-chia, which are Chinese terms. In southern Yunnan, the Shan call them Myen.

their treatments of the name, and their theories are not of much help.①

The term Lolo is a Chinese transcription made 800 years ago. It may not have been accurate when it was made, or it may have been a local term. Perhaps both Chinese and the Lolo language have changed in pronunciation during the intervening period. In the present state of our knowledge, it would be a mistake to offer theories of the origin and meaning of the name, since there are too many unknown factors. We may assume that the term is not of foreign origin, and that its etymology is obscure.

Although the name was used in the Yüan period, it did not become well established until the Ming. Then the *Nan-chao yeh-shih* gives a list of eleven

---

① Lacouperie, op. cit., pp. 480-81, derives Lolo from Lulu, and this in turn from Lo-kuei. This is incorrect, as Lo-kuei, a derogatory nickname, is more recent than either Lolo or Lulu.

Paul VIAL's explanation in *Les Lolos* …, 1898, that the Chinese reduplicated the syllable for euphony, is also incorrect. The earlier Chinese records wrote the name as Lulu-man, which was later contracted, and had the name been Lu, it would have been written Lu-man.

LIETARD considered Lolo as a corruption of No-so, a term used by the Lolo for themselves (*Au Yunnan*, "les Lo-lo p'o," 1913). But SHIROKOGOROFF (" Phonetic Notes on a Lolo Dialect and the Consonant L," *Academia Sinica, Bull.*, Vol. I, No. 2, p. 183) has shown that the syllables *no* and *so* vary so much in meaning among the Lolo that any etymological derivation is uncertain, which invalidates Lietard's explanation. Shirokogoroff suggests a number of hypotheses. The name may have a political origin (like Manchu), or it may have been given to them by their neighbors (like Tungus), or it may have been handed down from antiquity.

S. C. CLARKE, in *Among the Tribes of Southwest China*, follows a missionary named C. C. Hicks (" The Nou Su," *Chinese Recorder,* 41, pp. 211 ff.), in deriving the name from a basket used by the Lolo in ancestor worship, and calls it a contemptuous nickname given by the Chinese. This is very unlikely.

C. E. Jamieson, " The Aborigines of Western China," *China Journal of Art and Science* 1, pp. 376 ff., quotes CHANG Ying, a Chinese writer of the early 19th Cen., as saying that the Lolo were descended from a *kolo* ape, *kolo* being changed into Lolo. This is entirely unhistorical.

Lolo tribes subject to the Shan state of Nan-chao.[1] These tribal names are not racial, but mostly appear to have been given because of peculiar cultural distinctions such as dress, occupation, and customs. Sometimes they are simply the name of the ruling family. Tribes move, and families die out, so that the disappearance of a name does not imply the disappearance of the group. Among the independent Lolo, there are said to be twenty-six tribes of Black Lolo, thirty tribes of White Lolo, three tribes which are mixed, and two tribes of slaves.[2] Early Chinese records indicate a similar condition.

The designations black and white are very common among the peoples of Southwest China. The connotation must be separately determined in each case. Sometimes these names indicate the prevailing color of the costume, as among the Black and White Miao.[3] In southern Hunan, certain Miao tribes are called black because they are less civilized than the Miao who live near the Chinese settlements,[4] and this is also true of the Black and White Lisu, a people living along the Upper Mekong who are related to the Lolo.[5] In most cases, these names are seldom used by the peoples to designate themselves, but are applied

[1]　Chüan 2, pp. 25-27. Lietard, op. cit., considered most of these names as Chinese inventions, but this is unlikely. He gives more than twenty tribal names, many of which are almost identical with those of the *Nan-chao yeh-shih*.

[2]　Lietard, op. cit. His information is secondary, and he does not give further details. D'Ollone, who travelled through the Lolo territory in 1908-09, says, op. cit., that the tribes occupied well-defined territories and that trespassing was resented, so that he was frequently required to change guides.

[3]　Clarke, op. cit., p. 371.

[4]　Jamieson, op. cit., pp. 381-82.

[5]　A. ROSE and J. C. BROWN, " Li-su (Yawyin) Tribes of the Burma-China Frontier," *Memoirs, Asiatic Society of Bengal,* Vol. III, 1910-14, pp. 249-76.

to them by the Chinese.

But the Lolo are an exception to this statement, for they divide themselves into black and white groups. Some western observers have missed this division entirely.[1] In Yunnan, the Black Lolo consist of the ruling families, and all below them are White Lolo. In Ssuch'uan, the majority belong to the black division.

This distinction among the Lolo is an old one, for the *Man-shu* and the T'ang history divide the tribes into Black and White Barbarians.[2] The way in which this distinction is used may indicate a racial difference, and certainly indicates a difference in language between the two groups.[3]

Among the modern Lolo, the black and white groups are different physically. The Black Lolo are tall, and are sometimes reported as taller than Europeans. They have aquiline noses, well-developed brow-ridges, and on the whole are quite different from the Mongoloid type.[4] The White Lolo are more

---

[1] Jamieson, op. cit., p. 381. He says the term black refers to the color of the skin. This statement is repeated by Buxton, *The Peoples of Asia*, p. 156. As a matter of fact, the Lolo have a lighter color than most of the aborigines. This has been noticed by many observers, some of whom regard them as fairer than southern Europeans. And if the Black Lolo are so named because of their skin, what of the White Lolo?

Lietard derives the name Lolo from No-so, and as *no* means black, it was misinterpreted by the Chinese. This hypothesis has been discussed.

[2] The following tribes are mentioned in the T'ang sources: Wu-man, or Black Barbarians: Eastern Ts'uan (Lolo), Ai-lo, Nan-chao, Tu-ching-man, Ch'ang-kun-man, Shih-man, Shun-man, No-man, Tu-lao. Pai-man, or White Barbarians: Western Ts'uan, Nan-tung-man, Ching-lin-man.

[3] *Man-shu* 蛮书 , chüan 8, pp. 3-4. "The language (of the Wu-man) is entirely different from that of the Pai-man."

[4] Travelers from Marco Polo until the present have noted their fine features. E. C. Baber says that they are taller than Europeans, but this seems to be exaggerated. D'Ollone, op. cit., p. 51, says, " There was nothing of the Asiatic; the complexion was not yellow, but swarthy, like that of the inhabitants of southern Europe; the eyes, neither oblique nor flattened, were large, and protected by fine arched brows; the nose was aquiline, the mouth well cut...."

Mongoloid, possess an inferior physique, and a slightly different cephalic index.[1]

The Black Lolo form the ruling class, and the black division also rules among the Miao of western Kueichou. Black appears to be an aristocratic designation, and the Black Lolo do not marry outside their own group. In Yunnan, the Lolo chiefs sometimes marry their daughters to the sons of Chinese officials or into distinguished Chinese families.[2] Among the independent Lolo of Ssuch'uan, endogamy is strictly enforced.

A possible explanation of this situation is that the Black Lolo may originally have been a conquering group of a single racial stock, while the White Lolo were of different stocks which were subjugated and had the language of the conquerers gradually imposed upon them. This process seems still to be going on among the Lolo of Ssuch'uan. In Yunnan, the Black Lolo have been decimated by the Chinese in war, or have retired northward, so that in this province the majority of those called Lolo belong to the lower White group. A few ruling families have remained and accepted office under the Chinese.

Although the Lolo have been known to the Chinese for a long time, there is little information concerning them in Chinese sources. Often the facts have been confused, and because of the presence of other tribes, it is often hard to tell

---

[1]  Cf. A. LEGENDRE, " Far West Chinois," *TP*, 1909, tab. A-C. DIXON, *Racial History of Man*, p. 281, gives an analysis. See also V. K. Ting, " Man yu san chi."

[2]  For a description of such a marriage, see J. K. SHRYOCK, " Ch'en Ting's Account of the Marriage Customs of the Chiefs of Yunnan and Kueichou," *Amer. Anthro.* 36, No. 4, Oct.-Dec. 1934.

whether a mentioned tribe was Lolo or not. In this historic study, a starting point may be found in northwestern Kueichou, the Shui-hsi[①] district which was the home of the Lolo chiefs of the great An[②] clan.

During the Chou period, the region was part of the districts of Tsang-ko[③] and Ch'ü-lan.[④] This area was conquered by Chuang Ch'iao for the feudal state of Ch'u about the end of the 4th Century B. C. In 316 B. C., it was annexed to the rival state of Ch'in by Ssŭ-ma Ts'o. We know nothing of the inhabitants of the region at this time.

During the Han period, the district was a part of the kingdom of Yeh-lang,[⑤] which was the largest and most powerful independent state of southwestern China. A contemporary scholar, Wang Ching-ju, identifies the Yeh-lang with the ancestors of the Lolo on linguistic grounds.[⑥] This identification is strengthened by historical evidence.

During the latter part of the Eastern Han period, the district was ruled by chiefs from whom the Lolo An family of Shui-hsi claimed descent. The account

---

① 水西, approximately the modern 大定 and 黔西. The name Shui-hsi was first used during the Ming period, and the boundaries have varied at different times.

② The An clan 安氏 claimed descent from 济火 of the 3rd Cen. A. D., but the name An was not used before the Ming period.

③ One explanation of 牂 牁 is that it meant a stake to which boats were tied. During CHUANG Ch'iao's expedition, he is supposed to have tied his boat here. But CHÊNG Chên says that the name existed long before the time of Chuang Ch'iao. See 巢经巢文集, ch. 2: 1-2, 牂牁考. The extent of these areas is vague.

④ 且蘭 was a small state annexed by Han Wu Ti. It is the modern P'ing-yüeh 平越 of Kueichou.

⑤ *Han shu*, T'ung-wen ed., ch. 95, p. 1. 南夷人君长以什数，夜郎最大.

⑥ WANG Ching-ju, " A Comparative Linguistic Study on the Songs of the Bair-lang Tribe," *Academia Sinica, Nat. Res. Inst. of History and Philology, Mon. 8, Hsi-hsia yen-chiu*, pp. 15-54.

of this family is given in the *Tu-shih fang-yü chi-yao*.[1]

" Shui-hsi-hsüan-wei-ssǔ[2] is 300 li northwest of Kuei-yang fu.[3] The native chiefs of the An family[4] ruled here generation after generation. Their ancestors were descendants of Chi Huo.[5] In the third year of Chien-hsin (A. D. 226), when Chu-ko Liang made his southern expedition, the chief Tsang-ko collected provisions and built roads for the expedition. Chu-ko Liang memorialized the court and made Chi Huo the prince of Lo-tien.[6] He made his capital at P'u-li,[7] in the present district of P'u-ting-wei.[8]

"It was their custom to reverence ghosts, and those who officiated at these ceremonies were called 'ghost-lords.'[9] About the beginning of the K'ai-ch'eng period of the T'ang dynasty (c. 836), the ghost-lord A Feng[10] submitted. During the period Hui-ch'ang (841-46), he was made prince of Lo-tien. In the second

---

[1]　读史方舆纪要, by 顾祖禹 (1624-80), 桐华书屋 edition of 1879. An index to the second and third parts was published in Tōkyō in 1932 by AOYAMA Sadao. It identifies Ch'ing with pre-Ch'ing place-names. The passage translated is from ch. 123, pp. 16b-17b.

[2]　水西宣慰司. It was first established in the Ming period.

[3]　贵阳.

[4]　安氏.

[5]　济火. Sometimes, as in the *Ming-shih*, the name is given as 火济.

[6]　罗甸国王. Lo-tien was used for approximately as the Tsang-ko area after the Later Han period. The expression may have some connection with Lolo, as *Tien* means domain or country.

[7]　普里.

[8]　普定卫. It is about 45 li north of 安顺县. During the Sung period, it was known as 普里蛮部. During the Yüan period, it was called 普定路, and belonged to Yunnan. In the Ming period, the name was changed to P'u-ting-wei of the present An-hsün district. Under the Republic, the name has been changed to 定南汎.

[9]　鬼主.

[10]　阿凤.

year of the T'ien-ch'eng period of the Later T'ang (927), P'u Lu,[①] the prince of Lo-tien, paid tribute to the court on behalf of his nine tribes. During the period K'ai-pao of the Sung dynasty (968-75), a man named P'u Kuei[②] offered his territory and submitted. He also was made prince of Lo-tien. From Chi Huo to P'u Kuei there were already thirty-six generations. At that time, Sung Ching-yang,[③] a native of Chen-ting,[④] was ordered by the emperor to pacify the barbarians of the region. Therefore the court established the district of Tsung-kuan fu[⑤] for him in Ta-wan-ku-o.[⑥] The Yüan emperors created the offices of An fu[⑦] and Chang kuan,[⑧] and conferred them on different chiefs.

"In the fourth year of Hung Wu of the Ming dynasty (1372), the chiefs Ai Ts'ui,[⑨] Sung Ch'in,[⑩] and a native named An Sha-ch'i[⑪] submitted voluntarily. Ai Ts'ui was made the Hsüan-wei-shih of Kueichou, while SUNG Ch'in and AN Sha-ch'i were made sub-prefects. They established their position at Kuei-yang, but also ruled over their tribes in Shui-hsi. Ai Ts'ui was the strongest. When he

---

① 普露.
② 普贵.
③ 宋景阳.
④ 真定 the modern 正定.
⑤ 总管府.
⑥ 大万谷落.
⑦ 安抚.
⑧ 长官.
⑨ 霭翠 during the Yüan period, held the offices 四川行省左臣 and 顺元宣慰使 concurrently. See the *Yen ch'iao chi wen*, 3: 1.
⑩ 宋钦.
⑪ 安沙溪.

died, he was succeeded by his younger brother An Ti.[1] Then they assumed An as their surname. The An clan ruled forty-eight tribes of Lolo, whose chiefs were called 'heads.'[2] The Sung clan lived for generations near the capital of the district, ruling twelve tribes of barbarians, whose chiefs were called ' horse-heads.' The clan of the sub-prefect An ruled a single tribe of barbarians, whose chief was also called ' head.' "

"The An clan occupied the district of Shui-hsi for generations. On the south, it extends to the Lu-kuang;[3] on the east it bordered Tsun-i;[4] on the west it was bounded by the Ch'ih-shui;[5] on the north it reaches Yung-ning.[6] It forms a continuous tract of several hundred li. The mountains are rugged and the growth dense. It contains the fortified strongholds of Shui-hsi, Ta-fang,[7] Chih-chin,[8] and Huo-shao.[9] Ta-fang was the strongest and most important. They (the An family) exploited the natives, becoming stronger day by day.

"During the period Wan-li (1573-1619), An Ch'iang-ch'en[10] secretly sided

---

[1] 安的. T'ien Ju-chên (*Yen ch'iao chi wên*, 3: 3) says that Ai Ts'ui was succeeded by his wife, and later by his younger brother, An Yün 安匀. An Ti is not mentioned, and possibly Ku Tsu-yü is mistaken here.

[2] 头目.

[3] 陆广, a city on the banks of the Lu-kuang river, in the 修文 district of Kueichou. The Lu-kuang is the largest river of Shui-hsi. It rises to the east of P'u-ting, flows through the 修文 district, and empties into the 乌江.

[4] 遵义. This is the Ch'ing name.

[5] 赤水. The modern 毕节县. In the Ming period it was called Chih-shui-wei.

[6] 永宁. The present 叙永 district of Ssuch'uan. During the Yüan period, it was called 永宁路, and during the Ming, 永宁卫.

[7] 大方地. In the modern 大定 district. It is in the western part of Shui-hsi, near 毕节卫.

[8] 织金城. In the northwestern section of Shui-hsi.

[9] 火灼城. It is to the north of the modern district of 黔西. It is also called 火灼堡, or 火著.

[10] 安疆臣.

with the chief of Po,[①] who rose in revolt. The court was angry, and sent an expedition which defeated and killed Po.[②] An Ch'iang-chen became afraid, betrayed his former allies, and attacked them. The court praised his merit, winking at his earlier treachery.

"About the beginning of the period T'ien-ch'i (c. 1621), An Ch'iang-ch'en died, and was succeeded by his son, An Wei,[③] who was young and weak. The native chief An Pang-yen[④] forced him into a rebellion, along with the barbarian chief of Yung-ning, She Ch'ung-ming.[⑤] The court sent a punitive expedition which defeated She Ch'ung-ming, who escaped to An Pang-yen. The native chiefs of Wu-sa[⑥] and Chan-i[⑦] made a counter-revolt against An Pang-yen. The latter terrified the border districts of Kueichou and Yunnan. To the south, he

---

① 播酋, i. e., YANG Ying-lung 杨应龙, who led a revolt from A. D. 1595 to 1601. Yang's ancestor became chief of 播州 in the T'ang period, having taken the territory from Nan-chao. From the founder to YANG Ying-lung, 29 generations of chiefs held the position for nearly 800 years. See the *Ming-shih*, 312: 1-11.

② [omitted].

③ 安位.

④ 安邦彦.

⑤ 奢崇明. She was the name of a large Lolo clan along the Ssǔch'uan-Kueichou border during the Ming period. 永宁 Yung-ning is the modern 关岭县.

⑥ 乌撒, approximately the modern 镇雄 of Yunnan and 威宁 of Kueichou. The *Yüan shih ti li chih*, T'ung wen ed., ch. 61, p. 28b, says, "Wu-sa is a barbarian name. The old name was 巴凡兀姑, and it is now called 巴的甸. It includes the six tribes of Wu-sa and Wu-mêng 乌蒙. Later their descendants held the whole territory, adopting the name of their ancestor Wu-sa as their tribal name. They surrendered in the tenth year of Chih-yüan (1273), and the Wu-sa-wei was established in 1276." The Wu-sa were Lolo. The chief who revolted with An-Chiang-chen was An Hsiao-liang 安效良.

⑦ 霑益, in eastern Yunnan. During the T'ang period, it was occupied by the Po 播 and La 剌 tribes, who probably used a Shan language. Under the Nan-chao, the area was occupied by the Mo-mi 摩弥 tribe, probably allied with the Lolo. The chief connected with this revolt was Li Hsien 李贤.

invaded Kuei-yang,[1] and to the east, P'ien-yüan.[2] The native chief of Hung-pien[3] and the Miao tribes of the east and west made counter-revolts against him. The government forces attacked him on all sides, but met with no success.

"In the fourth year of T'ien-ch'i (1624), the viceroy Chu Hsieh-yüan[4] proposed that the Yunnan forces should attack Chan-i in order to prevent An Pang-yen's reinforcement from Wu-sa, and with another force at T'ien-sheng-ch'iao[5] and Hsün-tien[6] to block his retreat. The Ssüch'uan forces should attack Pi-chieh[7] to break his communications. Another force should advance from Lung-ch'ang[8] and Yen-t'ou[9] to seize his strategic positions. The Kueichou forces should advance from P'u-ting[10] and cross the Ssü-la River[11] direct to An Pang-yen's headquarters. Forces from Lu-kuang[12] and Ya-ch'ih[13] should attack

---

[1] 贵阳. A well-known city of Kueichou.

[2] 偏沅. A combination of 沅州 and 偏桥关. Under the Ming, the govern of P'ien-yüan 偏沅巡抚 was appointed to manage the affairs of the Miao, staying half the year in Yüan-chou and the other half in P'ien-ch'iao-kuan. The office was abolished under the Ch'ing. Under the Ming, it was one of the most important positions in southwestern China.

[3] 洪边 was first established during the Yüan period, about 8 li north of Kuei-yang. The rebel chief was Sung Wan-hua 宋万化.

[4] 朱燮元.

[5] 天生桥, northwest of 安顺县 in Kueichou. A place important strategically.

[6] 寻甸 in Yunnan. Under the Ming, it was called 寻甸军民府 which was later changed to 寻甸府.

[7] 毕节 northwestern Kueichou. It is an important center of communications between Ssüch'uan, Yunnan and Kueichou. The cliffs made it difficult to capture.

[8] 龙场. In the modern 修文县, Kueichou.

[9] 岩头.

[10] 普定 in the 安顺 district of Kueichou.

[11] 思腊河.

[12] 陆广 the modern Lu-kuang river. Cf. p.1314, note [3].

[13] 鸭池 the Ya-ch'ih river, one of the upper tributaries of the Lu-kuang.

at weak points. The Kuangsi forces should advance from Ssü--ch'eng[1] as a reserve. The main army should advance from Chan-i to attack him in front. But at this time the viceroy resigned his office because of the death of a parent.

"The viceroy resumed his office in the second year of Ch'ung-cheng (1629). He commanded the armies of Ssüch'uan, Hunan, Yunnan, Kueichou and Kuangsi to advance again. He ordered the Yunnan forces to advance on Wu-sa, and the Ssüch'uan forces on Yung-ning and Pi-chieh in order to cut communications. He himself led the main force stationed along the Lu-kuang, advancing on Ta-fang. At this time, An Pang-yen and She Tsung-ming were attacking Chih-shui, and had advanced far into Yung-ning. The viceroy ordered one government force to advance from San-ch'a,[2] one from Lu-kuang, one from Tsun-i, and sent a light force to encircle the ' bandits ' from the rear. The ' bandits ' could not resist this attack, and collapsed. An Pang-yen was killed in battle, while An Wei was besieged in Ta-fang. The 'bandits' were helpless, and offered to give up the territory of six tribes on the borders of Shui-hsi, and to open a highway through Pi-chieh as the conditions of surrender. The viceroy accepted these terms. He sent punitive forces to pacify the revolting Miao tribes of Pai-chin, Liang-chiang, Pa-hsiang, Lang-pai and Huo-hung,[3] in order to isolate Shui-hsi. An Wei died not long after, and his clan submitted and

---

[1]　泗城 in the modern 凌云 district of Kuangsi. It has been abolished under the Republic.

[2]　三岔, i.e., 三岔寨, north of the P'u-ting district.

[3]　摆金, 两江, 巴乡, 狼狈, 火烘. These five tribes cannot be identified at present. The names seem to be geographical.

surrendered their territory. The viceroy petitioned the court that the territory of Shui-hsi should be divided among the native chiefs and the Chinese who had taken part in the expedition, in order to divide the strength of Shui-hsi, and make it easy to handle. Thus Shui-hsi was once more pacified."

Of these tribal chiefs, the An and She were definitely Lolo, but whether the Sung and Li were Lolo is not known. It may be assumed that many tribes under the authority of Lolo chiefs were not Lolo. This passage indicates how great an effort the Ming dynasty was forced to make in order to 'pacify' the Lolo—an effort that required the armies of five provinces, commanded by the viceroy of South China. How far the exhaustion caused by this effort contributed to the final downfall of the dynasty it is difficult to say, but it should be considered a factor in the debacle which culminated in 1644.

Under the Ch'ing dynasty, the An Lolo chiefs of Shui-hsi were still strong. In the third year of K'ang-hsi (c. 1665), Wu San-kuei conquered An K'un,[1] and divided his territory into five prefec- tures. An K'un's wife fled to Wu-mang, where she gave birth to a son named An Shih-tsung.[2] Later it was decided not to employ Chinese in the local government, and An Shih-tsung was appointed Hsüan-wei-shih of the area in 1683. In 1702, the viceroy Wang Chi-wen[3] memorialized the court, saying that An Shih-tsung should be removed because of maladministration. Accordingly he was disinherited, and his territory brought

---

[1]  安坤. Cf. the Ch'ing shih kao, 土司传, 4:1b-2a.

[2]  安世宗. Cf. the Ch'ing shih kao, ibid., 4: 11b.

[3]  王继文.

directly under Chinese control.

There is an excellent description of the Lolo of this area in the *Yen-chiao-chi-wen*.[1] This book was written in 1560 by T'IEN Ju-ch'eng,[2] who served as a high official in Southwest China, and who had more than ten years' experience in dealing with the native tribes. The book has been used as a source by many later authors, but the description of the Lolo has been largely neglected.

"Lolo[3] was originally Lulu,[4] which was corrupted into the present form. There were two kinds. Those who live in Shui-hsi, Shih-'erh-ying,[5] Ning-ku,[6] Ma-ch'ang,[7] and Tsao-ch'i[8] are the Black Lolo. Those who live in Mo-i[9] are the White Lolo, and are also called 'White barbarians.' The customs are much the same, but the Blacks are the more numerous. The Lolo reverence ghosts, so they are also called ' Lo kuei.'

"In the time of the Shu Han dynasty (221-265), a man named Chi Huo was a follower of Chu-ko Liang at the capture of Meng-huo, and he was appointed Prince of Lo-tien. He was the ancestor of the present Hsüan-wei-shih of the An

---

① 炎徼纪闻 4.14a of the Chia-yeh-t'ang edition.

② 田汝成.

③ 罗罗.

④ 卢鹿.

⑤ 十二营, 30 li north of the 镇宁 district, Kueichou. The district was abolished in the Ch'ing period.

⑥ 宁谷, 30 li southwest of the 安顺 district, Kueichou. The district was abolished in the Ch'ing period.

⑦ 马场, along the Ma-ch'ang river, in the 平越 district, Kueichou.

⑧ 漕溪.

⑨ 慕役, A about 60 li south of the 关岭 district. Under the Yüan, it was a 寨, and under the Ming and Ch'ing, 长官司.

clan. Those who lived in Tzŭ -ch'i,[①] Yeh-lang,[②] and Tsang-ko,[③] were called by the name of their country. Those who lived in T'e-mo,[④] Po-i,[⑤] and Chiu-tao,[⑥] were called by the name of their prefecture. All were Lolo.

"The Lolo are stupid, and love their masters. Even when their masters were tyrannical and killed whole clans, they still supported their master's children, just as wives and concubines love their husbands, and never became their husband's enemies. Therefore from Chi Huo until the present, for more than a thousand years, they have been masters of the country from generation to generation. They are divided into forty-eight tribes, the chief of a tribe being called ' head.'

"The people have deep eyes, tall stature, dark complexion, and white teeth. Their hair is worn in a certain way,[⑦] and they go barefoot. They wear felt, *li*,[⑧] and a kind of reed belt about the waist. On the left shoulder hangs a piece of sheep-skin. They carry a long sword, and a case of arrows. The rich wear gold amulets. They are fierce, and love to fight. They are expert in the art of attack, and respect strength. In prosperity, they fish, hunt, and cut lumber, but in times of scarcity, they seek to kill and plunder. Therefore their armies are the best of

① 自杞.
② 夜郎.
③ 牂牁.
④ 特磨, the 广南 district of Yunnan. Under the Sung, it was called 特磨道.
⑤ 白衣.
⑥ 九道.
⑦ 椎结.
⑧ 戴笠, a conical hat made of bamboo splints.

all the barbarians. The proverb says, ' The Lo-kuei of Shui-hsi break heads and [then] wag tails.' This means that their reactions are brusque.

"They have also a script like the Mongol. They have neither chairs nor mats. When they eat, the meal consists of a plate of rice and a bowl of water. They take some rice with a spoon, roll it into a ball, and throw it into the mouth. After eating they rinse their mouths and brush their teeth, and they consider this hygienic. They shave the hair on the upper lip, but keep that on the face. The women wind their hair into a knot, and tie it with black tape. In their sexual orgies they respect no generations, and are not ashamed of this. When their fathers die, they marry their step-mothers. When brothers die, they marry the widows also. When a bride first sees her husband's parents, she does not prostrate herself, but with naked body she offers washing utensils. This is called *feng t'ang*.[①] Their dwellings are unlike the Chinese. They assemble like running wolves. They are suspicious, and always fighting each other.

"The customs of the White Lolo are similar to those of the Black Lolo, but their food is much poorer. They have cups and plates, and cook with a three-footed pot.[②] They fry (meat) with the hair still on, and tear it with their teeth while it is still bloody. Rats, birds, ant-eggs, locusts, and all kinds of worms (insects? ) are collected, burned, and eaten, just as if the people were pigs. They do not write, but keep knotted cords and notched strips of wood. Girls who were

---

① 奉堂.
② 三足釜.

renowned for licentiousness were much sought in marriage, because they were considered beautiful. They wrap the dead with cow or horse-hide and cremate them. Those who live in P'u-ting are called A-ho.[1] In their customs they are like the White Lolo. They sell tea for a livelihood."

The information concerning the area including the western districts of Kueichou and the northeastern districts of Yunnan before the T'ang period is very meagre. The country was moun- tainous and remote. Chinese influence had hardly penetrated beyond the southwest border of Chien-wei[2] and Shu-shih[3]; i. e., the modern district of I-pin.[4] The main road from Ssü- ch'uan to Yunnan used from the T'ang period until the present day skirted the eastern border of this area, passing through Hsü- yung, Pi-chieh, Chan-i and K'un-ming.[5] *The Man shu* calls this the northern route. Beginning with the Chin period (began in A. D. 265), the peoples of this area were known as the Ts'uan.[6]

"During the T'ien-pao period (742-55), northeast from Ch'ü- ching chou[7]

---

[1]　阿和.

[2]　犍为.

[3]　朱提. 朱 is pronounced like 殊, and 提 like 上支反.

[4]　宜宾.

[5]　叙永，毕节，霑益，昆明. The place-names given in the *Man shu*, Ch. 1, pp. 4-5, cannot be identified. But the book says that places along this route were inhabited by the Lulu and other peoples of Lolo affinities, e.g., 过鲁望第七程至竹子岭，岭东有暴蛮部落，岭西有卢鹿蛮部落。第六程至生蛮磨弥殿部落。此等部落，皆东爨乌蛮也。男则髻髻，女则散发。见人无礼节跪拜，三译四译乃与华通，大部落则有鬼主…

[6]　爨.

[7]　曲靖州. Under the T'ang there was no Chü-ching, and this reference should read 曲州 and 靖州. Chü-chou is near the modern 庆符, and Ching-chou is in the old 叙永 of Ssüch'uan.

and southwest to Hsüan-ch'eng,[1] towns and villages are visible from each other i. e., they are close together and cattle and horses are numerous in the fields. Those who live in Shih-ch'eng, K'un-chou, Ch'ü-o, Chin-ning, Yü-hsien, An-ning and Lung-ho-ch'eng[2] are called the Western Ts'uan. Those who live in Ch'ü-ching chou, Mi-lu ch'uan, Sheng-ma ch'uan and Pu-t'ou[3] are called the Eastern Ts'uan." [4]

According to the *Man shu*, Shih-ch'eng is the old Wei-hsien[5] which is fifteen miles from the modern Ch'ü-ching. Lung-ho-ch'eng is to the east of Ta-li. Therefore the area occupied by the Western Ts'uan was approximately from the modern Ch'ü-ching westward to Ta-li. The Ch'ü-chou and Ching-chou of the T'ang period were immediately south of the modern Ch'ing-fu and Chang-ning[6] districts of Ssüch'uan. Mi-lu is approximately the modern Lu-hsi.[7] Sheng-ma is near the modern Ch'ü-ching. The identification of Pu-t'ou is difficult, but it appears tox be south of the modern Chien-shui[8] on the Red, or Tonking River. Therefore the Eastern Ts'uan occupied a large area south of the Yang-tzü River,

---

[1] 宣城.

[2] 石城,昆州,曲轭,晋宁,喻献,安宁,龙和城.

[3] 曲靖州,弥鹿川,升麻川,步头.

[4] *Man shu*, ch. 4, p. 1a.

[5] Ibid., ch.2, p.2. 石城川，味县故地也。贞观中为朗州。开元初改为南宁州。州城即诸葛亮战处故地也。

[6] 庆符 and 长宁. Cf. p.1322, note[7].

[7] 泸西县.

[8] 建水县, i.e., of the 临安府. Concerning the identification of 步头 Cf. PELLIOT, "Deux itineraires . . .", *BEFEO* 4. 138.

from the I-pin[1] districts south nearly to the borders of French Tonking.

The Ts'uan have usually been identified as Lolo. The Eastern Ts'uan were undoubtedly Lolo, as can be seen from the description in the *Man shu*, but the Western Ts'uan appear to have been different. They belong to the group of White Barbarians, and were different linguistically and culturally from the Eastern Ts'uan. During the latter part of the T'ang period, both Ts'uan were under the rule of the Nan-chao state. The Nan-chao king Ko-lo-feng (A. D. 748-79) forced 20000 families of the Western Ts'uan to migrate to the Yung-chang area. The Eastern Ts'uan dispersed into the mountains and escaped a similar fate. Somewhat later they spread over the area formerly occupied by the Western Ts'uan.[2]

The problem is the origin of the term Ts'uan. The Western Ts'uan claimed that their ancestor came from the An-i[3] district of Shensi during the Ch'in period. This is a tradition which does not appear to fit the facts. From the 3rd Century A. D. the Ts'uan were among the ruling clans of the Yunnan-Kueichou area. When Chu-ko Liang made his expedition into Yunnan, he moved 10000 families of the Black Ch'iang[4] into Ssüch'uan, and he divided the remainder of

---

① 宜宾.

② *Man shu*, ch. 4, pp.2a-2b. 阁罗凤遣昆川城者杨牟利以兵围胁西爨，徙二十余万户于永昌城。乌蛮以言语不通，多散林谷，故得不徙...乌蛮种类，稍稍复振，后徙居西爨故地。Cf. also *Hsin T'ang shu*, 222B, p. 11.

③ *Hsin T'ang shu*, ch. 222B, p. 10. 西爨自云本安邑人，七世祖晋南宁太守，中国乱遂王蛮中。The *Yünnan t'ung chih*, ch. 189, p.21, says there was no such title as 南宁太守 under the chi. The place-name 南宁 was first used under the Ch'i and Liang dynasties, but the title of the office was 刺史, not 太守.

④ 黑羌.

the population among the larger clans, among which was the Ts'uan.[1] Possibly this clan became so powerful that the whole population came to be known to the Chinese by its name. Whether the ruling family was descended from Chinese or not it is impossible to say, for the tradition means very little. The name Ts'uan was not used after the T'ang period.

The Lolo of Yunnan have usually been identified with the Ts'uan, and the Lolo script was called Ts'uan script in the older Chinese books. But it is hardly correct to identify all the Ts'uan with the Lolo. Ts'uan was a political designation, used from the 4th to the 10th Century A.D., during which time it may have been applied to many quite different aboriginal tribes. The Eastern Ts'uan were nominally under the control of Nan-chao, but enjoyed considerable independence.

During the Ming period, the area in Ssüch'uan occupied by the Eastern Ts'uan during the T'ang period was known as the four Chün-min-fu,[2] Wu-meng, Wu-sa, Tung-ch'uan, and Chen- hsiung.[3] According to the Ming history,[4] these peoples were descended from the Lolo tribe called Wu-meng during the T'ang period. The history also states that under the Sung, a chief was given the title of prince of Wu-meng, and that the Mongols established chiefs called Hsüan-wei-shih in these places. Wu-sa was the most important, and a special

---

[1]   *Hua yang kuo chi*, ch. 4, p. 6.[诸葛亮]...移南中劲卒青羌万余家于蜀，为五部。所当无前，军号飞...，分其羸弱配大姓焦雍晏爨孟量毛李为部曲。

[2]   军民府.

[3]   乌蒙，乌撒，东川，镇雄.

[4]   *Ming shih*, ch. 311, pp.4-5. 东川芒部诸夷种类皆出于罗罗。厥后子姓蕃衍，各立疆场，乃异其名曰东川，乌撒，乌蒙，芒部，禄肇，水西。无事则互起争端，有事则相为救援。

official was stationed there. At the beginning of the Ming period, the area was conquered by the Chinese, but never very successfully, as the people always aided their relatives of Shui-hsi in their rebellions.

Wu San-kuei conquered this area for the Manchus, although they were obliged to reconquer it after his rebellion. During the Yung-cheng period (1723-35), the energetic viceroy O Erh-t'ai[1] recommended the abolition of the regime of local self-government under native chiefs, and a Chinese administration was substituted. As a result, all the Lolo chiefs rose in revolt, there were sanguinary battles before the rebellion could be suppressed, and large numbers of Lolo were killed. For this reason there are few Lolo remaining in this area at present.

Lastly, there is the area of the independent Lolo. To the northwest of the Ta-liang shan is the Chien-ch'ang Valley.[2] During the Han period, the northern part of this valley was called Chiung-tu.[3] In the sixth year of Yüan-t'ing (109 B. C.) it was organized as the Yüeh-sui-chün,[4] and this name continued in use under the Later Han, Chin, Liu Sung and Ch'i dynasties. The Later Chou changed the name to Hsi-ning chou,[5] and still later it was made Yen-chou.[6] In the third year of Hsien-t'ung (863), the district was annexed by Nan-chao, who first used the name Chien-ch'ang. The Nan-chao authorities brought in Black

---

[1] Cf. *Ch'ing shih kao*, 土司传，三，pp.1-2 and 四，pp.1-5.

[2] 建昌.

[3] 邛都.

[4] 越西郡.

[5] 西宁州.

[6] 严州.

and White Barbarians. It is not known whether these were Lolo. During the Sung period, the state of Ta-li which had succeeded Nan-chao lost control of the area, in which civil wars raged. When the Mongols conquered Yunnan, the chiefs of the area surrendered. The Ming annexed the area, and changed the name.[1]

The Chien-ch'ang Valley is followed by the main route to Southwest China and beyond. It was the route of the expedition of Chu-ko Liang, and all dynasties have endeavored to keep it open. The Han emperors were not overly successful in this, and even the T'ang could keep the road open for only a short period. The Lolo in the valley and in the districts among the foothills were subdued by the Chinese, and Chinese administrative districts established among them.

But there is little information concerning the Lolo of the Ta-liang mountains. Presumably they remained independent until almost the end of the Ch'ing period. During the Yung-cheng (1723-35) and Chia-ch'ing (1796-1820) periods efforts were made to subdue them, but apparently they were not successful. Lolo parties constantly raided the Chinese colonists, many of whom were carried away as slaves. About 1870, the Chinese general CHOU Ta-wu[2] marched into the heart of the Ta-liang mountains and set free thousands of captives. In the present century, the energetic general CHAO Erh-feng[3] proposed to conquer completely the mountain Lolo. The expedition was

---

[1]　This was frequently done after a change of dynasties. The new name was 建昌卫.

[2]　周达武.

[3]　赵尔丰.

postponed by the death of Kuang-hsü in 1908. Shortly after this, the Lolo killed a British missionary, and CHAO Erh-feng attacked them both from the northeast and the southwest. The two forces met in the mountains, and Chao was able to build a road across the range, along which garrisons were maintained. He prohibited the Black Lolo from keeping slaves. The government by native chiefs was abolished, and Chinese administrative districts were established. So at the very end of the Ch'ing dynasty, the independent Lolo country, made famous by Baber and d'Ollone, was finally subdued.[1]

This historical sketch of the three important areas occupied by the Lolo gives what can be gleaned about them from Chinese sources. A word may be said about certain peculiar features of Lolo culture.

With the exception of the families of chiefs, the Lolo are less advanced in material culture than their neighbors. They are semi-pastoral, but do not milk their cows. Agriculture is left to the slaves where these exist, and these can hardly be called Lolo. Their houses are huts of rammed earth, covered with fir planks and interlaced with bamboo strips. There is practically no house- hold furniture, and the only utensils are a few turned wooden bowls, bamboo baskets, and iron pans.

They appear to know no condiments except salt, which is a great delicacy. Their only textiles are a rough and primitive hempen fabric, and the tough felt used for cloaks. They appear to have neither money, weights, nor measures.

---

[1] Cf. *Ch'ing shih kao*, 土司传二, pp. 1-7.

There is no pottery, and this characteristic they share with the ancient peoples of this area, for the *Man shu* says that the Nan-chao had no pottery, but used containers of gold, silver, and bamboo.[1]

The felt cloak of the Lolo is not found among any of the surrounding peoples. The texture of the felt is rough and uneven, and the color is brown, blue, or the natural tint of the wool. Both men and women wear the cloak, winter and summer. It is mattress, blanket, and even roof. The antiquity of the cloak is attested by the *Man shu.*

"All the barbarians wear felt cloaks. Their other garments are similar to those of the Chinese, but the hoods are different. The Nan-chao used red damask (?) and others, gray. Their custom was to use a piece of cloth with the edges of one corner sewed together like a horn. Into this was stuffed a wooden cone. The device was then fixed to the back of the head, the hair twisted round it, and the remaining cloth wrapped about the head. Only the rulers and high officials were allowed to wear this. The lower officials and the warriors wore their hair in a knot on the forehead, and were not allowed to wear the hood. All wear felt cloaks, and go barefoot."[2]

The Nan-chao of the T'ang period spoke a Shan language. The modern Shan do not use felt in general, or felt cloaks in particular.

The well-known Lolo " horn " is a method of wearing the hair, which is

---

[1]　*Man shu*, ch. 8, p. 2b. 南诏家食用金银，其余官将则用竹单。贵者饭以箸，不匙。贱者，搏之而食。

[2]　Ibid.

thrown forward, twisted, and coiled on the forehead until it resembles a horn. No other group in Southwest China dresses the hair in this way, yet the *Man shu* shows that lower officials and warriors of the Nan-chao did this, which makes it probable that the bulk of the Nan-chao armies was formed of Lolo.

Among the Naga tribes of Manipur there is one group which dresses the hair in a horn similar to that of the Lolo.[1] As no other Asiatic groups wear the hair in this way, such a coincidence can hardly be accidental, and there is said to be a Lolo tradition that their ancestors came from that direction. Such questions cannot be settled with certainty.

Two other features of Lolo culture may be briefly mentioned, the disposal of the dead, and the cult of the ancestors.

All peoples are conservative about religion in general, and about the disposal of the dead in particular. The Lolo are surrounded by Buddhist peoples, but Buddhist beliefs and practices have made practically no impression upon them. Christian missionaries have had practically no effect. Since the Lolo have resisted all external religious influences in the past, it is probable that their method of disposal of the dead is of great antiquity. In contrast to other aboriginal peoples of China, the Lolo practice cremation. This was noticed by the Chinese as early as the T'ang period, for the *Man-shu* says, " The Wu-man (Black Barbarians) do not bury their dead. They burn a corpse three days after death,

---

[1]  T. C. HODSON, *The Naga Tribes of Manipur*, 1911, pp. 29-30. See also the plate facing p. 21. But if the twisted hair be considered a queue, there have been many northern peoples sharing this feature. Cf. Kurakichi SHIRATORI, " The Queue among the Peoples of North Asia," *Mem. Toyo Bunko*, No. 4.

and cover the ashes with soil. They keep only the ears. The Nan-chao keep the ears in golden vases, which are placed in a silver box and stored in a special room. At each season they are taken out and sacrifices are offered to them. The common people use copper and iron vases."[1]

The Wu-man included the Eastern Ts'uan who were the ancestors of the Lolo. The Lolo do not practice the preservation of the ears, but the practice of cremation is corroborated by Marco Polo, who visited the region. " When any of them die, the bodies are burnt, and then they taken the bones and put them in little chests. These are carried up the mountains and placed in great caverns, where they are hung up in such wise that neither man nor beasts can come to them."[2]

The Nan-chao are generally considered to have been Shan, although it should be noticed that Shan is a linguistic group, rather than a race. The modern Shan do not cremate their dead. In spite of Buddhist and Hindu influences, they bury them. This might indicate that culturally the Nan-chao were closer to the Lolo than to the modern Shan who are considered their direct descendants, or that the bulk of the Nan-chao subjects were Lolo. The *Man shu* also says that " the White Barbarians bury their dead like the Chinese, and plant trees about the graves."[3] This indicates that the terms

---

[1]　*Man shu*, chüan 8.

[2]　E. C. BABER, " China in Some of Its Physical and Social Aspects," *Proceedings of the Royal Geographic Society*, n. s., V, 1883, pp. 445-48, identifies the Coloman of Marco Polo with the Lolo, in which he is probably correct.

[3]　*Man shu*, chüan 8.

black and white involved differences in culture.

The T'ang history says that the barbarians revered the ghosts (ancestors?), and had " ghost lords " who ruled over them. Each family annually contributed an ox or a goat, which were sacrificed at the home of the " ghost lord." When they summoned the ghosts or sent them away, they carried arms, and at that time they made raids, or avenged their wrongs.[1]

All this historic and descriptive information may be brought to bear upon the theories of the origin of the Lolo.

The earliest theory is that of Lacouperie,[2] who held that the Lolo were a southeastern extension of the peoples of northeastern Tibet. He connects the Lolo with the Jung and Chiang of the old Chinese records. As he offers no substantial evidence to support this theory, it can be discussed more fully with that of Ting.

Vial and others connect the Lolo with the Tibetans on linguistic evidence. Unfortunately for this theory, such evidence is chiefly the comparison of a limited number of selected words. Our knowledge of the linguistic principles of the Sinitic group of languages has hardly advanced to the point where exact generalizations can be made upon the relations between these different languages.

V. K. Ting is the first investigator to place his hypothesis upon a physical

---

[1]　*Hsin T'ang shu*, lieh chüan 147. The same custom was formerly practiced by the Yakut. W. JOCHELSON, "Kumiss Festivals of the Yakut," *Boas Anniversary* Volume, 1906, p. 263.

[2]　Op. cit., pp. 480-81. VIAL, *Les Lolos*, 1898. See also J. DENIKER, *Races of Man*, 1900, pp. 381-82, and H. R. DAVIES, *Yunnan*, p. 337.

and historical basis.[①] During his prospecting tours in Yunnan, he was able to take measurements of a number of Lolo. The prevailing cephalic index that he obtained is dolicocephalic. He concludes that " historically the Lolo, in association with the Ch'iang, formed an important people in northwestern Ssüch'uan, Kokonor, and South Turkestan. In the last place they inter-married with the Iranian people known as the Yüeh-chih. The Iranian element may have found its way into the Lolo through the Ch'iang."[②] Ting appears to use the term Iranian in the same sense as Ripley.

In a later publication,[③] Ting said that the subjects he examined were mostly White Lolo, so that his findings are not surprising. The dolicocephalic factor corresponds to Dixon's Caspian type, which is the secondary dominant factor among the White Lolo.[④] As the White Lolo are a mixed group subject to the Black Lolo, the dolicocephalic factor may represent a strain of the older population of Mon-Khmer peoples.[⑤] Dixon based his analysis on Legendre's measurements, in which the brachycephalic factor prevails. The number of subjects examined by Ting and Legendre was not sufficient in either case for their evidence to be considered conclusive.

---

① 　V. K. TING, " Native Tribes of Yunnan," *China Medical Journal*, March, 1921.

② 　Ibid.

③ 　" Man yu san chi " (Travels in Yunnan), *Independent Review*, Nos. 34-36, 1933.

④ 　R. B. DIXON, *Racial History of Man*, p. 281. L. KILBORN and R. MORSE said to have made measurements of Lolo recently, but the results have not yet been published.

⑤ 　The Pnong, Moi, Kha, and other Mon-Khmer speaking peoples of Southeast Asia show a strong dolicocephalic factor. Cf. DIXON, op. cit., p. 276.

It is far-fetched to attribute the supposed Caucasoid features of the Lolo to an infusion of Iranian blood from the Yüeh-chih. The racial affinities of the latter are still a matter of dispute, but the most common opinion is that they were Indo-Scythians.[1] The fragmentary information of the *Ch'ien Han shu*[2] indicates that they were a nomadic people of Eastern Turkestan. About the end of the 3rd Century B.C. they were defeated by the Hsiung-nu. A part of the group migrated westward, conquering the Tocharians who had overthrown the Greek state of Bactria. About the beginning of the Christian era, they conquered northwestern India, where they were known as the Kushanas. A section of the Yüeh-chih did not migrate, but moved southward, mixing with the Ch'iang. After the Chinese had driven the Hsiung-nu from Eastern Turkestan, the Little Yüeh-chih were induced to return to their original locality.

It is now customary to attribute nearly everything in Central Asia during this period to the Yüeh-chih; but it is very uncertain whether they ever reached Ssüch'uan. The migration of the Lolo during historic times has been northward, and if the Yeh-lang were ancestors of the Lolo, they were already established at the time the Yüeh-chih began to migrate.

Buxton's theory[3] is based on Ting's measurements and on information

---

[1]  For a recent discussion of this point, see Sten KONOW, " Kharoshthi Inscriptions," *Corpus Inscriptionum Indicarum* 2, Pt. I, 1929, pp. xlix-lxxxii.

[2]  *Ch'ien Han shu*, chüan 95, translated by A. WYLIE, *Jour. of the Royal Anthropological Institute* 9, 1880, pp. 53-96.

[3]  BUXTON, *The Peoples of Asia*, pp.156-57.

supplied by Jamieson. The latter holds that the Lolo came from the Tibetan-Burman border, on the ground that they are the only people of southwestern China frequently associated with the horse.[①] Therefore Buxton connects the Lolo with his Nesiot race, corresponding to Elliot SMITH'S Brown race, a group reaching across to Western Asia and the Mediterranean. This theory differs from that of Ting in that the connection is southward around the Himalaya foothills. Although Legendre's measurements are more important than Ting's, neither Ting nor Buxton seem to have considered them, and Buxton does not appear to be familiar with the historical facts of the situation.

The traditions of the Lolo point to their origin on the Tibetan-Burman border. When they first came in contact with the Chinese, they were in northeastern Yunnan. An interesting report has come from this district. In the Chao-tung area are many earthen mounds, conspicuous on the plain. "Some of these have been opened, and in them have been found rough, unhewn stones, apparently placed as door-frames, and burned bricks of an unusually large size and marked with a peculiar pattern."[②] It is too early to speculate whether this has any bearing on Lolo origins. The Lolo of this area have a tradition that the mounds represent a pre-Lolo population, the P'u, whom the Lolo destroyed.

Lolo traditions indicate that they are not autochthonous to the Ta-liang mountains. They regard themselves as deprived of the rich valleys by the

---

① JAMIESON, " The Aborigines of Western China," *China Journal of Art and Science* 1, p. 381.

② C. C. HICKS, " The Nou Su," *Chinese Recorder* 41, p. 211.

Chinese,[1] and their retreat to the mountains continued as late as 1727. While traditions cannot be taken too seriously, it seems safe to say that the Lolo were not the original inhabitants of their present locality.

The division of black and white may have some bearing on the problem. The use of the term black to indicate superior descent existed among the peoples of northeastern Asia. The Western Liao kingdom founded by Yeh-lu Ta-shih called itself Black Kitan, indicating that the people were the original Kitan. The Mongols were at first divided into black and white, Genghiz Khan, along with his generals and ministers, belonging to the Black Mongols.[2] This would indicate connections with northern culture. The use of felt by the Lolo, and the ghost cult of the ancient Ts'uan point in the same direction. No suggestions can be made about the practice of cremation. It cannot be attributed to Buddhist or Hindu influence, and the use of fire in apotropaic rites is widespread.

The lack of pottery points toward the north, for there have been few historic peoples who lacked pottery, and among these are the Mongols. It is significant that pottery is not found among the Lolo, since they are surrounded by pottery-using peoples.

On the other hand, the Lolo, like the Chinese, are not milk-users. The peoples of Asia may be divided into two groups, each occupying contiguous territories, the milk-users, and those who do not use milk. To the milk-using group belong the

---

[1] E. C. BABER, " Travels and Researches in the Interior of China," *Royal Geographic Society, Supplementary Papers*, I, p. 121. D'OLLONE, op. cit., p. 107.

[2] [omitted].

peoples of northwestern Asia, the Tungus, Mongols, Turks, Tibetans, Hindus, Iranians, the peoples of the Near-East, and some of the Paleo- Asiatics. The Chinese, Japanese, Shan, Lolo, and most of the Mon-Khmer peoples do not use milk. Under such circumstances, the non-use of milk by the Lolo cannot be accidental. They possess herds but do not milk them. Had the Lolo originally been a pastoral people, it is very unlikely that such an important cultural trait would have been lost.[1] Chinese influence can hardly be considered in this connection, and the Lolo generally are unsympathetic to external influences.

There are other traits that point to the south, such as the practice of going barefoot, the use of poison arrows, and the Lolo " horn." On the other hand, the cross-bow, which is a typical weapon in southeastern Asia, is not found among the Lolo.

This discussion leaves the conclusion uncertain. Some facts point in one direction, some in another. The existing theories are based upon one of these sets of facts only. When the complexity of the ethnic situation in southeastern Asia is considered, as well as the lack of investigations made by trained observers, it is apparent that a great deal of work must be done before accurate classifications can be made.

[ 与 J. K. Shryock 合作，原载 *Harvard Journal of Asiatic Studies*,

Vol.3, No.2(1938), pp.103−127 ]

---

[1]　The Yakut still retain cattle under most unfavorable circumstances. JOCHELSON, op. cit., pp. 257-71.

# THE LOLO OF CHINA:
## Their History and Cultural Relations

The Lolo are one of the most important and numerous of the non Chinese peoples in the South-west of China. This interesting people long ago attracted the attention of anthropologists and explorers, and a considerable amount of material has been written about them. Most of this information deals with their present state of affairs, or about those who have acquired a large amount of Chinese culture. No serious attempt has been made to correlate these materials with the old Chinese records and the historical peoples who have successively inhabited this area. Such a study is imperative, because without a knowledge of their history, the present amount of information accumulated can hardly be intelligibly interpreted. But such an approach is beset with difficulties from the very beginning. The old Chinese records are sporadic and scattered, and themselves need to be coordinated and worked into a systematic whole.

The Lolo have been in their present habitat for at least more than a thousand years. Being a vigorous and warlike people, they have always constituted the upper stratum of the aboriginal population whereever they went. They occupied the key position in the movements of peoples in this part of China. Although they possess a script they have no history of their own.[①] The only source of information available concerning their past comes from the Chinese side. This makes the Chinese sources, although meagre and sometimes inaccurate, especially valuable.

The present study does not attempt to give a full account of the Lolo culture as a whole, but rather to treat specifically those topics from which historical comparisons can be drawn. Not all the materials here used are utilized for the first time, but all of them are examined in a new light, and often times with corrections of older misinterpretations. Special stress is laid on the historical reconstruction of the movements of peoples in Lololand and their connection with the Lolo.

---

[①]　The Lolo Script has attracted a great deal of attention among philologists. It is pictographic, some what modelled after the Chinese but lacks the elaborate laws of ideation. According to Chinese sources, it was invented by a Lolo named A-bi about 550 A.D., but the Lolo has three different myths concerning its invention. A-bi called it *Wei-shu*, e.g. "standerd script"; the Chinese called it *Ts'uan Wen*, e.g. "script of the Ts'uan". It is essentially a religious writing only intelligible to the pi-mo (their medicine men). Even the pi-mo of one tribe cannot read the script of the pi mo of another tribe, as shown by V. K. Ting in his *Man yu san chi* and D' Ollone in his *In Forbidden China*, pp. 106-107.

# The Origin of the Name "Lolo"

The name Lolo first came into use during the Yuan dynasty (1280-1368 A.D.). It was soon identified with the Lulu, a tribe of the Eastern Tsuan barbarians of the fifth to the ninth centuries A.D., Lolo being a corruption of Lulu.[1] Whether this identification is correct or not, we have no means of knowing, but the term Lulu has not been used since the Yuan period. The terms used by the Lolo for themselves vary considerably from tribe to tribe at present. The variations of the first syllable usually lie within the phonetic complex where the initial consonant is either *y* or *n* but rarely *l*. The following vowel fluctuates from the range of all the five vowels *a e i o u*. The second syllable is usually *so* or *su* with a few variations, and sometimes omitted altogether.[2]

The earliest interpretation of this term was given by Terrien de Lacouperie. In his *Language of China before the Chinese*,[3] he says: "Their name, formerly Lo-kwei in Chinese, altered into Lulu, and now Lolo or Kolo, had become a by-name for many of the mixed tribes which in the south west provinces owe their origin to the intermingling with tribes of the

---

[1] *Nan chao yeh shih*, book II, pp. 24-25. See also Pelliot, Deux itineraires de chine en inde, *BEFEO*, IV, 1904, p. 137.

[2] Here are some of the variations: No-su, Nou-su, Ngo-su, Ne-su,Nei-su, No-su, No, Na, Lei-su, etc. In Ssuchuan they are called *Man-tzu*, or more courteously *Man-chia*. In south Yunnan the Shahs call them *Myen*.

[3] *Transactions of the Philological Society*, 1885-7, pp.480-481.

Taic and Mon and other stocks. The variants in their name have come from the influence of the Taic Shan phonology, which makes *h* or *k* equivalent to *l* in its adaptation of foreign words beginning with the latter consonant." This linguistic interpretation is very misleading, because the nickname Lo-kwei (kwei means ghost in Chinese) is derogatory and of much more recent date than either the name Lulu or Lolo; and the *ko* is a mispronunciation of the Chinese character *lo* by European scholars.[①]

Paul Vial's interpretation is different though naive.[②] He says that the Lolo in Ssuchuan called themselves *No*, and those in Yunnan called themselves *Na*, that the Chinese transcripted it with their nearest character and doubled the sound for the sake of euphony. This can scarcely be the case. If the Lolo called themselves *No* or *Na*, the most probable thing for the Chinese to do was to call them *No-man, Na-man*, or *No-yi* or *Na-yi* (*man* and *yi* mean barbarians) as is usually done with all the south western tribal names. As a matter of fact, in the earlier Chinese records it was actually written *Lulu-man* or *Lolo-man* and later contracted into *Lo-yi*, etc.

Lietard's explanation of the derivation of the term is much more plausible.[③] He considered *Lolo* as a corruption of *No-so*, a term most of the Lolo use for themselves. According to Lietard *no* means black and *so* means

---

① 　The Chinese transcription is sometimes differently rendered. 猡 猡, 猓 猓 sometimes 猓 猡. 猓 is often mispronounced as *ko*.

② 　*Les Lolos* ... 1898.

③ 　*Au Yunnan, les Lo-lo P'o*, 1913.

man in the Lolo language. So *no so* means black man. But according to Shirokogoroff,[1] the meaning of these syllables do not always agree. For example in the Bus. dialect, the Lolo call themselves *no-so*, whereas black is *no*, and no means five. In the Ni dealect the Lolo call themselves *ni*, and black is *ne*. As to *so*, no such meaning as man is found in the Bus. dialect. Although these syllables are near enough, their variations make the etymological derivation very uncertain.

Furthermore Shirokogoroff conjectured that the name may be of a political origin (like Manchu), or that it may have been given to them by their neighbors (like Tungus), or that it may be a name handed down from great antiquity.[2] He suggested these three possibilities but hesitated to make a decision. To assume a political origin is most improbable. The Lolo were never a close-knit political entity. There is also no ground for assuming that the name was given to them by their neighbors, as the name they used to call themselves is too close to it.

As we know the name was in use nearly eight hundred years ago, we have to make allowance for the variations in the language of this isolated people. We must also remember that *Lolo* is purely a Chinese transcription. For the non-phonetic Chinese characters used phonetically, we must also make allowance for the inconsistencies involved. Taking all these factors

---

[1] *Phonetic Notes on a Lolo Dialect and Consonant L. Academia Sinica, Bul*. Vol. I, pt.2, p.183.

[2] Op. cit. p.184.

into consideration and together with the closeness of the Lolo term they used for themselves, it is fair to assume that the term is not of foreign origin. Its etymological derivation is obscure. Lietard's explanation failed to take into account the fact that most of the Lolo who called themselves *No-so* are not Black Lolo only, but also White Lolo. It has been remarked that the Lolo do not like to be called by this name. This is undoubtedly due to the fact that the term is sometimes used contemptuously in the mouth of the Chinese. They do not object to being called *Man-chia* or *Yi-chia* (*man* and *yi* mean barbarians, no better than Lolo in the Chinese sense), because the word *chia* is a courteous term used in address among the dialects of west China.[1]

## Present Distribution of the Lolo

Before going on to give a reconstruction of Lolo history, a few words should be said about the extent of the area they occupy. It is important because it will be the decisive factor in our choice of the descriptions from

---

[1]　E. C. Hicks, a missionary, gives another interpretation of the name Lolo. The Lolo used a bamboo basket about the size of a duck's egg in worshipping their ancestors. This ancestral basket is called *Lolo* by the Lolo themselves. So Hicks advanced the theory that the term Lolo, given to the No-so, "is a contemptuous nickname given to them by the Chinese in reference to their peculiar method of venerating their ancestors". This interpretation is followed by other missionary writers, such as S.C.C. Jarke in his *Among the Tribes of South west China*, Jamieson gives another story by quoting Chang Ying, a Chinese writer of the early 19th century. The Lolo were descended from a *Kolo* ape, and afterwards turned into Lolo. This is entirely unhistorical. (See C. E. Jamieson, *The Aborigines of Western China, China Journal of Arts and Science*. I. p.376.seq. )

Chinese sources about the peoples who occupied the Lolo territory successively in history. Only those who have been actually in this region will be examined and comparisons drawn.

The present population of the Lolo is estimated by various writers to be about three millions.[1] This number is not based on actual count and its reliability is very questionable. They are scattered over the mountainous regions of Yunnan and southwest Ssuchuan. To the west they reach the Burmese border. To the east they have penetrated into the western districts of Kueichou. To the south they have spread into the Ssu-mao districts of Yunnan well below Lat. 23°. In a northeastern thrust from northern Yunnan along the Ta liang (great cold) mountain ranges following the northeastern course of the Yangtzu River, they reach as far north as Chia-ting and Ya-chou. This narrow strip of land more than 200 miles long and less than 100 miles broad is extremely rugged and wooded and is known as the home land of the independent Lolo. Geographically the Lolo seem to be intrusive here, because on all three sides they are surrounded by non-Lolo tribes. The Tibetans, Sifan and certain Miao tribes are found on the west, Sifan on the north, and Miao on the southeast. This region from early Han times was known under the name of Chiung tu, Kung pu and Yueh sui and inhabited by various tribes which we shall deal with later.

---

[1] Terrien de Lacouperie,op.cit. p.479; Yang Chen-chih. *A Brief Account of the Lolo, Ling-nan Journal*, Vol. I, pp.134-152.

Immediately south of it are the Lolo who are under Chinese control but governed by their own chiefs. This includes the greater part of Yunnan and western parts of Kueichou. It must be understood that the area is not exclusively inhabited by the Lolo. The lower valleys are settled by Chinese immigrants and frequently interspersed with Miao and Shan villages. The Lolo are essentially a mountain people. They dread the lower valleys and especially the humidity and the lassitude of lower altitudes.

Physiographically this whole Lolo region is a southeastern extension of the Tibetan Plateau and the Himalaya ranges. It is traversed by the upper courses of the Mekong river and the Yangtzu with its tributaries. The mountainous nature of the country makes these rivers full of rapids and boulders which renders navigation impossible for any distance. The climate is temperate but quite rigorous in winter.

## Early History of Lololand

China has long been in close contact with the part of the country occupied at present by the Lolo, and wars have been incessant with the peoples of the region since the middle of the first millennium B.C. The failure of the ancient records to give any notice to such a vigorous and warlike people as the Lolo is rather striking. This is probably why d'Ollone thought the Lolo only became formidable during the last few centuries.[1] But one suspects that the Lolo are late comers to their present habitat, for otherwise the silence of the early Chinese records is inexplicable.

The surrounding tribes, which the Chinese called barbarians, have always played a conspicuous part in China's dynastic wars. So in the struggle between the Chou (B.C.1122-249) and the Shang (B.C.1766-1121) for the supremacy of China, a part of the aboriginal people of Ssuchuan and Yunnan were used by Wu Wang (B.C.1122-1114) the actual founder of the Chou dynasty. In the speech at Mu, as recorded in the Canon of History, he says: "...o men of Yung, Shuh, Keang, Maou, Wei, Lu, Peng and P'u, lift up your lances, join your shields, raise your spears, I have a speech to make."[2] The P'u became well known in early Chinese history and have been identified as inhabitants of Yunnan. [3] They were known later under the name Pai P'u, or the Hundred P'u.[4] The name P'u is probably a generic name for all the ancient peoples inhabiting this area. In works of the early Christian era,[5] different tribes of the P'u were described, such as the Ch'iu-liao P'u; the Tailed P'u having tails like the turtle's; the Mu-mien P'u, cultivating the cotton tree (mu-mien); the Wên-mien P'u, who tatooed their faces; the Chih

---

[1]    *In Forbidden China.*

[2]    *The Chinese Classics*, Legge's Translation ,vol .III, part II, pp.301-302.

[3]    Ibid., see Commentary.

[4]    *Yunnan Tung chih, Nan man chih,* Books 172-190. A little information may be found in English in G.E. Gerini, *Researches on Ptolemy's Geography of Eastern Asia*, 1909, AsiaTie Soc Monographs, No.1, PP.804-805.

[5]    Such as the *Hua Yang Kuo chih*; and such later works as the *Tung tien*, and others.

-kou P'u who pierced their lips, knocked out their teeth and went naked; the Hei-po P'u, who were much like the modern P'o-jên. Some are described as cannibals, others as piercing their breasts or having elongated ears. The tails of the Tailed P'u may be some kind of caudiform appendage like certain tribes of the modern Nagas. These descriptions may be in the main inaccurate, but there is not the slightest indication of Lolo traits. The modern P'u-man of Yunnan are regarded as the remnants of the ancient P'u.[1]

These peoples were in constant contact with the Chinese border states. In the year 611 B.C., the P'u threatened the powerful state of Ch'u and the latter contemplated removing their capital in order to avoid their onslaught.[2] But as a matter of fact the Ch'u always considered this region as their legitimate southern territory. [3]

Toward the fourth and third centuries B.C. we have more reliable historical data. Chuang Ch'iao of the State of Ch'u led an expeditionary force up the Yangtzu River, finally conquered T'ien (the region surrounding the modern capital of Yunnan province) and annexed it to Ch'u.[4] While he was on the expedition its rival state Chin annexed Shu (modern Ssuchuan province) and Pa (modern eastern Ssuchuan and western Hupeh provinces),

---

[1]　*Yunna Tung Chih*, op. cit.; and Davies, H.R., *Yunnan*, 1909, p.375.

[2]　*Tso chuan*, Legge's tr.p.273.

[3]　Ibid., p.624.

[4]　Wylie, tr. *JRAI*, Vol. 9, 1880, pp.53-96.

and Chuang Ch'iao's retreat was cut off.[1] He was obliged to settle down with his men and made himself king of the barbarians by assuming their garb and adopting their customs. Lietard regarded Chuang Ch'iao as a naturalized Lolo king, but there is no reason for regarding the people Chuang Ch'iap conquered as Lolo.[2]

During the time of the Former Han dynasty (B.C.206 Wylie, tr.A.D.23), the country conquered by Chuang Ch'iao evolved into the Kingdom of T'ien. To its east rose the Kingdom of Yeh-lang (the modern district of Chu-Ch'in, e.g. the Northeast of Yunnan province and West of Kueichou province). To the north in the Chien-chang valley was a people called Chiung-tu (the very home of the modern independent Lolo). T'ien and Yeh-lang were kingdoms of considerable size and power. They even asked the Han emperor's envoys such questions as "Whose kingdom is bigger, the Han emperor's or mine?" Intercourse between these kingdoms and the Han emperors was close, and not long later all were annexed to China.[3] There is nothing to indicate that these peoples were Lolo. The general mass of population seems to be the P'u tribes, organized under Chinese leadership.

A little north of the Chiung tu tribes (in modern Ya-chou, Ssuchuan

---

[1] Ibid. And also see Chi Li, *Formation of the Chinese People*, pp. 240-241, how Chin annexed Shu and the interesting debate which took place in the Chin court concerning this matter.

[2] Lietard, *Au Yunnan*, 1913. Rocher mistook Chuang Ch'iao for two different persons as his name mentioned in the *Chien Han shu* and the *Hou Han shu* is slightly different. Rocher: TP,X, 1899, p.15.

[3] Wylie, tr., op. cit.

province) was a tribe named Bair lang (in Mandarin P'ai-lang, means white wolf) during the Later Han dynasty (A.D. 25-220). This tribe submitted to the Chinese and in appreciation of the Han emperors' graces, they offered a song in which the original sounds were transcripted.[1] In a comparative study of this piece of song, Mr. Wang Ching-ju discovered that it has some bearing on the name of Yeh-lang.[2] He reasoned to explain why a tribe in the north was called Bait-lang (white wolf) and a tribe far south of it called Yeh-lang (night groom or man). There must be some connection. So he took Lietard's interpretation of *No-So* as black man and inferred that *yeh* is synonymous with *dark*, and *dark* is synonymous with *black*. *So* or *sou*, according to him, can be evolved from *sian. Lang*, in ancient times, could be pronounced *sian*. Proved to his own satisfaction, so Yeh lang is easily equated with Lolo. Such a linguistic somersault is entirely unwarrantable, but circumstantially there is some possible connection between Yeh-lang and Lolo. Geographically the Yeh-lang area was always occupied by tribes of Lolo affinities in later times,[3] and the arrogant attitude of the Yeh-lang toward the Han emperors also suggests the independent spirit of the modern Lolo. But we shall have to wait for more evidence before such an

---

[1]　*Hou Han shu* (History of Later Han dynasty) in the section *Hsi nan yi chuan* (Southwestern barbarians).

[2]　*A Comparative Linguistic Study on the Songs of the Bair-lang Tribe, Academia Sinica*, The National Research Institute of History and Philology, Monographs No. 8, *Hsi Hsia yen chiu*(Tangut studies), pp.15-54. An English summary may be found in pages 273-4.

[3]　Later in the fifth century, it was the home of the Eastern Ts'uan.

identification is possible.

The third century A.D. witnessed the famous campaign into Yunnan by the crafty general and statesman Chu ko Liang.[1] He conquered them by force but he won so much affection from them that he is still worshipped among many of the isolated tribes. Legends about him are widespread in this area. Many aboriginal chiefs claimed institution from him. At least we know four famous families of Lolo chiefs, the Cheng, Sha, Lung and An families in Yunnan and Kwei-chow claimed such a beginning.[2] Unfortunately Chu-k'o Liang did not leave any record or description of the peoples he conquered.

Soon after this the whole area of T'ien, Yeh-lang and Chiung-tu was consolidated into a kingdom called Ts'uan.[3] The Ts'uan was divided into an Eastern Branch who called themselves Wu-man (black barbarians) occupying eastern Yunnan and extending southeastward into Kuei-chou; and a Western Branch who called themselves Pai-man (white barbarians) occupying the region diredtly west of the Wu-man until it reaches the Mekong River. The

---

①     Cheng Shou, *San kuo ch'ih* (History of the Three Kingdoms), *Biography of chu k'o Liang*. See also Rocher and Jamieson, op.cit.

②     Jamieson, op. cit. The authenticity of their claims is very hard to ascertain as Chu-k'o Liang has become a culture hero among these aborigines.

③     I, VIII. See also Barbares Ts'ouan, *BEFEO*, 8, Nos. 3-4, pp. 334-335. Gerini held that Ts'uan (or Ts'wan) is indentical with Ptolemy's Doanai. "This coincidence in location of the Ts'wan with the Doan, or t'wan, and the Kau of the Annamese historians, coupled with the fact that Ts'wan, or Doan, is the Annamese pronunciation of the Chinese term Ts'wan, is sufficient evidence to show, I think, that they really were the same people. Similar coincidences in names and location also indicate them to be identical with Ptolemy's Doanai. It is therefore pretty certain that in our author's time a conspicuous portion of this people had already advanced into Eastern Laos or Dasarna, which they held under sway." op. cit. p. 126. The Difficulty in Gerini's identification is that the Ts'uan did not come into existence during the time of Ptolemy.

Eastern Ts'Uan (Wu-man) showed strong analogies with the modern Lolo, and one of its tribes, the Lulu, has been regarded as their ancestors. This division into an Eastern and Western or White and Black, branches is not merely a dualistic social distinction because their languages are quite different and each occupies large tracts of distinct areas. Socially there is a wide gulf between them and it also may imply a racial distinction. [1]

Whence and where the Ts'uan people came and how they destroyed the kingdoms of T'ien and Yeh-lang are questions we are unable to answer at present. During the third and fourth centuries of the Christian era, the Ts'uan were on the move toward this region. Most scholars regarded them as pushing from the north southward.[2] This was most probably implied by the name of their ruling class, the Ts'uan family. So far as present evidence goes, the founding of the Ts'uan did not involve great racial dislocation.

The term Ts'uan was only a political name derived from the ruling family. The Western Ts'uan claimed that their seventh ancestor was the governor of Chien-ning (in northeastern Yun-nan) during the Ch'in dynasty (265-420 A.D.) and that their original home was in the An-yi district of Shensi. [3] This tradition led to the general misconception of the southward invasion of the Ts'uan race. From other sources,[4] it seems that the Ts'uan family was a

---

[1]　It is especially apparent in the *Man shu.*

[2]　Terrien de Lacouperie, op. cit. pp. 480-481; V.K. Ting, *Man yu san chi.*

[3]　See VIII, I.

[4]　Such as the *Hua Yang kuo chih*, and *Ssuchuan tung chih*(Gazeteer of Ssuchuan province).

well-known family of Ssuchuan and many of its members rose to high official positions during this period. This seventh ancestor of the Ts'uan, like Chuang Ch'iao , took advantage of the chaotic conditions in China proper and made himself king of the barbarians. Thus the term Ts'uan-man came into use. Although the area was ruled by the Ts'uan family, the great mass of the people were of different racial stocks, and the modern Lolo is surely one of them.[1] The Ts'uan maintained their power by acknowledging the suzerainty of China until they were weakened by inter-tribal strife, and finally were conquered by the powerful kingdom of Nan-chao.

Before giving a brief history of Nan chao, the problem of the origin of the Shan race must be solved, because the Nan-chao has been identified as a Shan Kingdom.[2] Later writers have followed Terrien de Lacouperie in placing the cradle of the Shan race in Central China, Hupeh and northwestern Ssuchuan provinces. [3] This hypothesis was further developed by E. H.

---

[1]  The modern Lolo script is called by Chinese authors *Ts'uan wên*, e.g. Ts'uan script.

[2]  The Nan-chao was identified with the Shans purely on linguistic grounds, such as the word *chao* is a Shan word for *king*, or *kingdom*. The original name of Nan-chao was Meng-shê. It was situated on the south of the other five *chao*, so it was called Nan-chao by the Chinese. Among the modern Shans, the first syllable of the son's name is taken from the last syllable of the father's name. This is exactly like the names of the Nan-cho kings, such as: Hsi-nu-lo, Lo-shen-yen, Shen-lo-pi, Pi-lo-ko, and Ko-lo-feng, etc. (See E. H. Parker, *The Old Thai or Sha Empire of Western Yunnan*, *CR*, Vol. XX, pp. 337 seq.) There are also place names in Yunnan reminiscent of Shan etymology. There are a number of Nan-chao words, especially names of governmental offices and official titles, preserved in the *Man shu* and *Nan chao yeh shih* , but they have not been scientifically examined.

[3]  Terrien de Lacouperie, op. cit. pp. 448-452; and his Cradle of the Shan Race in A.S. Colquhoun, *Amongst the Shans*, 1885 pp. xxi lv.

Parker. [1] Weighty theories about the formation of the Chinese civilization have been put forward based on this hypothesis. [2]

Terrien de Lacouperie does not give any evidence to support his theory except the case of Ai-lao. [3] According to the History of T'ang dynasty (A.D.618-906), the Nan-chao claimed descent from the Ai-lao. Nan-chao is Shan, so Ai-lao must be Shan. According to the History of Later Han dynasty (A.D.25-220), the original seat of the Ai-lao was Lao-shan. Lao-shan is situated, according to Terrien de Lacouperie's identification, at the intersection of Honan, Hupeh and An-hui provinces, and extending westward forming the boundaries of Ssu-chuan and Shen-si provinces. In the year A.D. 47, the Ai-lao descended the Chiang and Han on bamboo rafts[4] and attacked the frontier barbarians Luh-to. In A.D. 51 they surrendered their

---

[1]　op. cit. and in his *Burma* , the first few chapters.

[2]　C. W. Bishop maintains in his *Geographical Factor in the Development of the Chinese Civilization* (*Geographical Review*, Vol. 12, 1922,pp.19-41 especially p. 34) how important/apart the Shan-Taic Race contributed to the building of the Chinese civilization, practically all writers have accepted this hypothesis naively. Some have cast doubts on this hypothesis but were unable to examine the Chinese sources. Davies said, in his *Yunnan*: "Whether the Shans ever extended over the provinces of China which lie north of the Yangtze is a question that can probably never be settled. Professor Terrien de Lacouperie is of the opinion that the Shan race was formed in the mountains between Ssuchuan and Shan-hsi out of a mixture of some northern tribe akin to the Chinese with a race of Mon-Khmer stock. This may be so, but M. de Lacouperie does not appear to give any reasons for this opinion." p. 378. A. Henry (1903) who had spent many years among the Shans, postulated a southern origin of the Shans race, but he was unable to utilize the Chinese materials, so his hypothesis remains unheeded by other writers.

[3]　See p.1353,Note[4].

[4]　Terrien de Lacouperie identified the *Chiang* with the *Yangtzu River*, and the *Han* with the *Han* River, a large tributary of the Yangtzu in northern Hupeh province which takes its source in the Ssuchuan-Shensi border. This identification is entirely unwarranted.

arms to the governor of Yueh sui.[1] In A.D.78 they rebelled, but were soon put down. Finally in 629 they established the great state of Nan chao. This is the supposed origin of the Shan race and its southward migration. [2]

If we examine the case more carefully we will discover all of Terrien de Lacouperie's evidence is based on false identifications. To place the Lao-shan at the intersection of Honan, An-hui and Hupeh borders is geographically most unlikely.[3] As Lao-shan may be identified with any place, the most important place name here involved is the well known district Yueh-sui where the Ai-Lao surrendered. It is too well known to be mistaken, so Terrien de Lacouperie omitted it entirely in his discussions. [4] Supposing Lao-shan is in the north eastern Hupeh border, it is at least 1500 miles away from Yueh-sui. For a primitive tribe to migrate 1500 miles in three years with a community of 77 chiefs, 51,890 families comprising 553,711 persons, fighting their way through hostile tribes, inhospitable mountains and impassable forests, and possibly with Chinese forces pursuing them almost amounts to an impossibility. Terrien de Lacouperie must be misled by the mention of the river Chiang and Han which he identified with the Yangtzu

---

[1]    Yueh-sui was a well known administrative district in the Han dynasties, situated in the modern districts of northwest Yunnan and southwest Ssuchuan provinces.

[2]    For a full translation of the Ai-lao myth, see *Si nan man chuan* tr. by A. Wylie, *Revue d'Extreme Orient*, Vol. I, 1892. For Terrien de Lacouperie's interpretation, see the works cited in p.1340,Note[3]. The Ai-lao myth given in the *Nan-chao yeh shih* is slightly different.

[3]    See map for Terrien de Lacouperie's identification.

[4]    Terrien de Lacouperie did not mention this place. It would be irreconcilable with his hypothesis.

river and its tributary the Han river in Hupeh province. Here the Chiang and Han should be identified with the Mekong river, not the Yangtzu and the Han rivers.[1]

Lao-shan is expressly stated, in the *Man-shu*, as situated in the Yung-chang area on the upper Mekong river, near the frontier of the district of Yueh-sui in Han dynasty.[2] According to the commentary of *Nan-chao Yeh-shih*, Lao shan (sometimes Ai-lao shan) is called Tien ching shan, situated in the same area.[3] The Chiu-lung mountain, which Terrien de Lacouperie placed in the Shensi-Ssuchuan border, is south of the city of Yung-chang according to the same book.

With these place names properly identified, one can clearly see that the original home of the Shan is in Yung-chang, southwest Yunnan (Long. 99° and Lat. 25°), not in north east Hupeh, Central China (Long. 115° and Lat. 32°). The southward invasion of the Shan is only a misinterpretation and is not substantiated by fact. So far as present evidence goes, the Shan have never been in the Yangtzu valley.[4] The aboriginal peoples which the

---

[1]　See the Commentary on this passage of the *History of the Later Han Dynasty* by Shen Chin-ban.

[2]　*Man shu*, chapter 3, p.4. "...Their (the Meng-she Chao, e.g. the Nan-chao) surname is Meng. In the first year of the Chen Yüan, they submitted a letter to the governor of Chien-nan district, Wei Kao. They said originally they were descended from Sha-hu of Yung chang... " The Sha-hu here is the Sha-yi of the Ai-lao myth, who bore ten sons. The word *hu* 壺 is a misprint of *yi* 壹 because of their close resemblance.

[3]　That is the Yung-chang area. See IX, Book I,p.5, *Commentary* by Hu Wei.

[4]　This view is substantiated by the passage in the *Nan-chao yeh-shih* on the P'o-jên (e.g. one of the Chinese names for the Shah). "P'o-jên is also called Po-yi or Pai-yi. Their natare can stand the heat. Their dwellings are mostly under the bushes (so they are called Po-jên). Originally they were barberians outside of the Lan-tsang chiang (Mekong River)..." Book II, p.24.

early Chinese came into contact with were chiefly the Miao and Yao (the Pan hu race claimed to be descended from a dog ancestor) of the Mon Khmer speaking stock.[1]

---

[1] There is no indication in the Chinese records that any of the early aborigines in the Yangtzu valley can be identified with the Shan. Terrien de Lacouoerie attempts to identify the Shan with Shang (or Yin) dynasty people; it is purely popular etymology. He also identified the state ch'u in Chou dynasty as Shan. (See op. cit. pp. 410-411). "In the chronicle of Tso, already mentioned, in 664 B.C., two words are quoted in support of as interesting legend similar to others well known elsewhere. The scene is in Ts'u (i.e. Hupeh, Ts'u is the same as ch'u)"

"A male child was thrown away by his mother's orders in the marsh of Mung: there a tigress suckled him. This was witnessed by the Viscount of Yun, whilst hunting, and when he returned home in terror, his wife (whose son the child was) told him the whole affair, on which he sent for the child and had it cared for. The people of Ts'u called 'suckling' *tou* or *nou*, and 'a tiger' they called *wu tu*, hence the child was called 'Tou-wutu', and he became Tze wên, the chief minister of Ts'u."

"The nearest approximation to these words are found in the Taic-Shan vocabularies, where 'suckle or suckling' is called *dut* (Siamnese), and 'a tiger' is *htso, tso, su*, etc. The connection here suggested by these vocables is further promoted by this fact that a large proportion of the proper names of that same state of Ts'u are preceded by *tou*, which seems to be a sort of prefixed particle. This is also a peculiarity of the Tchungkia dialect of some tribes-still in existence in the southwest of China and formerly in Kiangsi, where they represented the ancient ethnic stock of the state of Ts'u. And this Tchungkia dialect is Tai-Shan to such an extent that Siamese speaking travellers could without much difficulty understand it."

The laws governing the phonetic changes of Chinese and Siamese are still not fully known. Whether *htso, tso,* or *su* are derivable from *wu-tu* is still very questionable. The ch'u people at that time (6th Century B.C.) spoke a Chinese dialect. From the literature of this period, the ch'u dialect was not much different from the other dialects spoken in other parts of China. It is most gratuitous to consider the Ch'u dialect as Shan on this flimsy evidence. The proper names of Ch'u prefixed (?) with *tou* are not more than two or three. T. de Lacouperie's statement here is an exaggeration. The Chung-chia (another local Chinese name for the Shan) as we shall show later are everywhere to the south of the Miao-yao groups. Other writers go still further. W. W. Cochrane says that the Shans "actually form one of the chief ingredients that compose the so-called Chinese race". (*Shans*, Vol. I, p. 8) Cochrane also held that "the old name of this region (Ssuchuan) was Shuh, which *looked* suspiciously like the Shan word for 'tiger', and the Shahsof Burma belong to the 'tiger tribe'. This is entirely in ignorance of the meaning and etymology of the Chinese character *shuh*. For a discussion of the language of the Ch'u, see Eduard Erkes: *Die Sprache des alten ch'u.TP*, 1930, XXVII, pp. 1-11.

Dr. Chi Li identifies the ancient states of Wu and Yueh in the lower Yangtzu valley as Shan on the ground that they practiced tattooing. As tattooing is a trait widely distributed, it is very unsafe to use it as a criterion unless it is checked by other traits. The Shans are not the only people in southeastern Asia who practiced tatooing. The moi of Indo-China also tattooed their bodies (see Henry Baudesson: *Indo-China and its Primitive*

The Chinese only came into contact with the Shan during the early Christian centuries when they came to Yunnan. This point is strongly borne out by the present stratification of aboriginal peoples in south China.[1] We find everywhere the Miao-yao group is to the north of the Shan group, along the borders of southern Kiangsi, Hunan, Kuangsi and Kueichou. The same is true in Yunnan. The Lolo, Moso and Lisu (they are closely related to each other linguistically) are everywhere found north of the Shan groups.

The formation of the Shan race seems to be quite a recent affair as the homogeniety of their language shows.[2] Their home is probably in the Yung-chang area, southwestern Yunnan, and by the beginning of the eighth century A.D. they began to spread eastward into southern Kueichou, Kuangsi and even as far east as Kuangtung, and they mingled with the Mon-Khmer peoples. Southward they pushed along the Mekong and Menam valleys driving before them the Mon-Khmer speaking peoples and finally in the thirteenth and fourteenth centuries they reached the sea at what is now Siam. This great

---

*Peoples,* p. 119). The Moi are closely related to the Miao-Yao group of Southern China by possessing the Dog-ancestor myth (see Baudesson, op. cit. pp. 105-107). Linguistically and physically they are also related. The Wu and Yueh did not resist the Chinese advance but the Nan-Chao did, so Dr. Li was troubled with his explanation of this contradictory fact: "After they had reached Yunnan, the Shans evidently determined to make a last stand against the northern invading group, although they kept on their southward migration and give rise to the modern Siamese." (*Formation of the Chinese People,* p. 258) It would be much easier to assume that the Wu and Yueh were not Shans at all.

It may be added that the ancient Wu and Yueh and the modern Shans practiced tattooing to a great extent, but the people of Ch'u were never reported to have tattooed their bodies. It further weakens the identification of Ch'u as Shan.

[1]　See map II.

[2]　A. Henry, op. cit., p.97. Cochrane, op. cit., p.7 and note.

southward movement may be due to the downfall of the Nan- chao empire.

The first Nan-Chao king Hsi-nu-lo came to the throne in the year 629 A.D. He was of quite humble origin. In later works he was claimed to be descended from an Indian king, undoubtedly due to Buddhist fabrication.[1] Hsi-nu-lo was succeeded by Lo-shen-yen (A.D.674-713), Lo-shen-yen by Shen-lo-pi (A.D.714-729), Shen-lo-pi by Pi-lo-ko (A.D.730-749). In the year A.D.732 Pi-lo-ko conquered the other five *chao* and consolidated them into one empire. He still acknowledged the suzerainty of China and received his institution from the T'ang Emperor Yuan Tsung (A.D.713-755) and was given the name Meng-kuei-yi.[2]After him followed two of the most illustrious of the Nan chao kings: Ko-lo-feng (A.D.749-779) and Yi-mao-hsun (A.D.779-809).[3] At this time the Tibetans were the most powerful nation in the west and constantly at war with China. Nan-chao shifted its allegiance, being at one time with the Chinese and at others with the Tibetans, until finally during the Sung period (A.D.960-1278) all communication was entirely stopped.

During the reign of Ko-lo-feng, he forced 20,000 families of the Western Ts'uan to migrate southward to the Yung-chang area. Some writers regarded this as the southward movement of the Karen, but we have no

---

[1] See Pelliot, *BEFEO*, IV, 1904, pp.167-168.

[2] Meaning "returning to righteousness".

[3] Imousun of E. H. Parker, see op. cit.

evidence for such an identification.[1] The Eastern Ts'uan on account of their unintelligible language, all dispersed into the forests and the deep valleys, so they escaped this general forced exodus. Later, the Eastern Ts'uan migrated and occupied the original area of the Western Ts'uan and became powerful again. [2]

Under the Nan-chao were thirty-seven barbarian tribes. Only of the Ts'uan have we had much information. The Western Ts'uan were forced out of their territory by Ko-lo-feng, and only the Eastern Ts'uan occupied the Lolo territory at this time. Of all these tribes, it is also the Eastern Ts'uan which show the closest affinities to the present Lolo.

The Eastern Ts'uan were divided into seven tribes: (1) A-yu-lu, (2) A-mang, (3) Kwuei-shan, (4) Pao-man, (5) Lulu-man, (6) Mo-mi-chien and (7) Wu-tun.[3] It is the fifth tribe, Lulu-man, that was identified with the Lolo in the Yuan dynasty. [4] But the Lulu was not the most important tribe during the T'ang period (A.D.618-906). That position was held by the Wu-tun. According to the *T'ang shuh*, the Wu-tun occupied an area of about one thousand square *li* and were divided into several subtribes, especially the subtribe Chu-lo, who occupied the area of Chiung-pu and Tai-tun, the area

---

[1]　E.H.Parker, *The Old Thai or Shan Empire of Western Yunnan. China Rev.* XX, pp.337 seq.

[2]　See VIII, I.

[3]　See I.

[4]　IX, Book 2, pp.24-25. "Lolo are the descendents of the Lulu of the Ts'uan barbarians. Lolo is a corruption of the sound Lulu."

of the Ta-liang mountain range and the Chien-chang valley. it was also at the hands of the Wu-tun tribes in alliance with Chinese armies that the Tibetans suffered their most disastrous defeat.

The Wu-tun and a few other warlike tribes of Lolo affinities around the Ta-liang mountain area were mentioned in the *Sung Shih*, especially as wearing felt cloaks and dressing the hair into a knot on the head. Unfortunately information from this period is very scanty. When the Sung conquered the kingdom of Later Shu (modern Ssuchuan), the general, Wang Chên-pin, drew up a plan for the conquest of Nan-chao and submitted it to Sung Tai-tsu (A.D.960-976), the founder of the Sung dynasty (A.D.960-1278). Tai-tsu, aware of the troubles the T'ang had had with the Nan-chao, drew a line with his jade axe along the Ta tu river and said reluctantly: "Outside this line, the territory is not mine." So all communications with this region were prohibited.[1]

The kingdom of Nan-chao, after a succession of thirteen kings, was overthrown in the year 902 A.D. and was succeeded by the Ta-li (A.D.937-1094) of the Tuan fatally. In 1097 A.D. this was succeeded by the Later Ta-li, until the latter was conquered by the Mongols in 1253 A.D. The Mongol conquest was rather a bloodless one.[2] The most serious strife took place at the beginning of the Ming (A.D.1368-1644) and Ch'ing (A.D.1644-1910) dynasties. Most of the Black Lolo fell in these battles and those who remained retreated

---

[1] See IX.

[2] See III, Book 145.

northward. A few accepted the office of Tu-ssu (native chiefs)[1]

During the Ming period the Lolo (formerly Lulu) became prominent, and all the other Eastern Ts'uan tribes seem to have disappeared surreptitiously. They cannot all have become extinct within such a short time. No later Lolo tribal names correspond with the names of the Eastern Ts'uan tribes mentioned in the *T'ang shu* except the Lulu. The only explanation seems to be that these tribal names were names of the ruling families or clans. When the family died out or lost its power, so went with it the name, as in the case of the Ts'uan. The Lolo tribe being the most powerful later, its name became a generic name for them all.

From this brief account the movements of peoples in this part of China can be clearly visualized, The Pai P'u were perhaps the original inhabitants of this region, and later constituted the bulk of the population of the kingdom of T'ien founded under Chinese leadership, and their remnants are still to be found in Yumnan as the Pu-man. To the northeast of T'ien, the Yeh-lang showed strong affinities with the Lolo, but their exact relationship can not be ascertained. During the early centuries of the Christian era the Lolo seem to have dispossessed the Pai P'u. Where they came from, it is not known, presumably from the Tibetan-Burman border. At the same time the Miao -Yao group were migrating south-ward on the east in Kueichou and Kuanghsi. The Shan were also beginning to assert themselves and finally consolidated into

---

[1]  See IV, Books 300-319. V, Books 517-522.

the kingdom of Nan-chao in the eighth century. During the whole Nan chao and Ta-li period, the Lolo perhaps constituted the general bulk of the population in the north and the warrior class Lo-chu-tzu of the Nan-chao armies[1] might be chiefly recruited from them. After the fall of Ta-li and at the beginning of the Ming and Ch'ing dynasties, there was a general depopulation of the pure Lolo and a more thorough sinicization of the Yunnan area.

## Tribal Divisions

The political unit of the Lolo is the tribe. During the T'ang times the Eastern Ts'uan were divided into seven principal tribes, of which only the name Lulu survived. According to the *T'ang Shu* the smallest of these tribes were more than one hundred families each and ruled over by a chief called *Kuei-chu* (Ghost lord). These tribes were constantly at war with each other as the Lolo are at present. Sometimes an able chief of some tribe might attain supremacy and unite them into a loose political unit, as in the case of the Ts'uan. Such unions were of short duration.

As to what had become of the early Lolo tribes, we know nothing. It was not until the Ming period (A.D.1368-1644), that the name Lolo became well

---

[1] The Nan-chao armies were conscripted from all the aboriginal peoples. The Lo-chu-tzu were the shock troops selected from the local militia. See *Man shu*, chap.9, pp.2 seq.

established and their tribes recorded. The *Nan-chao Yeh-shih* gives a list of eleven Lolo tribes subject to the Nan-chao.[1] They are as follows: *Hei Lolo*, *Pai Lolo*, *Kan Lolo*, *Hai Lolo*, *Sa-mi Lolo*, *Ko Lolo*, *A-che Lolo*, *A-wu Lolo*, *Lu-wu Lolo*, *Lao-wu Lolo* and *Miao Lolo*. At present only the *Hei* (black) *Lolo* and *Pai* (white) *Lolo* are existing names, all the others having vanished. But the *Hei* and *Pai* are no longer tribal names. They are generic names of two types of Lolo and within each contain many tribes. Lietard, who had studied the White Lolo of Yunnan, considered most of these names as inventions of Chinese authors and impossible of identification.[2] But a closer examination of Lietard's tribes will reveal that most of them show close identity. According to Lietard's description of his tribes, the *Na-P'ou* corresponds to the *Hei* (black) *Lolo*, the *Na-P'ou* to the *Pai* (white) *Lolo*, and the *Ko-P'ou* to the *Kan* (dry) *Lolo*. He gives more than twenty other divisional names, and many are nearly the same as these given in the *Nan-chao Yeh-shih*, such as *Sa-m'e*, *Lou-ou P'ou*, *A-d'je P'ou*, *A-tcha P'o*, *Lo-ou P'o*, etc.[3]

Most of the tribal names found in old Chinese records are by no means indicative of racial characteristics. They are given to the natives because of some peculiar features in their dress or customs, occupation, place of their occurrence, and most common of all according to the names of their ruling

---

[1]　Book II, pp. 25-27.

[2]　*Au Yunnan*.

[3]　The *Yunnan tung chih* also gives some tribes that are not in the *Nan-chao yeh-shih*, such as: A-hsie Lolo, Pu-la Lolo, Ta-Lolo, Hsiao Lolo, etc.

families. Since all these things have changed, tribes have moved about, and ruling families died out, so their tribal names have changed. A little more fieldwork and study of their history will reveal most of their identities.

Among the independent Lolo of Ssuchuan, Lietard gives the names of twenty-six tribes of Black Lolo, thirty tribes of White Lolo, three tribes of mixed (e.g. black and white) Lolo, and two tribes of slaves. Lietard's information is only secondary and he does not give any further details of their settlements, social usages, etc. d'Ollone, who has travelled through their territory (in 1906-1909), indicated that the tribes occupied well defined territories and trespassing was resented, as he had frequently to change guides and respondents when passing from the territory of one tribe to that of another.[①] The same condition may have existed from very early times as is shown by the few indications from the early records. As the Lolo are a semi-pastoral people and enjoy hunting, whether they have any rights regarding pasture grounds or hunting territory, we know nothing.

Lietard is more conversant with the tribes of Yunnan. He says that each of the tribes bears the same tribal name, speaks the same dialect, wears the same costume, and is endogamous. Since Lietard is the first investigator to treat this subject, there is no other material for comparison. Tribal endogamy seems to be contrary to the old practice. During the T'ang dynasty, according to *man-shu*, the Black Barbarians intermarried among themselves

---

① D'Ollone, op. cit.

irrespective of tribal and political divisions. Even the Nan-chao, considered Shan at present but belonging to the category of Black Barbarians, intermarried with the noble families of the Eastern Ts'uan, e.g. the modern Lolo. How the present tribal endogamous system works out we have to wait for more investigation to see.

## The Dual Division of Black and White

The designation of black and white is a very common phenomenon among the peoples of southwest China. The term is often used in various shades of meaning and the exact connotation has to be determined in each case. Sometimes it is used to indicate the prevailing color of the costumes the people wear, as in the case of the Black and White Miao.[1] The term is also employed to convey the idea of the culture status of a people. Certain Miao tribes in southern Hunan province are called black because they are less civilized than their kinsmen near the Chinese towns. [2]The same is true with the Black and White Lisu, a people related with the Lolo on the Upper Mekong river.[3] Sometimes the term *shen* (raw) and *shuh* (cooked or tamed)

---

[1]　Clark, op. cit. p. 371.

[2]　Jamieson, op. cit. pp. 381-382.

[3]　Rose, Archibald, and Brown, J. C., *Li-su (Yawyin) Tribes of the Burma-China Frontier, Memoirs, Asiatic Society of Bengal*, Vol. III, 1910-1914, pp.249-276, ix pl.

is used in substitution. But in all these usages, one point is clear. The peoples so far concerned seldom used this term to designate themselves. They are designations applied to them by the Chinese.

The case is different among the Lolo. They actually styled themselves as Black and White.[1] But the situation is very delicate and observers often miss this division entirely. It is interesting that d'Ollone passed through the whole span of Lolo territory, and did not notice this division at all. He speaks about the noble families, serfs, slaves, but makes not a single mention of the Black and White distinction. Lietard spent many of his missionary years among the Lolo of Yunnan and considered it as purely a Chinese invention, saying that many of the Lolo in Yunnan do not know of such a distinction. As he got more information from Ssuchuan where the Black Lolo are much more numerous, he found such a division indubitably existed. He was forced to accept it but tried to account for it by a linguistic interpretation.[2] In Yunnan the Black Lolo only constitute the few ruling families (tu-ssu), so every where one meets are the White Lolo. The situation is somewhat reversed in Ssuchuan, where the majority are Black Bones (as they call

---

[1]    Jamieson (op. cit. p. 381) says that "they (Lolo) are termed black not because the black Miao are so named, but because of the dark nature of their skin." This is followed by Buxton in his *Peoples of Asia*, p. 156, "they (Lolo) are called 'Black' because of the darkness of their complexions." This is surely not the case. They are certainly fairer than most of the aborigines, as has been noticed by all observers. Some even regard them as fairer than the southern European. If they are so named because of the darkness of their skin, then how should we explain the term "White" Lolo?

[2]    His usual theory, the Lolo called themselves *No-so,no* means *black*, so the Chinese misinterpreted it and called them black.

themselves) and those recently reduced to serfdom can scarcely be called Lolo on the strict sense of the term.

If we turn to the history of this area, this division is a very old one. At least, it goes back to the ninth century during the T'ang dynasty, when we have documentary evidence. In the *Man-shu* and the *T'ang shu*, whenever a tribe is mentioned, it is invariably appended with the discriminatory term *wu-man* (black barbarians), or *pai-man* (white barbarians). The following is a table reconstructed from the different sources of this period.

Wu-man Black Barbarians

1. Eastern Ts'uan (Lolo)
2. Ai-lao
3. Nan-chao
4. Tu-ching man
5. Ch'ang-kun man
6. Shih man
7. Shun man
8. Mo man
9. Tu-lao

Pai man White Barbarians

1. Western Ts'uan
2. Nun-tung man
3. Chins-lin man

This division seems at least to be intended to indicate some racial affinity, as is shown by the manner in which it is used. How far it is accurate, we do not know. A linguistic difference seems to be involved. [1] If we compare the modern Black and White Lolo, their physical characteristics are quite contrasted. The Black Lolo are characterized by tall stature, sometimes reported taller than Europeans' aquiline nose, well developed brow ridges, and as a whole quite different from the Mongoloid cast in appearance. [2] The White Lolo are generally inferior in physique. The cephalic index is also slightly different between the two. [3] These physical differences at least give us some suggestions about the disentangling of this perplexing question. A careful study of this peculiar institution will undoubtedly reveal some of the secrets of the coalescence and disintegration of the peoples in this part of China.

The Black Lolo every where constitute the ruling chiefs, sometimes even among the Miao in Western Kueichou province. [4] To be called "black" is an indication of ruling aristocracy. They never intermarry with the White Lolo or with any other people. In Yunnan the Lolo chiefs sometimes marry

[1]    *Man shu*, chap. 8, pp. 3-4, "...The language (of the Wu-man) is entirely different from the Pai-man."

[2]    Their fine physical features are noted by all travellers from the time of Marco Polo down to the present. E. C. Baber remarked that they are taller than any Europeans, but this seems to be exaggerated. D'Ollone (op.cit. p.51) especially praised their fine features by saying: "There was nothing of the Asiatic; the complexion was not yellow, but swarthy, like that of the inhabitants of Southern Europe; the eyes, neither oblique nor flattened, were large, and protected by fine arched brows; the nose was aquiline, the mouth well cut... 'What superb redskins these men would make, with a plume of feathers or a warbonnet on the head ! '"

[3]    A. F. Legendre, *Far West Chinois*, tableau A-C, T'oung Pao,1909, T.10, facing page 642. Subject measured 19. For an analysis, see R. B. Dixon, *Racial History of Man*, p. 281. See also V. K. Ting, *Man Yu san chi.*

[4]    Jamieson,op.cit .p.381.

their daughters to the sons of Chinese officials and distinguished Chinese families, [1] but they themselves very rarely marry Chinese wives. Among the independent Lolo of Ssuchuan, endogamy is strictly enforced. d'Ollone wrote that the rule was as strictly observed as in the Indian caste. [2]

If the division of Black and White among the Lolo has some significance upon the racial question, it will be like the following. The Black Lolo are originally a conquering group representing an uniform racial stock. The White Lolo are people originally representing quite different racial stocks subjugated by the Black Lolo one after another, and having imposed upon them the Lolo language. This process is still going on in the independent Lolo country. But in Yunnan owing to the advance of the Chinese, the ruling nobility were either fallen in the field or had retreated northward. What is left behind are only those slaves (White Lolo) who do not care whom their masters are. A few ruling families have remained and accepted the Chinese office of Tu-ssu (native chiefs). This is the actual condition we find now in Yunnan and in the dependent Lolo country.

---

[1]　There is an interesting little book which Dr. J. K. Shryock and I are translating, *The Marriage Customs of the Tu-ssu(native chiefs) of Yunnan and Kuei-chou*, which tells now the ceremonies of *such* intermarriages are carried out.

[2]　D'Ollone, op. cit. p. 63.

# The Lolo Cloak and "Horn"

As far as material culture is concerned, the Lolo are much less advanced than their neighbors. They are semi-pastoral, but they do not milk their cows. Agricultural pursuits are left to the slaves, who are hardly Lolo. Their dwelling is a kind of hut made of rammed earth, covered with fir planks and interlaced with bamboo strips. There is nothing that can be called household furniture, no tables, chairs, etc. The only utensils are the few turned wooden bowls, bamboo baskets, and iron pans for boiling purposes. They know no condiments in the preparation of food except the salt which is considered as a great delicacy. The only textile they have is a kind of rough hempen fabric, woven with a method described as the "primitive of the primitives", and the tough felt they use for their cloak. They have no money, weights or measures. They have no pottery. This they shared with other ancient peoples of this region. The Nan-chao, according to the Man-shu, likewise had no pottery. All their containers were made of gold and silver and bamboo.[1] We may continue to enumerate their negative traits *ad infinitum*, but it will not help *us* out in our historical deductions. Here we will take two characteristic Lolo traits which are not shared by other peoples in this region at present

---

[1]  *Man-shu*, chap. 8, p. 1, "The culinary utensils of the Nan-chao are made of gold and silver. The officials and generals used bamboo containers. The aristocracy eat with chopsticks, but the ordinary people fetched their food with fingers."

and trace them to their earliest known origin and draw our conclusions: namely, the Lolo cloak and the Lolo "horn".

The most characteristic Lolo dress is the felt cloak which both men and women wear as a protection against rain and cold. This garment is usually of deep brown, sometimes blue or of the natural tint of the wool. The texture of the felt is very rough and uneven. This cloak is invaluable to the Lolo. He never doffs it, winter or summer. In sleep, it is his matress, blanket, and even roof. For the Lolo will stretch himself out comfortably in the first hollow he can find among the rocks when night falls, and will slumber peacefully in this wonderful cape. "The true home of the Lolo is his cloak."

This useful and expedient Lolo dress is not used by any other people who now surround them, so it may be considered a national Lolo attire. If we turn to the historical material, we find the ancient Nan-chao wore a similar felt cloak. The *Man-shu* says:"All the barbarians (e.g. Nanchao) wear felt cloaks; their other clothes are slightly similar to the Han (Chinese), but their headbags (coiffure) are different. The Nan chao (e.g. royalties) used red damask (the material cannot be ascertained with certainty),and all others used gray color. Their custom was to use a piece of cloth sewed with the edges of one corner together in the form of a horn. A wooden cone was stuffed into it. It was fixed to the back of the head and the hair twisted around it. Then the rest of the cloth was wrapped around the head. Only the royalties and the high officials were allowed to wear this. The lower officials and the Lo chu tzu (warriors) dressed their hair on the forehead into a knot, and they were not allowed to wear the head bag. All wear felt cloaks and go barefooted. Even the prime ministers and generals are not ashamed of going barefooted."[1]

The wearing of the felt cloak was evidently a national custom of the Nan chao. But this raises several interesting questions. The Nan-chao, from the linguistical evidences we possess, were unquestionably Shan. The use of felt and especially the cloak is foreign to all the Shans at present. Was this trait lost when they migrated to warmer climates? Or, was this originally a Lolo dress adopted by the Nan chao from their subjects? These are questions we are unable to answer at present, but as we go further we will find there are still more similarities between the Nan-chao and the modern Lolo.

Another notable one is the peculiar way the Lolo dress their hair, popularly known as the Lolo "horn". The hair is thrown forward, twisted and coiled into the shape of a horn resting on the forehead. In appearance it looks like a horn. It is peculiarly Lolo, and no other people at present in the southwest of China dress their hair in this fashion. The passage just quoted from the *Man-shu* shows that the lower rank officials and the Lo-chu-tzu of the Nan-chao armies wore the same kind of coiffure. This further substantiates our statement that the warrior class of the Nan-chao army were chiefly Lolo.

If we turn to the Naga tribes of the Manipur, the Marrings have very similar methods of dressing their hair. "The men comb their hair from

---

[1]    Chapter 8, pp. 1-2.

behind and from the sides, and gather it into a horn-shaped protuberance above the centre of the forehead; round the base of their horn are usually wound strings of beads of various kinds, and transfixing it crosswise is a steel bodkin-shaped instrument with a sharp point about fifteen inches long and flattened for about a third of its length at the other extremity..."[1] The ornaments of the coiffure are somewhat different, as may be expected, but the shape and the method of making the coiffure are exactly the same. As there is no other people in Asia known to have dressed their hair in this fashion, the striking coincidence cannot be accidental. The situation is very tempting, especially as the Lolo have a tradition that they came from that direction. It would be rash to speculate now on this single evidence that the Marring Naga and the Lolo are in some way related.

## Disposal of the Dead

All peoples are very conservative in the manner of burying their dead. It is a trait that is likely to persist for ages, and can only be changed by radical religious influences from the outside. Since the Lolo have resisted all religious ideas in the past,[2] their treatment of the dead may be a custom

[1]　Hodson, T. C., *The Naga Tribes of Manipur*, Macmillan, 1911. pp. 29-30. See also plate facing page 21.

[2]　The Lolo are surrounded on all sides by Buddhist peoples but they have resisted the advance of Buddhism into their beliefs. Christianity met the same fate in spite of the incessant efforts of the missionaries.

dating back to great antiquity. In contrast to other aboriginal peoples of China, the Lolo practiced cremation. This custom goes back at least to as early as the T'ang dynasty, for the *Man-shu* says: "The Mung-shê and Wu-man do not bury their dead. They burn the corpse three days after death and cover the ashes with soil. They only keep the two ears. The Nan-chao keep the ears in golden vases. The golden vases are put in a silver box and stored in a special room. At every season they are taken out and sacrifices offered to them. The common people use copper and iron vases."[1] The Wu-man included the Eastern Tsuan, e.g. the progenitors of the modern Lolo. Although the custom of keeping the ears of the dead in metal vases is not present among the modern Lolo, the practice of cremation was corroborated by Marco Polo. He says: "When any of them die, the bodies are burnt, and then they take the bones and put them in little chests. These are carried up the mountains, and placed in great caverns, where they are hung up in such wise that neither man nor beasts can come to them."[2] This statement was again substantiated by the Grosvenor expedition in 1876.

"Before reaching Lao-wan-tan we were shown ledges on inaccessible cliffs on which coffins of a very small size were to be seen. I, however, did not observe any. These are supposed to be relics of a bygone barbarous age before the Chinese occupation. When asked how they were ascertained to

---

[1]  *Man-shu*, chap. VIII, pp. 3-4.

[2]  Baber, E. C. , *China,in Some of Its Physical and Social Aspects. Proceedings RGS*, n.s., Vol. V, 1883, pp. 445-448. Baber's identification of the *Coloman* of Marco Polo with the Lolo, I think, is valid.

be coffins, the natives replied that the monkeys, which in summer are very numerous, throw them down the cliffs. It is a source of wonder to the Chinese how they could have been placed in these inaccessible situations."[1]Grosvenor was travelling along the outskirts of the Lolo territory in western Ssuchuan which was occupied by the Lolo in former times. Cremation is an idea abhorrent to the tribes of southwest China. It was never mentioned in the ancient records. Its practice by the Lolo serves as a sure guide for their identification and correlations.

This brings out another question. The Nan-chao were considered Shan, but the present Shan do not cremate their dead. They bury their dead in spite of Buddhist and Hindu influences.[2]This point once more shows that the Nan-chao are more related culturally to the Lolo than to the modern Shan who are considered their direct descendants. The *Man-shu* further says that "the Pai-man bury their dead like the Chinese and plant trees around the graves". This substantiates the discussion of the dual division of black and white, that they were originally contrasted in culture.

---

[1]　Ibid., p. 446.

[2]　Milne, Leslie, *Shans at Home*, 1910, pp. 89-97.

# The Ghost Cult of the Tsuan and the
# Ancestor Cult of the Lolo

Next we may take the ghost cult of the Ts'uan and the ancestor cult of the modern Lolo. It is said in the *T'ang shu* that the barbarians revered their ghost (perhaps ancestors) and had ghost lords (kuei-chu), who ruled over them. Every year each family contributed an ox or goat and sacrificed them at the home of the Kuei-chu, who presided over them. When they summoned the ghosts or sent them away, they carried arms. This is the time they made their raids and revenged their wrongs.[1]

The most important cult of the modern Lolo is their ancestor cult. We owe our sole knowledge of this to Lietard who gave quite a detailed account.[2] It appears to be similar to the ancient ghost cult. The chief ceremony takes place in the first or second moon. The families in turn engage a *pi-mo* and invite the villagers to a dance. A pig and a goat are killed. Rice and wine are prepared. They are first offered to the ancestors and then eaten communally. The rituals are quite long and very elaborate.

---

[1]　See I. The same custom was also present among the Yakuts in ancient times. "During the summer, in olden times, every rich man arranged a kumiss festival, at which all members of the clan assembled and were entertained. Other people, and frequently whole clans, were invited; and during the festival, defensive and offensive leagues were concluded." W. Jochelson: *Kumiss Festivals of the Yakut and the Decoration of the Kumiss Vessels*. Boas Memorial Volume, 1906, p. 263.

[2]　Lietard, *Au Yunnan*, 1913.

The details of the Ts'uan ghost-cult-we have no means of knowing as the information conveyed to us by the *T'ang Shu* is very sketchy, but the essential points seem to be very similar to those of the Lolo ancestor cult. The kuei-chu seemed to be a sort of sacerdotal chief who officiated both at religious ceremonies and in secular affairs. His supersession by a class of priesthood in religious matters is a natural development. The ancestor cult is the most important cult of the Lolo, just as the ghost cult was to the Ts'uan. We are not in a position to say very much on this subject, as our information both on the ancient cult and the modern cult is very scanty. Many writers seem to have overlooked this practice among the Lolo entirely.

## The Problem of Lolo Origin

Having made a general review of the history and the probable movements of the Lolo and examined a few of their characteristic cultural traits in comparison with those of the historical peoples who surrounded or related to them, we are now in a position to examine whether they have any bearing on the problem of Lolo origin or not. Before going on, a review of the existing theories concerning this problem will be clarifying.

The earliest one to speculate on this question is perhaps Terrien de Lacouperie, who says: "The Laka Lolos were a southeastern extension of the populations of northeastern Tibet..."[1] In this, he connects the Lolo with the ancient Jung and Chiang of the Chinese records. As he did not produce any substantial evidence to support his hypothesis, we shall discuss it more fully in connection with V. K. Ting's theory.

In a similar fashion Paul Vial and many other writers connect the Lolo with the Tibetans. [2] The evidence is primarily linguistical, e.g. by comparison of a very limited number of selected words. The scientific relationship of the so-called Sinitic group of languages is still something to be established, so comments are hardly needed in the present state of our knowledge.

V. K. Ting is the first to establish his hypothesis on a physical and historical basis.[3] During his prospecting tours in Yunnan, he was able to secure a number of measurements of the Lolo. The cephalic index, as obtained from these measurements, is prevailing dolichocephalic. So he concludes that "historically the Lolos in association with the Chiangs, formed an important people in Northwest Szechuan, Kokonor, and South

---

[1] Op. cit. pp. 480-481.

[2] Vial, Paul: *Les Lolos*, 1898.

Deniker, J., *The Races of Man*, 1900. "The Lolo or Nesus, as they call themselves, of western Sechuen and the north-east of Yunnan, with whom we must connect the Kolo or Golyk or the country of Amdo (east of Tibet), perhaps represent it in its present form, if the portrait of them drawn by Thorel is correct. With slight figure, brownish complexion, they have a straight profile, oval face, high forehead, straight and arched nose, thick beard even on the sides of the face and always frizzy or wavy hair. Their language, however, fixed by a hieroglyphic mode of writing, appears to belong to the Burmese family..." (pp.381-2)

For H. R. Davies' classification, see op. cit. p.337. V. K. Ting's classification is somewhat based on Davies', which is adopted by Dr. Chi Li in his book (op.cit.), p. 255.

[3] Ting, V. K., *Native Tribes of Yunnan. China Medical Journal*, March, 1921.

Turkestan. In the last place they intermarried with the Iranian people known as Yuechi. The Iranian element may have found its way into the Lolos through the Chiangs."[1] Here Ting is using the term "Iranian" in the same sense as Ripley.

From the details Ting published later in his *Travels in Yunnan*,[2] we learn that the subjects he measured are perhaps practically all White Lolo. So, his findings are hardly surprising. The dolichocephalic factor corresponds to the Caspian type, in Dr. R. B. Dixon's terminology, which is the secondary dominant factor among the White Lolo.[3] As the White Lolo is a much mixed group subject to the Black Lolo, the dolichocephalic factor may represent a strain of the older population of Mon-Khmer speaking peoples.[4] If we examine Legendre's measurements, the brachycephalic factor prevails. Since the number of subjects measured were small in both cases, neither can be considered as conclusive.

To attribute the long headedness and the supposed Caucasoid features of the Lolo to the infusion of Iranian blood, e.g., the Yuehchi, is too far

---

[1]   Ibid.

[2]   Ting, V.K., *Man yu san chi,* Independent Rev. s, Nos. pp. 34-36, 1933.

[3]   Dixon, R. B. :"The Lolo are divided into an aristocracy and a class of common people, and the two groups appear to differ in their physical characteristics. The aristocracy is very similar to the population of Kwangtung, the Palae-Alpine factors being in the majority, with the Alpine type secondary. The common people, on the other hand, show a still stronger dominance of the Palae-Alpine type, the Alpine being displaced as a secondary type by the Caspian." *Racial History of Man*, p. 281. Dixon based his analysis on Legendre's (op.cit.) measurements.

[4]   The Mon-Khmer speaking peoples, the Pnong, Moi, Kha, etc. of S.E. Asia all show a strong dolichocephalic factor. Se Dixon, Ibid., p. 276.

fetched. First of all, we do not know racially who the Yuehchi were. Were they Iranians, Scythians, Huns, Turks, or Turco Tartars?[1] From the fragmentary information furnished by the *Chien Han Shu*[2] the Yuehchi were originally a pastoral nomadic people inhabiting the eastern part of Chinese Turkestan. About the end of the third century B.C. they were defeated by the Hsiung nu (the Huns) and a large part of them migrated westward and conquered the Tocharians who were responsible for the overthrow of the Greek state of Bactria.[3] During the beginning of the present era, they conquered Northwest India, and were known there as the Kushanas, who had much to do with the transmission of Buddhism into China. A small portion of the Yuehchi did not join the western exodus but retreated southward and mixed with the Chiang. They were known later as the Little Yuehchi. When the Chinese drove the Hsiung-nu from Chinese Turkestan, the Little Yuehchi were induced to return to their original place again. This happened about the end of the second century B.C. The Yuehchi

---

[1]    The racial affinity of the Yueh-chi is still a question of much debate. The bibliography is extensive. For the latest discussion see, Sten Konow, *Kharoshthi Inscriotions*, Corpus Inscriptionum Indicarum, Vol. II, Pt. I, 1929, pp. xlix-lxxxii. The general opinion seems to be that the Yueh-chi (Kushanas) were Indo-Scythians.

[2]    History of Former Han dynasty.

[3]    Shortly before the Yueh-chi came to Bactria, the country seemed to have been occupied by a people known to the Greeks as Tocharians (Tukhara of the Indian writers and Tu-huo-lo of the Chinese). They were responsible for the overthrow of the Greek kingdom in Bactria. Where the Tocharians came from, it is not certain—presumably from the same direction as the Yueh-chi, e.g. western Chinese Turkestan. Some identify them with the Chinese Ta-hsia, and others with the Yueh-chi. Recent discoveries in Chinese Turkestan show that the Tocharians spoke an Indo-European language more related to the Western group, e.g. Greek and Latin, than to the Eastern group, e.g. Iranian and Sanskrit. These discoveries give much color to the theory of the Central Asiatic origin of the Indo-Europeans.

hypothesis is too much exploited by recent scholars, and everything in Central Asia is credited to them. Whether the Little Yuehchi had penetrated so far south as Southwest Ssuchuan or not is very problematical, as we have shown before that the migration of the Lolo since historical times is a northward instead of a southward one. Moreover, if we consider the Yeh -lang as Lolo, they were already an established race during the time when the Yuehchi began to migrate.

The theory of L. H. D. Buxton [1] is based on Ting's measurements and the information supplied by C. E. Jamieson. Jamieson says that the Lolo came from the Tibetan-Burman border, on the ground that the Lolo are the only people in southwest China frequently associated with the horse. [2]Buxton connects the Lolo with his Nesiots, who were indirectly related to the longheaded population of Western Asia and the Mediterranean area, corresponding to Elliot Smith's Brown race. The only difference with Ting is that the connection is a southward one around the Himalaya foothills. Both Ting and Buxton seem not to have taken Legendre's measurements into consideration, though they are more important than Ting's. And Buxton seems not to be familiar with the historical facts which are inextricably connected with the problem.

If we now turn to the traditions among the Lolo themselves and see

---

[1]  Op. cit. pp.156-157.

[2]  Op. cit. p. 381.

what they say about this problem, we find that according to the various versions recorded, they all point to their coming from the Tibetan-Burman border. How far this tradition may be substantiated, we have no means of knowing. The Lolo, as they were first known to the Chinese, were in the North-east of Yunnan. In this very spot C. E. Hicks made an interesting report. In the Chao-tung area there are many earthen mounds conspicuous on the plains. "Some of these have been opened, and in them have been found rough unhewn stones, apparently placed as door frames, and burned bricks of an unusually large size and marked with a peculiar pattern."[1] How much has it any bearing on the question of the origin of the Lolo, it is too early to speculate. According to Hicks, the Lolo in this area have a tradition that these earthen mounds represent a native population, the P'u, whom the Lolo destroyed. Archaeology must have a great part to play in the future.

Nor are the Lolo autochthonous to the Ta-Liang mountains, according to their own tradition. If the stories recorded by Baber[2] and d'Ollone[3] contain some truth, they have always regarded themselves as vanquished and deprived of their rich valleys by the Chinese. Their retreat to the mountains continued as late as 1727 in the Ching dynasty. Popular traditions may contain some historical truth, but cannot be taken too seriously as

---

[1]  Hicks, E. C., *The Nou Su... Chinese Recorder*, Vol. 41, p.211.

[2]  Baber, E. C. , *Travels and Researches in the Interior of China. Royal Geographical Society*, Supplementary papers, Vol. I., p. 121.

[3]  Op. cit. p. 107.

authentic history. One thing seems to be fairly certain that all their traditions indicate that they are not the original inhabitants of their present habitat.

If we take the few ethnological traits which we have treated before to see whether they have any bearing on the problem, first let us take the dual division of black and white. The use of "black" to indicate orthodox descent or blue-blood was quite prevalent among the older peoples of northeastern Asia. The Western Liao kingdom founded by Yeh-lü Ta-shih called themselves Khara Kitan, e.g. Black Kitan, in order to indicate that they were the original Kitan. The Mongols were also first divided into black and white Tartars. Genghiz Khan and his generals and ministers all belonged to the Black Tartars.[1] This cannot be considered as evidence of possible connections, but it may serve as suggestions to the solution of the problem. The use of felt by the Lolo and the practice of the "ghost cult" by the ancient Tsuan are also in accord with the northern nomadic peoples. As to the practice of cremation, no possible suggestions can be made at present. It certainly cannot be attributed to Buddhist or Hindu influence, because the Lolo have never been Buddhists.

There are two other negative traits which point to entirely different directions, namely the lack of pottery and the milking trait. The Lolo are surrounded by pottery making peoples on their south and east, but they have never mastered that art. Most of their pots, bowls, and containers were made

---

[1]　See *Mung ta pei lu* (Accounts about the Tartars). What the Black and White Tartar divisions indicated is still a subject of much debate. For a discussion see *Researches on the Wu-liang-haand the Tartars*, 1932, pp. 31-37.

of wood. Occasionally they possessed a few pieces of pottery, but they are of Chinese importation. We know very few people in the Old World who lack pottery except a few of the nomads, as the Mongols. Its absence among the Lolo is rather conspicuous, for it cannot be attributed to isolation or to some other cause.

The few ethnological traits mentioned above seem to indicate their connections with the north, but there is one strong negative trait that excludes them from that direction. They are not milk users. The peoples of Asia may be divided into two groups: those who use milk and those who do not, and each occupies a contiguous territory. All the northwestern Asiatics, the Tungus, Mongols, Turks, Tibetans, Hindus, Iranians and all the peoples of the Near East, and the Paleo-Asiatics, constitute the milk using group. The Chinese, Japanese, Shan, Lolo, and most of the Mon-khmer peoples belong to the non-milk using group. Its absence among the Lolo cannot be accidental. Flocks they possess, but milking is unknown. If they were originally pastoral peoples, such an important and essential trait could not be easily and entirely lost.[①] It cannot be attributed to Chinese influence; as a matter of fact, they have adopted very few Chinese traits. There are also other traits that suggest southern connections, such as going barefooted, the use of poison arrow and the Lolo "horn". But the cross bow is conspicuously

①　Such as the Yakuts who retreated to northern Siberian tundras within historical times where the climate is most unfavorable for cattle breeding; but they still retain their cattle under very adverse conditions. See Jochelson, op. cit. pp. 257-271.

lacking although it is a typical weapon in southeastern Asia.

Taking all these facts into consideration, the origin of the Lolo is still a mystery. Most of the theories are based on one set of facts, sometimes with disregard for the others. The question cannot be settled at present, and more field work will be needed in order to put these conflicting facts into their proper settings.

## Bibliography Abbreviations to Periodicals

ASB          Asiatic Society of Bengal

BEFEO        Bulletin de l'Ecole francaise d'Extrême Orient

BMSAP        Bulletins et Memoires Société d'Anthropologie de Paris

CR           China Review

JRAI         Journal of the Royal Anthropological Institute of Great Britain and Ireland

JRASNCB      Journal of the Royal Asiatic Society, North China Branch

MC           Missions Catholiques

RGS          Royal Geographical Society

TP           T'oung Pao

Baber, E. C.

Travels and Researches in the Interior of China. *RGS*, Supplementary papers, 1882, pp. 1-201.

Bonifacy

Etude sur les coutumes et la langue de Lolo et de La-qua dy Haut Tonkin. *BEFEO*, VIII, 1908, pp. 531-558.

Bonin, Charles-Eude.

Vocabulaires. Mantse de Leang-chan. *TP*, IV, 1903, pp. 124-126.

Bourne, F. S. A.

Report by Mr. F. S. A. Bourne of a Journey to South-western China, presented to both Houses of Parliament by Command of Her Majesty, June 1888. *China*—No.I.

Bridgman, E. C.

Sketches of the Miau-tse. *JRASNCB*, III, 1859, pp. 257-286.

Charria, S.

Les Inscriptions Lolo de Lou-k'ian. *BEFEO*, V, 1905, pp. 195-197.

Clark, George.

Translation of a Manuscript Account of the Kwei-chau Miao-tzu, written after the subjugation of the Miao-tzu about 1730. In A. R. Colquhoun, *Across Chrysé*, 1883. Vol. II, Appendix, pp.363-394.

Cordier, Henri.

Les Lolos, etat actuel de la question. *TP*, VIII, 1907, pp. 597-688.

Crabouillet, P.

Les Lotos (du Se-tschoun). *MC*, V, 1873, pp. 71-2, 94-5, 105-7.

Davies, H. R.

Yunnan: the link between India and the Yangtze. 1909 Appendix VIII. The Tribes of Yunnan, pp. 332-398.

Deveria, M. B.

Les Lolos et les Miao-tze, a propos d'une brochure de M. P. Vial... *Journal Asiatique*, 1891, pp. 356-369.

Francois, C.

Notes sur les Lo-lo du Kien-tchang. *BMSAP*, V, 1904, pp. 637-647.

Gutzlaff, C.

Tibet and Sefan. *Journal RGS*, XX, 1850, pp. 191-227.

Henry , A.

The Lolos and other tribes of western China. *JRAI*, XXXIII, 1903, pp. 96-107.

Hicks, C. C.

The Nou Su... *Chinese Recorder*, Vol. 41, pp 211.

Hosie, A.

Three Years in Western China. 1890. Chap. VI.

Jamieson, C. E.

The aborigines of Western China. *China Journal of Arts and Science*. Vol. I, 1923, pp 376.

Laufer, B.

The Si-hia Language, a Study in Indo-Chinese Philology.
*TP*, XVII, 1916, pp. 1-128.

Legendre, A. F.

Far West Chinois. Races aborigines-les Lolos-etude ethnologie et anthropologie. *TP*, 1909, pp. 340-380, 399-444, 603-665.

The Lolos of Kien-tchang, western China. *Annual Report, Smithsonian Institution*, 1911, pp. 569-602.

Liu, C. H.

On a Newly-discovered Lolo MS from Szechuan, China. *Man.* 1932, XXXII, No. 268, OP. 235-6.

Lietard, A.

Le district des Lolos A-chi. *MC*, XXXVI, 1904, pp. 93-96, 105-8, 117 -120.

Notions de grammair Lolo (dialects A-hi). *BEFEO*, IX, 1909 pp. 285 -314.

Notions de grammaire Lolo (dialects A-hi). *TP*, XII, 1911, pp. 627 -663.

Essai de dictionnaire Lolo francais, dialecte A-hi. *TP*, XII, pp. 1-37, 123-156, 316-346, 544-558.

Vocabulaire francaise Lolo.*TP*, XIII, 1912, pp. 1-42.

Au Yunnan les Lolo P'o: une tribu des aborigenes de la Chine meridionale. *Bibliotheque Anthropos*, Vol. I, 1913.

Madrolle, C

Quelques peuplades Lo lo. *TP*, IX, 1908, pp 529-576.

Maire, Henri

La mission des Lolos. *MC*, XIV, 1882, pp. 505-7.

Mueller, H.

Beitrag zur Ethnographie de Lolo. *Abessler Archiv*, III, pp. 38-68.

Ollone, Vicomte d'

In Forbidden China. 1912.

Ecritures de peuples non chinois de la Chine. 1912.

Playfair, G. M. H.

The Misotzu of Kweichou and Yunnan from Chinese descriptions. *cr*, V, pp. 92-108.

Rocher, Emile

Histoire des princes dy Yunnan et leurs relations avec la Chine d'apres de documents historique chinois, traduits pour la premiere fois. *TP*, X, 1899, pp. 1-32, 115-154, 337-368, 437-458.

Shirokogoroff, S. M.

Phonetic notes on a Lolo dialect and consonant L. Academia Sinica: *Bulletin of the National Research Institute of History and Philology*, Vol. I, Part II, 1930, pp. 183-225.

Sculie, G., et Tchang Yi-tchou, tr.

Les barbares soumis dy Yunnan Chapitre de Tien hi. *BEFEO*, 1908,

VIII, pp. 149-176, 333-379.

Starr, F.

Lolo Objects in the Public Museum, Milwaukee. *Bulletin*, Vol I, 1910 11, pp. 210-220, 8 pl.

Terrien de Lacouperie

On a Lolo MS Written on Satin. *Journal RGS* n.s., Vol. XlV, 1882, pp. 119-123.

Lolo not connected with Vei characters. Athenaeum, 23, September, 1882.

The Language of China before the Chinese. *Transactions of the Philological Society*, 1885-7. pp. 394-538.

The beginnings of Writings in Central and Eastern Asia, or, Notes on 450 Embryo-writings and Scripts. 1894.

Ting, V. K.

Native Tribes of Yunnan. *China Medical Journal*, March, 1921.

Vial, Paul

Un tournoi chez les sauvage Lolos. *MC*, XX, 1888, pp. 445-448.

Etude sur l'ecriture des Lolos du Yunnan. *Le Lotus*, IX, 1890, pp. 30-49.

Les Gni ou Gni-pa tribu lolo te du Yunnan. Miscellaneous notes scattered in *MC*, XXV (1893) and XXVI (1894).

Les Lolos histoire, religion, moeurs, langue, ecriture. Etudes sino -orientales, fascicule A, 1898. (Reviewed in *CR*, XXIII, pp. 182-3, by E. H.

Parker; and TP, IX, 1898, pp. 413-6).

Dictionnaire francaise-lolo, dialecte gni, tribu situe, etc. province du Yunnan. 1909.

Wylie, A., tr.

History of the Southwest Barbarians; tr. from the Tseen Han Shoo (History of Former Han Dynasty) Book 95, by A. Wylie. *JRAI*, IX, 1880, pp. 53-96.

Si nan man chuan, *Hou Han Shu*, book 116 (Section on the south western barbarians in the History of Later Han dynasty); tr. by A. Wylie. *Revue d'Extreme Orient*, Vol. I, 1882.

Zaborowski, S.

Les Lolos et les populations du sud de la Chine d'apres le ouvrages chinois. *Revue de l'Ecole d'Anthropologie de Paris*, XV, 1905, pp. 86-95.

Photographies de femmes Lolo Miao-tse et de natives de la ville de Yunnan. Collection de chaussures de sud de la Chine. *BMSAP*, 1901, pp. 140-143.

## Roman numbers referred to in the
## notes are to the following Chinese works

1. *Nan man, Hsin T'ang shu, lieh chüan*147 (Southern Barbarians,

New Official History of the T'ang dynasty).

2. *Man i, Sung shih, lieh chüan*252-5 (Barbarians, Official History of Sung dynasty).

3. *Shin Yuan shih, chüan* 145. Barbarians of Yunnan, Hu-kuang and Ssuchuan (New Official History of Yuan dynasty).

4. *Tu ssu, Ming shih, chüan* 300-319 (Native chiefs, official History of Ming dynasty).

5. *Tu-ssu chuan,Ching shih kao, chüan* 517-522 (Biographies of native chiefs, Draft History of Ching dynasty).

6. *Hua Yang Kuo Chih* (History of the country of Hua Yang) Compiled during the 3d century A.D.

7. *T'ung Tien* (a cyclopaedia compiled by Tu Yu of the T'ang dynasty) Section on Barbarians.

8. *Man Shu* (Book of Barbarians) by Fan Cho (9th Cent. A.D.) See Pelliot, *BEFEO*, IV, Nos. 1-2, p. 132, Note 5.

9. *Nan-chao Yeh-shih*, tr. into French by C. Sainson, 1904.

10. *Huang Ching chih kung tu* (Atlases of the Tributary Countries of Ching dynasty) compiled during the beginning of the 18th Century.

11. *Nan man chih* (Records of Southern Barbarians). Gazetteer of the province of Yunnan, Books 172-190. Comp. during 1826-1835.

12. *Nan man chih*. Supplement to the Gazetteer of the province of Yunnan, Books 159-199. Comp. in 1901.

13. *Man Ssu ho chih* , by Mao Chi-lin (1623-1716). It is a book about the native chiefs of Kwei-chou, Yunnan, etc. A full supplement to the Official History of the Ming Dynasty.

14. *Yang Chen chih:* A Brief Account of the Lolo. Ling nan Journal, Vol. I, pp. 134-152.

15. *Ting: Man yu san chi* (Travels in Yunnan and Ssuchuan). *Independent Review*, Nos. 34-56, 42. 1933.

Ancient tribal and place names referred to in the thesis are in red. Those underlined are names in the T'ang period.

```
Terrien de Lacouperie's identifi-
cation of Lao-shan.  See page 18.


Actual location of Lao-shan
```

MAP 1

MAP 2

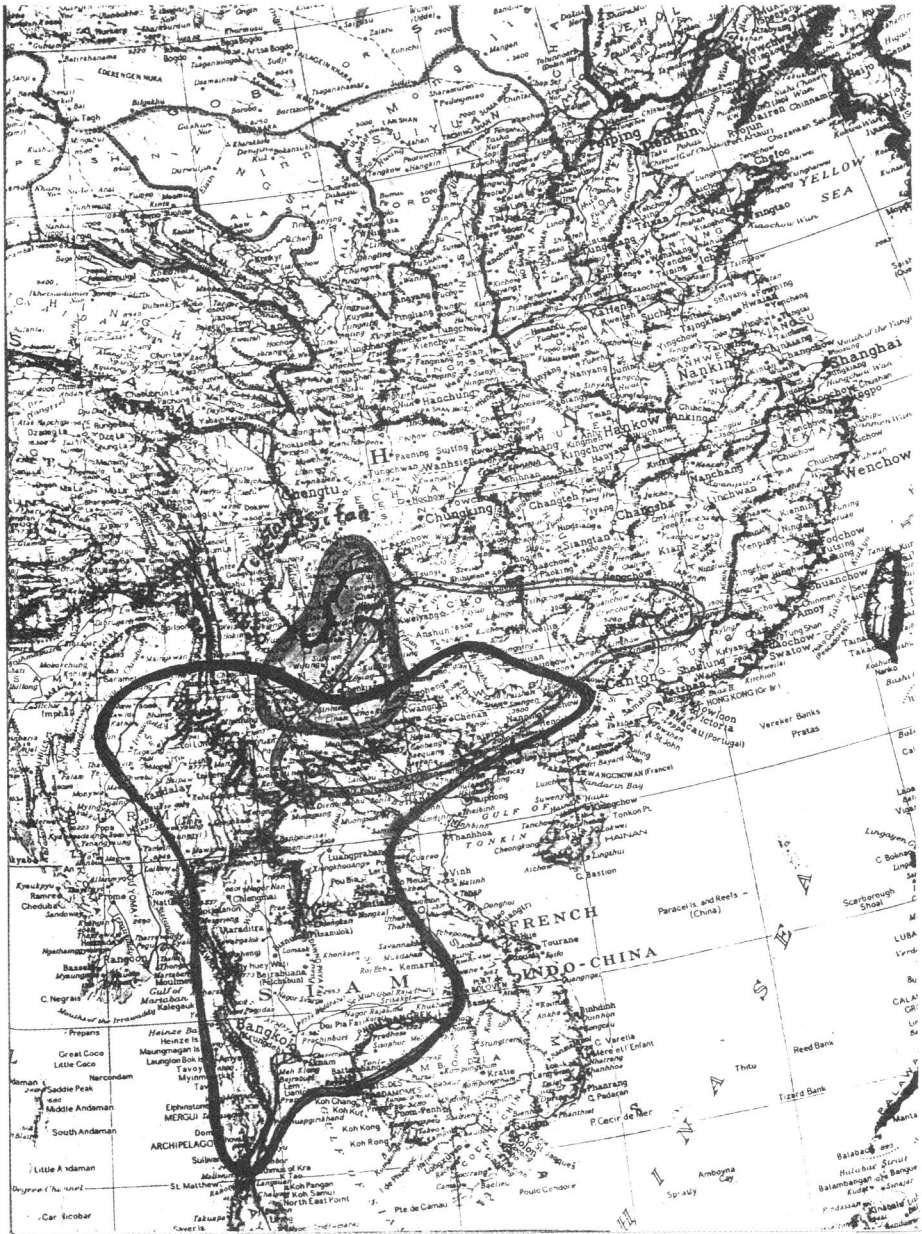

Lolo

Miao-Yao group

Shan

The distribution of these three groups, here represented in the map, is chiefly based on Ryozo Torii's *Geographical distribution and present condition of the Miao tribe in China* (in Japanese) J. G. Tokyo, G. S., 1903, pp. 385-400, 465-574; H. R. Davies' *The Tribes of Yunnan*, 1909; C. E. Jamieson, *The Aborigines of Western* China, 1923; *Gazetteer of Upper Burma*; and many of the works given in the Bibliography.

（此为 1934 年冯汉骥先生在宾夕法尼亚大学人类学系就读
期间所完成的硕士论文，打印稿今存
Van Pelt Library, University of Pennsylvania ）

（原载张勋燎、白彬编：《川大史学·冯汉骥英文卷》，
四川大学出版社，2015 年，第 21—76 页）

# MARRIAGE CUSTOMS IN THE VICINITY OF I–CHANG

## Forword:Chinese Marriage Customs

This material concerning local marriage customs in the vicinity of I-Ch'ang was collected by Dr. FENG Han-yi in 1938.

I-Ch'ang is located on the north bank of the Yangtse River, 397 miles above Hankow, and 1,000 miles from the sea, in the province of Hupeh. It was formerly a treaty port, and according to Couling, contained about 40,000 inhabitants. The district was not thickly populated. I-Ch'ang was important chiefly as a port of transit, though beans, grain, sesamum seed, vegetable tallow and wood oil were exported. The gorges of the Yangtse begin about ten miles above the city.

The material was collected in the country districts about I-Ch'ang. As such places are conservative, the customs reflect the situation in the closing days of the empire, which ended in 1911.

Dr. FENG had the advantage of being a native of this district himself, and was able to secure information through his family connections. He consulted about a dozen elderly men and women who were accustomed to act as masters-of-ceremony at marriages, and in addition, attended eighteen marriages himself while collecting the material.

The material presented here was intended as a preliminary study, but unfortunately it must be the final form as well. The hostilities between China and Japan made the area about I-Ch'ang a battlefield for several years, and most of this time the city was held by the Japanese. Not only did this interrupt Dr. FENG's investigations, but it has probably made it impossible for him, or anyone else, ever to complete them. The society in which these customs flourished has ceased to exist, and in so far as a custom was peculiar to the locality, it is probably lost. Nevertheless, the material includes a complete account of what was regarded as a normal marriage.

So far as the authors are aware, the only other detailed study of Chinese marriage customs is "Les cérémonies du mariage," by Paul SERRUYS, in *Folklore Studies*, Vol. III, 1944, published by the Museum of Oriental Ethnology of the Catholic University of Peking. This study is concerned primarily with customs in the vicinity of Ta T'ung , in the province of Shansi, in North China.

The authors are indebted to Professor Derk BODDE, of the University of Pennsylvania, for valuable suggestions.

In pre-Buddhist China, social theory left no place for the unmarried, either men or women. Even in religion, there were no instances of celibacy in devotion to a god, or in monastic orders.

It was the duty of parents to arrange for the marriage of their children as soon as the latter had reached the marriageable age, and when such marriages were not arranged, the responsibility for such negligence rested with the parents. This situation seldom arose, since the desire for male children who would carry on the family line was an incentive to early marriage.

Although certain marriage rites had a religious significance, no supernatural sanction was required, and no priest need be present. The ritual was strict, and the legality of the marriage demanded certain recognized forms. Because of the paternal clan organization, marriage is forbidden to couples bearing the same surname; this regulation is strictly enforced and seldom violated. Marriage is permitted between relatives who do not bear the same surname, provided that they belong to the same generation of the clan. But this does not mean that the couple are required to be of approximately the same age, since the generations are reckoned from some remote ancestor, and with the lapse of centuries, there may be representatives of twenty generations alive at one time.

The authors wish to express their gratitude to the American Council of Learned Societies for a grant which made this study possible.

## The Betrothal:Taking the Eight Words: *Na pa tzǔ* 拿八字

The consideration and provision of a future mate begins as soon as a child is born. While the child is small, the parents seldom take an active part in such negotiations, waiting for someone else to take the initiative. This often comes from a maternal uncle, but a friend or neighbor is acceptable. In a majority of cases, the first action comes from some relative, though not of the immediate family. A matchmaker is an important figure at later ceremonies; he must eliminate friction and antagonism between the two sides and act as a liason official. Complications frequently occur, so that few care to accept the responsibility of such a position within their immediate families.

The matchmakers are called *mei* 媒, and must be men, though the original suggestion may have come from a woman. There must be two *mei*, and so the man to whom the idea originally occurred finds another with the same interest and standing, who acts with him. In the various ceremonies connected with marriage, for which the general expression "happy events," *hsi shih* 喜事, is used, everything should be in pairs as far as possible, and there should be no single object or action. The two *mei* should have the same interest in and knowledge of both sides of the prospective marriage.

Having reached this point, the two *mei* consult as to whether the proposed match would be a good one. Both families should have about the same social and economic status, though it is better that any advantage should lie with the family of the future husband. A man would be at a disadvantage if he married into a family superior to his own, but every man desires that a daughter should marry into a better home than her father's. Such considerations are called *liang mei* 量媒, "measuring by the *mei*."

If the *mei* consider the match suitable, the next step is for them to visit the family of the girl. After an exchange of greetings and preliminary conversation, one of the *mei* speaks to the following effect:

"Please accept our congratulations upon having such a good and beautiful daughter. We are anxious to learn whether she has been 'written on red.' If not, we would remind you that the LI family has a fine boy, and you know that their 'gate is high and large.' As the ancients said, 'When a girl is born, she should be engaged into a family whose gate is high.' We should like to 'write on red' for your daughter, and inquire whether you are willing."

As the betrothal contract is written on specially prepared red paper, the phrase "write on red," *t'i hung* 题红, is equivalent to a betrothal. Red is the appropriate color for happy events, and accordingly must be used as much as possible at a marriage. A high gate indicates a mansion and a powerful family, and the Chinese expression is *kao mên ta hu* 高门大户.

If the parents of the girl do not approve the match, or intend to betroth their daughter into some other family, they can easily make excuses which will not offend the matchmakers. But if the parents of the girl like the idea, they will reply in approximately this manner:

"If Mr. CHANG desires, will he please exchange our little girl for some wine?"

This phrase refers to the fact that matchmakers consume considerable amounts of both wine and food. A proverb says, "If you love to eat and drink, become a matchmaker," and another, "The matchmaker has eight mouths," referring to a minimum of eight feasts to which he must be invited before the marriage ceremonies are finished.

Then the two *mei* visit the family of the boy, saying:

"Congratulations! Congratulations! You have a fine boy, who ought to marry a beautiful girl. There is a girl in the WANG family, and you cannot imagine what a darling she is. You know how illustrious the line of the WANGS is. The rules of their family are strict, and the education within their home is good. As the saying runs, 'A boy should marry a girl from a refined family.' You are aware how refined the WANG family is. If you desire, we will be glad to put ourselves at your service."

If the LI family do not like the match, the father may reply that he prefers to wait until the boy is older, or gives a similar acceptable excuse. If he approves the match, he replies somewhat as follows:

"If Mr. WANG does not consider us too poor, and you two gentlemen are willing to put yourselves to such trouble, please do as you wish."

Naturally the father of the boy is aware that the two *mei* have already secured the consent of the girl's parents. The direct question concerning the betrothal would not be put until after some preliminary conversation on general topics not connected with marriage.

When the matchmakers have secured the consent of both sides, they seek an opportunity to obtain from the girl's family the "oral eight words," *K'ou pa tzǔ* 口八字.

The "eight-words" are four expressions of two words each which give the year, month, day and hour of the girl's birth, the characters being taken from two lists known as the Heavenly Stems and the Earthly Branches. The eight-words given the *mei* at this time are spoken, so that if the match should not be made, less embarrassment is caused since nothing has been committed to writing.

The eight-words of the girl are given to the boy's family, who take them, together with the eight-words of the boy, to a fortuneteller skilled in this subject. He examines them to see whether the two sets are compatible. This is an elaborate procedure, the principle being that of analogy with the meanings of the terms. If the two sets of words are not compatible, the proceedings are automatically stopped, and since all has been oral to this point, no damage has been done.

If the two sets of eight-words apiece are compared and found compatible, the agreement is called *Shang hun*上婚 . The boy's family will then choose a fortunate day—selected by a fortuneteller, or by means of the calendar, which lists the proper and improper days for various occasions.

The first invitations for this date are then sent by the boy's family to the two matchmakers, written upon a special red card. When the matchmakers receive these cards, they inform the family of the girl. Then the family of the boy sends an invitation to the father of the girl. From the time this invitation has been sent, the fathers of the two children call each other "related family" *Ch'in chia* 亲家.

On the morning of the chosen date, the two matchmakers first go to the family of the girl. The eight-words of the girl have already been written upon a special red card eight inches high and three inches wide. The words are written in the middle, parallel to the long side. The size of the card is symbolic, eight representing the number of words, while three corresponds to the *San yüan ho hun* 三元合婚. This phrase cannot be translated literally, but means to submit the horoscopes of a proposed betrothal to the three powers: Heaven, Earth, and Man.

This red card is placed in a red envelope, nine inches high by three and a half inches wide. A phrase of four words is written in the middle of the envelope. Either of two phrases may be used, both taken from the Book of Odes, and both indicating a long and happy life together for the couple. The phrases are *Ch'ang fa Ch'i hsiang* 长发其祥, "May their felicity long pour fourth," and *Po shih ch'i Ch'ang* 百世其昌 "May their prosperity extend to one hundred generations." The envelope symbolizes an expression, *po nien chieh lao* 百年偕老, meaning "to reach one hundred years together." These cards and envelopes are carried in stock in all stationary stores.

Card and envelope are placed in a red lacquered box ten inches long, four inches wide, and one or two inches deep, called *pai t'ou ho* 拜投盒 "visiting-card box." Large families usually possess such a box, but it can be borrowed from a neighbor.

The girl's father is invited to the ceremony, but never attends. Instead he sends a messenger bearing the visiting-card box, who accompanies the two matchmakers to the home of the boy's family. As they reach the gate, firecrackers are set off in welcome.

When the three enter the house, they are met by the father of the boy, who is congratulated by the matchmakers, and they bow *tso i* 作揖 to each other.

The messenger places the visiting-card box containing the eight-words on a table in the center of the hall before the family ancestral shrine, and opens the box without removing the card on which the eight-words are written. He offers congratulations to the boy's father, and they exchange bows.

The father of the boy then sets off firecrackers, lights a pair of red candles, and burns sticks of incense before the family shrine and ancestral tablets, bowing three times before the shrine.

This ends the ceremony, and the guests rise and offer greetings and best wishes for the future marriage and for the parents of the pair. The father of the boy then removes the eight words of the girl from the box, placing it in a secure spot, for it is the evidence of the betrothal contract. These eight-words are popularly called *hung kêng pa tzǔ* 红庚八字 "red birth date eight-words," or *T'ung kêng pa tzǔ* 童 ｜ ｜ ｜ ｜ "the child's birth date eight-words."

The procedure just outlined may be considered the minimum requirement, such as would be used by a peasant family. A well-to-do man will give presents to the girl betrothed to his son as a part of this ceremony of the eight words, and these are called "betrothal presents," *p'ing li* 聘礼. Such presents are always in pairs, and they may include earrings, finger rings, bracelets, pieces of silk (usually two pieces sufficient for making two garments for the girl), and 100 "dragon" and "phoenix" betrothal cakes—so called because of the images stamped on them, the dragon being male, and the phoenix female. While the minimum ceremony is fixed by custom with little or no variation, there is no definite standard with regard to betrothal presents, which may be of great value or eliminated entirely.

Although there is no resort to legal machinery—for instance, the betrothal is not registered with the courts—the ceremony is legally binding. It would be exceedingly difficult to dissolve such a betrothal, and the person initiating such a step would lose considerable social standing, no matter what reasons were advanced. Even an incurable disease would not generally be considered sufficient grounds for breaking a betrothal. Should a girl become blind or lame, her parents may request the two matchmakers to arrange for the cancellation of the contract, but this is a gesture which it is considered honorable for the parents of the boy to refuse. Such misfortunes on either side would be held due to fate, and not matters permitting human readjustment. Indeed, the parents of the boy would acquire prestige for making such a refusal. But in case of the death of either the boy or the girl, the betrothal would be automatically cancelled without further ceremony.

These childhood betrothals may take place any time between a few months after birth to the time the children are three or four years of age. After that, it is considered rather discreditable for a child to remain unbetrothed. This is usually due either to poverty, or to the bad reputation of the family. As a result, it may be difficult for a boy or girl to make a good match in later life, for there is an implied reflection upon the social standing of the parents.

The preliminary negotiations for a betrothal may take place at any time during the year, but the actual betrothal ceremonies must be held within fifteen days after the Chinese New Year. The New Year period is a time of festivity, and for the peasants, the only such period permitting long preparation. The house is well stocked with food, and it is easy to prepare a feast. It is a time of inactivity for farmers, between the autumn and spring plantings. The ceremony is usually held on a day with an even number for its date—the sixth, eighth or tenth day of the month.

One or more tables are prepared for the feast, to which neighbors, relatives, and friends are invited. As most of these must be entertained during the New Year period, a double purpose is achieved, for the engagement feast will also serve as the spring feast. The feast is usually held about noon, but if the family of the girl live so far away that the invitations cannot reach them in time for them to arrive at noon, the event may take place about dark. At this feast, the seats of honor are occupied by the matchmakers.

After this, the two families seldom call on each other, and the affair is not discussed again until the engaged couple have grown and are ready for marriage. But if the families are related—though having different surnames—calling would continue as usual. The kinship status will not be altered until the marriage is consummated, although the boy and girl will avoid each other before the marriage.

Among the peasants, the girl is generally one or two years older than the boy, but it is not considered good for the girl to be more than four years older than her husband. If the marriage takes place when the boy is eighteen, the girl will then be twenty and fully mature, becoming immediately an economic asset to her husband's family as a worker.

## Filling in the Age: *T'ien Kêng* 填庚

When the boy is between sixteen and eighteen years of age, arrangements must be made for his marriage. The family of the boy always takes the initiative, giving notice to the matchmakers about a year in advance. They, in turn, notify the family of the girl, in order that preparation may be made for her also. A year is needed for adequate preparation.

When a father has decided that his son's marriage is soon to take place, he takes the eight-words of both the boy and the girl to a fortuneteller, in order that the latter may determine whether the coming year contains a favorable date for this particular marriage. Sometimes it is necessary to wait as long as two years before a suitable date can be secured.

If there is a satisfactory date, the boy's father sends a formal card to the two matchmakers shortly before the New Year, announcing that his son intends to visit his future father-in-law during the coming season in order to offer his New Year's greetings. The date for this visit must be the second, fourth, sixth, or eighth day of the New Year. The matchmakers in turn inform the family of the girl of the proposed visit.

On the day fixed, the matchmakers come to the house of the boy to accompany him, his father, and a messenger. The messenger carries four packages of delicacies and a visiting card box containing the following articles: an invitation card to the girl's father, a New Year's greeting card from the boy's father, an "age book" of dragon and phoenix design *kêng shu* 庚书, a pair of writing brushes, and a pair of ink sticks. All must be new and hitherto unused, and must be wrapped in red paper.

The birth date of the boy—his eight-words—is written vertically on the right side of the age book, the left being left for the corresponding data for the girl. The age book is placed in a red envelope on which is written *T'ien tso chih ho* 天作之合, "The union is made by Heaven."

When the house of the father of the girl has been reached, the father of the boy and the matchmakers exchange bows and New Year's greetings with the father of the girl. The boy kowtows three times to his future father- and mother-in-law. The messenger places the presents and the visiting card box on a table which has been prepared in the center of the hall.

The father of the girl takes the visiting-card box to an interior apartment, where he removes all the cards. He fills in the girl's birth-date on the left side of the age book and replaces it in the box, but keeps the other cards.

The father of the girl has prepared a feast of one or two tables, to which he has invited outside guests as an honor to the boy's family and the matchmakers. At this feast the boy and his father occupy the seats of honor, with the matchmakers ranking just below them.

When the feast is over and the guests are leaving, the girl gives a present to the boy, not in person, but through an intermediary. This present consists of two pieces of needlework and a handkerchief in a case. The father of the girl must give a present, *li shih* 利市, usually one or two dollars, to the messenger who carried the visiting-card box, and this present must be wrapped in red paper.

The father of the girl will return the visit of the father of the boy on the date specified on the invitation card presented in the visiting-card box. He is accompanied by the two matchmakers, and by a servant carrying four packages of delicacies. This is usually done two or four days (an even number) after the first visit. This return visit is called *kuo lu* 过路, "crossing the road."A similar feast is held, and a present given to the one who has carried the gifts. These feasts are held at noon.

During the period between the exchange of the eight-words when the boy and girl were small children and the time of filling in-the-age, perhaps fifteen years, the two families seldom visit each other. The fathers may meet at the house of a third party, and on such occasions they call each other "relative," but assume no special attitude. But when the children reach marriageable age, a new and closer relationship is assumed, and the two ceremonies of filling in-the-age and crossing-the-road are the first steps in this new attitude. They also serve as a notification to the parents of the girl that the boy has matured and is ready for marriage.

# Requesting Assent: *Ch'iu k'ên*

Although these ceremonies suggest to the family of the girl that the father of the boy considers his son ready for marriage, no formal request has been made as yet, and such a ceremony is necessary.

The formal request for the actual marriage is called "requesting assent," *Ch'iu k'ên.*

About two months after the ceremony of filling in the age, the father of the boy will invite the matchmakers to a feast, at which he will request them to announce formally his intentions to the father of the girl. The matchmakers then go to the father of the girl and speak about as follows:

"The 'relative on the male side' (the formal title by which the father of the boy is called by the girl's father) has asked us to inform you that, as the children are gown, he desires, and assumes that you desire also, that they should be happily married this year."

The "relative on the female side" (i.e., the father of the girl) will then reply in this manner:

"Our girl is still young, and is ignorant of management. If she goes now, we fear that she will be a burden to her mother-in-law. We think it best to wait another year."

The matchmakers then reply:

"As the old saying goes, a boy ought to marry when he has matured, and a girl also. Even though your daughter lives to the age of one hundred, she must go to her husband sometime. Since she must be married eventually, why not allow her to go now? We consider that the sooner this happy event takes place, the better."

Then the "relative on the female side" will say:

"If the family of the boy is determined to get the girl this year, they can have her. But please tell them that we will be unable to give the girl anything (i.e., a dowry) this year. All we can spare is the girl herself. Please request the parents of the boy not to complain because we give the girl nothing."

The terms for the father and mother of the boy which are used in this speech, *Ch'in yeh* 亲爷, and *Ch'in ma* 亲妈, are, strictly speaking, titles used by the younger generation in directly addressing the father-and mother-in-law to be. They are used by the older generation on the principle of teknonymy.

The speech by the father of the girl is the sign of consent. The matchmakers the term *mei-jên* 媒人 is sometimes used as the equivalent of *mei*—make some complimentary remark and then change the subject of conversation. The father of the girl may then invite the matchmakers to a simple meal, but this is optional. After this the matchmakers return to inform the boy's family that the consent has been obtained, and the preparation for the marriage ceremony is begun.

But the family of the girl may not consent, and may even delay the marriage for years; in that case the family of the boy can do nothing but wait. There are two common reasons for such a delay.

The first is economic. The girl's family is required to give a dowry with the girl, the amount of which depends on their social status. It may be necessary for them to postpone the marriage until the dowry can be provided; this is particularly necessary when there are other daughters. All the daughters must be treated impartially in this matter in order to avoid family troubles and injurious gossip, although obvious changes in the family fortunes might result in lessened or increased dowries without causing difficulties—provided the dowry given is appropriate to the position of the family at the time. But should a man be financially embarrassed, he would probably postpone the marriage of a daughter.

The second common reason for delay is affection between mother and daughter. When a mother is unusually fond of a daughter—especially the youngest—she may oppose an early marriage, particularly because the marriage and the new life may be a difficult ordeal for the girl, and the mother may not desire her daughter to experience it too early.

# Announcing the Date: *Pao Ch'i* 报期

After the consent of the girl's family has been secured, the father of the boy prepares for the announcement of the date of the marriage. The approximate or exact date has already been communicated unofficially to the family of the girl, but the time has now come to make a formal announcement.

Before selecting the exact date, the menstruation period of the girl must be known, for it would be considered disastrously unlucky should the girl be menstruating at the time of the marriage. A popular couplet of four words to each line expresses the general feeling:

*Ch'i ma pai t'ang* 骑马拜堂

*Chia pai jên wang* 家败人亡

"When the bride is 'riding a horse' at the time of the marriage, the family will fall and its members be destroyed."

The phrase "riding a horse" is a symbolic expression used as a substitute for a more direct reference to menstruation. The information concerning the girl's period would probably be secured by the girl's parents informing the matchmakers that certain days of each month would be inconvenient for the ceremony.

At this time the family of the boy will engage a tailor, who then makes all the clothes for both bride and groom. The tailor visits the home of the girl in order to secure the measurements.

The traditional date for the announcement of marriages is the sixth day of the sixth month. On this day, tenants send their first fruits to their landlords. The day comes during a lull in the farming season, when rice and cotton have been planted, but two months before harvest. On the day of announcement, the two matchmakers are invited to the home of the boy for breakfast.

The gifts to the girl on the announcement-of-the-date usually include the following:

Two suits of clothes, one for summer and the other for autumn.

Two sticks of rouge.

Two boxes of face powder.

Two bottles of perfume.

One fan—an exception to the rule that objects must be in pairs. The fan may be either round or folding.

These gifts are for the girl herself. There are also gifts for her relatives, which will include four packages of delicacies or 100 cakes of dragon and phoenix design.

The "wedding date announcement card," *ch'i tan* 期单, is designed by a fortuneteller, or by a scholar expert in such matters. A number of directions and requirements must be given on this card, particularly with regard to certain taboos. The taboos depend upon the date, and that in turn upon the eight words of the boy and girl, so that the taboos vary. Should it be discovered that the appropriate taboos have not been properly announced, great trouble would result, both in quarrels between the families, and in serious misfortunes of the sort known legally in the West as "Acts of God."

The system is quite complicated, requiring an expert to manipulate it. Tables of days, months and years must be examined, and the names of animals used in the Chinese cycles carry with them, by analogy, the characteristics of these animals. SERRUYS (*op. cit.*, 98, 99, 142) gives tables, diagrams and examples.

These taboos, a literal translation of which would be meaningless, include the following:

*Chou T'ang chih T'ang* 周堂值堂, and *Pai hu chih mên* 白虎值门. The second phrase means "The white tiger arrives at the gate." The white tiger is a symbol of discord, and must be shut out of the premises by the seal and the carpet, both of a fortunate color, red. When this taboo is in force, the gate of the groom's house must be sealed with red paper, and the ground over which the bride enters must be covered with a red carpet.

*Chou T'ang chih wêng* │││翁. The parents of the groom must leave the house at the moment the bride enters the gate, and remain absent during the marriage ceremonies.

*Chou tang chih nü fu mu* │││女父母. The bride's parents must avoid their own house at the moment the bride is leaving it.

*Pai hu chih chu* ||| 厨. The cook must avoid the house at the moment of the bride's entrance. The last word in the phrase, meaning kitchen, is also used for a wooden cage in which criminals were placed.

In these formulas, the words *t'ang*, *wêng*, and *chu*, meaning house, old man, and kitchen, appear in a cycle given by SERRUYS, and their significance in these formulas depends on their position in the cycle.

*Hsiao li yüeh* 小利月. A "small month" contains only twenty-nine days, and the phrase is also used for premature birth. The bride may not return to visit her parents until one month after her marriage.

The card must also announce the time of the "putting-up-the-hair." In childhood, a girl's hair is braided and hangs down the back. When puberty is reached, the braids are tied in a knot on the back of the head, but the hair over the forehead is plaited right and left from the center of the forehead and brought back to the knot at the rear of the head. This distinctive style of dressing the hair for an unmarried girl is called *fên pien t'ou* 分辫头.

The putting-up-the-hair consists of eliminating the two plaits in front by combing all the front hair straight back from the forehead to the knot. This is the custom for married women, and the ceremony is a matter of importance to women. The affair takes place from ten to three days before the marriage, and the card announcing it is specific, giving such information as the hour of the ceremony, the direction which the girl will face, and the woman who will dress the hair.

The announcement card containing all this information is written on deep red paper and placed in a red envelope. Down the middle of the face of the envelope are written the words "to announce beforehand the good date," *yü pao chia Ch'i* 预报佳期.

The envelope containing the card is then placed in a visiting-card box together with the personal card of the boy's father. The delicacies, cakes and presents are placed in a special box, *ho* 盒, carried by two men.

The matchmakers and those carrying the gifts leave the house of the boy's family after their formal breakfast, and go to the home of the girl. There they offer congratulations to the girl's father, who receives them, and entertains the matchmakers at luncheon. This ends the ceremony of announcing-the-date.

## The Dowry: *Chia lien* 嫁奁

In a Chinese family, a girl is considered an outsider, because she will eventually leave the family. ( Under the law of the empire, a daughter could not inherit real property. ) On the other hand, her father must provide her with a dowry at marriage.

As the dowry passes outside the family, a daughter is regarded as a financial liability, *p'ei ch'ien huo* 赔钱货. Her father can seldom give her real estate, lest her brothers complain. Therefore the dowry usually consists of money, and of other things easily carried.

These gifts vary with the economic position of the family, but there is a general idea of a minimum dowry fixed by custom. Most of the objects are for the furnishings of the bride's new room in her husband's home, and for her trousseau. A bride is called a "new person," and all the objects in her dowry must be new. The furniture for the bridal apartment will include certain pieces, but there are different sets, such as the "small complete set," *hsiao Ch'üan T'ao* 小全套, "double boxes and wardrobe," *shuang hsiang shuang kuei* 双箱双柜, and "four boxes and four wardrobes," *ssŭ hsiang ssŭ kuei* 四箱四柜. The first of these sets includes the following pieces:

1. A double bed. There are many kinds of beds, cheap and expensive. At present it is permissible to buy a Western spring bed.

2. A large wardrobe for clothing.

3. A red-lacquer wooden chest.

4. A table, with four bench seats.

5. A dresser, with a chair.

6. A table for personal washing utensils.

7. A rack for clothes.

8. A brazier, with a stand and other accessories.

9. A commode.

10. Two wooden bathtubs, one for the man and one for the woman, lacquered. These tubs would seem small from a Western point of view, and are called "foot tubs."

11. Wash basins.

12. A teapot, with ten cups and ten spoons.

13. A mirror.

14. Two porcelain jars for holding candy, etc., which are placed on the dresser.

15. A box containing a lady's toilet accessories, powder boxes, etc., which is placed on the dresser.

16. Two lamps.

17. Two cotton-padded quilts.

18. Two embroidered pillows.

19. Bed curtains, with ornamental front pieces.

This "small complete set" includes what might be called the minimum requirements for respectability. A wealthy man would add considerably to this list. The cost of this "small complete set" might vary from one hundred to five hundred dollars, Chinese currency, before inflation, depending on the kind of materials and the quality of the workmanship. Woods vary in price, and leather is still more expensive. While these things may be bought ready-made in a large town, they are usually made by local carpenters who are contracted for the occasion, and who begin work on the marriage furniture in the spring. In the country districts, such a man may be a farmer who will make the furniture in his spare time.

The groom's parents seldom provide anything save the room, and all the furniture and decorations are given by the bride's parents. Accordingly, the guests who come to admire the presents praise only the bride's parents. The women in particular examine everything, making the arrangements the subject of their gossip for many days thereafter, and discussing the generosity or niggardliness of the bride's parents. Many brides urge their parents to give them as much as possible, for it would add to their prestige in their new families, especially among the wives of the husband's brothers. A girl who brings a large dowry will be looked on with favor by her husband's parents. Moreover, the woman will probably be obliged to live with these household goods for the remainder of her life. These objects cannot be taken away from her, and she will always take pride in them, although it is especially at the time of the marriage that she desires to make a good showing. As a result, the girl may even quarrel with her parents in order to secure a good dowry.

The other objects given to the bride usually consist of clothes and ornaments. There is no fixed requirement for these things, but the clothes would probably include from eight to sixteen suits, sufficient for the four seasons of the year, if the bride's parents can possibly afford the outlay. In fact, the parents of the groom do not expect to provide any clothes for their son's wife for several years, and it would be a disgrace to the bride's parents were her trousseau insufficient.

The material of the clothes varies, poor people using cotton cloth, while the rich may use wool, silk and fur, sometimes furnishing the bride with more than a hundred suits.

The personal ornaments will include bracelets, rings, hairpins and earrings. Among the rich, these will be of gold; among the moderately well to do, of silver; while the very poor will have none at all.

The preparation of the trousseau is a serious and troublesome affair. Although the bride may have her preferences, she is unable to select or buy the things herself, for all this must be done by her father or brothers. Itinerant tailors may be brought to the house, and several may be employed on the task for one or two months.

The date of the marriage is usually in the tenth month—about November—though it may be as much as a month earlier or later. During this marriage season of late autumn and early winter, the marriage gongs are frequently heard throughout the countryside. It may be noticed that in ancient China the season for marriages was the spring; the reason for the change of time appears to be economic. November is a time of plenty, and is a season of inactivity for the farmers, since the harvest is over. The weather is still warm enough for people to go about without serious inconvenience from the cold, yet cold enough to preserve meats and other foods for some time. The latter condition is sometimes a serious problem, for it may be necessary to keep pigs and goats killed for the occasion four or five days without any means of artificial refrigeration.

There is also a more personal reason for choosing this time of the year. The period following the marriage is a very difficult one for the bride. She is suddenly thrust into an unfamiliar environment. Not only is she unknown to her husband's parents and relatives; she has never even seen her husband before the marriage. Naturally she is obliged to make difficult adjustments. But as the marriage takes place at a time of relative inactivity and enjoyment, she has an opportunity of fitting into her new situation under favorable circumstances, before farming begins again in the spring.

But should the fortuneteller decide that no autumn date is favorable, marriages may take place in the spring and summer. A man may desire his son to marry at sixteen, and discovers that the only favorable date is in the spring, after which there will be no suitable opportunity for several years. But this is unusual, and dates are commonly found in the autumn.

## Preparation for the Marriage Ceremonies

The family of the groom must begin their preparations for the marriage at least one year before, and the plans must be made even earlier.

Rice and other foods must be accumulated and stored long before the occasion. The fattening of the pigs must begin a year before, and while properly fattened pigs can be bought, it is much more economical for a man to do this himself.

The number of pigs required depends on the number of guests; and this in turn, upon the social status of the family. A man will usually be able to estimate the number of guests long in advance, so that he can prepare accordingly. Goats and chickens must also be prepared; farmers usually prefer to do this themselves, rather than go to the expense of buying them at market. The quality of feasts varies with the host. Some men value above all the praise given by the guests for lavish entertainment, while others care little about it.

All the invitations to those who are to act as ushers and officials at the marriage ceremonies must be sent out before the New Year, and are usually sent with the New Year presents. This gives these people, particularly the women, time to make adequate preparation, and to borrow formal costumes and ceremonial gowns from relatives and friends if they do not possess the things themselves. These officials and ushers are usually relatives, and their exact functions at the marriage need not be fixed until later.

All the things needed which cannot be made in the home, including food for the feasts, presents for the bride, and clothes for the groom, must be purchased one or two months before the ceremony. Since the bride is called *hsin niang* 新娘, "new woman," and the groom *hsin lang* | 郎, "new man," all that they wear at the marriage must be new. It may be necessary to make a number of trips to the nearest market town, and some of these things must be made to order. A cook must be engaged about the beginning of the year, while a sedan chair, carriers, and musicians must be arranged for as early as possible.

There is usually little choice about the chair-carriers and the musicians, for there are probably unions or corporations or gilds of sedan-chair-carriers and musicians in the district, which monopolize their specialty, and would cause trouble if outsiders were imported, going as far as fights and lawsuits. Such monopolies by gilds are based not on law but on precedent and tradition, which are generally recognized and acquiesced to, even by the courts. It is possible to import men from outside, but only with the approval of the local gild, which may be secured by paying a percentage of the cost. The gild, in turn, furnishes everything needed for the marriage procession, including sedan chairs, banners, and ornamental umbrellas.

Five or six days before the marriage, everything needed for the feasts must be assembled. A large number of tables and benches must be borrowed from neighbors. The cook provides the bowls, plates, spoons, chopsticks, and other utensils, and with his assistants, comes to arrange the kitchen. A butcher is hired to slaughter the pigs and goats. Other servants, such as those who wait on the tables, and those who serve tea and tobacco, are brought together and instructed. A temporary shed or porch for the convenience of the guests is erected before the house. Bamboo mats shield them from the sun as they sit outdoors.

One of the more important officials at the marriage is the chief usher, *chih K'o* 知客, "he who knows the guests." Besides supervising the servants and assistants, he sees that the guests are properly placed at the tables. This is not an easy task. The tables are square, seating eight guests each. There are two seats of the first honor, two of the second honor, and four accompanying seats without distinction. To place a guest or relative who should have a seat of the first honor in one of the lower places would be a serious affront. Therefore the chief usher must have a wide acquaintance, a polished appearance, a respectable character, a likable disposition, must be a good conversationalist, and above all, must know intimately the positions of the guests and their relationship to the host. Obviously it is not easy to find such a man.

As the guests are being seated, there will be considerable protesting and polite withdrawal as the chief guests refuse the seats of honor, so that eventually they must be compelled to take the highest position. The chief usher, while seating the guests at one table, must remember at the same time those who are sitting at the other tables. For example: suppose a guest has an uncle, who would rank above him in the family, sitting at another table; it would be improper for that guest to occupy a seat of honor, and he must wait for another table.

The women are not served with the men, but in a separate apartment. Accordingly there is a woman who acts as chief usher for the ladies, having approximately the same duties as her male counterpart.

## The Exchange of Presents: *Kuo li* 过礼

The ceremony of the exchange of presents takes place from two to four days before the marriage.

At this time, the household furniture to be given by the parents of the bride is moved to the home of the groom. The matchmakers inform the father of the groom how many men will be needed to carry the things, and he sends the correct number.

The family of the groom sends presents to the bride in return, and conventional gifts to her family. But as most of these gfits are to the bride, who will bring them with her to her new home, they do not represent a loss to the groom's family.

One type of gift appears peculiar to West China. It consists of two paper objects called *ho-lao-yeh* 盒老爷, literally, "old-worthies-of-the-box." One of these objects is a representation of a hill about two feet high, two feet long, and one foot wide, made of red and gold paper, with paper flowers. On the hill are small human figurines, and a "Ch'i lin (unicorn) presenting a baby." On each side is a red paper banner. On one banner is written *Pai liang ying mên* 百辆盈门 "May hundreds of chariots fill the gate," and on the other, *Tzǔ sun Ch'ien i* 子孙千亿, "May there be millions of descendants."

The two boxes, or *ho-lao-yeh*, differ only in the sentences written on a small piece of gilt paper which tops the contrivance. The two sentences are complimentary, and a literal translation means little. They are:

*Wên ting hüeh hsiang* 文定厥祥"May the civil arts determine their good fortune."

*Chên tzǔ shih nien* 贞字十年 "May there be ten years of true words."

There appear no records concerning these *ho-lao-yeh*, and their origin is unknown. The complimentary title *lao-yeh*, "old worthy," refers to the human figures. At present, while these *ho-lao-yeh* are a part of the ritual of marriage gifts to the bride, they seem to be ornamental, and the original significance has been lost.

On the day of the exchange of gifts, the *ho-lao-yeh* bearing the first inscription is placed in a box or case carried by two men. The box is suspended from a pole which rests on the shoulders of the men. At the ends of the box are hung a large piece of pork weighing from five to ten pounds, or a pig's head, and a fish—usually a carp from three to five pounds. In the box are also two bottles of wine, 100 to 400 cakes of dragon and phoenix design, two boxes of "tea fruits," two boxes of tea leaves, a goose or a duck (the goose is correct, but the duck is often substituted for it) and a chicken. The goose and the chicken are usually returned. The contents of this box are for the bride's family.

In another box, along with the second *ho-lao-yeh*, are the presents to the bride herself. These include:

1. Two suits, of four pieces each, of padded cotton; two coats and two pairs of trousers.

2. A coat for formal occasions.

3. An embroidered red skirt.

4. A red coat. With this would go insignia of rank, if appropriate, such as the "phoenix hat," etc.

5. A bride's veil, *kai t'ou* 盖头, of red feather cloth, three and a half feet long.

6. A pair of red stockings.

7. A cloth belt for the trousers.

8. A pair of shoe laces.

9. Four red artificial flowers.

10. Two pieces of rouge.

11. Two boxes of face powder.

12. Two bottles of perfume.

13. A pair of earrings.

14. Two finger rings.

15. Bracelets. The rings and bracelets will be of gold or silver, depending on the circumstances of the family.

All these gifts will be brought by the bride to her husband's home, and if she does not intend to wear certain of them, they may be returned by her parents immediately with the box. Items 2, 3, 13, 14, and 15 may merely be borrowed for the occasion. This list may be considered the minimum requirement, and the rich would augment it considerably.

In addition to these gifts, there are sent the following:

1. Three feet of red cloth, in which the carpenter wraps his axe.

2. Silk threads of five colors; four threads of each color. These threads are wound around two pieces of green cardboard shaped like a lotus leaf.

3. A bronze mirror.

4. Three pairs of *hsi chu* 喜烛, "happy candles".

5. A taper, *nien tzǔ* 捻子, made of cotton cord about three inches long, wound around the end of a piece of bamboo two feet long. The cord has been coated with wax, and is used to light the candles.

6. Two strings of firecrackers.

7. Two boxes of hairpins, used by the bride in "raising the hair,"called *li shih* 利市.

8. A set of invitation cards, called *ho mên shu* 合门书 for the bride's parents.

9. An invitation card for the bride's younger brother, called for this occasion *hsiao eh'in chia* 小亲家, who accompanies the bride's furniture to the home of the husband.

10. Personal calling cards from the parents of the groom. They are called *pai T'ieh* 拜帖.

These calling cards are a necessary accompaniment for anything sent to the bride's family. They are only a formality and are not received.

These things are placed in a box containing four shelves. On the first shelf are the ornaments, on the second and third are clothes, and on the fourth are the cards and cakes. On the outside of the box are written a pair of sentences on red paper:

*Wu sê yün lin mên ssŭ ts'ai* 五色云临门似彩

"Clouds of five colors come to the door as good fortune."

*Ch'i hsiang ch'ê yung p'ei ju Ch'in* 七香车拥辔如琴

"The seven-perfumed chariot rushes on, the bridles tinkling like the music of lutes."

The procession of carriers—perhaps twenty or thirty men—headed by the two matchmakers, leave the home of the groom early enough to reach the home of the bride between nine and ten o'clock in the morning. The matchmakers enter to offer congratulatory greetings, while the boxes containing the gifts are placed in the center of the main hall. The parents of the bride and their kinsmen open the boxes and remove the gifts. The goose or duck, and the chicken—both of which must be alive—are immediately returned, together with the visiting-cards. Those ornaments and clothes which the bride would not actually wear at the ceremony are also sent back at once, or else placed in the boxes with the bride's trousseau.

If the parents of the bride are dissatisfied with the way things have been done—if the gifts are unsatisfactory, or if the ceremonial acts have not been properly executed—the moment has now arrived for them to voice their complaints.

The matchmakers attempt to offer satisfactory explanations, speaking for the groom's family, and smooth matters over. As a result, the bride's parents sometimes shift their wrath to the matchmakers, putting the blame on them. In this trying situation, the matchmakers must remain diplomatic, never losing their tempers or replying in kind.

Should the matchmakers become quarrelsome, they would be accused of improper conduct by both sides, although the groom's family would do so chiefly in order to placate that of the bride. The matchmakers—*mei*—would become moldy, unlucky, *mei* 霉. In such an affair, the bride's family are always the aggressors, while the groom's family are acquiescent and submissive. A popular saying expresses the situation: *T'ai t'ou chia nü êrh , ti t'ou chieh hsi fu* 抬头嫁女儿, 低头接媳妇, "One gives a daughter in marriage with the head raised, but when a son is married, the head is dropped,"

If the matchmakers are suave and conciliatory, the complaints are usually answered satisfactorily. Some families are extremely particular at the marriage of a daughter, requiring that all their wishes be met, and refusing otherwise to send the bride's household furniture. On the other hand, some reflect that in any case, gifts extorted from the groom's family must be sent back with the bride. Therefore they make few requests, lest the future relations between the two families should be strained.

When all matters have been settled, the furniture and trousseau are given to the carriers who have accompanied the matchmakers, to be carried to the groom's home. But the wash basin and bathtubs, and the curtains for the bed, are carried by a man furnished by the bride's parents. This man must be treated with considerable respect, and receives an unusually large gift of money from the groom's family. The bride's family also send the carpenter who has made the furniture, accompanied by a man carrying his axe, which has been drapped in red cloth. This man is usually the carpenter's apprentice.

The carpenter goes to the groom's house to assemble the furniture, of which the bed is the most important piece. A Chinese bed has over the top a central beam, called *liang* 梁, which is the word used for the ridgepole of a house. When the carpenter is adjusting this beam, he lifts the axe wrapped in red cloth, and shouts, "*Kao shêng*" 高升, "Raise higher." In addition to its literal meaning, this phrase is a demand for a gift. The assistants and helpers join with the carpenter, crying, "Certainly." The groom then makes the carpenter a gift, wrapped in red paper. This proceeding is repeated twice, so that the carpenter receives three gifts. This is called *lien shêng san chi* 连升三级, "to raise successively three ranks," and is considered a favorable omen for the groom's future success. But if the carpenter considers the gift too small, he may extort larger sums from the groom by continuing to cry "raise higher," and the groom is obliged to continue his gifts. If the demands of the carpenter are not met, he refuses to adjust the beam until he is satisfied, and such a refusal would be a very unfavorable omen.

But the carpenter is obligated to cry "raise higher" at least three times, for otherwise the groom's family would consider it an unfavorable omen. In one instance, where the carpenter was a close friend of the family of the groom, it was feared that he would not make this demand, because he might dislike to accept money from old friends, and so the matchmakers were instructed to ask the carpenter to make the cry as many times as possible, even though he should decline the gift.

The carpenter must be careful in making and assembling the bed, for should there be any mishap at this time, it would be unlucky, and he would be discredited and blamed. But if everything goes off satisfactorily, the carpenter occupies a seat of honor at the marriage feast.

The bride's parents appoint someone to accompany the furniture, and to take the keys of the chests and wardrobes to the groom's house. This person is called the *hsiao Ch'in chia* 小亲家 "small kinsman," or *ya chia lien* 押嫁奁, "he who deposits the bridal trousseau." Usually this person is a younger unmarried brother of the bride—a boy between eight and fifteen. Should the bride have no younger brother, her brother's son or daughter may be substituted, but never her younger sister.

When the "small kinsman" reaches the gate of the groom's house, firecrackers are set off, and he is received with great attention, bows and congratulations being exchanged. The groom's mother has left her apartment and is sitting at one side of the main hall. The "small kinsman" goes to her, and after bowing, says,

"Kinswoman-mother, *Ch'in ma* 亲妈, you have felicity. We have prepared for the new *ku-yeh* 姑爷 a few rough pieces of furniture and poor clothes, but please do not laugh at these things." Then he presents her with the keys, and bows once.

*Ku* indicates an aunt on the father's side, while yeh, is a title of respect used for an older person. *Ku-yeh* would properly be used for the husband of the father's sister. The use of this title by the "small kinsman" is not strictly correct, therefore, since the groom and the bride's younger brother are of the same generation.

The mother of the groom accepts the keys, bows, and says,

"Please tell your parents *Ch'in yeh* and *Ch'in ma* that the things they have prepared are so fine and complete, they must have required a large amount of time, and caused them considerable trouble. We are exceedingly thankful for these things, and request you to tell them so." After saying this, she retires.

Then follows a feast, at which the seat of the highest honor is occupied by the "small kinsman." After the feast is ended, he begs permission to leave. The parents of the groom present him with "happy money," *hsi Ch'ien* 喜钱—a few dollars—and an embroidered handkerchief and case.

That night, the parents of the groom open the boxes in the "new room," before an assembly of close relatives, consisting chiefly of the wives of the father's brothers, of the mother's brothers, and the sisters of the father and mother. This is called *chao hsiang* 抄箱,"searching the boxes." While opening the boxes, they must repeat sentences of good omen, such as: 抄箱 抄箱. 金玉满堂. 打开宝库. 千仓万箱. "Search the boxes! Search the boxes! Gold and jade fill the hall. Open the precious treasury. A thousand stores and ten-thousand boxes!"

When the bride's parents pack the trousseau, they must see that the upper-most and lower-most articles in each box are trousers. The word for trousers, *k'u* 裤 is a homophone of the word for treasury, 库. It is the duty of the tailor to inform the ignorant of the correct way of packing these boxes, so that when they are unpacked by the groom's parents, the first and last articles met are trousers, which have a favorable name, signifying future wealth for the married pair. In the words of a proverb: "*Yao tê fu, hsien K'ai k'u* "要得富,先开库. "If one desires wealth, first open the treasury."

When the boxes are packed, all articles are placed facing downwards, but after the search, all must be facing upwards.

The search is also the time when the bride's furniture and clothes are discussed and criticised by the relatives of the groom, particularly the women.

When the search is finished, the groom's parents place a package containing money in each box. This is called *ya hsiang Ch'ien* 押箱钱, "money to hold down the box."

## Raising the Courtesy Name: *shêng hao* 升号

The ceremony of "raising-the-courtesy-name" is an initiation rite, equivalent to the ancient *kuan li* 冠礼, the rite of becoming an adult, found in the *Book of Rites*. The *kuan* was a conical cap worn in ancient China, and still found among Taoists, which was a sign of manhood. The ceremony was called "capping," and appears to have died out, but its place has been taken by the raising of the courtesy name. After this rite, the boy ceases to be a child, or minor. Among young people, a mature man who has not married is often jokingly called a child.

The modern rite is somewhat different from the ancient, being connected with the Chinese system of personal names. A Chinese man has at least three names. When he is born, he receives a *ju ming* 乳名, "milk name." When a few years old, he is given a *P'u ming* 谱 | ,"generation name."

Each family or clan possesses a poem of perhaps twenty syllables, each syllable of which is used as the designation of a generation, permitting of twenty generations before repetition is necessary. For example; if a man's name is WANG Shih-jung, WANG would be the surname, Shih would indicate the generation of the clan to which he belonged, while jung would be his personal name. This is the name which would be placed in the family records.

There may be two forms of the courtesy name, the *tzŭ* 字 and the *hao* 号. A man may possess both, but habitually uses only one of them. Both courtesy names must be complimentary extensions, allied in meaning, of the personal syllable in his generation name. To continue the example: if the syllable *jung* in the generation name is the word meaning "glory," the man might be given such courtesy names as Yao-kuang, "brilliant light," for his *tzŭ*, and Hua-T'ang, "Flowery hall," for his *hao*.

The raising-of-the-courtesy-name is held on the day before the marriage, probably as a matter of economy, for the initiation rite appears to have no necessary connection with the marriage. The ancient capping ceremony was held when the youth had reached the age of twenty, and the marriage took place later. But while a man might remain unmarried indefinitely, he necessarily came of age. However, the two ceremonies have become associated in modem practice, so that in effect, the initiation rite has become one of the ceremonies incident to marriage. There is no record of how or when this change took place.

On the morning of the day of this ceremony, the gate of the house and the door of the bridal chamber are decorated with ornamental couplets written on red paper. The following couplet is typical:

堂上行周官六礼/阶前颂王纪三章

"In the hall, the six rites of Chou are being performed;"

"In the court, the three verses of WANG Chi are being sung."

Above the lintel of the door is placed a tablet with these words:

诗咏关雎

"Sing the 'Kuan-chü Ode' of the *Book of Poetry*."

On the door itself is fastened the following couplet:

易曰乾坤定矣/诗云钟鼓乐之

"*The Book of Changes* says that the male and female principles are determined."

"*The Book of Poetry* says,' Rejoice her with bells and drums.'"

Above the door is fastened a strip of paper with the magic formula:

姜太公在此诸神回避

"CHIANG T'ai-kung is here; all spirits must flee."

About ten yards in front of the main gate there is fastened on a wall or pole the inscription:

麒麟到此

"The *Ch'i lin* (unicorn) has arrived here."

The following couplet is placed, one half on either side of the door of the bridal chamber:

金屋人间传二美/银河天上渡双星

"Within the golden chamber, men admire the two beauties (bride and groom) ."

"The twin stars are ferried over the silver river in heaven."

The last line refers to the story of the shepherd boy and the weaving damsel, a pair of stars, who are allowed to meet as lovers once a year, on the seventh day of the seventh month, by crossing the Milky Way, which in China is called the Silver River.

On the lintel is placed the inscription, *T'ien tso chih ho* 天作之合, "union is made by Heaven". On the door is fastened the "double happiness" symbol, *shuang hsi* 双喜. All these inscriptions are written on red paper.

In the center of the main hall, before the family shrine, is placed a square table having an embroidered cloth for a frontal. On the table is placed the groom's courtesy name, or *hao*, written on a strip of red paper about two feet long and eight inches wide, or on a red or black lacquered tablet of the same size.

The ceremony is held about nine or ten o'clock in the morning, and is performed by the head of the family—probably the father of the groom. He lights incense, candles, and burns paper money to honor the family spirits and the ancestral tablets. These acts, however, are merely an accompaniment of the rite called *kao-tien* 告奠, "to announce (to the ancestors) with sacrifice."

Musicians outside the hall make music and blow the trumpet. Three salutes are fired, and firecrackers set off. Within the hall, the head of the family stands before the table. On his left stands a man bearing a tray on which are three empty wine cups, while on his right another man carries a flagon of wine. The head of the family pours wine into a cup, takes it in his hands, bows toward the ancestral tablets, and pours the wine on the ground. This is done with each cup, three times in all. This rite is also called *San chên san tien*, 三斟三奠, "to pour three libations." The head of the family then kowtows four times, *ssǔ ta li* 四大礼, or eight times before the family shrine, remaining in front of the table.

The groom is then dressed in his formal attire, which is entirely new, even to the underwear. In his hair are tied two red threads, which symbolize the saying, *Ch'ien li yin yüan i hsien Ch'ien* 千里因缘一线牵 "Although a thousand *li* apart, (the pair are) united by a thread."

On his breast, inside the formal coat, hangs a small bronze mirror about three inches in diameter. This custom rests on the belief that the mirror can counteract the evil influence of widows and "four-eyed persons," (i.e., pregnant women). In spite of the power of the mirror, widows and pregnant women are usually excluded from the marriage ceremonies.

From this time, the youth is considered an adult. His milk name is discarded forever, and he is now addressed by relatives and friends by his courtesy name. While this initiation ceremony is short and simple, and has become a part of the marriage ceremonial, there can be little doubt that it is a survival of the more complicated ancient ritual.

During the marriage ceremony, the groom is called *hsin lang* "new man," or *hsiao têng K'o* 小登科, "the little *têng-k'o*." *Têng-K'o*, "advance in grade," was a term used in connection with the old state competitive examinations, indicating that the first degree had been obtained. Possibly the expression is applied to the groom as a favorable omen for a successful career.

The day on which the courtesy name is given is also that on which guests are received and congratulations offered. After the raising-of-the-courtesy-name is finished, the "new man" takes his seat on the right side of the hall, while the head of the family places himself upon the left. When a guest arrives to offer congratulations, the musicians outside the hall play a short passage. The guest advances from the doorway down the middle of the hall. As he does so, the groom and the head of the family join him on either side, all three standing before the table, facing the ancestral tablets.

They then bow together, and the guest offers his congratulations to the head of the family. As he retires, the chief usher cries, "Let tea be offered," and the guest is given tea and tobacco. After this he goes to the *li kuei* 礼柜, "wardrobe for gifts," and presents his wedding gifts.

One or more men are appointed to take charge of this reception of gifts. They must be men with a wide acquaintance, for they must recognize and remember the names of all the guests. It would be very embarrassing to ask a guest his name, when he had come to offer congratulations and gifts. The man in charge keeps a record of the guests, and of their gifts.

These wedding gifts from the guests are usually money, and the amounts may vary from a half-dollar to thirty dollars. The acceptable amount depends upon gifts which have been made to the guest by the host on previous similar occasions. In every family a gift book is kept, in which are recorded all gifts given and received, whether in money or in other things, and the size of a gift for a given occasion will depend upon the contents of that book. For example, a guest, on consulting his gift book, finds that since he last made a gift to the head of the family, he has received from him three gifts of one dollar each on separate occasions. Accordingly, he is obligated to make a gift of three dollars at the marriage. This is the usual custom of giving among friends: the giving and taking should be equal, and if this is not so, the offender eventually loses his friends. Such a loss involves not only friendship, but a loss of face on such occasions as a marriage.

Among closely related kinsmen the understanding may be somewhat different. A man may have given to his father's sister gifts amounting to ten dollars. On the next occasion she returns this amount, and adds an equal sum, which places him under a similar obligation. In any case, a gift received amounts to a debt which must be eventually repaid. When an occasion demanding such a return arrives, such as a marriage of a son or daughter, the appropriate gift must be made, even if the money has to be borrowed.

Such gifts are called *jên Ch'ing* 人情, "human relations," and form a large item in the family budget. Should an unusually large number fall due in a certain year, it may require great effort to secure the necessary funds. On the other hand, if a man has previously made a large number of such gifts to others, he may actually make money by his son's marriage. The number of return gifts which fall due may exceed the amount he is obliged to spend on preparations.

On this occasion, the feasts begin about noon, and may last until four o'clock. The number of guests usually requires more than one sitting, of from four to ten tables. For this reason the feasts are called *liu shui hsi* 流水席, "flowing water feast," (i.e., continuous).

The feast consists of nine courses. The first course will be either *yu yü* 鱿鱼, cuttle fish, or *hai shên* 海参, sea slugs. When this dish is served, the chief usher will visit each table, offering wine, and saying that the feast will be a poor one.

The fifth dish consists of *yüan-tzǔ*, 圆子, meatballs. When the meatballs are served, the groom, accompanied by the chief usher, visits each table, offering wine, and requesting the guests to enjoy the feast. The guests rise, and the groom bows once, and then leaves. The reason for this proceeding is that the term *yüan*, meatball, also means round, to come together, and therefore is a favorable omen at the moment of the groom's greeting to his guests.

The last course will be *yü*, fish. The word *yü* meaning fish is a homophone of *yü* meaning surplus. There is a popular phrase:

*Fu kuei yu yü* 富贵有鱼.

Literally, this means, "Riches and position have a fish;" but the real meaning is, "Of riches and position may there be a surplus." Fish, therefore, is a favorable omen at the last course.

The majority of the guests and friends leave as soon as the feast is over, but close friends and kinsmen may remain at the house for several days, until all the marriage ceremonies are over. A popular and influential man may have more than a thousand guests, while even a poor man will have nearly a hundred.

These affairs are occasions when the peasants become acquainted and mix with each other. There are many introductions, and much chatting and laughter. Ordinarily, a peasant has little chance of meeting a man who lives ten miles away. He very seldom visits a market town unless he has something to sell, and even on such occasions, has little chance of forming new friendships. And if this is true of the men, it is still more true of the women, who are practically confined to the home and nearby fields. Consequently, the occasions of marriages, funerals, and birth rites are the only opportunities most peasant women have for social intercourse.

At these feasts, the sexes are strictly kept apart. The women feast in the inner hall by themselves, and do not mix with the men either before or after the feast, but sit about in the women's quarters. However, the feasts given the women are the same as those given the men.

There are a few necessary changes in the proceedings involving the women. When a woman guest comes to offer congratulations, the assistants shout, "A woman guest," and the musicians play as they do for men. Women guests are received by the hostess—usually the wife of the head of the family—who, when she hears the guest has arrived, receives her in the main hall. The ceremony there is the same as for men, save that the place of the head of the family as host is taken by the hostess. The groom behaves as he does with men guests. After the ceremony of offering congratulations, the woman guest retires to the inner hall, or women's apartments, where she is served tea and tobacco by women helpers or assistants.

Women do not go out as guests so frequently as the men, and the women who go to a wedding would probably be kinswomen, such as the sisters of the father and mother of the groom, the mother's brother's wives, and so on. They usually arrive a day or so early.

## Doing up the Hair: *Shang t'ou* 上头

The ritual so far described has been connected chiefly with the male side, and indeed, at the marriage, the family of the groom take the initiative in most matters, while the family of the bride play a largely passive part. Marrying out a daughter is considered a loss, a happy event with a sorrowful background. Daughter and mother shed many tears at parting, though fewer tears are shed on parting from the father, and still fewer over the brothers. While there must be preparation for the marriage, it is much less arduous than the preparation in the groom's family. Guests may come to the girl's family to offer congratulations and gifts of money, but this is not necessary, and no face is lost by the family if no guests arrive. In any case, the number will be small in comparison with that at the marriage of a son, and the guests will usually be close kinsmen. The parents of the bride do not escape the burden of feasts entirely, but have fewer than the family of the groom.

Just as the rite of becoming an adult is a prerequisite to marriage for the man, so it is also for the woman. The initiation ceremony for girls is called *shang t'ou* "doing up the hair," and has already been mentioned, though not described. It has the same significance as the ancient rite of *chi li* 笄礼 "pinning," from the *chi*, or hairpin, used in the ceremony as the mark of womanhood. This ceremony is discussed in the *Book of Rites*, and is a different rite from raising-the-hair, though the purpose is similar.

The date on which the modern ceremony will take place is stated on the announcement-card already described—one, two or three days before the wedding. The hour also is announced on the card, but is always in the forenoon.

On the day of the ceremony, the girl bathes, and dresses in clothes which are entirely new. Then she sits facing a given direction, which has been announced on the card, on which is also stated the element to which the birth year of the girl belongs. The woman appointed to perform the ceremony then enters.

The sixty-year cycle of the Chinese is connected with the ancient theory of the five elements—metal, wood, water, fire and earth. The year cycle is divided so that each element is connected with twelve years, which are in turn held to belong to that element, though in each year there is a mixture of elements. This ancient philosophical speculation about what we would call physics is exceedingly complicated, so that it requires expert knowledge to apply, and has colored Chinese thought and customs since the Han period. If the announcement-card prepared by an expert states that the doing-up-of-the-hair must be performed by a woman whose birth year belongs to metal, then such a woman must be found.

It is also desirable that the woman should be a relative, not too old, not a widow, with many children, and generally considered to be happy and fortunate. However, the proper birth year is the primary requirement, and if a relative with the right birth year cannot be found, a friend will do, if she meets the other conditions.

This woman sits directly facing the girl. She places a new red cloth about the girl's shoulders, and powders the girl's face. Taking one white thread, and one green, she places one pair of ends between her lips, and holds the other in her fingers. These threads she manipulates by twisting so that they pull out any unwanted hairs, from both the forehead and the eyebrows. The line of hair across the forehead should be straight, and the eyebrows should be narrow and smoothly curved. This process is neither pleasant nor excessively painful.

The woman then pulls the girl's hair straight back from the forehead, and gathers it into a round knot on the back of the head. There are many styles of these knots, so that the girl is able to choose the one she prefers. Artificial flowers are arranged about the knot, and the girl puts on the earrings, bracelets, finger rings, formal coats, and other ornaments sent by the family of the groom. Those women who are entitled to do so put on the *fêng kuan* 凤冠 "phoenix hat," and the *hsia p'ei* 霞佩 "embroidered shoulder piece with tassels."

Then the girl's father lights candles and sticks of incense before the family shrine in the main hall. Firecrackers are set off, and the ceremony of announcement before the ancestors is performed, in a manner similar to the ceremony of the courtesy name already described. The girl's father stands before the altar, flanked by men holding the wine cups and the flagon. He pours a cup, bows, and makes a libation on the ground. Three libations are made in this manner, after which the father prostrates himself (the kowtow) four or eight times before the shrine.

Then two gifts under fourteen years of age lead the bride into the hall in order that she may perform the family rites. She kowtows four times to the tablets of the ancestors, and to all the relatives of a higher generation and status, beginning with her parents and including her older brothers and their wives, and her older sisters. She kowtows kneeling on a red cloth, performing the ceremony as the names are announced. In announcing these names, kinship terms, not personal names, are used; for example, "wife of the second younger brother of the father."

When this ceremony of official admission to the family as an adult has been performed, a table is placed before the family shrine, and a family feast is held. The girl sits in the seat of honor, wearing a red shawl, and facing the entrance. On either side are the two girls who accompanied her on her entrance into the hall, who might be called bridesmaids. Other girls, her friends, are invited to the feast. But the affair is rather gloomy, as the girl constantly weeps, and refuses to eat. This is called *pan nü* 伴女 "accompanying the girl."

When this feast is over, her girlhood is ended, and she is a woman. From now on, she will be called *hsin niang* "new woman",or *hsin fu* 新妇 "new bride." Early on the day of accompanying-the-bride, a couplet written on red paper is placed, one half on either side of the gate. The most common couplet is the following:

菱花绶带鸳鸯簇

"On the water-chestnut belt of silk, pairs of mandarin ducks cluster." This refers to an embroidered silk belt, on which mandarin ducks—a symbol of married felicity—are figured, together with flowers.

金尾屏风孔雀闲

"On the screen, known as the golden tail, the peacock struts leisurely." This refers to a story of the T'ang period. TOU I, the father of the Empress TOU, had two peacocks painted on a screen, and announced that his daughter would marry the suitor who could pierce the eyes of the peacocks with arrows. To each suitor two arrows were given. Only the future Emperor Kao- tsu, founder of the T'ang dynasty, succeeded. The girl died before the T'ang period and was made Empress posthumously. The phrase "pea-cock-screen" has come to mean the selection of a husband or son-in-law.

# Accompanying the Groom: *Pan lang* 伴郎

The ceremony of accompanying-the-groom is held on the night immediately before the marriage day, and is the climax of the pre-nuptial celebrations. Most of the guests who come to offer congratulations remain for this event, which is a jolly affair, and the feasts given in connection with it are the best of the series.

The ceremony begins shortly after dark, and is held in the main hall, in which the family tablets are placed. On the tablets are the names of deceased members of the family. A square table is placed before the tablets for the feast. Another table is placed a few feet in front of the first, and on the ground before it are cotton cushions covered with a red cloth.

On these cushions kneels the man who is performing the rite *hsing li* 行礼 which is usually considered as the kowtow 叩头. *Hsing li*, however, is not the exact equivalent of the kowtow, and means "to perform the rite," or in this ceremony, merely "salutation." *Hsing li* is therefore rendered "prostration."

Down the front of this second table hangs an embroidered red satin cover. On the table is a pair of red marriage candles about two feet high, and a pair of twisted tapers, *nien tzŭ* 捻子, for lighting them.

The whole hall is gay with candles and lanterns and is filled with a crowd of men and women. Firecrackers are set off, and music is played by musicians outside the hall. The head of the family, *chia chu* 家主, who is the father or uncle of the groom, comes forward to perform the announcement ceremony. As before, this includes the lighting of incense, burning paper money, and the three libations. After this, he prostrates himself four or eight times before the family tablets. During this procedure, the groom stands beside him.

Then the head of the family retires, and the groom comes forward. He prostrates himself four or eight times to the ancestral tablets, and four times to his parents. These prostrations are likewise made toward the tablets, but intended for the parents. In the same way, all the other prostrations are made toward the shrine, though they may be in honor of some particular person. A master of ceremony calls the names of those to be honored in this way, these being all members of the clan of higher generations than the groom. With the personal name is announced the degree of kinship. Then are honored the father's sisters, the mother's brothers and sisters, grandfather's sisters, and the grandmother's brothers and sisters. More distant kinsmen are honored with prostrations only if they are present, but the kinsmen mentioned are honored by name even though absent.

It may be noticed that in this last group are apparently included non-members of the clan, bearing a different surname. But under the cross-cousin marriage which prevailed in ancient China, the sisters of the mother and grandmother would have married into the clan. The modern custom apparently reflects a situation after the cross cousin-marriage had been dropped, if it ever existed in western China.

It is a serious affront to omit calling the name of any kinsman, no matter how distant, if he is actually present, and at the recital of each name, the groom is obliged to make four prostrations. After the list of kinsmen is exhausted, the ceremony is repeated for each of the matchmakers, and one set of prostrations is offered to the group of helpers, musicians, cooks and carriers. It is obvious that such a series of prostrations is exhausting physically to the groom, particularly when the clan is large, and there are many visiting kinsmen. So it is often remarked satirically that a wife is acquired by the kowtow.

When this performing-the-rite is finished, the matchmakers are requested "to light the (marriage) candles," *fa la* 发蜡. Each takes a taper, and they stand to the right and left of the table. First they light the tapers, then the candle nearest them, and then, as it is usually difficult to set the flame burning, the farther candle. It will probably be necessary to do this several times before the candles are fully lit. While lighting the candles, the matchmakers chant, each one in turn singing a verse of four lines, the matchmaker on the left beginning. The matchmaker on the left sings:

喜烛辉煌

照耀华堂

子孙千亿

长发其祥

"The marriage candles glow brilliantly, brightly lighting the flowery hall. May there be millions of descendants! May this good fortune long continue."

The matchmaker on the right sings:

雝雝鸣雁

旭日始旦

士如归妻

迨水未泮

"The wild geese call over the marsh at dawn; the man goes to be united with his wife; the distant ice is not yet melted." This verse is from the *Book of Poetry*.

After this ceremony of singing and lighting the candles, the matchmakers are invited to arrange the guests at the table. They accompany the groom to the table. The groom, flanked by the two matchmakers, stands facing the table, which involves facing the shrine. They are accompanied on either side by two servants, one holding a tray bearing two wine-cups and two pairs of chopsticks, the other bearing a pot of wine. The matchmaker on the left takes a pair of chopsticks, and the one on the right, a wine cup. They bow as they take the things, walk to the table, bow again, and place the chopsticks and cup on the table before the seat reserved for the groom. They then bow, walk backwards to their place, and bow again. This procedure is repeated with the other chopsticks and cup, for the groom must have two of each object he uses. As the matchmakers make their various bows, the groom, who has remained before the table, bows with them. He is then ushered to his seat.

There are two boys, under fourteen years of age, who accompany the groom at this ceremony, somewhat after the manner of the best man at Western marriages, and who are called *pan lang*. They are usually younger cousins of the groom, and have been engaged to perform this service a year before the marriage. These youths are dressed in formal or official clothes, and are seated by the matchmakers with the same ceremony with which the groom was seated. They sit on the same bench as the groom, the elder on his left, and the younger on his right. The left is the side of honor; but while this is sufficiently true throughout China for foreign observers to consider it a peculiar feature of Chinese culture, it is not universal throughout the country, either today, or in the past.

The bench on which the groom and his best men sit is covered with a red felt cloth, and their feet are placed on a *tou* 斗, a measure for grain, usually translated "peck." This receptacle is made of wood, and is square in section, with the top smaller than the bottom. For this occasion it is filled with cotton seeds, or some other grain, and in it are also placed two eggs which have been colored red—somewhat like the Western Easter eggs—

and two red turnips. The measure is sealed with red paper, and the top covered with a bamboo sieve, on which the feet of the three rest.

The remaining seats at the table are filled by seven other boys, three sitting opposite the groom and the best men, and two on each side. This is called the accompanying-the-groom table, or feast. The feast formally consists of nine courses, but there is a tenth added course called *pang* 榜—a term used for the list of successful candidates at the old government examinations.

This dish consists of a large circular piece of raw pork placed in a big porcelain bowl. The meat is not eaten by the guests, but is the property of the cook, who takes it home with him after the feast is over. It is a choice cut, usually from the hind leg of the pig. The bowl containing the raw pork is covered with red paper, and on the top is placed a branch of cypress. In this area of China, the term for cypress *po chih* 柏枝 (in North China the expression is used for arbor vitae) has the same sound as 百子 "a hundred sons."

On the cypress branch are hung nuts of the gingko tree, and peanuts which have been painted red. Also on the branch are the figures of two cranes playing with lotus flowers.

The whole dish is placed on a large tray, at either end of which is a large red candle. In front of the bowl is a red artificial flower placed in a small porcelain cup, called the *ling pei* 令杯 "command cup."

The course is brought to the table with the following ceremony. First come the musicians, headed by two gong players. They strike their gongs once, then twice, then three times, and repeat. Then come two trumpeters, followed by two men playing the Mongolian horn *la-pa* 喇叭 and two men setting off firecrackers. The last man in the procession is the cook, bearing the tray with the things on it pressed against his breast.

The procession starts in the kitchen, passes through the main door, and with the musicians playing, makes six circuits around the table at which the guests are sitting. The first three circuits are made counter clockwise, and the next three, clockwise. Then the tray bearing the bowl is placed in the center of the table, with the command cup before the best man to the left of the groom. The musicians gather behind the groom, playing as loudly as possible, and the groom is obliged to give each one a package containing a gift of money. They stop deafening his ears only when a good deal of money has been exacted.

Then the best man on the left of the groom opens the "command" or "order," *K'ai ling* 开令, by singing the following song:

开令开令

开开天门

一开金玉满堂

二开荣华富贵

三开百子千孙

四开长发其祥

五开五子登科

六开六合同春

七开麒麟送子

八开八仙闹海

九开九九长寿

十开状元榜眼探花郎

十一开花结果

十二开果团圆

花结果果团圆

花果团圆万万年

"Open the command! Open the command!

Open the gate of Heaven.

The first opening: gold and jade fill the hall.

The second opening: glory, splendor, riches and rank!

The third opening: a hundred sons and a thousand grandsons!

The fourth opening: long flourish his good fortune.

The fifth opening: five sons successful in attaining degrees!

The sixth opening: all the world (literally, the six points of the compass) shares in spring.

The seventh opening: the Ch'i-lin (unicon) presents sons.

The eighth opening: the eight immortals bustle across the sea.

The ninth opening: the double nine; longevity!

The tenth opening: the three highest graduates in the examinations!

The eleventh opening: the flowers bear fruit.

The twelfth opening: the fruits are closely united (as husband and wife.)

The flowers bear fruit, and the fruits are closely united.

Flowers and fruits closely united for ten-thousand ten-thousand years!"

When the best man on the left has finished this song, he passes the command cup to the best man on the right, who continues the song as follows:

门前放三炮

必有状元到

打的黄绫伞

坐的八人轿

"Three salutes are fired before the gate;

A *Chuang-yüan* (winner of first place in the triennial Palace Examination) must have arrived.

There is borne before him the yellow silk umbrella,

And he rides in a sedan chair carried by eight men."

The best man on the right then passes the command cup to the boy next to him, who takes up the song.

门口桅子立得高

脱下蓝衫换紫袍

取了亮顶戴纱帽

脚踏银镫步步高

"The flagstaff before the gate stands high;

Take off the blue shirt, and wear the purple gown.

Remove the transparent button, and put on the gauze hat.

The feet are placed in the silver stirrup; a step and a step higher."

The cup is then passed to the next boy, who continues with the first ode of the *Book of Poetry*.

关关雎鸠

在河之洲

窈窕淑女

君子好逑

"The cry of the osprey (symbolic of marriage)

On an islet in the river:

A modest, retiring and pure woman;

The prince is well-mated."

The songs may continue for four or six rounds, or even more. The number of rounds depends upon the best man on the right side of the groom, who "closes the command." If he possesses an extensive repertoire, he may continue the singing indefinitely by refusing to stop until the other boys have exhausted their memories.

No song may be repeated, and if a boy attempts to sing a verse that has already been rendered, or admits that he is unable to sing a new one, he is called *shih kê* 失格 "to lose the standard." A boy may know twenty songs, but if they are well known, his repertoire may be exhausted by others in the first three rounds, and so it is better to memorize songs that are not common.

In fact, the affair is really a singing contest among the boys, testing their courage, poise and calmness. The marriage is forgotten, and a boy may sing a song bragging of the number he can remember, or a verse ridiculing the other boys. There is considerable nervous tension, and a boy who knows many songs may forget them when his turn comes to sing.

The tension is increased by the fact that all the guests, both men and women, gather in the hall to witness and enjoy the contest. There will be laughter, praise, and criticism. If the best man on the right is able to exhaust the repertoires of the others before he himself is obliged to close the contest, he becomes the hero of the evening. To end the contest, he sings:

收令收令

收在府门

四水归大海

令酒归壶瓶

"Close the command! Close the command!

It is closed at the gate of the palace.

The four waters return to the great sea:

The command wine goes back to the jar."

When this song is finished, he passes the command cup to the best man on the groom's left, who takes the flower. He sings:

一朵花儿鲜又鲜

插在新郎帽旁边

插在左边生贵子

插在右边生状元

"This flower is fresh; as fresh as can be.

It is placed (lit., inserted) on the side of the groom's hat.

Placed on the left, a noble son will be born.

Placed on the right, a man who will win first place in the examinations will be born."

Then he places the flower on the hat of the groom. The singing contest is over, and the boys may enjoy the feast.

After this, recently-married young women try to secure the red eggs and turnips in the measure which is under the feet of the groom. Those who get eggs and eat them will bear sons, while those who get and eat the turnips will bear daughters. The groom, joining in the fun, presses down with his feet on the sieve in order to squeeze the arms of the young women. There is laughter, screaming and joking, in which the onlookers share.

That night, the two best men sleep with the groom in the bride's new bed. This is called *ya ch'uang* 压床 "pressing the bed."

# Bringing the Bride: *Ch'ü Ch'in* 娶亲

On the day of the marriage, everyone concerned, including the groom, rises before dawn. Dressed in his formal wedding costume of new clothes, he first makes an act of reverence to the family tablets, to the accompaniment of trumpets and gongs playing and the continuous sound of firecrackers outside the hall.

When this is finished, the groom enters a sedan chair generally carried by four men, although the son of an official may be borne by eight carriers.

A number of ceremonial emblems, *i chang* 仪仗, may be carried before the sons of those having official titles; such inscriptions might be the *luan chia* 鸾驾, "bell chariot," the *P'ai pien* 牌匾, "insignia plaque," and the *tui tzǔ ma* 对子马, "horse with *tui tzǔ*" (a pair of balanced complimentary inscriptions). The ordinary peasant has the minimum requirements for the processions, consisting of a large red umbrella, two embroidered banners, two long trumpets, two Mongolian horns, two gongs—each borne by a single man—and two men setting off firecrackers and firing guns. This company marches before the sedan chair of the groom.

Before the procession accompanying the groom sets forth, a number of other functionaries have already left on their journey to the home of the bride. These include the carriers of the visiting-card box, two masters of ceremonies called *hsiang Ch'in chê* 相亲者 or more colloquially, *t'o shou Ch'in chia* 讬手亲家 and the two matchmakers, and the two boys who act as best men. With the exception of the bearer of the visiting-card box, they ride, either on horseback or in sedan chairs each borne by two men. This group is also accompanied by six or seven empty chairs in which members of the bride's family will return to the house of the groom; the number of chairs required is specified in advance by the bride's family.

In addition, there are two men who carry a box containing two bottles of wine which are used in offering the gift of geese, and the "old worthy of the box" which has been described, and which bears the inscription *Chih tzǔ yü kuei* 之子于归. Another box contains the *hsi yên* 喜筵, "happy feast," together with a package of money as a gift to the cook of the bride's family. If this gift should be forgotten, there are a number of ways in which the cook could cause trouble. All these set out for the home of the bride at an earlier hour than that of the procession of the groom.

In the sedan chair of the groom there is a pair of wooden geese. This is a survival of an ancient custom in which gifts of geese were made to the father of the bride at a marriage or betrothal. Now, however, the custom survives only as a symbolic gesture, with wooden models substituted for real birds.

Immediately following the chair of the groom in the procession, is the chair to be occupied by the bride. It is borne by four or eight men, covered by red satin, and decorated with rich embroideries and tassels.

With trumpets sounding, and the noise of gongs and firecrackers, the "bridal-welcome procession" takes its way toward the home of the bride. Anyone who meets it must move aside, even the magistrate, or other local officials.

As the procession nears the home of the bride, the guns are fired in order to notify her family that the groom is arriving. The functionaries who have preceded the bridal procession, but who have not actually entered the bride's home, now advance, and at the signal shots, the bride's family prepare for the reception of the procession.

First arrives the man bearing the visiting-card box which contains the card of the groom's father. It is inscribed "With respectful congratulations, from your younger brother," and is presented to the father of the bride.

Then arrive the masters of ceremonies appointed by the groom's family, who are received with formal bows by two corresponding functionaries representing the bride's family. They are followed by the men bearing the old-worthy-of-the-box and the "happy feast," who deposit their burdens in the center of the hall. Then come the two matchmakers, who offer congratulations, and who are served with tea and tobacco.

Then appears a man carrying a second visiting-card box containing the card of the groom himself. The groom's name is preceded by the phrase *jou wan shêng* 柔晚生"weak late born,"(i.e., of a younger generation), and bears the words "Respectfully arrived today to welcome (the bride)." The groom does not yet call himself "son-in-law," because he has not yet received the bride.

When his card has been received, the groom's sedan chair arrives, and waits outside the main gate, with the chairs of the best-men on either side, so that there is a row of three chairs. The *chieh fêng* 接风, masters of ceremonies (literally, "those in charge of the ceremony"), come through the gate and stand on the steps facing the sedan chair of the groom. There may be two or four of these men.

At this moment, the cook of the bride's family may place a table bearing food before the groom, and this is called *hsia ma yên* 下马宴 "feast upon dismounting." It appears to be nothing more than a device on the part of the cook to secure gifts from the groom. The groom gives a package containing money, and the cook disappears.

Then the groom and the best-men exchange bows with the masters-of-ceremony, and the former leave their chairs. The latter bow again as an invitation to enter, and this also is returned. They forthwith enter the hall, the groom and the best-men walking in a row, with the masters-of-ceremony following. On reaching the seats, the latter bow once more, as an invitation to sit down, and after the bow has been returned, the three seat themselves. The whole ceremony, without words, is called *San i san jan* 三揖三让 "threefold request and refusal."

The groom and the best men sit upon a bench covered with red felt, which is placed in the center of the hall before a table. As in the ceremony of accompanying the groom, a grain measure, filled with cotton seeds in which are hidden red eggs and red turnips, and covered with a sieve, serves as a footstool for the groom and the best-men. When the three are seated, the masters-of-ceremony, the matchmakers, and the guests take their seats on the sides of the hall.

Tea and poached eggs with sugar are served three times, the masters of ceremony from the bride's family saying, "Please." It would be a breach of form for the groom and the best-men to eat or drink these refreshments, and would make them a laughing stock later; so they merely raise the cups toward their lips. The guests, particularly the women, gather in the hall to look at the groom, and gossip about him.

As the groom enters the hall, the foreman of the chair carriers brings the wooden geese into the hall, and places them on the table behind the groom with their heads facing away from the door. When the tea-ceremony is finished, a master-of-ceremony from the groom's family turns the geese around in the opposite direction, and pours a libation of wine on the ground. This is called *tien yên li* 奠雁礼 "the ceremony of offering the geese."

Then the master-of-ceremony substitutes the old-worthy-of-the-box inscribed *Chih tzǔ yü kuei* 之子于归, for the one inscribed *Wên ting chüeh hsiang* 文定厥祥. The latter had been brought to the bride's house at the time of thc exchange of gifts, and is now placed in the box in which the former was brought, in order to be returned to the house of the groom.

After this has been done, the groom and the best men rise and leave. On rising, they turn toward the family shrine and bow once, accompanied by the masters of ceremony. Then they turn, walk together to the door, face the tablets once more and bow—a ceremony which is repeated before they leave the hall.

As soon as the groom leaves his seat, recently-married girls, hoping for sons, rush to secure the red eggs hidden in the grain measure.

The groom returns to his sedan chair and waits.

At this ceremony, one of the duties of the masters-of-ceremony is to aid the groom, insuring that he perform the rites correctly.

Sedan chairs are then brought into the hall for the *sung Ch'in po* 送亲婆, and the *pan niang* 伴娘.

The first expression means "ladies who escort the bride (literally, relatives)" and there are two such women. They are guests of honor, and are usually selected from among the sisters of the bride's father, the wives of his brothers, and the wives of the older brothers of the bride. They must be happily married, and must not be widows. They are selected for the office at the beginning of the year—that is, about ten months previously.

The second phrase means literally "accompanying the bride," and is the term for a single servant who accompanies the bride to her new home, remaining with her after the marriage for a period from ten days to six months, depending upon the economic conditions in both families.

When these women have entered their chairs and been carried from the hall, the bride's sedan chair is brought into the hall. It is called the *hua chiao* 花轿 "flower-chair," or *ts'ai chiao* 彩 "ornamented chair." All male guests and everyone not a near relative leave the hall. Outside the hall, the sound of music and of firecrackers is continuous.

The bride enters the hall, and her kinsfolk endeavor to make her enter the bridal chair. Over and over again she refuses, weeping loudly. Her father and mother add their tears to hers. Finally her older brothers or sisters pick her up and place her in the chair. This proceeding is a required act of modesty, and is called *T'ao chiao* 套丨,"declining the (bridal) chair." It also marks the end of her pleasant life as a daughter, and the beginning of the hard life of a wife.

When she enters or is placed in the chair, her feet rest on the grain measure, about which chopsticks are scattered. The phrase for chopsticks is *k'uai-tzŭ* 筷子 which is homophonous with 快丨 meaning "to bear sons rapidly."

As soon as the bride is in the chair, the door of the chair is locked and sealed with a strip of red paper. The business of getting the bride into her chair may take anywhere from twenty minutes to several hours, depending upon the temperaments of the bride and her parents.

When the bridal chair has been carried from the hall, the bearer of the visiting card box presents another card from the groom on which is written "with respectful gratitude," but now the groom describes himself as *mên hsia hsü* 门下婿 "your son-in-law." The groom has become a son in law, having received the bride.

As soon as the groom's card has been received by the father of the bride, the procession starts the journey to the home of the groom. The groom's chair is carried in front, followed by that of the bride. The musicians play, the gongs are beaten, and fire crackers are set off continuously along the route.

But the procession must use a different road from that by which it came. This is popularly referred to in the sentence, "The new pair will not walk the old road."

By this time, the ladies-who-escort-the-bride, who had left the home of the bride before the bridal procession started, arrive at the home of the groom. Their chairs are carried directly into the hall and are placed facing the family shrine. There the two are met by four or eight women representing the groom's family, in full formal dress. These women are called *chieh fêng chê* 接风者, the same title as the male masters of ceremonies. Bows are exchanged, and the two women leave their chairs. On leaving, they again exchange bows. Then the ladies from the groom's family place the ladies-who escort the bride in the seats of honor, where tea is served to them three times with rigid formality. One lady of the groom's family carries a plate bearing the teacup, while another holds the tea pot. These pairs stand in two rows, on the right and on the left. A pair on the left advances to offer tea; then a pair on the right advances. The pair on the left will then retire, and then that on the right. At the next offering the order of advance is reversed. All the female guests stand grouped at the side of the hall to watch this "ceremony of the masters of ceremonies" *chieh fêng li* 接风礼. Should one of the ladies representing either family make the slightest mistake, it would cause much amusement, and be called *shih kê* "to lose the standard."

After the tea ceremony, tobacco is served once, and the reception is ended. The ladies-who-escort-the-bride are taken to the room of the bride, deep in the interior of the house, to rest. This room is called *tung fang* 洞房 literally, "cave room."

## The Completion of the Marriage: *Yüan Ch'in* 圆亲

This ceremony appears to be equivalent to the ancient *ho chin* 合卺 "to drink the wedding cup" ceremony.

Early in the morning of the day of the marriage, after the bridal procession has left on its journey to the home of the bride, the family of the groom invite two women, called *yüan Ch'in* literally, "to complete the marriage," to spread the bed for the bride and groom. These women are engaged for the task some time in advance, at the beginning of the year. They must be of an age commanding respect, virtuous, not widowed, and *tzŭ sun man T'ang* 子孙满堂, literally, "their sons and grandsons fill the hall."

Paddy stalks are spread on the bed, to make it soft. Then the cotton quilt prepared by the bride's family is spread upon the bed. As the things have been placed on the bed the day before, the spreading is merely ceremonial, the women going around the bed making the covers smooth, As they move about this task, cakes, dried lungan nuts, peanuts which have been stained red, and ginko nuts are placed in the bed. Later, girls hunt for these and eat them, in the hope that they themselves will bear children.

As they spread the bed, the women sing the following propitious verses:
One sings,

铺床铺床

金玉满堂

先生贵子

后生姑娘

"Spread the bed! Spread the bed!

May gold and jade fill the hall.

First, bear noble sons;

Afterwards, bear girls."

The other sings:

铺床铺饼子

养儿戴顶子

铺床铺桂圆

养儿点状元

"Spread the bed! Spread the cakes!

Bear sons who will wear the (official) button!

Spread the bed! Spread the lungan nuts!

Bear sons who will achieve highest honors in the examination (*the shuang-yüan)*."

The first sings again:

铺床铺得平

养儿一大群

"Spread the bed, and spread it smooth:

Bear a large number of sons."

The second rejoins:

铺床铺得宽

养儿做高官

"Spread the bed, and spread it wide:

Bear sons who will become high officials."

This ends the ceremony of spreading-the-bed.

In the bride's room are placed a pair of red wedding candles, a pair of hanging door screens, a pair of wine cups, and a pair of teacups. These things are used by the completion-of-the marriage women at the time of the drinking-of-the-wedding-cup. The articles are placed on the new table in the center of the room.

When the sedan chair containing the bride arrives, an incense table is placed outside the main entrance to the hall. On it are a small measure of rice (a *shêng* 升, which is a tenth of a *tou*), a pair of candles, and three sticks of incense which are stuck in the rice. There are also three cups of wine for libations.

A man is appointed "to send back the spirits." An ordinary man is not appointed to this post, which requires a scholar having a *hsiu ts'ai* 秀才 degree, approximately equivalent to a Western Bachelor of Arts.

When the bride's chair arrives, this man, wearing academic costume, stands before the incense table to send back the spirits. The candles and incense sticks are lighted, firecrackers are set off, and paper money burned. The libation of wine is poured onto the ground. Although the man is a scholar, not a magician, he bows from before the incense table toward the bridal chair, and recites the following magic formula:

日吉晨良

天地开昌

男家车马

请进高堂

女家车马

请转回乡

姜太公在此

诸神回避

"The day is fortunate and the morning auspicious;

Heaven and earth open their glory.

Chariots and horses of the man's family,

Please enter the high hall.

Chariots and horses of the woman's family,

Please return to your native place.

CHIANG T'ai-kung is here;

All spirits avaunt."

Or the man-who-sends-back-the-spirits may recite the following formula:

日吉晨良

天地开昌

新人到此

车马回乡

钱财白如银

回奉车马神

天煞归地界

地煞入幽冥

自从归过后

长享天地春

姜太公在此

诸神回避

"The day is fortunate and the morning auspicious;

Heaven and earth open their glory.

The new person (the bride) has arrived here.

Her chariot and horses return to their native place.

Money and wealth shining like silver

Are offered to the spirits of the chariot and the horses.

The baneful influences of heaven turn earthward,

And the baleful influences of earth enter Hades.

Until they have returned,

Long may universal spring be enjoyed.

CHIANG T'ai-kung is here;

All spirits avaunt.

Either formula may be used by the man who sends back the spirits, though the second is fuller and more explicit. When the formula has been recited, the man throws a handful of the rice at the bridal chair.

This ceremony of sending-back-the-spirits is performed while the procession is entering, and the chairs do not stop. The groom's chair is carried into the hall, with the bride's chair immediately following. The groom leaves his chair, which is immediately carried out, but the bride remains in her chair. All male guests, widows and "four eyed" (i.e., pregnant) women must leave the hall, only the groom and the other women remaining.

The bride is locked in her chair, and at this time, the head of the chair-carriers comes in and opens the lock. He is given a package of money, and leaves the hall.

Then the entrance is closed, and the ceremony of the-completion-of-the-marriage is begun. The completion-of-the-marriage ladies light the wedding candles in the *hsin fang* 新房, literally, "new room" (i.e., the bridal chamber), and return to the hall to conduct the *hsin ku niang* 新姑娘, "new woman," from the bridal chair. The bride always refuses to come out. The completion-of-the-marriage ladies (who represent the groom's family) then ask the escorters-of-the-bride ladies (who represent the bride's family) to request the bride to leave her chair.

The latter reply: "*Ch'in ma* (an honorary form of address), you are the honored guest of both families."

The former says: "When the man is the stronger, the girl will enjoy happiness."

Then the escorters-of-the-bride ladies help the bride from her chair, giving her to the completion-of-the-marriage ladies, who lead her to the groom.

The bride and groom then go to the bridal chamber. At first they walk shoulder to shoulder, but on entering the "new room," the groom should enter half a step ahead of the bride. Sometimes the bride tries to get in first, in the belief that the one who succeeds in entering first will be the stronger. Should she succeed, it is an omen that the husband will be henpecked. Accordingly, the completion-of-the-marriage ladies endeavor to see that the groom enters first. But sometimes the escorters-of-the-bride ladies try to get the bride in first.

When the bride and groom have entered the room, they may perform a ceremony called *chiao pai li* 交拜礼 "ceremony of mutual salutation," which consists of bowing or kowtowing four times toward the new bed. However, this is optional, and is usually omitted.

After this, the bride and groom sit shoulder to shoulder on the same bench. The completion-of-the-marriage ladies bring two cups of wedding wine. Each drinks half a cup, and then they exchange cups, each drinking the remainder of the wine in the cup.

Then the completion-of-the-marriage ladies lead the couple to the bed, on which they sit side by side. The ladies give each a piece of candy. Each takes half a piece, giving the remaining half to the other person. Then the completion-of-the-marriage ladies let down the curtains of the bed, so that the two cannot be seen from without, and it is assumed that they embrace and kiss. This ceremony is called *Ch'ih chiao pei chiu* 吃交杯酒 "the exchange of the cups of wine."

While this ceremony is going on, the musicians are playing outside, and firecrackers are set off continually. All the male guests must wait outside until the ceremony is concluded. Then the gates are opened, and everyone, irrespective of age or sex, rushes into the bridal chamber to see the bride, and to ask for cakes, which have been prepared by bride's parents. They are given mostly to young people and children.

Those who want cakes, come before the bride and bow. The bride bows in return, and the maid who has accompanied her from her home gives a cake to the asker. Some mischevious boy or girl may demand more, and at this, everyone will try to secure cakes in a rush. The maid must have enough for all demands. The bride must also present to each of her two maids an embroidered handkerchief with an embroidered case, and sometimes, a pair of shoes. Failure to do this would cause dissatisfaction, and injure the bride's reputation. The horseplay may last throughout the afternoon, boys returning again and again for cakes.

## Presenting the Bride: *Sung Ch'in* 送亲

After the sedan chair of the bride has left her home, her father—called, in referring to the marriage, *nü Ch'in chia* 女亲家—sends representatives to the home of the groom. These are men, and their number varies—two, four or six. These men are called escorters-of-the-bride *sung Ch'in* and are selected from among the male relatives of the bride's father.

They are preceded by a servant bearing the visiting card of the bride's father, who presents the card to the father of the groom-called *nan Ch'in chia* 男亲家. The card is inscribed, "With hearty congratulations; your related younger brother, so-and-so, bowing."

When the groom's father receives this card, he sends two men to the gate to welcome the escorters-of-the-bride, and as in the case of the ladies who also bore the title, the business is called *chieh fêng*. These two men may be relatives or friends of the groom's father, but they must be thoroughly familiar with etiquette. They stand just outside the gate, on the steps, and when the male escorters-of-the-bride arrive, the two groups exchange bows.

The former then lead the latter into the hall, where they all bow before the family tablets, the representative of the groom's family leading in the ceremony. The escorters-of-the-bride are then placed in seats of honor on either side of the hall, while the masters of ceremonies sit as hosts. Tea is served three times, and also three poached eggs with sugar, followed by tobacco.

By this time the feast is ready, and the escorters-of-the-bride are ushered to the tables. They stand in the middle of the hall, with the masters-of-ceremony on both sides. Two servants appear, one carrying a large plate on which are chopsticks and wine cups, while the other carries a jar of wine. The master of ceremonies on the left side takes a pair of chopsticks from the plate, while the one on the right takes a wine cup. After bowing, they walk to the table, and place the things at the seat of honor. They bow, and walk backwards until they reach their original position, when they bow again. Then the senior escorter-of-the-bride is invited to take the seat. This procedure is repeated for each individual, until all the escorters-of-the-bride are seated. Then the other guests are seated, and finally, the masters of ceremonies sits as hosts in the lowest seats. Each table seats eight persons.

At the same time, a feast is held for the women in the inner hall, at which the seats of honor are reserved for the female escorters-of-the-bride, who represent the bride's entire family, but particularly the mother of the bride. The female escorters-of-the-bride are conducted to their seats with the same ceremony by female masters-of-ceremony. When the other women guests are seated, the female masters-of-ceremony take the lowest seats.

When the first dish is served, representatives of the host and hostess (i.e., the parents of the groom) visit each table, bow once, and ask the guests to help themselves to the food. These representatives are usually the brothers of the groom's father, for the men; and their wives, for the women. When the representatives of the host and hostess come to a table, those sitting there rise in deference. This ceremony is called *shang ts'ai* 上菜 "placing the food," and after it has been performed, the guests begin to eat.

When the sixth dish is served, the groom visits each table, accompanied by a master of ceremonies. The groom bows and remains silent, but the master of ceremonies, speaking for him, requests the guests to take more wine. This ceremony is called *chin chiu* 晋酒 "serving the wine."

When the last dish is served, a string of firecrackers is set off. The escorters of the bride and the guests leave the tables, and are ushered to the guest room, where tea is served.

## Handing Over the Bridee:*chiao Ch'in* 交亲

After the tea has been served, the escorters-of-the-bride ladies ask permission of the groom's mother to hand over to her the bride and the dowry. The groom's mother waits in the main hall, and the escorters-of-the-bride come to her and sit in the guests' seats. Tea is served, after which the ladies bow to the groom's mother, who returns the bow. The escorters-of-the-bride then address the groom's mother as follows:

"*Ch'in ma* (an honorary form of address), your temper is mild, your manners are respectful, your nature is virtuous and good, and you are especially skillful in teaching young people. This girl (i.e., the bride) is still young, and rather stupid, inexperienced, and not expert in managing affairs. Please train and teach her carefully."

The groom's mother replies:

"*Ch'in ma*, you are too modest and courteous. The girl comes from a well known family, and certainly has been well trained. Please tell her parents that her life here will be easy."

Then the escorters-of-the-bride ladies hand to the groom's mother the keys to all the boxes brought as the bride's dowry.

Following this ceremony, the escorters-of-the-bride ladies ask permission to leave. They advance to the center of the hall and bow once, the groom's mother replying. Their sedan chairs are carried into the hall, and they enter them.

The groom waits outside the gate of the house, and as the sedan chairs pass, he bows to the ladies, and they nod in reply. As the chairs leave, firecrackers are set off in honor of the ladies. This is a moment when the bride weeps, because all the members of her own family have now left her in a strange and trying environment.

When the ladies have gone, the male escorters-of-the-bride come to the hall to make their farewell. There the father of the groom, or his representative, is waiting. Bows are exchanged, and the guests again offer congratulations, and thanks for the feast, after which they leave.

As they descend the steps—their chairs are not brought into the hall—a string of firecrackers is set off. Again the groom waits outside the gate, bowing as they pass. They enter their chairs, and return to their homes.

# Making a Disturbance in the Room: *Nao fang* 闹房

The ceremonies of the marriage day which have been described are usually finished by noon, or at the latest, by three o'clock in the afternoon. They are succeeded by several hours of inactivity. The important ceremonies are over, and some guests are departing. The cooks and other servants are cleaning up the debris and preparing to go home.

About dark, preparations are made for a jollification in the room of the bride. Candles are lit, and a feast table placed in the center of the room, while both men and women crowd into the apartment. During the fun, the bride cannot leave her room, or at least is not supposed to do so.

Everyone is permitted to enter; old and young, relatives and friends, higher or lower generations. Even an elder brother, or brothers of the father of the groom, are allowed to "make a disturbance in the room." This affair is called *san T'ien wu ta hsiao* 三天无大小 "three days without respect of old or young." For three days there is a period of license, during which anyone may enter the bride's room to look at her.

The groom and bride sit on the same bench at the table, the visitors filling up any available room. The groom serves wine three times to the guests, and then the bride does likewise, after which they serve wine to each other.

There is constant joking, fun, and license, with or without limits. When the parents of the groom desire to keep the fun within limits, the affair is called *wên ming nao fang* 文明闹房, "cultured new-room brawling." The fun is relatively refined, and no obscene words or actions are permitted. But when the hosts have no objections, the "new-room brawlers" may say or do anything they like, and this is called *yeh man nao fang* 野蛮闹房, "barbaric new-room brawling." There is a belief that the more unrestrained the disorder, the more prosperous the life of the newly-wed couple will be. A few instances of cultured joking may be given.

A guest may say he has heard that the bride's right foot is larger than her left. Another may contradict this, claiming that her left foot is the larger. A debate is started, which is settled by compelling the bride to hold up her feet for comparison and measurement. To a modern girl, this would mean little; but an old-fashioned girl would find the incident very trying, as it would offend her modesty. As she stretches out her feet, jokes are made about their size and shape, and she may be asked to take a few steps so that the question may be settled. Finally, in order to end the incident, someone may remark, "To rise ten thousand feet, one must start from the ground. Lotus flowers blossom at every step." This may be taken as a congratulation, or as a joke.

The same procedure may be followed with regard to her arms, which she will be obliged to stretch out for measurement. Or there may be a dispute as to whether the bride or groom is the taller, which is settled by compelling them to stand back to back, with an accompaniment of constant joking. This is "cultured" brawling.

When "barbaric" brawling is permitted, there are no limits whatever, except in handling the bride. Anything may be said. A male guest may throw himself on the bridal bed to give a realistic and amusing imitation of the bride's behavior when she is alone with her husband. Most of those present are under the influence of liquor to some extent, and even though the intention is to keep the fun within limits, matters sometimes get beyond control.

The origin of this "disturbance in the room" is difficult to determine. It may be ancient, but the first historical references to it are from the fourth century of our era. Considering the condition of China at that time, it has been assumed by some modern scholars to be of foreign origin. Others have suggested that it is a survival of "marriage by capture." It may be noticed that the word used for "barbaric" as a type of brawling is *man* 蛮, which is the name for the non-Chinese tribes now found only in southern and southwestern China, but formerly spread over a wider area.

The brawling, disorder and joking is usually ended shortly after midnight. The guests leave, and the newly married pair close the door and go to bed.

Women guests, and especially young girls, gather outside the door, or at some other point of vantage, where they endeavor to hear what is taking place in the room. In particular, they desire to find out who opens the conversation between bride and groom. There is a common belief that should the groom speak first, the first child will be a boy; while should it be the bride, the child will be a girl. Many jokes are based upon this belief. The women also want to hear the married couple's conversation so that they can ridicule and mimic it later. As the couple know this, the bride sometimes refuses to speak at all, no matter how the groom teases her, and she may refuse to go to bed until as late as possible.

During the first night, the lights, which are generally candles, must not be extinguished.

## Seeing the Old and the Young: *Chien ta hsiao* 见大小

Shortly before dawn on the following morning, the maid who has accompanied the bride from her home sets off a string of firecrackers before the door of the bridal chamber. The firecrackers have been prepared by the family of the bride, and brought from her home by the maid. The purpose of this ceremony is to announce to the bride that it is nearly dawn and she must arise. It would be discourteous were she to arise later, as well as a subject for joking. The ceremony is called *ching fang* 惊房 "to startle the room."

When they hear the firecrackers, the groom and bride arise and dress. The maid brings a basin of warm water to the groom for him to wash, and in return he gives her a package of money. Then she brings another basin of warm water for the bride. There is a belief that after sexual intercourse it is dangerous to wash in cold water. The married couple dress in full ceremonial costume, and leave their room, going to the main hall, in which are the family tablets.

Candles and sticks of incense are lit before the tablets, and firecrackers are set off. The couple worship together before the tablets, performing four obeisances. They then make four obeisances before all members of the family of higher generations who are present; the parents, grandparents, uncles, aunts, and other kinsmen of the groom. The master of ceremonies calls the names in order of precedence, and the couple make obeisance together before each person. In a large family, it may take several hours to perform this ceremony, which is of the nature of a public announcement to the family that the marriage has been consummated. The announcement is made to both the living and the dead.

When this ceremony is finished, the maid prepares a pot of sweetened tea, which is placed on a tray, together with ten tea cups. The groom and bride then serve the tea, first to the parents of the groom, and afterwards to all the kinsmen present. On accepting the cup of tea, each gives in return a package of money, called tea-money, which may vary in amount from ten cents to a few dollars. If there are many well-to-do kinsmen present, the married couple may collect an appreciable amount of money on this occasion.

The couple are obliged to serve tea to all representatives of higher generations of the clan. The kinsmen belonging to the same generation may demand that they be served also, as an amusing trick on the married couple. But the couple may counter by demanding that they be given a definite amount of tea-money before they serve the tea.

## Going to the Kitchen: *Hsia chu* 下厨

When the ceremony of serving tea has been finished, the bride returns to her room, where she exchanges her ceremonial dress for an ordinary working costume. Then she goes to the kitchen, to prepare her first meal as a married woman in her husband's home. She sweeps the floor of the kitchen, and then approaches the stove.

A fish has been prepared for her by the cook. She places the fish in the pan with the head pointing toward the front of the stove, and the tail toward the back. This is considered to be an omen that she will always do her work thoroughly, or as it is said, she will always "have head and tail" *yu t'ou yu wei* 有头有尾. In the sentence *fu kuei yu yü* 富贵有余 "There will be a surplus of riches and honor," the word for surplus has the sound of the word for fish, and therefore the cooking of the fish is held to be an omen of riches and honor in abundance.

Green vegetables have been mixed with rice flour for the bride to cook. This dish is called *chêng ts'ai* 蒸菜, "steamed vegetables," and is considered an omen of plenty.

The cooking of this meal by the bride is purely a ceremony, and everything has been prepared for her in advance, so that she does no more than place the articles on the stove. The object is to provide favorable omens for future happiness.

After this, breakfast is served to the guests, and usually amounts to a substantial feast.

## The Retturn Home: *Hui mên* 回门

On the third day after the wedding, the groom and bride together visit the parents of the bride and her relatives. Gifts, which may include tea, fruit, candy, and eggs, are placed in a box or case that is carried by two servants. On this visit, the groom and bride ride in ordinary sedan chairs, each carried by two bearers.

When they arrive at the hall, candles are lit and firecrackers set off. The married couple make four obeisances to the parents of the bride, and then to those of her kinsmen present who belong to higher generations of the clan than the bride.

It may be noticed that in this ceremony, no obeisance is made before the tablets of the bride's family. The groom is under no obligations to his wife's ancestors, and she has left their clan, so that no announcement need be made to them.

When this ceremony is over, the parents of the bride appoint a man to accompany the groom on visits to the homes of the paternal uncles of the bride. The brothers of the bride's mother are not members of the bride's clan, and may indeed be kinsmen of the groom. Under the cross-cousin marriage, which formerly prevailed in China, the brothers of the bride's mother would be the groom's paternal uncles, who would have already been reverenced by the married couple. The cross-cousin marriage, however, while it is still permissible, is no longer general.

In the halls of the bride's paternal uncles, the groom makes four obeisances before each uncle. This ceremony is called *hsieh Ch'in* 谢亲, "thanking for the bride." The groom also presents each of the bride's uncles with two boxes of candy and from four to ten eggs; this is called *ch'uan ch'a* 传茶 "to deliver the tea (i.e., the gifts) ." On receiving the gifts, each gives the groom a package of tea-money in return.

When the groom has returned to the home of the bride, her parents prepare two tables for a feast. The groom and bride are seated in the places of honor, while other guests are invited to sit with them. This is called *p'ei hsin ku yeh* 陪新姑爷, "accompanying the newly-wedded man." The expression *ku yeh* is used for the groom by the bride's family, and literally means "husband of the father's sister." It is inaccurately applied to the groom, but is a complimentary title, raising him a generation.

After the feast, as the married couple return to the groom's home, they receive a number of gifts. Well-to-do families may present the bride with gold earrings, finger rings, bracelets, ten pairs of shoes and ten pairs of socks. To the groom may be given a pair of shoes and a pair of socks, while the bride's parents give a certain amount of tea-money.

In addition to these things there is given the needlework done by the bride before the marriage. This may include a fan-holder for the groom's father, a tobacco pouch for his mother, handkerchiefs and pen holders for his younger brothers, and handkerchiefs or sleeve-protectors for his sisters. All these have been made and embroidered by the bride. The whole collection is placed in a box and carried to the groom's home. It is called *T'ien chuang* 添妆 "added dowry."

When the couple reach the groom's home, they find chopsticks scattered from the gate to the door of their room. The new wife picks up all the chopsticks as she enters. The act of picking up the chopsticks is considered a favorable omen for quickly bearing sons.

The date of the visit to the bride's home is fixed, depending upon the date of the wedding, and is specified on the schedule sent by the family of the groom to that of the bride before the marriage. If the month has twenty-nine days, the return visit must not be made until a month later than the wedding. Twenty-nine-day months are unlucky for the bride's parents, and must be avoided. Should the groom's family ignore this belief, and misfortune come to the bride's family, they would be held responsible. If the month has thirty days, the return visit may take place on the second or third day after the wedding.

## Thanking the Matchmakers:*Hsieh mei* 谢媒

The matchmakers hold a unique and important position in Chinese marriage, which is not legally correct without them. Beginning with the exchange of the eight characters, and ending with receiving the bride, they are required at every step at least where the Chinese customs have not been changed by Western contacts.

Their position is also exceedingly difficult, requiring considerable tact and ability in the adjustment of difficulties. A proverb expresses their task: *Hui tso mei ti mei liang t'ou* 会做媒的媒两头 "Those who are expert matchmakers have two heads (i.e., they must please both families)." Since they transmit proposals from both sides, they are responsible for removing dissatisfaction and complaints, and must make both families happy. When they perform their office successfully, they are called 媒两头, but when they fail they are called 两头媒. This alteration in the word order changes the meaning of the phrase, indicating that they are criticized and scolded by both sides. Although they enjoy many feasts, it is said that they are obliged to use both their legs and their tongues. Another proverb says, *Wu huang pu Ch'êng wei* 无谎不成媒 "Without lying, there is no success for a matchmaker."

When the wedding is over, their responsibility is ended, and they are rewarded for their efforts. On the second day after the wedding the family of the groom prepares a feast, at which the matchmakers sit in the seats of honor. After the first dish has been served, the host—usually the father of the groom—comes to their table, bows once, and asks them to help themselves. After the fifth dish, the groom comes, bows once, and requests them to take more wine. This is the last feast for them, and is called "Thanking the matchmakers."

## Sending the Hair Grease: *Sung Shu t'ou yu* 送梳头油

After an even number of days following the wedding—four, six, eight, or ten the—parents of the bride prepare a new porcelain bottle filled with mustard seed oil. This is taken to the bride by one of her brothers, or if she has no brothers, by her father.

The sending of the oil or grease is merely an excuse for visiting the bride, and the real purpose is to learn whether she is well treated by her husband's family. As this is a delicate task, it is performed by a brother or by the father. He may be invited to remain at the husband's home for a meal, or he may return immediately after seeing the bride.

Irrespective of the wealth or position of the families, this ceremony is always performed. It is the last of the ceremonies which may be considered as parts of the marriage.

［与 J.K.Shryock 合作，原载 *Harvard Journal of Asiatic Studies*, Vol.13, No.3-4(1950), pp.362-430］

# 附录：川康科学考察团日记（1939年7–8月）

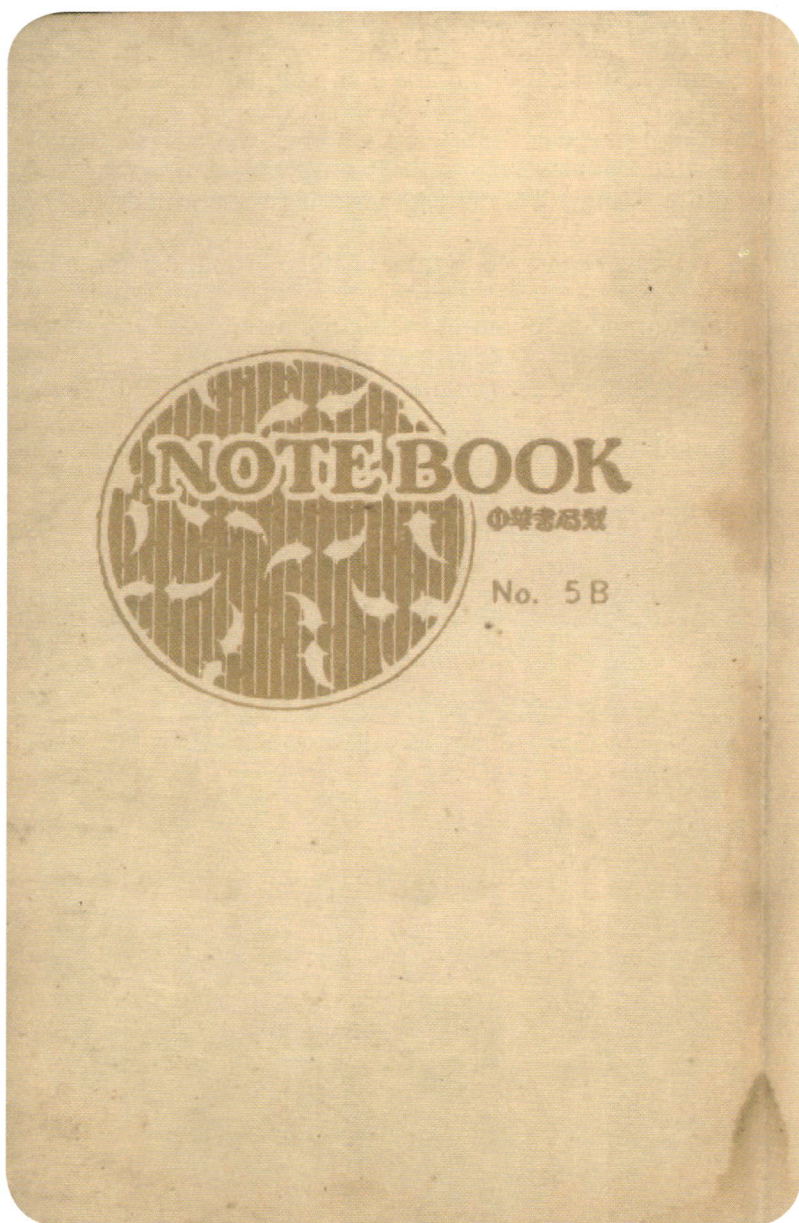

NOTE BOOK

No. 5B

馮漢驥考察日記 第一冊

管理中英庚款董會

川康科學考察團

July 16, 1939　　　转载.

　　于十五日晨由成都乘汽车往雅安.
带勃移霍默戎一人, 颇辛苦. 车于八点
始开行, 十点至旧县, 适早餐, 由此间往
西南之车均于此交打尖, 此一大站也.
汽车至新津, 须渡此两次始至. 两河至
此相会, 河床平坦, 而水流甚急, 故渡
颇险, 故该有"壮志吞天下"之"难过新津
渡"之语. 由新津至邛州, 九十华里, 司
马相如过卓文君家也. 由此面西行则
地势渐高, 冈岭起伏, 远望西山, 诸峰峻
拔, 川西平原, 至此尽矣. 再西行几十里至
名山之百丈驿, 亦即自白话也. 再九十里
经名山县城至雅安.

　　蜀工后一出邛州南门, 过南桥大邑, 即
邛水也. 三十里至蜀工埧, 相传即汉武间
蓝王收云南, 凿石开道, 费工万馀, 故名.

今由公路通之，已不觉其险峻矣。

由荥山修埔至城十五里至金鸡关，雅安之隘要也。下金鸡关为姚桥，汉高君碑在焉，惜石已剥蚀。至雅安时公路局，已七时许。进大庙时，为旧雅尺，因武侯平羌于此，故又名平羌尺。有义渡，岁别有浮梁通之。至雅城时已上灯，先至四川旅行社访方君，至则闻已搬至慢礼言。至则闻员已外出，方君往蜀家山中学开国措会议。与岑君同去晚膳，多数饭店已停业，因连未下雨，断屠已三日矣。依绍绍风雅雨，已不觉矣。晚膳后拟与岑君赴国务会议，天黑路崎，颇不易行，行至半途，彼苦已返，因同回慢礼会栖宿。

今日晨起整理行装，坚礼所赠之物，印挨捂名，午饭往观东城西新修犯之洞，慢人之御兽室也。晚平山新月，有映现连北之希望。

July 17.                         晴、热

近数日以来，天气甚热，晨起尚有八十度，言为雅安数十年来所未有也。中午热至九十四度（室内）。

昨晚于山新月观寨，见其为一平台地，形如新月，四週陡绝，为自卫之隘。意以为原始人类所造卜居之地，当必有遗址在。今晨亲至其地观察，见雅安市在其内弦，上起建新村，台上之平地悉为馆款。现等新弦凌至台地之项，于挖整题基时，得青石磨光之石斧一in situ，其他之粗厚陶片甚多。此斧余想为一stray artifact，因无他所得也。石之上为流水冲刷堆积台，厚约二尺余。然查台地之四周陡视，别无所得。此地甚有为一新石器时代遗址之可能，但尚须试掘也。

午膳时黄郢之团长来同午膳，见有
一鸡，彼尝似脱子心痛也。下午四时
後至南门外之筹和栈乘肩舆视，为
街头所阻。後见女场之黄君，为湖南
人，询其有无古物，云有旬题颇色。
承赠女一。偕其同至近行场察视，工
人正在挖填，均为流水冲积之圈石
与黄沈，颇不易概挖。旬雄云即復
不见之墓中浮也。墓均已概挖去，制做
不時。饰粽核之名墓一，云为宴墓，中
空无所有。双人，是筹粽材，建中有石
石底，墓上有园境，其代似不甚久。
此地有一特供即特宜置於高浴只
练，经约尺许之旬雄中，上筑以烧碍，
四周一有碍，不知属於何民族也。
晚同，新闻员谭英華林学臣二
人由夷宁到雅。

July 18.　　　　　　　陰雨.

　　昨晚作定今晨同围文旦人同往调查姚桥调查僕孝廉高君碑. 今日阴,田尚未雨,但七热. 迳袤青衣江唉,至汽车站,候人力车未成. 此袤之人人车夫多偽十日大之助章,且偽外他人,又人人吃稚地. 車共不過十馀輛,故頗不末值也. 至汽車材已小雨,於茶肆中之候,雨退方行,约十一時至姚桥,高孝廉澍於坊雪之兄也.

　　姚桥二衣孝廉鄉,以高孝廉而得名也. 姚桥镇午,以其地皆姚姓,约四百家,故名. 姚姓相传为明末围西時由苏州遷此,其些子孙蕃衍,遂全有其地.

　　高孝廉澍在公外百馀步,離青衣江約半里,基在坊处. 澍為三,其在坊已全全无在,其左坊為坊来至是,惟其中坊為原物,但其右部已完全塌去. 此澍高約文至六尺,為红砂建。其下之碑文忽全无，其现在所见者，为后来之翻刻者。其上有汉刻者，为浅浮雕，角上之人物为透雕。其样式与新津所发现者相似，何为汉魏间之作品也。祠前十余步，有石狮二，立相左右，其左已倒。数十年前曾发现墓外石虎二，现移枝镇内之景贤祠内。

July 19.　　　　大雨，午後停

昨日午後即雨，晚後更大，天气轉涼。晚间大雨如注，竟宿未停，今日午後始稍住。雅河暴漲，幾与岸平，庚後停止。雅安數星期以来，苦旱，秧田均已龟裂，此大雨後，農民均欣欣有苦色。

上午因大雨未停，故未外出，寫信给陸瑞及御儂。

下午國昔寺家由經濟組招待，不意其厨師於大雨傍中逃去，亦一趣事也。先是彼李之国員晨夕責罵厨子，迫於苦求，其逃去，亦宜也。其厨子逃後，無人作飯，不能招待，乃由任美商国社會組共同招待，予乃建議在外招待，费用元住，經濟組之無责也，於此可見。

本次聚餐，原為討論生活動电影而来，但此电影之孙君，因赴天全攝水未

到. 莽组长提议将歌比公分关于天, 但邵团
长以为不可, 言彼亦须保西其权利, 会遂
无结果而散.

　　会成往观青衣江大水.

July 20.　　　　　阴晴.

　　昨夜大雨一阵, 晨起放晴晴. 晨起
讨论组织会议, 议决事多起. 有记录.

　　午饭後, 往调查传慈禧太后之生地.
地在中正街之前道界街内. 小屋一间,
傲红色. 现作无缐电台之機器房. 傍之
左有院侧, 自傳与隔陸之李家大夫第有
一桥相通, 言李家女为慈禧之传耶姊妹
也. 女不便從前面走而出进, 故以桥
相通也.

　　雅安一瞥. 四川月報, 11:3, P.18J.

　　至将府家提款写

　　至月心山调查有無被水沖去之芑物

　　往张家山農林组参观従事所摇等之標
本. 同将兄家张家山对面有家洞数号.

July 21. 晴，热。

早餐后，方君顷暮君赴名山调查，予与镇诚往范仙阁，因志西公路院同谷初报，又大雨之后，前此长多，如有造地方有颈害，籍此签祝。再午，初俑惜等二来，借此以视之，然吾行长缚也。

出西门，沿飞行场下换脚行，至与茔坪之下迂陵，水尚高，故颇危险，所谓宋村废是也。与茔坪为一大河滩，约数百畝，田尚肥沃，有居民数十家。与茔坪之西省有颈害之石榔四且，均有公路摇蹬大半，与飞行场所发现之石玫相同，土人所谓害玫也。

与茔坪西为龙揭盖，其地积大渴陵未水峯。俗称龙坑，径约二公尺，深约一公尺馆，长围而光滑，有仙人工铜振咒，位於河峯之红砂石上，大概时可没之。

相传李二郎追蟹龙至此，龙入石中，揭石运龙，今石盖龙坑与蟹股痕，俨然尚在也。

由此而上十许里至一峡，崖壁峭削，蹬出云表，高约数千尺。盖修神为治水而凿之处，费工独多，故称多工。其左岸公路通之有瀑洞，终岁衔滴，号大旱不竭。水大时有如瀑布，此一水帘洞也。二郎神祠即在多工峡首，颇为险峻。川主官在洞上，形势险峻，公路出其左，危崖在其右。川主神为赤面，璿琅宫，所塑均青面糖羊，赤面马体，与他乡之川主不同，询之，言为试像也。川主像前有井，言为黑色，投物其中，则从多工河流出。揭开盖视之，已为污土填满，亦道士欺人之说也。川主庙前有锡碑，川主庙在崇之顶，此井乃庙顶也。於上而之楼上歇观之，亦有相似。

川王庙下游为下阔，狮子陂之尾口为上阔，阔之中有镇数十家，至芦山及天全均必经此打尖。天全芦山之侨，必折引道。天全芦山之侨二处此相会。

司马相如读书台，临南龙观山，相传相好通印简斯榆窗想此读书。

四望楼，城内月心山麓，相传为苏轼苏辙读书室，侍前曾有大暑铭，今已无存。楼旁有东坡池。又有苏公井为，相传左卅後，现已不知其所，相传苏间携二子锦雷簟夫，雁後有象傷出，味甚甘洌，固名。

July 22.　　　　晴，云

　　今日未出调查，早膳后"唇钱张二围员径東门外警祝一建筑，因昨日至陶家山时即见之而未详为何建筑也。据二人相告，为吴京张姓之祠园，祖孙后人聚祭於此，建筑甚宏伟华丽，略乃为川中地亩，不同好。

　　午心卸围卷未续，掌地之地质组黄奇。於本日午后还難至

　　午心四时许方场二君自名山调查回。晚间闲坐误会，讨论在乂宏后果调查再行出發时间，定廿三日休息一日，清理行装及整理材料。

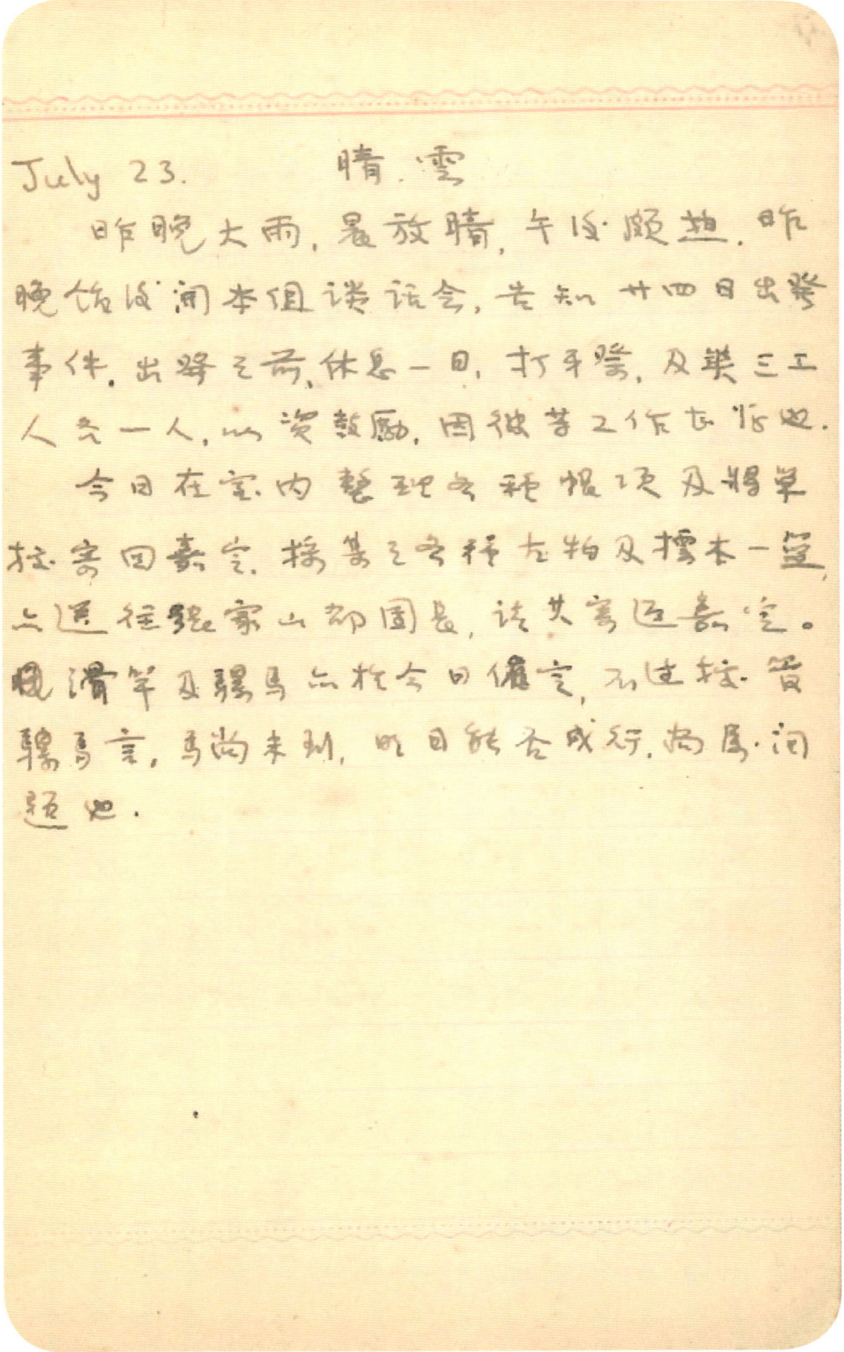

July 23. 晴.雲

昨晚大雨，晨放晴，午後頗熱。昨晚飯後開本組談話会，告知廿四日出發事件。出發之前，休息一日，打牙祭，及奖三工人各一元，以資鼓勵，因彼等工作甚好也。

今日在室内整理各種帳項及將單據寄回嘉定。採集之各種古物及標本一筐，亦送往張家山郭團長，請其寄返嘉定。雇滑竿及騾馬亦於今日備定，不過據管騾馬言，馬尚未到，明日能否成行，尚屬問題也。

July 24.　　　　　　晨雨，午後·晴.

　　昨宵大雨，晨仍雨不止、至九時後·雨停，馬夫始來，將大半之行李綁於駝鞍之上，以備明日清晨起程. 滑午走固起程，每人賠伙食之用.

　　午後往張家山兄鄧王之園地，商給明生學校房金事. 商定每組給廿元，由園芳作甫.

July 25.　　　　雨

　　昨夜大雨，至今日整日未停。午后雨稍小，因滑竿马使均已催好，不得不起程。柠檬乃冒雨而行。出南门，沿途皆泥泞，行甚缓。至下午三时份，始至观音桥，离雅安四十里而已。住于此地一小学内，已放假，地方尚传讹。晚饭后即就寝。今日气候颇阴冷。

　　观音桥地方颇为伤瘠，居民仅数十家，未作调查工作。

July 26.　　　　　　阴,云,又微雨.

　　晨五时起,雨已停,乃催其他诸人起身.预备起程,予与方君先行,其时约七时也.行数里,及遇路崩,不得过.因近日来大雨,各处山崩中甚多,此其甚者也.而雨已阻隔大数十人,予等乃下背筐行,泥又深,此时云散不浮跣稿矣.有一僧与一女子,陷入泥中不得出,所携之锄,已带倾入泥中,乃大呼帮忙,旁均不理,予乃属工人援之出.此家有人在艾麦场锄搜曰泥,作为修路,实则籍以锄草.方君乃取笑曰,如误认此女子为一美人,尽力救之出,免返溺猪火,二所不难.予乃笑曰,当如此女士者,不觉相与大笑.因忆晚在书时,适读此女士之意意也.

　　由此上山,二十里至吉子阁,又向马阿湖.此地为着名之迤区,不通现已断信.

此地草木青葱，亦为繁茂，及匪人土匪猖
獗，又为荣经与雅安交界之地，所谓三
不管者也。岭上有牌坊，指明荣雅分
界之处。其略形势有如灌川之娘子岭，而
无其高峻。岭之西墅有岗棚，藉以窥
匪徒之出入者。

下山二里许至麻柳沱，场名小，而
饭店甚多，因此处为自雅安之第一站，
离雅城适百七十里，一日之程也。

二十里至荥经辖城，过南门之铁索
桥，为十余年前取城石所建者。荥经
横亘于荥河与经河交流之处，即二河
之冲积地也。城垣已于十余年前毁
去，街道曰长街一条，东西向。人口约
二千户，一万人。营铁匠极多，因此处
出铁也。

辖城四面皆山，往时与番贩统之，

於荥东会流，直东北流入天全号与天
全河会（飞仙阁上十馀）而为青衣江.

　　高翚生言农林经济二组均有要
竹瘴疾发生，故每间一日各国员均服
金鸡纳霜丸二粒.

July 27.　　　　晴

昨夜整夜大雨，黎明时始霁，早饭后日出，乃与方君同往斟䥶厂道故城。另有记。

下午往逰梓桐观，即文昌宫，主持女为一僧人而非道士。以道宇而任佛僧，真佛道相通也。僧人已往毛屋山，留杂役一人而已。由文昌宫下望莹径之上有填垔为屏蔽处，自然之城堡也。

回城畤已五时，因好云垂他乡古陵，乃以调查，乃决定明日起程往陷溪。

锋张谭三国员往调查鄧通之铜山，主其地以因阻水未能达，乃与故龆老人谈鄧通之故事而逝。言通之捵铜时，诸事均无方储，惟缺火。与佛寺为告以十里外方得，通乃亲往十里外取之，候其至，已锋死，而通所印佛前之灯，方正明处。

至文昌宫時於河灘上捡得陶片一塊,
火候与 polish 的颇特别,作淡红色,不似
现代所製也.

晚晚宿寒潭县束闻误甚多.

午時的会野堂郡之家委员来误,力好
宗離妻子之地甚远,益欲听其乱言子也.
颇百有趣.

July 28.　　　　晴

昨晚微雨，天明以刀雲開日出。五時半，收拾率行，預備起程。七時半至宴重頃乃呂諸名余翻辞行，切未起，八乘滑竿行。出西冽，過鹿角壩，應刀溪十五里至磨背頂，滑竿夫欲小息，此地出虫茶，味畧苦而色青黃如醫油。往來之行旅必飲之，言其能清食也。虫茶刀係一種虫形如蠶，喂以苦蕎，其所裏之矢，即為虫茶。其刀正如醫矢，色黑而精刀。售價頗昂，约一角一两。

由此沿溪而進，十餘里至大通橋，為一小鎮，居民數十家，地方拘清靜。又數里至安善壩，有碑甫存，而無居民。好衆之所谓壩者，石過溪澗中之一小坪而已。安善壩即為涪溪輈境。

再十里至黃泥鋪，為漢源西北之

之要镇，居民百馀家，为过大相岭必宿之地。昔时设讯，历代皆有兵戍之。现亦有兵一连戍之，以保护相岭之安全。滑竿夫及力夫至此，均需齐牌乞打手号，因明日过岭，均须用力故也。此地有药属合作社旅馆，尚简单，不过亦是出事。在此地住宿，详情明日过山。黄泥铺今名凤仪堡。

凡苦人滑竿夫过岭，必在祭经割肉往城隍庙内敬神，以祈保佑平安过山。由于祭则有节至黄泥铺而食矣。

鸡上崖。过大通桥数里即至。原云梯也，其崖临大关山之险，至此始为平坦，肩挑背负，多憩止于此，故名。现有居民数十家，但楼上亦多于黄泥铺，不仅此也。

July 29.　　　　　晴

　　天繁明即起早餐，六时成即起行。今日天气晴朗，颇宜行走。由此断上山，十里至小洞山，高数百步，颇曲险，其上係施戍，甚险，二经时重要阅口之一也。又十里达大洞山，洞甚高，两面陡绝。上有店数家，备支省竿夫主必领气及饮食。大洞印即嵘阁，大小二洞相伴为何元所创，建食及器屋百件间，阿顺庇节。清顺佑间举人刘道贞破张献忠之前锋扼此。昔司马芰卿挥从巴菪洞入谕西南夷，即此地。岩阻岭迴，蟻缘蛇伏，虚曲如行鬼园。復有溷涂夏纬颓箐，吞紫霍雨。腥风义蒙，到处险峻。　老饽有其候询，康熙中威信公岳钟琪征西过此所建。穴名凍雪巷

　　绝顶第一峯名相公岭，缥缈如在天外。如遇天明气清，远望民勞诸山，历历在目。

大有一览众山小之概，不愧为卬在苐一
一览山也。

其阳有九折坂，昔王阳为益州刺史，
行部至此，歎曰，奉先人遗体，奈何数乘
险，寻谢病去。及王尊为刺史，至此曰，此
非阳所畏道耶？叱其驭曰，驱之。故世
谓王阳为孝子，王尊为忠臣。故杨升菴
有九折刺史坂，七擒孟获桥，之句。

July 30. 晴

昨晚宿于城内文庙之中心小学，经济组先已在此，故得同住，然校中颇有不洁之处也。闻经济组来此时，经县府交涉始得来此，然校门则久不开也。校内不许作饭，故诸事殊多不便。只得在隔壁文昌宫小学内借用厨房。

晚间访老先生数人，谈当地之掌故。

夜间一时许，大风忽作，声震屋宇，乃起关窗，历半时而止，此即所谓焚风耶。

晨六时起床，厨房厨子以迟起，故至九时始早餐。询其故，云不能独回，乃申叱之。军警武亦加以申叱，防以后有此事再发生也。

早餐后往出东门调查此处河谷之构成状况及有无石器发现之可能。后至川主庙玉渊书院，其地有泉，云即焚香

水，傍有宋碑，拓以匠像。再至古城，
已荒无足体。

午饭往西门及南窑视。汉原城基南
冲积斜坡，颇陡。东南西三面有温以湖
上围之东西两涧冲胖绝壁，高几百丈，
大西之城堡之险，未有如此者。

July 31.　　　　　　晴

上午往离东约三里之太傅庙，实为武威庙，奉蜀汉时之马忠。其庙原在城内，后时移于城外。今每岁六月十二迎神，今乙年未举行矣。此地之供奉马忠，或此君任马之司有因缘也。庙内势纪事碑，不过当湖记太傅庙之始，碑末复有重刻词，但此不知为何时物也，甚年代似甚近。

下午来县，翻阅县志，又缮正亲书。

晚饭后阅谈话会，商议以日起行事。

汉原有一属水，即不闻南门，因南门有他似女陷，俗谓美女怀孕，若开南门，则清溪之士子，将大发忧患，不逞于宦。土人言之凿凿。当廿四年红军之役，二十四军将城门打开，数城内之女子，果有异动，于是乎闭之。我昨日曾至南门警视，则半闭半掩，固不便妨少行人而已。不

遇南门左旁之缺口，有对面之猛虎
间视之，晃似其的彻也。

Aug. 1.　　　　　晴

　　早餐後，予於方君先行。出西门下擂後上山至擂虎嘴。下山至冷飯溝，为一客白厩来刮客最多之地。滑竿夫在此加多。至富莊午飯。富莊之上，有客莊。或以谓富莊俗称客莊，非也。富莊附近，有野生之仙人掌，他處则未见也。自過冷飯溝心，莊鎮较他处为密。

　　下午三時至泥頭，古称延化也，己為城續多考。地势並不险峻，山势既平。任此地之中心小学。

　　晚近以来，雨至期前下大雨，河底暴漲，为数十年所未有。冲毀之田包为其甚多。如泥頭下之營沙坎，田畝冲去大半，及房宅二十餘家。

　　自冷飯溝下行己出風沙河，相信即沙和搞吃人之處也。大概因沙林濱门而名，实与此神话无涉也。

　　溪峒将之女子，青年中多尚有缠足。且缠亦多颇有缩小。豆腐西施，颇有不少也。

　　五将之泥设，为古飞延塔，凡遇飞延赛者，心拈此福，以偷次日返山。清华寄录学费，每人三角。魏住此地之中心小学。

Aug. 2.　　　　　陰.

　　晨起吃麵及雞蛋, 食後即行. 予与方君至高橋畔, 繞道至九老洞. 離正路上山約二里許. 洞在東雲庵北之西溝中, 石質為流水沖成之洞也. 甚深. 惟其中空無所有, 有泉水自其中出, 不能居人. 稍事參視後, 即返正路.

　　三時過飛越嶺, 俗稱鳥雅嶺. 此嶺甚高峻, 石為上下. 在頂上遠望印峽諸山, 极壯觀.

　　下嶺時因雨甚滑, 六月為雨季, 雲起即有雨, 特以下午為甚. 由嶺上下山十四里至化林坪. 有居民五六十家, 前清時為化林营, 是時有居民五六百家. 寧今則由此遷越巂書, 為必宿之地.

　　信沿理之小路即由此分路, 由大路亦由此上山, 由小路即由右西之岔中

缘溪而上. 由此沿溪之此翻山, 高则相
等, 而逆了号寺大相绕, 两途程亦稍近.
由西向东则易之, 由东向东则难之,
因全为上坡也. 今则败煤之好所往
好路, 了无稽查, 而其化之上专商人,
专由大湾, 因为绕土匪之子, 不易行之.

化林坪之对面之岩上, 有一石, 形似
人, 相传往昔有一女子上山研菜, 而身不
净, 急于石上, 而月经之滴于石上, 其后
受日精華, 遂而粗怪, 土人称之曰甩
神. 其后常至镇上作祟为妖, 镇人
执镜击碎其首, 其煙遂息. 而今行人
尚能目指其家也.

至化林之小学中, 绝岩狙因昕日在
岭上通雨疮行至坪, 故休息一回, 被云
住匠里.

Aug. 3.　　　　晴

　　清晨四时三刻即予各团员起，明月尚
正明，因今为夏历六月十九日也。因坪在岭
上，气候甚冷，夜间盖厚棉被冷，晨起另
着皮衣。起时因天气晴吼，万里无云，对面
之雪山毕露，景亦雄伟壮丽，各团员均甚
鹜喜，为摄影二张。化林坪之地势虽为险
要，西面望之甚伺，有一大峡阅，茜夫万入
之枢，诚为守飞越荥将之要塞也。

　　六时始早膳内行，至雪喻崖时，始为
大水冲去，颇难行。由此而至大渡口，田
甚房至，碾罄冲去左右，以笑隆场（诸圮
铺）而言，原有庇铺百余家，今止余一二
十家而已。由此沿尹公崎下至沈村，冲刷
之田畴甚多。尹公崎始居入大渡河，即入沈
边界，沈村前有土习驮牧其地，其衔令
徂为小泻。

由沈村对岸上坡，至虎耳崖，其旁有观音，均就岩石雕刻。言亚西童谓，往来行人，多於此祈平安，故香火右盛。此处之险係在半岩中鑿出。下为沪沱急湍，百丈巉崖，上为峭壁至高仞之险岩，仰首不能见其巅。行人至此，俯视仰望，真觉心寒而慄。僧人真能利用心理，無怪其香火之盛也。半岩中有横磴，间则山崩，而土人则以为观音菩萨之殛罚也，强之以狼而身殒石。由此下即冷磧，市场颇盛，百物均有，险阨而三会之区，故为繁盛。而往来行旅之必打尖之地也。

尹公潘与大凌河会合之南辈，有沈村，为沈迪土司驻牧之地。火之司之後人会其祸现在宁宫政分枝。土司食衡尚存。冷磧而经，聆迤土司之地，土司同姓，现尚住冷磧镇中。

川康公路至冷碛出大渡河，盘旋于数千尺之山腰之中，险要之情形，殆无以复加。同行有言如作车此等山顶上行，则宁坐滑竿，不乘汽车。予笑曰，川省乃因噎废驢车？乃相与大笑。不过其险峻之情形，则可想而知矣。

由冷碛至泸定之旧路，因在公路之下，多为掘公路之土石所掩盖，多有不可通行之处，有处必需绕越始通过，亦甚危险，驮行者之马，有处须将行李取下，空马而过。但公路亦不能尽通，有时须绕道山上，上下须起地而行，其惊心怵魄，有不可形容者。因思甲在雅安出发时，多勇气甚大，至此有意气沮丧，不顾再往前进者。可见青年大半在初起时志向甚大，一遇阻碍，则易于消沉也。予意此起不过小小阻碍，将来的更有更甚于此者，决不可因此而自

险大逼窄耳。但无论如何，此山路之险峻、艰巨、工程之浩，即可想而知。现工程之土工全已竣工，惟石工正在开始，其工程之艰巨，当更甚于土工也。有许多地方，须全从岩石中挖出一道道也。

约四时半至泸定道桥，住于省立小学，地方尚在属营房，校长亦极勤招待，遂在此住下。

公路由二郎山逶迤下降，至冷碛时已出大渡河，但尚山顶，但由此渐渐下降，至泸定而降至河谷之底。

Aug. 4　　　　晴

化林坪至泸定七十五华里，一日程，但气候相差七区。化林坪于盛夏之时，则有如初冬，固其地甚高，下山至大渡河谷有二十五里，而坡度七陡。岭碛与泸定则有如内地之炎，然迟旱间则甚凉。

泸定之地势，则七平凡，位于山潜之 alluvial cone 之上，如腾中山洪暴发，则有被冲之虞。且泸定之重要，则在铁索桥，为康西四十四道，行旅必经此渡河，至于泸定之本身则无险可守也。

泸定之人口，接杨存最近调查，约五千余户，至多不过二万五千余人。人民除汉人外，在靠之南部者，有猓猡，约二百余户。披甄。此外大半为土著，属于何种民族，现尚不得而知。县城之四郊及此部，均为彼等。服装语言均已汉化，闻尚能说彼原有之语言，尚须详细之调查也. 猓猡亦多汉化, 多里白二种, 但均已失其先犷之性, 奉政府之号令惟谨, 大似大凉山之猓夷也.

　　缚之北有鱼通, 藏人称曰鱼通佳. 尚保存其原有之风俗习惯. 其特别之习惯, 为偿物时以偿带勒颈前. 相传武侯南征胜, 徵役等运粮, 而无人押送, 故特制此法, 使被苦偿物时不得知後面有人押送, 因如偿负, 如回顾则所负之物必回顾也.

　　嵐乌, 嵐高, 乌泥, 嵐安等地, 均为汉化土人所居最多之地, 但现在自称为汉人, 而不愿认其为土人矣. 此等地带, 均与鱼通相接.

　　李勣曾言此地之苄麦甚好, 每一株三穗. 但人民健讼, 故外方人谑之曰, 以一穗完租, 一穗自用, 一穗讼人. 盖讼费甚輕, 败不均输与胜,每以讼人为荣，今则增加讼费，而由败诉者担负，故争讼之风稍息。但乡人健讼，故是一事，而荸荠一株三穗，又是一事，乡老则言之凿凿，实为不察也。予在沿道田中观察，从未有见一株荸荠生三穗者，即间有生两穗者，其一穗亦不成遂。人言之不可遽信，有如此者。

嶺碛之同土司，相传尝赏戴红顶，此係异数，固先御间该土司以花椒磨成如意二柄进贡，适值慈禧太后六旬万寿，深得其赏鉴，故有此异数。而花椒又为当地之特产者为最佳，磨成如意，允称别具匠心也。

Aug. 5. 晴

今日五时印起，六时起程，十五里至咱哩，盖咱哩土千户驻牧之地也。土司古姓，原为鱼通人，自清末改流后，坐吃山空，又吸食鸦片，已贫不能举火，现与余其第一人，约二十左右，其兄已捻数月前殁，讨债务垫门，尚未能归葬也。在其家慰问后，略事询问，即至底上早餐。

大童坝上冷竹间下，河中有一洲，上有方圆之墙硬之陈名一。相传为诸葛亮扎营之地，土人称为诸葛营，但经上视之，毫无陈迹，但无论如何大水，均不将其淹没，土人颇以为异。

过冷竹间后，狂风大起，予所乘之滑竿，几为挹去，跨在半山行，下临窝灞，颇有危险。今日太阳特别热，山高谷深，亦知其必心有大风也。

由冷竹关上十三四里，康定河由此出泸河，行谷甚狭，宽中间才数十武，两岸岩石壁立，至上午九时尚不浮见阳光也。沿沟行一二里即至瓦斯沟，尚民五十徐家，二百八十徐人，均为客民。瓦斯沟向属咱哩千户所。沟上尚有番民七八家，均汉化，碉楼尚隐约可见。自下望之，颇为险峻，昔为军事必争之地，名大岗，因其为通藏孔道之锁钥，故征金川时，当力争之。

沟水亦为清冽，但甚冷，流甚急。予团自出成都以来，未尝沐浴，因往河中避静沈沐，因中往返二多，予团不惧，脱衣时堕入河中。衣履尽湿，幸日记小提包，尚未失落。衣履既湿，二团之大汔其狼。

此家园山高行隧，矢晓腾车须心风，住拖此地之小学中，西山飘狂风一阵，屋瓦皆震。沟下有铁椿桥一，本桥自已折，多年失修，有行不得也哥哥之概。此号通重道。

Aug. 6.　　　　　晴

　　由瓦斯薄西上，山绕峥嵘，两岸岩石，壁立千仞，河谷坡度甚大，故水流湍急，溅花眩眸行人。太阳光线，映之溅花，有时成虹，颇有奇观。两端声之大，真如百万鸣蝉，壁岩陡立，故回声甚大，行人相语，需以大声出之，方能听见也。壁航下绝壁有传雍正十三年二月果亲王题"西南佛障"四大字，刊于大岩石之上。果亲王好弄文墨，于此可见一斑。

　　两岸多白花岗石 Granite.

　　仙人掌，此地称观音掌，初见于富庄附近，至船越岭下即不再见。过岭至冷碛则渐，沿途而上，几偏山皆是。西行过瓦斯薄时绝迹，可见此地之乾燥温暖也。仙人掌上生一种梨形之实，大小二如梨，不过其上生刺甚多，取之稍不慎，即为所伤。此实在夏历八月间成熟，色黄，其中之实颇甘美，土人言其性凉，並称之曰仙人桃，为其地之特产。

火草在康定附近有之，由雅安至瓦斯沟则未已也。

明正土司之祖先，原为 Mi-nyag 之酋
长。相传一日，其祖先出猎，于 Jedo 山顶
见一鹿，射之，其鹿带箭而逃，其先追之，见某地有两
河交流之地，颇平坦，有遗箭于此之意，
遂在现在天主教真原堂起一衙，以貯藏
其家，断则久居于此，又在其旁另一衙，
即后来之土司官衙，现在 139 师所驻之
地是也。天主堂现之旧衙，别通称之曰
旧衙门，十余年前尚有人知之，今则无
人能道其详矣。

明正土司藏语曰 gyala，意有铁山
之意。"明正"之意及起源，则不得而知。
明正土司汉姓姓甲，有人附会请雍正间
果亲王使藏，道经鑪城，有其士妇私，
已而生子，故以甲为姓，甲者，果亲王头半
也。不知甲字乃借由 gyala 而来，与
果亲无涉，人言之凿凿，有如甲云。

晨

打箭炉原有四十八家锅庄，有时正原有百姓地雄人，对扎土司之家，今有的朕守，皆来投居在以四十八家之下。锅庄原为支持铁锅之三石椿，故曰锅椿，讹为锅庄。锅庄原指以正土司之四十八家，但以凡大庄房，均称之曰锅庄。寡有之四十八家锅庄，多已畜式微，只剩二十馀家，其中之最大者，为包元二家。包官藏名曰 Wa(s)(y)chab，包家信黑教，Wa(s)(y)为黑教之神名，cha 为救之意，今则土人别讹为"瓦斯家"。其何以取汉姓曰包，则不得而知。元家以其祖名 trowobam，故曰元。

打箭炉最老之庄房，则为罗家，相传已三百馀年，三层，庙式甚高，远望如一小喇嘛寺。罗家藏名 Norbūzonqbö，意为"美珠"。相传汉人与唐藏人易茶马，始於 Norbu-ganqbö，漢人運茶至店宴，藏人用牦牛運入藏，其最初交易之所，即現在之羅家之屋中也。Norbu-songbo 為藏人，故在打箭炉為客家，故其地位在原四十八家锅庄之下。四十八家頭人在明正土司家中，均各有身分職務稱，而羅家獨無，後乃專門為土司衙中各房屋刷石灰，每年一次，故又稱 Sagahrgoba，即石灰頭人之意也。現羅家之人均已亡故，只餘寡婦二人，已招贅。

　打箭炉之名稱，漢人則相傳為武侯南征，於此鑄箭，故有此稱。此乃全係附會之詞，不足為典據。推打箭炉而譯用藏語為 Dartsido，或 Tǎchido，而各有涵意自不同。如為 Dartsido，Dar 為“騾馬”之意，tsi 為第之音，do 為碼頭之意。明正土司驻牧於此，又因為貿易之埠，故稱此地 為"第一等遠之碼頭"。明正土司自尊其驻牧之地之稱也。如曰 Tǎchido，其義則又不同，da 代表大炮山，有水自其中出，chi 為折多山，有水自其中出，二水至此会流，do 即兩河会合之三角州也。打箭炉為二水会流之地，故稱 Tǎchido。以意度之，Tachido 為此為正，如 箐木日（Chamiko）乃甚顛倒也。

四十八家鍋莊，康语白 Aja-kaba zhi-ju-zhe-je。Aja 非康语，或為 gyarong 语，今未可知 至於藏语之 kalon 尤 Lhumbo。毒為孫人 取在 Jyelbo 之下，Bön 之上，土司之王家是也。

　　打箭炉之喇嘛寺，古首推珍吉寺，為明正土司之家廟也。明正家之珠寶，多金此寺之中，家為紅教，故大殿上供蓮花大师。此寺為康定寺之最大者。自謂佛法僧三者皆備，何以為佛法僧之均皆備。依佛言，則其後殿中所供之釋迦牟尼，為於薩 PoTaLa 工文戌公主所塑之像，按言其与之完全相似。故以佛言，為康中第一。以法言，則殿中之全部藏經，皆從控薩求来，而化东喇嘛寺中所藏者，自為億格所所翻来。又有金水所写經一部，特為珍貴，非但大喇嘛憚自大者日不得閱看，故以經法言，又為康中第一。佛像及經均供於大殿旁之小殿中，為全寺最尊之所，申曰佛前有小金刺塔三四座，高四五尺，似為銅而鍍金也。上鏤以古称宝石，言文中有舍利子，价值连城．
多为明正土司所藏．经为 Būma taichü
（莲花海）所取回．佛像之左供有金
刚表一枚，上有凹，似白人之足球，高
约一二尺．为寺中镇寺之物．相传金
刚自后山岩上以足踢落，岩石往下
榭坠停止之处，即起寺焉．故寺称
曰寺寨，義为金刚表日也．

　　所谓傳巧，係指 Būma taichü，
为此寺之开山祖师．相传为明正中土
司之嗣，栈建颇巴世將於西藏取经，
又监修寺務之石拱桥．圆寂后，将
其肉身塑泥镀金，供於大殿莲花大
师之前，进為白殿之精．兄弟昂生生
於殿中，偶延生者，亦知中，以为係
一世喇嘛生於其上也．圆有向扎之
僧，故此僧言，又为康中第一巴．

大殿之右有護法堂，入其内亦觉香烟缭绕，惨淡無光，一神秘之地也。殿中不见神像，惟见各種供俸之物。其他則阴森可怖，殆無天日，外人不得入内也。言每年跳護法神一次，有一喇嘛享司之，跳時凡默絕數日，继以圈勒其頸，至以出血而止，继以怠躍而起，身披人不能勝之盔甲，预言季中一年之事。如季中喇嘛有不信者，則以黑線捌之，則季中必将其逐出也。

季中共有喇嘛六十人。

打箭炉寺庙中香火之盛，莫过於
将军庙。因番汉均言其十分灵验，故
能如此。其像為铁铸，神有喇嘛主
之。汉人中传说，将军名郭達，為三国
時诸葛亮之偏将，尝铸箭於此死而
為神，土人祀之。雅州府志，即為此
说者。又有以為郭達係战争思拇之
将，能铸铁炮，暴死於此，死而為神。
按此皆無如汉人之传说，郭達实属
為佛喇嘛教中之神，藏语為 Dam
chen dor gee leqbǎ。Dam 為有信
之义，chen dor gee 為金刚，leqbǎ 為善。
在佛教中原為习铁匠之神。喇嘛
言其神像，係從郭達山中岩石中跳出，
非人手所铸也。郭達山康名 Dzom
draq，（坐姐儸挌），义為全美之白岩石。
与郭達铸箭無涉也。

按郭达铸器之说，当以汉人古以为
其习铁之之神，故附会至铸器，而又
附会至诸葛亮。

跑马山 Dey tok (on peace).

督吉寨寺 Dorqee draq
南无寺 Shamo tsi 义为仙女顶．
　　黄教庙也
康定共有七庙（"喇"嘛寺），以上二者
为最大．

汶川之瓦寺土司，汉人相传以为昔日
有喇番僧至此，居人 瓦以为寺，故称
瓦寺．此大相枧而附会之词。瓦寺土
司为乌思藏人，其中有一族名 Wahsü，
瓦寺者，Wahsü 之译音也．或者瓦寺

土司原为 wahsü 族人，因驻牧其地，
故称瓦寺。wahsü 族中之语言，与
其他藏语，稍有不同，现在属藏之
牛厂中多为此族。

在乾嘉以前，通属宝之路，原绕
由冷竹阁上山绕大阁，至山顶道水
再至河谷。现在沿河之峡，仍绕乾
嘉以后所开者。

以外闻人所知，喇嘛对人民之间隔，亦
为和谐，不但在宗教上为人民所仰赖，而在
经济及政治上，亦为人民所尊敬。故近来
言康地之书，鲜有言喇嘛与人民之冲突
者。然考康地之情形，此实不然，人民与喇
嘛之纠纷，牲有所闻。今乃举一案件，以为
例。

康定嫩第五区1头为康人 Losangpengtso，
以前为团练，操区内之政权，已有十八九
年，据估，号召马队至千人之谱，故其势力
颇为侮。第五区之内有喇嘛寺五，而以
Owaka 寺为最大，而对于人民，颇有所微
嗜，Losangpentso 乃起而反抗之，言人民
既已有政府当差，不应再对喇嘛，受诸
迫之微嗜，不然人民则会两层受负。而喇
嘛则言，彼等传已来，已经如此，今则何
得一旦取消，而喇嘛亦何所得食。Losang

pantso 则言，纵使前清如此，有何证据。况今已为民国，地土皆为国有，喇嘛非政府官吏，何得擅自征税，故双争相持不下。及喇嘛乃以巨金至省府运动，并运动大刚喇嘛（Owaka 亦为黄教），乃诬 Losangpongtso 欲反抗政府，控之于康定省府，省府乃下之于狱，并其他六人亦下之狱。及川康建设考视团来此，五匠人民亦曾日向之控诉，某团曾亦电刊之康，未曾得覆。闻今已释五人，而 Losangpongtso 及其他一人尚繋狱中也。当七人下狱之始，适五匠之人民数百，咸至省府请愿，统为对待日，告游戟之始末。此案在刘文辉大案件之下，至今繋狱中已半年，尚未解决也。

甘孜之孔撒女土司，现方二十一二岁，尚未婚嫁。其父亦均已亡故，按例当由遇伊承继。由尊院令至甘孜将，曾认其为义父。不道现因婚姻问题，尚禁狱中。

按之屦人之婚例，颇为自由，男女情愿，即可成眷属；而男女之离异亦易，男女一方不愿，即可分离。不过土司之婚姻，则非与土司不可。再屦中择婿之风特盛，有子女则使之习"别嘛，而择能女婿以承家篙，而牛亨使之。

孔撒女土司名 Tāchingwangmu，以待嫁之青年，自欲觅一乘龙佳婿，以承继其土司之家篙。昌班详仪仗隔追甘孜将，有其 妻珞 名陈若伊希等老 玉秸（藏名太夫）青年，係藏人，年轻倜傥，二人情投意合，遂定白首之约。岂岂不致上式开婚也。仍遣人至康定囧伖 Wascha 之女主人向副文耀说项。Wascha 之女主人，也为糕昭细粹练，曾至北平上海，故举止大方。

后等如风，伊乃言之於刘夫人经道主席，主席
别言及婚姻乃彼二人之自由，如彼二人愿意
改在则无不可。Teching wangmuu 得此意，乃
举备婚嫁，不意当成婚之日，新印乘马至宝
土司寓所之际，当地之驻军团长张家强印与
其弟张家麟突加袭捕，而驻时抄王司之宅中，
出字镜五百馀支，数百年榻下之金佛甚伙及
其他珠宝甚伙。抄没乃电西昌刘文辉言此
谓此句诸藏人谋叛政府。孔撒土司辖之
人民，有枪二千馀支，其势力颇不可侮，政府
对之，早有注意。今则新娘新郎尚絷狱中，
有禄调来源之馆注之伙，好事多魔，吉事竟
成祸事，未知将来有圆室之时否。

前言之 Losangpengtso 言，"剌嘛"即以百胜诉，乃将 Owaka 村之差役加之於 Otieh 村之下。Otieh 村为 Losangpentso 之本村，有人约一百八十馀人。原有牛差22，马差三匹半。今剌再加上 Owaka 之马差四匹半，牛差21，共现有牛差四十三，马差八。以以前之差役，人民以苦不堪言，今又增加田 Owaka 之差役，若折银算，每人约担负藏洋十元之谱。但在"剌嘛"皃威，政府亦徒而助之，人民则敢怨而不敢言矣。而"剌嘛"则高揚言人民属於枯若，生殺由的，不与 Losangpengtso 彼等可置之於死地，即全匣之人民，亦可生殺由之也。且藏院各護送班祥之重柜，缘追隨於剌嘛之尊卸，几无所後加，人民则真以剌嘛之言為是，只知有剌嘛，而不如有政府矣。

康地官吏出行或运输，所徵人民之牛马差，通称乌拉，茗不得其义。询之汉人，则称曰为唐名，询之唐刊人，则答曰为汉词。民乃知乌拉，原非为差之义。当岳钟琪征西藏时，因运输困难，乃徵为民差，且对鞭挞甚惨。当唐人被鞭挞之际，因不雅民语，则自称乌拉，义为诉饶语其怜惜之词，故自遭鞭挞，叫以"乌拉"，習而久之，故自二称康人当差之人，通为乌拉娃。唐语称当差曰 chê jie. Chê 当为民语之差之讹. 牛差曰 Kū ma chê, 马差曰 Ta chê.

西人所五 Hor states 者, 即蒙古人之义. 藏
人呼蒙古人为 Horpa, 因此之土司有为蒙古
人, 故呼之为 Hor. Horpa 为後起之名词,
现在呼蒙古人别为 Sokba. 相传成吉斯汗
有第五子封此地为王, 後又有之子, 成为现
在道孚甘孜间五土司之祖. 五土司即

Hor Kanqsar
 "   Beri
 "   Drango
 "   Driwo
 "   Mazur

此五土司之中, 惟 Kanqsar 及 Beri 存在,
Drango 之林遂当奉时改流, Driwo 於大金寺
之役, 周通藏嫁遂被殺, Mazur 绝嗣, 改合
於 Kanqsar.

孔撒女土司伝说任母之义孚之, 其母与人
私通, 生一子, 其祖母将其通杀. 现已立, 代子现

随其兽往拉萨。后·亲王母之祖母限有辟绿，
其祖母父二品招赘书，现尚存。

德亲王母数年前与其枧文（雷揽佛）之偿私通，欲
统成为婚姻，不过其属下之大陇人等亟端
固反对，因其破土司婚姻之成例也。后·亲王
母不听，一日好偿目其妆楼下，大陇人等伏
於闇击杀之。后·亲大怒，亲至属官诉之当局，
当局二任愿之言者为之择一乘托佳婿也。